ANCIENT INDIAN TRADITION & MYTHOLOGY

Translated by
A BOARD OF SCHOLARS

Edited by
Prof. J.L. SHASTRI

VOLUME 32

ANCIENT INDIAN TRADITION AND MYTHOLOGY SERIES

[PURĀṆAS IN TRANSLATION]

Volumes Released

ŚIVA 1-4
LIṄGA 5-6
BHĀGAVATA 7-11
GARUḌA 12-14
NĀRADA 15-19
KŪRMA 20-21
BRAHMĀṆḌA 22-26
AGNI 27-30
VARĀHA 31-32
BRAHMA 33-36
VĀYU 37-38
PADMA 39-48
SKANDA, PARTS I-XVIII, 49-66

Volumes Under Preparation

SKANDA, PARTS XIX-XXIII
BHAVIṢYA
BRAHMAVAIVARTA
DEVĪBHĀGAVATA
KĀLIKĀ
MĀRKAṆḌEYA
MATSYA
VĀMANA
VIṢṆU
VIṢṆUDHARMOTTARA

THE VARĀHA PURĀṆA

Translated and Annotated by
S. VENKITASUBRAMONIA IYER

PART II

MOTILAL BANARSIDASS PUBLISHERS
PRIVATE LIMITED • DELHI

First Edition: Delhi, 1985
Reprint: Delhi, 2003

ISBN: 81-208-0362-0

Also available at:
MOTILAL BANARSIDASS
41 U.A. Bungalow Road, Jawahar Nagar, Delhi 110 007
8 Mahalaxmi Chamber, 22 Bhulabhai Desai Road, Mumbai 400 026
236, 9th Main III Block, Jayanagar, Bangalore 560 011
120 Royapettah High Road, Mylapore, Chennai 600 004
Sanas Plaza, 1302 Baji Rao Road, Pune 411 002
8 Camac Street, Kolkata 700 017
Ashok Rajpath, Patna 800 004
Chowk, Varanasi 221 001

UNESCO COLLECTION OF REPRESENTATIVE WORKS—Indian Series.
This book has been accepted in the Indian Translation Series of the UNESCO Collection of Representative Works, jointly sponsored by the United Nations Educational, Scientific and Cultural Organization (UNESCO) and the Government of India

Printed in India
BY JAINENDRA PRAKASH JAIN AT SHRI JAINENDRA PRESS,
A-45 NARAINA, PHASE-I, NEW DELHI 110 028
AND PUBLISHED BY NARENDRA PRAKASH JAIN FOR
MOTILAL BANARSIDASS PUBLISHERS PRIVATE LIMITED,
BUNGALOW ROAD, DELHI-110 007

PUBLISHER'S NOTE

The purest gems lie hidden in the bottom of the ocean or in the depth of rocks. One has to dive into the ocean or delve into the rocks to find them out. Similarly, truth lies concealed in the language which with the passage of time has become obsolete. Man has to learn that language before he discovers that truth.

But he has neither the means nor the leisure to embark on that course. We have, therefore, planned to help him acquire knowledge by an easier course. We have started the series of Ancient Indian Tradition and Mythology in English Translation. Our goal is to universalize knowledge through the most popular international medium of expression. The publication of the Purāṇas in English Translation is a step towards that goal.

PREFACE

The present Volume contains the Varāha Purāṇa Part II (Chapters 137-218) in English Translation. This is the thirty second volume in the Series on *Ancient Indian Tradition and Mythology*.

The project of the series was planned in 1970 by Lala Sunder Lal Jain of Messrs Motilal Banarsidass, with the aim to universalize knowledge through the most popular international medium, viz. English. Hitherto, the English translations of eight Purāṇas, namely Śiva, Liṅga, Bhāgavata, Garuḍa, Nārada, Kūrma, Brahmāṇḍa and Agni have been published by us.

This Purāṇa, like most of the other Purāṇas, is of encyclopaedic character. Like the first part, this part of the Varāha Purāṇa contains topics of diverse nature. Nevertheless there is a sort of unity under diversity. The early chapters which open this part contain stories on the efficacy of holy places in India. They tell us how by resorting to these even a creature of low species can attain godhood. To illustrate, a vixen and a vulture are hit by the arrow of a hunter. They die at holy Saukara and are born as the prince of Kaliṅga and the princess of Kāñcī. A wagtail falls in the Ganges and is born as the son of a rich merchant who renounces the world, goes to Saukara and attains liberation. Holy places include streams, pools, wells, peaks of mountains etc. and are associated with the episodes throwing light on their efficacy.

Most prominent among the holy places are Mathurā, Gokarṇa, Badarī and Dvārakā. Their efficacy is supported by the anecdotes which ancient tradition has handed down to us. We learn that devotees are liberated, ghosts are relieved, gods are absolved of curses. A Śrāddha at these centres can transport manes from hell to heaven.

Since the Purāṇa is Viṣṇuite in character, a number of chapters are essentially devoted to the worship of lord Viṣṇu in the form of idols. Various kinds of idols are enumerated. They are of wood, stone, clay, copper, bronze, silver or gold. The procedure of worship is the same as prevails among Vaiṣṇava devotees even to-day.

Much emphasis is placed on the performance of Śrāddha. The subject is very mysterious. It begins with a narrative on the origin of Śrāddha, proceeds with the description of the ritual, the qualities of the Brahmin to be fed and the articles to be used at the rite. The account presents sufficient material for research in this field.

Quite interesting and informative is the story of Naciketas who visits the abode of Yama and returns home. His description of Yama, Yamaloka and Yama's attendants is very thrilling. Extremely horrid is the sight of sinners undergoing torments resulting from their evil deeds. Most dreadful is the scene where demons and Yama's men fight with each other. It is strange to learn from Yama's instructions to his messengers that they have to assume different shapes, as of a snake, fever etc. to perpetrate death. The topic is very important inasmuch as the Purāṇa devotes twenty chapters to this.

In the miscellany of topics we can include Reflections on Sexual Relations, Efficacy of Chastity, the Awakening and others.

Acknowledgement of Obligations

It is our pleasant duty to put on record our sincere thanks to Dr R.N. Dandekar and the UNESCO authorities for their kind encouragement and valuable help which render this work very useful. We are grateful to Dr S. Venkitasubramonia Iyer, professor of Sanskrit (Retired), University of Kerala, for his critical Introduction, lucid translation, useful glossary and notes. We also thank those persons who have offered suggestions for improving the same.

—*Editor*

CONTENTS

PART II

ABBREVIATIONS

Common and self-evident abbreviations such as Ch(s)-Chapter(s), p—page, pp—pages, V—Verse, VV—Verses, Ftn—footnote, Hist. Ind. Philo—History of Indian Philosophy are not included in this list.

ABORI	*Annals of the Bhandarkar Oriental Research Institute*, Poona
AGP	S. M. Ali's *The Geography of Purāṇas*, PPH, New Delhi, 1973
AIHT	*Ancient Indian Historical Tradition*, F. E. Pargiter, Motilal Banarsidass (MLBD), Delhi
AITM	*Ancient Indian Tradition and Mythology* Series MLBD, Delhi
AP	*Agni Purāṇa*, Guru Mandal Edition (GM), Calcutta, 1957
Arch.S.Rep.	Archaeological Survey Report
AV	*Atharva Veda*, Svādhyāya Mandal, Aundh
Bd. P.	*Brahmāṇḍa Purāṇa*, (MLBD), Delhi 1973
BG	*Bhagavadgītā*
Bh. P.	*Bhāgavata Purāṇa*, Bhagavat Vidyapeeth, Ahmedabad
Br.	*Brāhmaṇa* (preceded by name such as Śatapatha
BS. P.	*Bhaviṣya Purāṇa*, Vishnu Shastri Bapat, Wai
BV. P.	*Brahma Vaivarta Purāṇa*, GM, 1955-57
CC.	*Caturvarga Cintāmaṇi* by Hemādri
CVS	*Caraṇa Vyūha Sūtra* by Śaunaka; Com. by Mahidāsa
DB	*Devi Bhāgavata*, GM, 1960-61
De or GDAMI.	*The Geographical Dictionary of Ancient and Mediaeval India*, N. L. De, Orienta Reprint, Delhi, 1971
Dh. S.	*Dharma Sūtra* (preceded by the author's name such as Gautama)
ERE	*Encyclopaedia of Religion and Ethics*—Hastings.
GP	*Garuḍa Purāṇa* Ed. R. S. Bhattacharya Chowkhamba, Varanasi, 1964

GS	*Gṛhya Sūtra* (preceded by the name of the author such as Āpastamba)
HD	*History of Dharma Śāstra*, P. V. Kane, G. O. S.
IA	*The Indian Antiquary*
IHQ	*The Indian Historical Quarterly*
JP	*Purāṇa* (Journal of the Kashiraj Trust) Varanasi
KA	*Kauṭilya Arthaśāstra*
KP	*Kūrma Purāṇa*, Veṅkaṭeśvara Press Edt. Bombay, also Kashiraj Trust Edt., Varanasi 1971
LP	*Liṅga Purāṇa*, GM, 1960; also MLBD, Delhi, 1981
Manu.	*Manusmṛti*
Mbh.	*Mahābhārata*, Gītā Press, Gorakhpur, VS 2014
MkP	*Mārkaṇḍeya Purāṇa*
MN	*Mahābhārata Nāmānukramaṇī*, Gītā Press Gorakhpur, VS 2016
MtP.	*Matsya Purāṇa*, GM, 1954
MW	*Monier Williams Sk. English Dictionary* MLBD, Delhi, 1976
NP.	*Nāradīya or Nārada Purāṇa*, Veṅkaṭeśvar Press, Bombay
PCK	*Bhāratavarṣīya Prācina Caritrakośa*, Siddheshwar Shastri, Poona, 1968
Pd. P.	*Padma Purāṇa*, GM, 1957-59
PE	*Puranic Encyclopaedia*, V. Mani, English, MLBD, Delhi, 1975
PR or PRHRC	*Puranic Records on Hindu Rites and Customs* R. C. Hazra, Calcutta, 1948
ṚV	*Ṛg-Veda*, Svādhyāya Mandal, Aundh
Śat. Br.	*Śatapatha Brāhmaṇa*
SC or SMC	*Smṛti Candrikā*—Devanna Bhaṭṭa
SEP	*Studies in Epics and Purāṇas*, A.D. Pusalkar, Bharatiya Vidya Bhavan (BVB), Bombay

CHAPTER ONE HUNDRED AND THIRTYSEVEN

The Vulture and the Jackal

Sūta said:

1. Hearing this elaborate account of expiations pertaining to the devotees (Earth said):

2. What you have said about the great expiations for the welfare of your devotees, is pleasing to me.

3. It behoves you now to tell me, O lord, the means of acquiring *dharma*.

4. What is the holy vow to be performed in Kubjāmraka and which is the holy spot that brings pleasure to the devotees ?

Varāha said:

5. Listen to what you have asked of me, which is of a highly secret nature, namely the most sanctified spot for the devotees.

6. Kokāmukha is a great spot, so too Kubjāmraka, so again Saukara which gives release from *saṁsāra*.

7. Holding which spot I raised you from the underworld and where the river Gaṅgā flows.

Earth said:

8. To which worlds do those who die in Saukara go ? What merit is acquired by bathing there or drinking its water ?

9. What are the sacred Tīrthas (places for bath) in Saukara. It behoves you to tell me all this for the sake of establishing *dharma*.

Varāha said:

10. Listen to what I say in reply to what you ask, namely where the people dying in Saukara go.

11. What merit accrues to those who go there or die there and the tīrthas therein.

12. Listen to the merit that those who go to Saukara get.

13. Those who die there send to heaven seven generations of their ancestors and fourteen generations of their successors.

14. By merely going there and seeing me, one takes birth for seven lives in a big family,

15. Affluent in wealth and grain, handsome and virtuous and ever devoted to my service.

16. He who goes there without committing any offence and lives there till death,

17. Assumes a form with conch, disc, mace, lotus and bow in four hands and goes to Śvetadvīpa.

18. I shall tell you, O Earth, what happens to the man who bathes in these *Tīrthas*.

19. One acquires enormous religious merit by bathing in the Cakratīrtha where the Cakra (disc) is installed.

20. Going to Cakratīrtha taking only limited food and in all austerity,

21. And taking there ritualistic bath on Dvādaśī day in the month of Vaiśākha, one takes birth in a large and affluent family and remains in it for ten thousand ten hundred years.

22. He becomes a great devotee dedicated to my service, gets initiated and avoids all offences.

23. By this he crosses the ocean of *saṁsāra* and attains a four-armed form holding disc, mace, conch and lotus.

24. He who dies there gets a form similar to mine, and excels in my world.

25. Hearing these words of the Lord, Earth said with hands folded over her head.

26. In the tīrtha Saukara, the moon propitiated you. Tell me about this, as I am eager to know.

27. At these words of Earth, Viṣṇu, the respository of all *māyā*, spoke to her in a voice like thunder.

28. O Earth, listen. I shall tell you the reason why I was worshipped by him.

29. I was pleased with him and I revealed to him my original form which is difficult even for the gods to see.

30. Soma could not stand the effulgence of this form and he fell down senseless.

31. Then closing his eyes and folding the hands over his head, he desired to speak but could not.

32. Seeing this condition of this lord of the Brāhmaṇas, I prompted him in sweet words.

33. O Soma, with what aim do you perform this severe penance? Tell me what you have in mind. I shall grant that for your pleasure.

34. On hearing my words, the lord of luminaries, who had come to Soma-Tīrtha, spoke thus.

35. O great god, the master of yoga and the lord of yogins, now that you are pleased and have come here,

36. May I have firm and eternal devotion for you as long as these worlds exist.

37. May the form you have given me be visible in all the seven islands of the earth.

38. Let it be *soma* that Brahmins drink in sacrifices and may they attain the divine supreme path.

39. On new moon day when I am weak, let there be oblations for the manes, and may I become pleasant to look at after that.

40. Let my mind never turn to what is unrighteous. Let me be the lord of all herbs.

41. If you are pleased, O great god without beginning, middle or end, may this be granted to me.

42. Hearing these words of Soma (I gave him the boon) and disappeared there.

43. Thus did Soma perform penance and get supreme attainment at Somatīrtha rare to get.

44-46. I shall tell you the result that accrues to a devotee of mine of righteous conduct, who takes bath in Somatīrtha where the great Soma performed penance standing on one foot.

47. Remaining like that with upturned face for five thousand years and doing severe penance, Soma attained great brilliance.

48. He became free from the effect of all his offences.

49. He who performs oblations in the Somatīrtha is born a Brahmin well-versed in Veda and Vedāṅga for three thousand three hundred years.

50. He becomes wealthy, virtuous and well known and a devotee not committing any offence. He finally gets liberated from *saṁsāra*.

51. O fair one, I shall tell you the sign by which Somatīrtha can be identified by a devotee.

52. On the Dvādaśī day in the bright half of the month Vaiśākha, when darkness sets in and nothing is visible,

53. Moonlight is seen on the earth without, however, the moon being there.

54. Such is the wonder of the place which I have to tell you.

55. This is the indication by which the Somatīrtha in Saukara can be known, where all beings get release.

56. I shall tell you another thing which shows the wonderful greatness of this place.

57-58. By the prowess of this place of mine, a female jackal who happened to die there without any desire, was born as a highly beautiful princess, supremely virtuous and proficient in all the sixty four arts.

59. On its eastern side is the tīrtha called Gṛdhravaṭa, where a vulture which died without any desire, became a human being.

60. Hearing these words of Lord Nārāyaṇa, the holy Earth spoke for the welfare of the devotees of Viṣṇu:

61. What a power does this *tīrtha* possess, by which two beings in the animal kingdom, namely a vulture and a jackal, attained human form!

62. O Janārdana, tell me what befalls a person who bathes or dies there.

63. What identification do they get who die there without any desire?

64. Hearing these words of Earth, Viṣṇu, the foremost knower of everything righteous, spoke to Earth in sweet words.

65. Listen, O Earth, I shall tell you what you seek to know, namely how these two beings attained human form.

66. When due to what I had ordained, Kṛtayuga was over and Tretāyuga had set in,

67. A virtuous king by name Brahmadatta was ruling in the city of Kampilla.

68. He had a handsome and righteous son named Somadatta.

69. Once the prince went for hunting in the forest full of tigers and lions for the sake of his father.

70. While he was wandering, being not able to get any game, he came across on his right a female jackal.

71. The prince hit her with an arrow and she fell down in great pain.

72. Being wounded by the arrow and tormented by the heat of the sun, she went to a Śākhoṭaka tree.

73. Then she gave up her life without any desire in the Somatīrtha.

74. Meanwhile, the prince felt thirsty and reached Gṛdhravaṭa for taking rest.

75. He saw a vulture on the branch of a banyan tree and then hit it with an arrow.

76. It fell down dead being pierced in its heart.

77. The prince was delighted. He plucked out its wings to feather his arrows and went home.

78. The vulture died there without any desire, and after a long time, it was born as the son of the king of Kaliṅga.

79. He was handsome, virtuous and learned and always delighted the people.

80-81. The jackal was born as the daughter of the king of Kāñcī. She too was beautiful, virtuous, cuckoo-voiced and proficient in all the sixtyfour arts.

82. O Earth, due to my favour, Kāñcī and Kaliṅga became very friendly and closely attached to each other.

83. In due course, the marriage of the prince of Kaliṅga with the princess of Kāñcī was conducted in the proper manner.

84. The King of Kāñcī bestowed on them numerous gems and jewels and elephants, horses and women.

85. Honoured well by him, the king of Kaliṅga also went to his capital with his son and daughter-in-law.

86. The couple lived in extreme happiness like Candra and Rohiṇī.

87. They delighted themselves in temples, gardens and other places of enjoyment.

88. If the princess did not find her husband by her side even for a moment, she felt extremely anxious.

89. Similarly, the prince too felt the same if he could not find the princess near him even for a moment.

90. Day by day, their love waxed like this and there was no difference between them in any matter whatsoever.

91. The prince, by his intelligence and nobility pleased all his subjects and all the ladies in the harem.

92. By the couple everybody was made happy.

93. Their mutual love steadily grew up and their intimacy was like that between Indra and Śacī.

94. The loving princess once made a request to her husband:

95. O famous prince, I wish to ask you something which you may tell me because of your love.

96. Hearing these words of his wife, the prince of Kaliṅga said in sweet words:

97. O fair princess, I shall tell you in truth whatever you wish to know.

98. Truth is the source of all Brahmins, Viṣṇu is established in truth. The source of that is penance, the kingdom is established by truth.

99. I will never speak falsehood, I have not said anything false so far in my life.

100. I shall give you elephants, horses, chariots, vehicle, gems and wealth. I shall even raise you to the very position of the ruler.

101. Hearing these words of her husband, the princess of Kāñcī held his feet and said.

102. I don't wish to have gems or elephants, horses and chariots. I don't wish to rule the kingdom so long as you are there.

103. I wish to sleep for a short while at noon without being seen by anybody.

104. During the time of this vow, even the father-in-law and mother-in-law and any one like them shall not see me.

105. Those in my own household may, however, at times see me sleeping.

106. Hearing these words of his wife, the prince of Kaliṅga agreed to what she said and spoke to her:

107. Be assured, O my love, that none will see you in your bed during your vow.

108. As time was passing, the king of Kaliṅgs having become old, installed his son on the throne.

109. He gave the kingdom, as is wont in his line, after making it free from all troubles.

110. After receiving this gift from the king, he used to sleep alone without being seen by anyone.

111. In due course, he begot five children resplendent like the sun.

112. Such is the human world under the spell of my *māyā* that everyone revolves like a wheel in accordance with one's own actions.

113. A human being is first born, then he becomes a boy, then a youth in the prime of life, and after that attains old age.

114. Whatever deed a boy does without knowing it, does not bring upon him any sin.

115. While he was ruling the kingdom happily and free from trouble, seventyseven years passed.

116-117. In the seventyeighth year, on the Dvādaśī day in the bright half of the month of Mādhava, when the sun was at the zenith, the desire came upon him to see his wife.

118. He thought: Who is worshipped by her and what is her vow to sleep in loneliness. A vow during sleep is not heard of anywhere.

119. This is not ordained by Viṣṇu or Śiva, nor do we find it in the dharmaśāstra of Manu.

120. A detestable action can never be *dharma* even for yogins. There will be none who will do like this.

121. We do not find in dharmaśāstra of Bṛhaspati or Yama anything ordaining a vow for a woman in sleep.

122. Enjoying as much as she liked and eating meat, taking tāmbūla and wearing red garments,

123. Having fragrant unguents and numerous gems, what is the sort of vow she performs?

124. Certainly my wife will be angry if I see her. All the same, I should know what vow she practises.

125. Perhaps she wants to acquire the power of attraction of the Kinnaras or to become a yogīśvarī to go wherever she likes.

126. Or she is having sexual urge for another person.

127. While he was thinking like this, the sun set and night began giving pleasure to all.

128. When night was over and day set in, the bards began singing rhapsodies.

129. As the sun rose for the welfare of the world, the king was roused by the sound of conchs and drums.

130. The desire to see his beloved was still there in his mind.

131. He then took bath and wore silken clothes and gave orders to keep away people from him.

132. Any one who touches me during my vow will be punished according to the rules of law.

133. Issuing the order in this manner, the king went to the place of vow of his beloved in order to see her.

134-135. He found her there crying with severe headache and asking herself.

136. What wrong did I do that I am now in this despicable state ?

137. My husband does not know that I am helplessly suffering like this. What will he or my relations think of me ?

138. What shall I tell those who are my constant companions ?

139. How has all this come about ? What will my husband say ? What will others say ?

140. The vow which is not properly done will be defective. But I shall once go to Saukara and there I shall utter what I have in my mind.

141. Hearing these words of his beloved, the king embraced her and said:

142. What do you say ? Why do you condemn yourself. Why should you be sorry when you can be happy ?

143. Are there not doctors adept in the eight kinds of treatment, who can control your headache ?

144. Under the pretext of observing a vow, you have been hiding your severe headache.

145. The head is aching because of the disturbance of wind, phlegm, bile or blood or all these together.

146. It can also be due to exciting bile in place and out of place by eating meat.

147. The head can be bored, blood expelled and anointed. How then can the ache remain ?

148. Why is it that without telling me about this, you undergo all this suffering under the guise of vow ?

149. You now speak of going to Saukara. What is the secret for you there ?

150. Then that beautiful and bashful lady held her husband's feet and told him:

151. Be pleased, O king, not to ask me this question. My former life was full of bad deeds.

152. Hearing these words of his beloved, the king of Kaliṅga spoke to her with composure.

153. O beautiful lady, why should you hide anything from me. Tell me the truth.

154. She then told the king softly with eyes wide with wonder.

155. The husband is virtue, the husband is glory and the husband is the most dear. So what the husband asks should certainly be told.

156. Still I don't wish to say what I have in mind because it may cause sorrow to you.

157. My distress remains in mind. You are a handsome king ever remaining happy.

158. You have numerous wives like me in the harem. You can have any food you like, so too clothes and jewels.

159. You can drive in any vehicle, or on the back of elephant or horse. So even without me you can have a life of pleasure.

160. Your command is unviolable and you have everything for your pleasure. So it is not necessary for you to ask me about my illness.

161. O noble king, you are my god, preceptor, husband, sacrifice, *dharma*, wealth, desire, fame and heaven.

162. So when you ask me anything, I should tell you the truth. That is the duty of all obedient wives.

163. But the happiness of the husband should not be disturbed by a wife. Therefore, please don't ask me about my pain.

164. Hearing these words of his wife, the king of Kaliṅga spoke being distressed at her ailment:

165. Happy or unhappy, the husband should be told what he asks.

166. No virtuous wife will hide from the husband any matter private or public, good or bad.

167. Even if it is a sin committed out of passion, if the wife hides it, she is never considered virtuous.

168. Considering all this, O great lady, tell me the truth. You will not be committing any sin by telling me the truth.

169. Hearing these words of her husband, who was standing on *dharma*, she replied:

170. It is said that the king is god, the king is preceptor and the king is Soma. Therefore, in the name of *dharma* I should tell you what you ask.

171. If I should not keep it secret, install your eldest son on the throne, as is the usual practice.

172. Then come along with me to the place called Saukara.

173. Hearing these words of his wife, the king of Kaliṅga agreed to her proposal and said:

174. As you say, I shall give my kingdom to my son as I got it from my father.

175. The king and the queen in full agreement with each other, left that place.

176. Then seeing the chamberlain, he asked him in a loud voice to dispel the crowd that had gathered there. All those who had collected there out of curiosity were asked to leave the place.

177. Then a tumult was heard inside the palace.

178. Why are we being sent out from here ? We have come here for our own purpose. Why should there be a command like this ? Perhaps we are not to know the reason.

179. Then he ate sumptuous food and took rest with his wife for a while.

180. Then he sent for his ministers and asked them to make arrangements for the coronation of the son.

181. He also asked them to decorate the capital in an auspicious manner.

182. Then he went near the oldest minister, who was well-versed in polity, and told him.

183. O revered minister, I wish to coronate my son tomorrow. Please make arrangements for all the necessary rituals.

184. The arrangements have already been made, they said. What you proposed to do is agreeable to us also.

185. Your son, O king, is interested in the welfare of your subjects and he is always just and considerate.

186. Your proposal really gladdens us. So saying the ministers left and the sun set.

187. He spent the night well and was roused in the morning by music and the rhapsodies of the minstrels.

188. When the night was over and the sun rose up, the son was crowned at an auspicious time.

189. Giving him thus the kingdom and smelling him on his head, he told him.

190. Although you have now become the king, listen to what you should do.

191. If you wish to acquire great merit and liberate your manes, you should be a liberal giver and abstain from injury.

192. But one who molests another's wife should be punished, so also one who kills children.

193. Do not entertain desire for another's wife particularly when she is a Brahmin. Close your eyes if you see a beautiful lady who is another's wife.

194. Don't desire the wealth of another or any ill-earned wealth. You should protect the land with cleverness and justice.

195. Be always enterprising and follow the advice of the ministers. The report of a minister should be carefully considered.

196. Take care to protect your person. See that the subjects as a whole, and Brahmins in particular, are happy.

197. Indulgence in the seven kinds of pleasure may bring about great harm.

198. Wealth should never be squandered. Unpleasantness with ministers should be avoided particularly by those that are interested in the welfare of the subjects.

199. Do not prevent me from going away renouncing everything, but observe all that I have said.

200. Hearing these words of his father, the prince held his feet and said piteously:

201. What are kingdom, treasury and army to me. Without you here, I may not be able to have any activity.

202. You have crowned me king, but I don't consider it great without you.

203. I know only to play as other boys do. I do not know the administration of the kingdom, which only experienced kings know.

204. Hearing these words of his son, the king of Kaliṅga spoke to him words of consolation.

205. I do not know why you say like this. The citizens will instruct you as to what you should do.

206. After advising the son in this way, the king started for Saukara.

207. Seeing him leave like that, the citizens with their families followed him.

208. The elephants, horses, chariots and women in the harem gladly followed him.

209. After a long time, he reached Saukara and there he made large gifts of money and grain.

210. O Earth, as time passed, they became more and more purified.

211. Then the handsome prince spoke pleasantly to the princess of Kāñcī.

212. Now a thousand years of my life is over, please tell the secret about which I asked you before.

213. Hearing these words of her husband, she laughed and told the king:

214. It is all as you say. You fast for three days and then you will know the truth.

215. The king agreed: O my beloved, I shall do what you say. That is to my liking also.

216. Then he took the prescribed twig, twelve fingers in length, and after bathing took the vow of fast for three days.

217. For three days they observed fast according to rules and after bathing, put on new silk.

218. Then they bedecked themselves and offered worship to Viṣṇu.

219. Then she removed all ornaments, offered *naivedya* to me and then told the king.

220. O my lord, come along so as to know the secret. Then holding his hand as in wedlock, she spoke sweetly to the king.

221. I was formerly a vixen and I was hit by the arrow of Somadatta when he was hunting.

222. See here the stump of the arrow well lodged in my head, as a result of which I have developed headache.

223. I was then born in the Kāñcī royal family and I was given to you in marriage. By the prowess of this place I attained all this.

224. Hearing this, the king of Kaliṅga said to her remembering his previous life.

225. I was a vulture who was hit by the same Somadatta by a single arrow.

226. Then I was born as the king of Kaliṅga and attained great prosperity and this kingdom.

227. All this was because I died without any desire in this holy place.

228-229. The devotees of Lord Nārāyaṇa and all the other people there, hearing about this, began to perform rites there without any sense of loss or gain.

230. Those who died there without any desire went to Śvetadvīpa with a four-armed body, all of them holding conch and various weapons.

231. The women also went to Śvetadvīpa and enjoyed all pleasures there.

232. I have thus told you about the greatness of Saukara.

233. Those who perform rites here and die without desire go to Śvetadvīpa.

234. Now listen, O Earth, what results from a bath in Śākhoṭaka tīrtha.

235. For twelve thousand and twelve hundred years they enjoy pleasure in the Nandana garden.

236. They then come down to the earth and are born in a big family of my devotees.

237. I shall now tell you the result of merely bathing in Gṛdhravaṭa.

238. For nine thousand nine hundred years he delights himself in the world of Indra with the gods.

239. Then coming down from Indraloka, he is born as a devotee with full detachment.

240. I have thus told you the result of bath in this tīrtha which you desired to know.

241. Hearing these words from Lord Nārāyaṇa, Earth asked him again in sweet words:

242. Due to the result of which action is this tīrtha attained for bath or for death? Be pleased to tell me this.

Varāha said:

243. O goddess, listen. Due to the defect of some action, one is born as an animal.

244. But due to merit acquired in former lives by deeds like bath in sacred spots, and by liberal gifts etc, one happens to die there.

245. The action performed in a former life, whether it is big or small, gives its effect without fail.

246. Even by the very sight of a sacred spot at some time or other and even alone, what is weak becomes strong and what is strong becomes weak.

247. The result of action is mysterious because what is little becomes enormous.

248. That is the reason of being born as a human being and attaining kingship.

249. The jackal and the vulture, by their death in the *tīrtha*, got their sin removed and attained memory of their former lives and went to Śvetadvīpa.

250. I shall now tell you about the tīrtha called Vaivasvata where Sun-god performed penance.

251. In order to get a son, Sun performed severe penance and Cāndrāyaṇa for ten thousand years.

252. Then for seven thousand years, he lived on air alone.

253. I was very much pleased by this action of Sun and I asked him to seek a boon, as he was devoted to me.

254. Choose a boon which you have in mind.

255. Hearing these words, the mighty son of Kaśyapa, spoke to me in sweet words:

256. If you are pleased with me, then give me the boon of my getting a child by your favour.

257. I was glad to hear this uttered by him in all purity and seriousness.

258. You will beget a twin, Yama and Yamunā.

259. After giving this boon to Sun I disappeared due to my yogic power. Sun too returned to his abode.

260. One who attains merit by austerities at Saukara, eating but little and bathing there, remains in the world of Sun for ten thousand years.

261. The virtuous man who dies there never goes to the world of Yama, because of the power of this *tīrtha*.

262. Thus have I told you about the benefits of bath and death at Saukara.

263. This is the narrative of all narratives, the action of all actions. This is to be recited as authority during the worship of sandhyā.

264. This is the glorious mantra dear to all devotees.

265. This should not be imparted to a wicked person, a fool or one who is not a devotee, nor to a Vaiśya or Śūdra who does not know me as the Supreme being.

266. This should be recited in an assembly of learned men or

in a hall full of Brahmins proficient in Vedas. It may be imparted to those who are initiated and who know the *śāstras*.

267. O blessed goddess, thus have I told you about the merit that accrues from Saukara.

268. He who recites this rising up early in the morning, gets the result equivalent to contemplating on me for twelve years.

269. He does not take birth again, but attains eternal liberation. He who reads even one chapter of this, liberates ten generations of his ancestors.

CHAPTER ONE HUNDRED AND THIRTYEIGHT

The Story of the Wag-tail

Sūta said:

1. After hearing about the greatness of Saukara and the benefits drawn from it and its capacity to change one being into another.

2. The goddess who knew everything about *dharma* was wonderstruck and felt much gratified.

3. She then asked Lord Viṣṇu: How great is this tīrtha Saukara of yours ! Whichever being dies here without desire becomes a human being.

4. What other story do you propose to tell me about Saukara. I am very much curious to know.

5. What merit accrues to a person who sings there or renders instrumental music ?

6. What merit is acquired by one who dances there or what by one who keeps awake all the time. What is the effect of making gifts of cow, food and water there ?

7. What benefit is got by cleaning, anointing, offering flowers, incense, lamp and *naivedya* ?

8. What is the effect of other actions like *japa* and sacrifice performed there ? Please tell me all this for the sake of your devotees.

9. Hearing these words of Earth, Lord Hari spoke in sweet words.

Varāha said:

10. O fair goddess, I shall tell you what you wish to know, the sacred deeds that bring about happiness.

11. In Saukara a wag-tail bird ate too many worms as a result of which it was suffering from indigestion.

12. By this action, it fell down dead.

13. Then came there many boys to take it for playing and they were running for it.

14. They began to quarrel among themselves each attempting to get it for himself.

15. Then one of them took it and threw it into the river Ganges saying that it was of no use to them.

16. The wag-tail happened to fall in Āditya tīrtha in the Ganges.

17. As a result of this, it was born as the beautiful son of a Vaiśya who had performed numerous sacrifices and was very wealthy.

18. Intelligent, pure and devoted to me he was, and twelve years passed in this manner.

19. Once when his father and mother were together, he bowed to them and made a request.

20. If I am dear to you, please grant me a boon I ask for.

21. I should not be said 'No' either by you father, or you mother. I swear by my preceptor.

22. Hearing these words of the son, the parents were very glad and they told the dear son.

23. Whatever you say and whatever you have in mind, be confident that we will fulfil.

24. Thirty thousand milch cows are here and you can make a gift of any of them.

25. If you do not wish to have trade which is our occupation, you may gift away all wealth to your friends.

26. You can gift away quite unhampered all the grain and money.

27. We shall bring here aristocratic girls of our clan to choose one as your bride.

28. If you wish to perform sacrifices, you can do the same according to the rules laid down for Vaiśyas in this regard.

29. If you wish to be a farmer you have here eight mighty bulls and eight thousand ploughs.

30. If you wish to feed Brahmins sumptuously you can do it as you like.

31. Hearing these words of his parents, the virtuous boy held their feet and said:

32. I don't wish to make gifts of cows. I have not thought of my friends. I don't wish to have a bride and I don't wish to have the merit of sacrifices.

33. I don't wish to enter trade or farming and cattle-rearing. Nor do I wish to host anyone.

34. There is only one thing that I desire and that is to go to Saukara, the place of Lord Nārāyaṇa.

35. Hearing these words of their son, the two devotees of mine began to weep. (The mother said):

36. How is it that you think of Lord Nārāyaṇa now? That is, of course, good to you at the proper age.

37. Even now I have to run after you to make you eat. How is it that you think of going to Saukara now ?

38. My breasts are still full of milk for you and I still wish to fondle you. How is it that you think like this ?

39. During sleep when you turn on the bed you call 'mother' even now. How is it that you have this desire ?

40. The women hold you when you play. No offence has been committed in temples or homes.

41. No relation or servant has spoken to you anything harsh. You have with you the cane when you are threatened or made angry.

42. I do not find any reason for your renunciation.

43. Hearing these words of the mother, that delighter of the Vaiśya clan, spoke to her in sweet words:

44. I have always been attached to your person. During pregnancy I was in your womb. As child I was playing over your shoulders.

45. I have suckled your extensive breasts and, sitting on your lap, I have soiled your whole body.

46. O mother, be kind to me. Give up the grief of parting with the son.

47. People come and go. When once gone, they are never seen again.

48. From where is one born ? What relation has he ? Whose

is a mother or father? I happened to fall in your womb and thereby into the ocean of *saṁsāra*.

49. Thousands there are of fathers and mothers and hundreds of sons and wives in numerous lives. Who are they and who are we?

50. Therefore, O mother, don't feel sorry. The parents were surprised at this and they said:

51. What a great secret is it that you speak about.

Then the Vaiśya boy told his parents in sweet words:

52. If you think that there is a secret in what I said, then ask me about it at Saukara.

53. There I shall tell you the secret about me if you ask there in Sūryatīrtha.

54. They agreed and resolved to go to Saukara.

55. Arrangements were made for everything regarding the journey to Saukara, the place of the lord of Ābhīras.

56. Twenty thousand cows were sent there in advance.

57. People went in front with all materials, whatever in the house that could be offered to Lord Nārāyaṇa.

58. Then on the Trayodaśī day in the month of Māgha, he called together all his people.

59. They all started together at an auspicious time, cleansed themselves and took bath with lord Nārāyaṇa in mind.

60. Meditating on Nārāyaṇa for a long time, they reached my temple on the Dvādaśī day in the month of Vaiśākha.

61. After bathing there and propitiating the manes and putting on the dress prescribed for my devotees, they moved forward with twenty thousand cows.

62. They were received duly by my devotee named Bhaṅgurasa.

63. He was given twenty milch cows all of them sacred and auspicious.

64. The king was giving gifts of money and gems every day and feeling happy with his wife and son.

65. While he was spending the days like this, the rainy season set in which makes all plants grow.

66. The Kadamba, Kuṭaja and Arjuna trees flowered profusely. Women separated from their husbands were feeling extremely sad.

67. The waterfalls produced roaring sound in some places and gentle sound in others.

68. There were the subdued sound of flowing rivers and the cooing of peacocks. The fragrance of Kuṭaja, Kadamba and Arjuna flowers was spreading everywhere.

69. The blowing wind gave delight to the peacocks but agony to women in separation.

70. As the rainy season with its drums of thunder passed, the autumn season set in and the Agasti star (Canopus) rose.

71. The ponds became clear and smelt of lotuses and lilies which blossomed producing fine fragrance.

72. The wind was pleasant with fragrance and coolness and the smell of the Saptaparṇa flowers excited lovers.

73. When the autumn was over and the month of Kārttika started, on the Ekādaśī day in the bright half of the month.

74. The couple took bath and dressed themselves in silk and then spoke to the son;

75. "We have now stayed here for six months and the auspicious Dvādaśī day has come. Why don't you tell us the secret which you have been hiding from us."

76. Hearing the words of his parents, that dutiful son spoke in sweet words:

77. What you say is true. Tomorrow morning I shall tell you this secret.

78. This Dvādaśī, O my parents, is particularly dear to Viṣṇu and it is very auspicious and it brings about the well-being of the devotees of Viṣṇu.

79. The initiated yogins among the devotees of Viṣṇu are delighted on the Dvādaśī day of Kārttika and they make gifts.

80. By these gifts meant to propitiate Viṣṇu, they are able to cross the dreadful ocean of *saṁsāra*.

81. As he was telling them this, the night came to a close. After worshipping *sandhyā* at dawn,

82. He had the ritualistic bath, and putting on silken garments, bowed to Lord Viṣṇu.

83. And holding the feet of his parents, told them:

84. I shall tell you, my parents, the purpose of our coming here. It is to give you the secret of this Saukara.

85. I belong to the species of birds and I was born as a wag-

tail. I ate numerous flies and worms and I began to suffer from indigestion.

86. Because of that I was unable to move and, seeing this, boys took me in their hands to play with.

87. They made fun of one another and I was moved from hand to hand, but soon a quarrel arose each saying, 'I saw the bird first'.

88. One of them snatched me away and threw me in Ganges. That happened to be the Somatīrtha and I breathed my last there.

89. Since I died there without any desire, by the power of that place, I was born, O mother, as your son on this holy day.

90. Thirteen years have passed since then and I have been hiding this truth from you all the time.

91. I have now told you the purpose of our coming here.

92. I shall now engage myself in what I have to do. I bow to you, O father, be pleased to return.

The parents said to the son again:

93. Whatever deeds you do to propitiate Lord Viṣṇu, the same we shall also do.

94. They became my devotees for a long time and performed actions laid down for liberation from *saṁsāra*.

95. In the end they died there and due to their determination and by the power of this place, they were liberated and they reached Śvetadvīpa.

96. All the attendants who had come there with them were endowed with health and wealth.

97. They acquired the smell of lotus, became yogins and felt happy by the prowess of this sacred spot.

98. Thus have I told you about this great story.

99. Such is the prosperity which this place bestows on those who go there. Even what is originally an animal goes to Śvetadvīpa attaining liberation.

100. He who reads this in the morning every day, liberates ten generations of his ancestors and ten generations of his successors.

101. This should not be read before fools or those who decry the śāstras or within the hearing of wicked people. It is best to recite it in solitude at home.

102. This should be recited before Brahmins who are well-versed in Veda, before devotees of Viṣṇu and those who are learned in śāstras.

103. It liberates from *saṁsāra* the pure and the humble.

CHAPTER ONE HUNDRED AND THIRTYNINE

Greatness of Saukara—the benefits of Service in worship

Varāha said:

1. O goddess, listen. I shall tell you what merit accrues to a person who smears (the floor of the temple with cowdung).

2. He remains in heaven for as many thousands of years as the number of steps he smears with cowdung.

3. If he does this for twelve years, he is born in a family rich in money and grain.

4-5. He then goes to Kuśadvīpa and lives there as a great devotee of mine for twelve thousand years, honoured by the gods.

6. At the end of his life in Kuśadvīpa he is born as a king who upholds *dharma*.

7. He then becomes a great devotee fully dedicated to my service and adept in all śāstras.

8. He constructs many temples and ultimately reaches my world.

9. I shall tell you what world is attained by collecting cowdung.

10. He who does this remains in heaven for as many thousands of years as the number of steps he goes to collect it.

11. Then he delights in the śālmaladvīpa for eleven thousand eleven hundred years.

12. Then leaving Śālmala he is born as a virtuous king and a great devotee.

13. He who carries cowdung for use in the temple remains in my world for twelve thousand years.

14. Now know the benefits that accrue to a person who bathes me, applies unguent and offers water.

15. He lords in heaven for as many thousands of years as there are drops in the water offered.

16. From heaven he descends to Krauñcadvīpa and from there he descends to be born as a king.

17. And then by his own merit he goes to Śvetadvīpa.

18. I shall tell you now, O Earth, about what befalls a man or woman who does the cleaning of my temples.

19. The pure devotee, free from all faults, remains in heaven for as many hundreds of years as there are particles of dust expelled by his sweeping.

20. From heaven he descends to Śākadvīpa and, remaining there for long, is born as virtuous king.

21. Then enjoying all pleasures in the world, he goes to Śvetadvīpa and remains in my eternal worship.

22-23.. Listen now to what I tell you about the result of singing in my service.

24. He who sings for me remains exalted in the world of Indra for as many thousand years as there are syllables in the song.

25. He becomes handsome, virtuous, accomplished and proficient in Veda. He always sees Indra, the lord of gods.

26. He remains my devotee even while living in the world of Indra, always worshipping me.

27. Then from the world of Indra, he passes on to the garden Nandana and makes himself happy there in the company of Devas.

28. Then he is born in this world amidst Vaiṣṇavas always singing my glory in great devotion.

29. And then by my favour, he reaches my world.

Sūta said:

30. Hearing these words of Lord Mādhava, Earth exclaimed with folded hands:

Earth said:

31. How wonderful is the efficacy of singing ! Who are those who attained salvation by this means ?

Varāha said:

32. In a hermitage there, an outcaste was living as a devotee of mine keeping awake for a long time.

33. O fair goddess, though an outcaste, he had good qualities and was deeply inmersed in devotion, singing my praise for many years.

34. On the Dvādaśī day in the bright half of the month of Kārttika, when all were asleep, he wandered about playing on Vīṇā.

35. While he was thus awake, he was caught by a Brahmarākṣasa. The outcaste was week and the Brahmarākṣasa strong.

36. Grief-stricken, he was unable to move. He then spoke to the Brahmarākṣasa.

37. I am a mere wanderer. Why did you do this to me ? The Brahmarākṣasa then told him, being desirous of eating a man.

38. I have been going without food for ten days and now I have been given the food.

39. I shall eat you now with your flesh and blood and satisfy myself with this that Providence has given me.

40. Hearing the words of the Brahmarākṣasa, the outcaste who was still engaged in singing in devotion asked him to do what he liked.

41. I have now become your food given by Providence. You do what you think proper.

42. But I am now engaged in keeping awake and singing in praise of the Lord.

43. Let me finish my worship according to the rules and then you can eat me.

44. This vow of mine is for the propitiation of lord Viṣṇu and, when this is over, you may eat me.

45. Hearing these words of that outcaste, the Brahmarākṣasa who was extremely hungry, spoke to him in harsh words:

46. "Why do you try to cheat me by saying that you will come to me later. Can any man live after falling into the mouth of Death ? You wish to get out of it and then come back".

47. Hearing these words, the outcaste said again:

48. "Although now I am an outcaste because of my bad actions in my previous life, I am a pure man in my mind.

49. Listen to my promise of returning to you after my vow which is for the good of the world. I swear truly that I will return to you. So please release me.

50. The whole universe is based on truth, all the worlds rest

in truth. The sages who speak of Brahman get their attainments through truth.

51. By truth is a girl given in marriage, the Brahmins speak truth, kings win by truth.

52. Heaven is attained by truth, salvation is got by truth. The sun shines by truth and the moon sheds light by truth.

53. If I do not return to you, I will incur the same sin as accrues to a person who does not take bath on Ṣaṣṭhī, Aṣṭamī and Amāvāsyā days.

54. If I do not return to you, I will incur the same sin as accrues to a person who shares bed with the preceptor's wife and the king's wife.

55. If I do not return to you, I will incur the same sin as accrues to a person who is a beggar or a liar.

56. If I do not return to you, I will incur the same sin as accrues to a person who kills a Brahmin or drinks liquor or who does not complete a vow undertaken".

57. The Brahmarākṣasa was pleased at these words of the outcaste, he bowed to him and allowed him to go.

58. Released thus by the Brahmarākṣasa, the outcaste with determination again moved about singing my glory out of devotion.

59. When the day dawned, the singing and dancing were concluded, and uttering the name 'Nārāyaṇa' the outcaste began to return.

60. Then a man suddenly appeared there and spoke to him in appealing tone:

61. O good man, where are you going in such haste. That is the place of goblins and don't lose your life by going there.

62. Hearing these words of that man, the outcaste said:

63. I have to honour an agreement with the Brahmarākṣasa who wanted to eat me. I am speeding to him now.

64. Then the man told him in all earnestness.

65. O you poor outcaste, don't go to that place where lives that Brahmarākṣasa. It is not sinful to violate truth if it is to save your own life.

66. Then that austere outcaste said, determined to court death:

67. I shall not do as you say. I shall never sacrifice truth, come what may. That is my resolve.

68. The whole universe rests on truth, the family is established in truth, truth is the highest *dharma* and the soul has its basis in truth.

69. I shall never give up truth and take to falsehood. I bow to you. Be pleased to go.

70. The outcaste, who was thus firmly wedded to truth, went to that Rākṣasa, bowed to him and said:

71. I have now come to you. Eat me quickly. By that favour I shall be able to go to the abode of Viṣṇu.

72. Eat my body as you like and drink my warm blood. You are so full of hunger. Satisfy yourself and do me thus good.

73. Hearing these words of the outcaste, the Brahmarākṣasa told him:

74. I am pleased with you. You have upheld truth and righteousness. You have got this commendable mind, although being an outcaste, you do not know the rules.

75. Hearing these words of Brahmarākṣasa, the outcaste who was standing on truth, spoke to him endearingly.

76. Although I am an outcaste not entitled to perform rituals, I should always stand by truth.

77. Hearing these words of the outcaste, the terrible Brahmarākṣasa spoke to him again:

78-79. If you wish to save your life, give me the benefit of your having sung the glory of Viṣṇu throughout night. I shall then release you instead of eating you.

80. The outcaste then replied to the Brahmarākṣasa:

81. I am not able to know what you mean. You said that you will eat me. And now you want the fruit of my singing the praise of God.

82. The Brahmarākṣasa then said: Give me the merit of your singing for one watch of the night. Then I shall release you so that you can go to your wife and children.

83. At these words of the Rākṣasa, the outcaste who treasured the merit of his singing, told him with an air of determination.

84. O Brahmarākṣasa, I shall not give you the merit of my singing which you ask for. You may eat me and drink my blood.

85. The Rākṣasa then replied: Give me the merit of your singing once before Lord Viṣṇu. By that I shall be liberated.

86. The outcaste was wonderstruck at these words of the Rākṣasa and asked him:

87. What wrong did you commit that you became a Rākṣasa ?

88. The Brahmarākṣasa then spoke in great sorrow:

89. I was a Brahmin by name Somaśarmā belonging to the Caraka clan.

90. Without knowing the rules and *mantras* I used to perform sacrificial rituals for the credulous, because of my greed.

91. When once I was performing a sacrifice in this way, I was stricken by pain in the abdomen and I died as a result.

92. When, thus, the five-day long sacrifice was interrupted, a great sin befell me.

93. I became a Rākṣasa because of this objectionable deed.

94. Whatever I did without mantra, without proper accent, without following the code, the resultant form of all that I could see then.

95. By my own faults I became this Rākṣasa. It behoves you to liberate me from this by giving me the merit of your singing. Liberate me, this despicable self, by the song in praise of Viṣṇu.

96. The saintly outcaste was moved by these words of the Brahmarākṣasa and so he agreed and spoke to him:

97. O Rākṣasa, if it will make you pure and get you release, I shall give you the merit of my faultless singing.

98. He who faultlessly sings songs before Viṣṇu crosses all berriers. So saying he transferred to him his merit.

99. The Rākṣasa, thus getting the merit from the outcaste, became pure like the moon in autumn.

100. The outcaste continued to be a singer of my glory and, in the end, attained Brahman.

101. Such is the result, O Earth, that a person who sings for me gets.

102. He who sings on the Dvādaśī day of Kārttika, renounces everything and reaches my world.

103. He who sings songs in my praise during the period when I am awake, becomes detached from everything and attains my world.

104. I have thus told you about the efficacy of singing by which one is able to transcend this world.

105. I shall now tell you about the instrumental music which confers a position equal to the Gods.

106-107. By means of Śampā tāla or Sannipāta[1] one goes to the abode of Kubera and remains there for nine thousand nine hundred years.

108. Then from the abode of Kubera he moves about as he likes and finally reaches my world by the efficacy of the tālas like Śampā.

109. O Earth, I shall tell you now about the efficacy of dancing by which one is enabled to transcend the world.

110. He goes to Puṣkaradvīpa and moves about there as he likes for thirty three thousand years.

111. He becomes handsome, virtuous, valiant and always treading the right path. He gets release from *saṁsāra*.

112. He who dances for me with vocal and instrumental music, goes to Jambūdvīpa and is born there as an emperor.

113. He becomes an ardent protector of his subjects and remains a staunch devotee.

114. He who offers me flowers in ritualistic worship and places them on my head as much as it can hold,

115. (He) reaches my world by the efficacy of this action of his.

116. Thus have I told you what is conducive to the liberation from *saṁsāra* for my devotees.

117. He who recites this early in the morning liberates ten generations of his ancestors and ten generations of his successors.

118. This should not be read in the midst of fools or before wicked people. It should be read only before devotees who seek release.

119. This should not be read to the indifferent, the cruel and those who go to temple simply seeking food, if you wish for good.

120. This is the greatest of all *dharmas* and the greatest of all actions.

121. Don't read even a chapter of this to one who despises the śāstras if you wish to go to my world.

1. These are different kinds of keeping time-measure.

CHAPTER ONE HUNDRED AND FORTY

The greatness of holy spots in Kokāmukha

Earth said:

1. I have now known about the temples of which you spoke to me. But I wish to know in which place you reside for ever.

2. Which is that most exalted place where you remain as an idol? Which is the exalted place where the performance of actions leads to the attainment of the highest end?

Varāha said:

3. O you goddess, fond of devotees, I shall tell you about the places where I reside.

4. I have formerly told you about Kokāmukha. There in the Himālayas is a broad rocky surface called Badarī.

5. There is a spot called Lohārgala resorted to by the king of the Mlecchas. These are places from which I do not move out even for a moment.

6. This is the place where I am installed, although I am the entire universe and there is nothing in which I am not present.

7. Let those who wish to know the secret about me go to Kokāmukha soon.

8. Earth was glad to hear these words of the Lord. Holding her hands over her head, she spoke to him:

Earth said:

9. O lord of the worlds, I have great curiosity to know how Kokāmukha is great. Be pleased to tell me.

Varāha said:

10. There is no sacred spot greater than Kokāmukha, none more pure than Kokāmukha, no position higher than Kokāmukha's, nothing more dear than Kokāmukha.

11. He who goes to Kokāmukha never returns to *saṁsāra*. Whatever action is performed there, becomes conducive to the soul.

12. Among all the places about which you have asked, O Earth, a place which equals Kokāmukha never has been and never will be.

13. There in Kokāmukha is my hidden form.

Earth said:

14. O great lord, the refuge of devotees, be pleased to tell me about all the secrets of Kokāmukha.

Varāha said:

15. O goddess, listen. I shall tell you what you desire to know about this charming Kokāmukha.

16. There is a waterfall called Jalabindu in the mountain which is important. By performing rites there one reaches my world.

17. There is another waterfall in Kokā called Viṣṇudhārā which is like a club.

18. If one fasts there for a day and night and then takes bath, he acquires the result of a thousand Agniṣṭoma sacrifices.

19. He never fails in his duty and he attains full benefits. He is then born in a big family of my devotees.

20. One who gives up life at Viṣṇudhārā, doubtless sees this form of mine.

21. There is a place in Kokāmukha called Viṣṇupada dedicated to Varāha which is not known to many.

22. He who offers libations there after fasting during the night, will be born in Krauñcadvīpa as my devotee.

23. One who gives up life there, renounces everything and reaches my world.

24. Then there is the lake called Viṣṇusaras where I have played with you raising you up with my tusk.

25. One who bathes there early in the morning, becomes free from all sins and goes to my world.

26. In Kokā there is Somatīrtha where there is a spot of five slabs with the name of Viṣṇu marked therein.

27. One who bathes there after fasting for five days, is born as my devotee in Gomedadvīpa.

28. One who gives up life there, becomes free from all sins and sees me.

29. In my region in Kokā, there is Tuṅgakūṭa where water falls from the mountain in four streams.

30. One who takes bath there after fasting for five days goes to Kuśadvīpa and then to my world.

31. There is the place called Anityāśrama sacred for rituals which is not well known even to gods, why then speak of mortals?

32. One who bathes there after fasting for a day, is born as my devotee in Puṣkaradvīpa.

33. One who dies in this holy spot becomes free from all sins and goes to my world.

34. Then there is the highly holy Agnisaras where water falls from the mountain in five streams.

35. One who bathes there after fasting for five days, is born as my devotee in Kuśadvīpa.

36. One who dies there after performing the important rites, goes from Kuśadvīpa to the world of Brahmā.

37. There is the great spot called Brahmasaras where water falls in a single torrent on a slab.

38. One who bathes there after fasting for five days, becomes my devotee in Sūryaloka.

39. One who dies there goes from Sūryaloka to my world.

40. There is then the place called Dhenuvaṭa where a single torrent falls from a rock.

41. My devotee may take bath there after fasting for seven days.

42. He then gets the merit of having bathed in seven oceans and he may remain my devotee in all the seven islands.

43. My devotee who gives up life there, transcends the seven islands and reaches my world.

44. There is the place called *Dharmodbhava* in that holy region where a single torrent falls from the hill-top.

45. One should take bath there after fasting for a day. If he is a Śūdra he will be born a Vaiśya.

46. One who gives up life there, enjoys the fruit of all sacrifices and then reaches me.

47. There is the holy spot called Koṭivaṭa where a single torrent falls at the foot of a banyan tree.

48-49. One who bathes there after fasting for a night remains my devotee with all prosperity for as many thousands of years as there are leaves in that tree.

50. One who gives up life there after severe austerities, attains the colour of fire and reaches my world.

51. There is the place called Pāpapramocana where a single torrent falls shaped like a pot.

52. One who bathes there after fasting for a full day is born as a Brahmin proficient in all the four Vedas.

53. One who gives up life there resorting to the stream called Kauśikī and one who takes bath there after fasting for five days,

54. Revels in the world of Indra following the rules of my devotees.

55. One who gives up life there transcends the world of Indra and reaches my world.

56. There is another important spot called Yamavyasanaka where there is a torrent in the river Kauśikī.

57. One who takes bath there after fasting for a day, does not meet with adversity.

58. The devotee who gives up life there, becomes free from all sins and reaches my world.

59. In the same place there is a spot called Mātaṅga where there is another torrent in the same river Kauśikī.

60. One who takes bath there after fasting for day will be born in Kimpuruṣa and become fully purified.

61. One who gives up life there, transcends Kimpuruṣa and goes to my world.

62. There is another spot there called Vajrabhava where again, there is another torrent in the river Kauśikī.

63. One who takes bath there after fasting for one day, will be born in the world of Indra.

64. By the merit of the bath there, he gets a body like Indra's holding the weapon Vajra.

65. One who gives up life there meditating on me, transcends the world of Indra and reaches my world.

66. At a distance of three krośas from there, is the spot called Śakrarudra in the expansive rock in Kokāmukha.

67. One who takes bath there after fasting for three days, will be born in Jambūdvīpa where Jambū is rooted.

68. (One who gives up life there), transcends Jambūdvīpa and reaches my world.

69. O Earth, there is another important spot there by going where people cross the ocean of *saṁsāra*.

70. That is known as Daṁṣṭrāṅkura and is at one extremity of Kokāmukha. This is not so well known to people.

71. One who bathes there after fasting for a day, will be born as my devotee in Śālmalidvīpa.

72. One who gives up life there, transcends Śālmalidvīpa and reaches my world.

73. There is the spot called Viṣṇutīrtaha which brings about good to my devotees.

74. In it from the middle of the mountain in Kokā, there are three torrents.

75. He who bathes there snaps all ties with the world and goes to the world of Vāyu remaining in airy form.

76. The devotee who gives up life there, transcends the world of Vāyu and reaches my world.

77. There is a great spot called Sarvakāmikā where there is a famous rock at the place where the river Kauśikī enters Kokā.

78. One who performs bath there after fasting for a day will be born in a big family of devotees with the memory of the past.

79. By merely bathing there one attains whatever is desired in heaven or earth.

80. One who gives up life there, gives up all attachment and goes to my world.

81. There is the spot called Matsyaśilā in Kokāmukha where there are three torrents in the river Kauśikī.

82. If while bathing there, one sees a fish, it should be understood that I have gone there then on my own accord.

83. Seeing the fish there, the devotee shall offer water with honey and fried grain.

84. One who bathes there reaches Padmapatra to the north of Meru.

85. One who gives up life in Matsyaśilā, transcends the peak of Meru and reaches my world.

86. The Kokāmukha region extends over five yojanas. He who knows this is never stained by sin.

87. I shall tell you now another thing, O Earth ! I stand in the beautiful Kokāmukha facing south.

88. I remain there in human form with the face of the boar and complexion like sandalwood.

89. With the face raised on the left and the left tusk held up, I see the whole universe and my devotees there.

90. The sinless persons meditate on me there and perform actions meant to secure liberation.

91. If a person happens to die in Kokāmukha, he never returns to this world but attains a form similar to mine.

92. This Kokāmukha is a great place, the greatest secret and the greatest attainment.

93. I tell you the truth that what is acquired by the processes of Sāṅkhya or Yoga will never be equal to what is acquired by going to Kokāmukha.

94. I have thus told you what you desired to know. What else do you wish to ask ?

95. He who reads this liberates ten generations of his ancestors and ten generations of his successors.

96. After death, he will be born in a family of pure devotees and will be solely devoted to me.

97. He who listens to this early in the morning, snaps all potentialities of his future lives and becomes my staunch devotee.

98. He who recites this account of the greatness of Kokāmukha early in the morning reaches my Supreme abode. There need be no doubt in this matter.

CHAPTER ONE HUNDRED AND FORTYONE

The greatness of Badarikāśrama

Varāha said:

1. Now listen to another secret on the surface of the Himavat mountain, namely the holy place Badarī which is not easily accessible even to Devas.

2. People do not reach there by their actions, however difficult to perform they may be. They reach only by devotion this place which liberates all.

3. It is not easy to reach this place of mine in the rocky peak full of snow. But he who is able to go there will be really gratified.

4. In that heap of rocks there is Brahmakuṇḍa. O Earth, I remain there in that snow.

5. The man who bathes there after fasting for three nights attains merit equal to performing Agniṣṭoma sacrifice.

6. And, if after performing the vows and with full control of the senses, he gives up life there, he crosses Satyaloka and reaches my world.

7. In that place, there is the spot called Agnisatyapada, where water falls in torrents from three peaks.

8. He who bathes there after fasting for three nights becomes truthful, clever and devoted to my service.

9. He who dies there too, crosses Satyaloka and reaches my world and enjoys there.

10. In Badarī, there is my hermitage known as Indraloka where I was most sincerely propitiated by Indra.

11. Here too from the peaks water falls in big torrents in a broad slab which is dear to me.

12. He who bathes there after fasting for a night becomes truthful and pure and remains high in Satyaloka.

13. And he who gives up life there after performing the vow called Anāśaka, crosses Satyaloka and reaches my world.

14. There is the tīrtha called Pañcaśikha in Badarī where water falls from five peaks.

15. He who bathes there attains the merit of Aśvamedha sacrifice and delights himself in the company of.Devas.

16. He who dies there after performing all austerities, crosses Svargaloka and remains high in my world.

17. In that great place of mine there is the spot called Catuḥsrotas where water falls in streaks, one each in the four directions.

18. He who bathes there after fasting for a night delights in heaven and becomes my devotee.

19. And if he dies there after performing all austerities, crosses heaven and reaches my world.

20. There is another spot called Vedadhāra there wherein from the mouths of Brahmā emanated the four Vedas.

21. Four big peaks are there in that place in the Himālaya and from these four torrents fall.

22. He who bathes there after fasting for four nights gets the capacity to easily master the four Vedas.

23. And if he dies there standing in my service, he crosses the world of Devas and reaches my world.

24. Then there is another spot called Dvādaśādityakuṇḍa, where the twelve Ādityas were settled by me.

25. There on a big slab fall twelve streaks of water facilitating service to me.

26. He who bathes in any one of these twelve streaks, goes there where the twelve Ādityas lord.

27. And if he dies there, he crosses the place of these Ādityas and remains high in my world.

28. There is the spot called Lokapāla where the guardians of quarters were settled by me.

29. There in the middle of the mountain is a pond from where by splitting the rocks arose Soma.

30. He who bathes there on the Dvādaśī day in the month of Jyeṣṭha, delights with guardian deities of the quarters and becomes my devotee.

31. And if he dies there, remaining in my service, he crosses the world of these guardian deities and reaches my world.

32. There is a very holy spot called Merorvara from where the Mount Meru settled itself.

33. Three torrents bright like gold fall from there but become invisible at the place where they fall.

34. He who bathes there after fasting for three nights, delights himself in the peaks of Meru and becomes my devotee.

35. And if he dies there, he crosses the Meru and reaches my world.

36. There is another important tīrtha called Mānasodbheda where water gushes forth piercing the earth.

37. Even Devas do not know about this place, but men know since the water comes forth from under the earth.

38. He who bathes there after fasting for a full day and night delights in the heavenly Mānasa and becomes my devotee.

39. Then there is the holy spot called Pañcaśira where Brahmā clipped off one of his heads.

40. Five ponds are there amidst big rocks in the place of five heads.

41. The one in the centre has water red in colour and this represents the head cut off by Brahmā.

42. He who bathes there after fasting for five nights, delights in Brahmaloka and becomes my devotee.

43. And if he dies in this Pañcaśira after performing Jalacāndrāyaṇa and remaining steadfast in my service,

44. He becomes clever and prudent and free from desire and stupor, and crossing the Brahmaloka reaches my world.

45. There is another tīrtha named Somābhiṣeka, where Soma (Moon) was crowned by me as the king of Brahmins.

46. O Earth, I was propitiated there by the Moon by austerities numbering fourteen crores.

47. He attained great powers because of this. The whole world is now dependent on him, as also the cereals and all herbs.

48. Skanda, Indra and Maruts are born from him and also disappear in him, and everything will be of Soma.

49. There is a spot called Somagiri where there is a torrent of water falling in cavity.

50. He who bathes there after fasting for three nights, delights himself in the world of Soma.

51. And if he dies there after performing austerities, he crosses Somaloka and reaches my world.

52. In that sacred Badarī there is the holy Urvaśīkuṇḍa where Urvaśī was born out of the right thigh.

53. There I was performing penance for the sake of Devas. None knew me.

54. A long time passed as I was performing penance there. Even the gods like Indra, Brahmā and Śiva did not know me then.

55. Result is certain in Badarī and I performed penance for many thousands of years.

56. In fact, I continued like that for millions of years.

57. As I was in this secret place, Devas could not see me and they became very sad.

58. O Earth, while I was engaged in that penance, I could see every one, but none could see me because of my power of illusion.

59. Then the gods went to Brahmā and told him that without Viṣṇu they could have no peace of mind.

60. Hearing the words of Devas, Brahmā said that I was concealed from them by the enveloping Māyā.

61. Then Devas, Gandharvas, Siddhas and Saints became very much pleased.

62. Headed by Indra they came where I was and said:

63. "O Lord, we are all unhappy being forsaken by you. Save us by your blessing".

64. I then cast a glance at them and they became happy.

65. He who bathes in the Urvaśīkuṇḍa after fasting for a

night, gets absolved of all sins and delights in the Urvaśīloka for all time.

66. And he who gives up life there remaining in my service, becomes freed of all merits and sins and merges in me.

67. He who thinks of this holy Badarī reaches the abode of Viṣṇu never to return.

68. He who listens to this or recites this remaining truthful, celibate and free from anger,

69. Or remaining in contemplation and he who understands the secret of such contemplation,

70. And understands the self, attains supreme beatitude.

CHAPTER ONE HUNDRED AND FORTYTWO

Action in Privacy[1]

Sūta said:

1. Hearing these words of the Lord, Earth, desirous of *dharma*, propitiated him with folded hands.

Earth said:

2. O Mādhava, be pleased to listen to what this servant of yours with tender nature has to say.

3. Women do not have the stamina to do all that you said now without taking food.

4. So tell me how these can attain happiness even if they take food with your blessing.

5. Hearing these words of Earth, the Lord laughed and said:

Varāha said:

6. O fair goddess, it is good that you asked me about this secret conducive to my devotees.

7. She who is my devotee, if she feels anything impure, may touch my image wherever it is.

1. This relates to women in their monthly period.

8. If, while performing austerities, the need for food is felt, it can certainly be taken with mind set in me.

9. If a woman gets menses (in the course of her austerities), she does not incur sin if she takes food after uttering this mantra with hands folded over the head: "I in my monthly course, bow to the great Lord who is unborn and has no beginning or end.

10. There is no harm in her doing things after taking food with this mantra.

11-12. Taking bath on the fifth day (from the occurrence of menses), if she duly performs worship with mind solely set in me and without thinking of worldly life she may attain manhood.

Earth said:

13. Men or women are really neither men nor women (of the type they ought to be). How can they be liberated from the bondage of worldly life?

Varāha said:

14-15. Controlling all their sense organs and steadying their mind, if I am meditated upon steadfastly, it is *Sannyāsayoga*. One that does it, whether it be a man, woman or hermaphrodite, attains supreme bliss.

16. I shall tell you another thing, please listen. The mind, intellect and thought are not usually within the control of man.

17. But he, who with the power of knowledge, is able to fix it unflinchingly on one object and keep it in poise, is not stained by anything.

18. He who has the poised mind set in me, does not incur the result of any action even if he takes all kinds of food and drink, prescribed or prohibited.

19-20. If the mind, intellect and thought are poised and set in me, then one is not affected by whatever one does, like the water on the lotus leaf.

21. O Goddess, let the mind be well poised whether it is for the whole day and night, for an hour or even for a moment.

22. One attains the supreme aim if the mind is well poised even if he does all kinds of things day and night.

23. What fear has he who always thinks of me, awake or asleep, hearing or seeing?

24. I praise him who has nothing else in mind, be he a Caṇḍāla doing heinous deeds or a Brahmin who has strayed into the wrong path.

25-26. Those who perform sacrifices knowing *dharma* well, endowed with proper knowledge and mind set in me, those who always think of me and perform actions dear to me and those who, in dedication to me, sleep well free from care, and those who are tranquil in mind, all of them are dear to me.

27. Those who do actions, good or bad, thinking of themselves alone, are very base men and they bring upon themselves suffering.

28. It is the mind that leads to ruin in this world, and it is the same mind that is the cause of liberation also. O Earth, therefore, let me be attained with the mind set on me.

29. Dedicating *Jñāna* (knowledge) and *Yoga* (action) to me, let me be worshipped with steadfast devotion.

30. He who with due austerities has the mind always set on me, comes near me and becomes eligible to be in me.

31. The rule that a woman should be cohabited with after her monthly course, was laid down by me for the sake of progeny.

32. If one does not cohabit (with his wife) soon after her period, with full concentration of mind and wishing my blessing, ten generations of the ancestors and ten generations of the descendants are harmed.

33. Let one approach the wife with a sense of duty to his ancestors and not with the motive of carnal pleasure or impelled by lust.

34. Let not a second woman be touched even if urged by uncontrollable passion, so too a third and never a fourth.

35. After cohabitation, let one not have the curiosity to see the women laying in the bed, in order to maintain purity.

36. When once the thing is over, my devotee shall bathe in water and change his cloth.

37. He who cohabits before the stopping of the monthly course, doubtless makes his manes drink semen.

38. A man cohabits with one woman (for the sake of *dharma*) with a second due to passion. He who does it with a third or fourth is indeed a depraved person.

39. This is a rule which I have made for the entire world.

40. Soon after the period, cohabitation is laid down for the sake of the manes. He who cohabits at this time (alone) is considered celibate enough.

41. The man who wanders away at this time without cohabiting with the wife, due to anger or delusion, incurs the sin of killing the embryo.

42. I shall tell you another thing, O Earth, please listen. It is knowledge relating to *Cittayoga* and action relating to *Karmayoga*.

43. People reach my place by action, also by singing of me; so too by contemplation. There is no other course (for this).

44. Jñāna, Yoga and Sāṅkhya are all based on the mind and those that follow the path I have shown, will achieve their aim.

45. O Earth, during the monthly period, one may remain for three days on air alone.

46. On the fourth day such actions as conducive to the attainment of the aim, may be done, but none else.

47. The head should be cleansed by bath, white cloth should be worn, and the mind should be made steady.

48. The prescribed deeds may then be done. Those who do so are dear to me indeed.

49. Then after worshipping me they may take food and bow to me with hands folded over the head.

50. The mantra for this is: "You are the first of all beings and you have no end. O Lord, we who were in our monthly course, bow to you. We have fasted for three days and we bow to you now when the menstrual flow has stopped."

51. O Earth, the women after their course become purified by this mantra and they may do the actions that are to be done after bath as well as those to be done before bath.

52. In this way man or woman does not get any harm and those who do actions laid down by me are dear to me.

53. And they become more and more inclined to do what is dear to me, even if they be defiled by association with the monthly period.

54. And those desirous of attaining the supreme, may give up everything and with full control of the senses and deep concentration of mind, meditate on me.

55. They get the result, be they men, women or hermaphrodites, irrespective of their knowledge and actions.

56. People who are caught in *Saṁsāra* do not know me yet. Those who are engaged in devotion to me alone know me.

57. Fathers and mothers in thousands, and sons and daugthers in hundreds, revolve like a wheel and as a result of this stupefaction, they are unable to know me.

58. The world is enveloped by ignorance and subjected by delusion. It is also bound by many attachments. It is difficult to wean the mind clear from all this.

59. The mother goes away, the father goes away, so too the sons and servants.

60. They are born according to their own deeds.

61. Even those with knowledge, if they are deluded by *saṁsāra* remain (in my world) for a short while only, a few months or years, and are born again and do not remain with me.

62. But he to whom the *Nyāsayoga* (dedicating everything to me) is known, releases himself, no doubt.

63. He who listens to this (account) early in the morning soon after waking up, acquires great attainments and goes to my world.

64. Thus I have told you the secret about which you asked me for the favour of devotees.

CHAPTER ONE HUNDRED AND FORTYTHREE

Greatness of Mandāra

Varāha said:

1. O fair goddess, I shall tell you now about another place which is important to my devotees. Please listen.

2. This is known as Mandāra and is situated on the right side of river Gaṅgā, on a plateau in Vindhya.

3. In Ṭretāyuga will be born the brilliant Rāma and he will consecrate me there.

4. Hearing these words from the mouth of Lord Nārāyaṇa, Earth desirous of *dharma*, spoke to him in sweet tone.

Earth said:

5. O great Lord, you were pleased to tell me about the holy place called Mandāra.

6. What rites do people perform there and to what worlds do they go?

7. What are the secrets about Mandāra? I am eager to know all this. Please tell me.

Varāha said:

8. I shall tell you all that you ask, the rites in Mandāra and the secrets.

9. I was playing there when the Mandāra tree was in flower and I placed one of its beautiful flowers on my chest.

10. Then in the place where the Mandāra was standing in the mountain, eleven ponds appeared.

11. I remained in that place beneath the Mandāra for the sake of devotees.

12. It is an attractive spot with a beautiful slab where I stood beside that tree.

13. You may know the wonder of this Mandāra. It flowers only on the Dvādaśī and Caturdaśī days.

14. And this occurs during the noon. No flower can be seen in it on any other day.

15. The man who bathes in the Mandārakuṇḍa attains supreme bliss.

16. He who dies there after performing austerities, goes to my world.

17. On its northern side is the hill called Prāpaṇa where three torrents fall on the southern side.

18. This is known as the Snānakuṇḍa in that place and here the water that falls on the south flows northwards.

19. He who bathes there after fasting for a night delights himself on the southern peak of Mount Meru.

20. And he who dies there giving up all attachments, reaches my world.

21. On its north-eastern side is the spot Vaikuṇṭhakāraṇa where a torrent falls green in colour.

22. He who bathes there after fasting for a night, reaches heaven and enjoys with the gods.

23. And he who gives up his life there after full gratification, liberates his whole family and reaches my world.

24. On its south-eastern side on the peaks of the Vindhya is an even fall of water entering into a deep pond beneath.

25. He who bathes there after fasting for a night, delights himself on the eastern side of Mount Meru.

26. And he who gives up his life there with mind set in me, cuts off all connections with worldly life and reaches my world.

27. On the eastern side of Mandāra is a Koṭara where a torrent falls in the shape of a mace.

28. He who bathes there after foregoing five meals, delights himself on the eastern side of Mount Meru.

29. And he who gives up life there after performing austerities, crosses the peak of Meru and reaches my world.

30. On its southern side is Vindhyavinissṛta where five torrents fall in the shape of maces.

31. He who bathes there after fasting for one day and night, delights himself on the southern peak of Mount Meru.

32. And he who gives up life there after performing austerities, crosses the peak of Meru and reaches my world.

33. In the south-western side of Mandāra falls a torrent shining like the sun.

34. He who bathes there after fasting for a day and night delights himself on the Western side where (the star) Dhruva shines.

35. And he who gives up life there remaining in my devotion, gets freed from all sins and delights himself in my world.

36. On its western side is the deep lake called Cakrāvarta.

37. He who bathes there giving up five meals, delights himself freely in the peaks of Meru.

38. And he who gives up life there, crosses all peaks of Meru and delights himself in my presence.

39. On the north-western side of this rocky place in the Vindhya, there are three torrents, also shaped like maces.

40. He who bathes there with mind set on me, delights himself in all peaks (of Meru).

41. And he who gives up life there giving up all attachments, reaches my world.

42. At a short distance from it on the southern side is the deep lake called Gabhīraka.

43. He who bathes there after fasting for eight nights, enjoys himself freely in all islands.

44. And he who gives up life there remaining in devotion to me, leaves all these islands and reaches my world.

45. On its western side is the great Parama where seven torrents fall into a deep lake.

46. He who bathes there after fasting for a day and night, delights himself freely in the world of Indra.

47. And he who gives up life there remaining constant in my service, gets free from all attachments and reaches my world.

48. Now listen to this namely that Syamantapañcaka is in this mount Mandāra.

49. I remain in the heap of rocks in Mandāra at the top of the mountain Vindhya.

50. The cakra (disc) is on the right, gadā (club) is on the left, śaṁkha (conch), lāṅgala (plough) and musala (mace) stand in front.

51. I have told all this to you and for the sake of devotees.

52. Being deluded by my Māyā, people do not know this, except the pure devotees and those who resort to this Varāha.

CHAPTER ONE HUNDRED AND FORTYFOUR

Greatness of Someśvara, Muktikṣetra, Triveṇī and others

Sūta said:

1. Hearing about the greatness of Mandāra, Earth, who was desirous of *dharma*, was full of wonder and asked the Lord.

Earth said:

2. By your favour I got an idea of Mandāra. Be pleased to tell me now about what is even more important than that.

Varāha said:

3. Listen to me, O goddess, for what you wish to know. I shall tell you about Śālagrāma.

4. In Dvāparayuga in the clan of Yadus in which is the leader Śūra,

5. To whom is born Vasudeva of righteous actions,

6. Whose wife is the highly beautiful Devakī,

7. To her I will be born known as Vāsudeva to the Devas destroying all enemies.

8. In that place of Yādavas was a Brahmarṣi by name Sālaṅkāyana.

9. He was wandering in all ten quarters to worship me and then performed penance at the peak of Meru for getting a son.

10. He then went to Piṇḍāraka and from there to Lohārgala and so on for a thousand years.

11. As I was in my form together with Śiva, he could not see me in any of those places.

12. O Earth, I was together with Śiva, and Sālaṅkāyana was performing penance.

13. In that mount Śālagrāma, Śiva united with me remains as a stone.

14. I, of course, remain there in the form of the mount and all the stones there represent me.

15. All these stones are fit for worship, particularly those which have the cakra-marks in them. And Śiva remains in the form of a Liṅga in a temple in that hill.

16. There are stones there marked by the liṅga and also those marked by cakra. The hill itself is in the form of a liṅga and is lorded by Someśvara.

17. This is because it was established there by Soma (Moon) and named after himself. He performed penance there for a thousand years for release from a curse.

18. When he was freed from the curse, he regained his effulgence and strength and then extolled Śiva,

19. Who emerged as a giver of boons from Someśvara.

Soma said:

20. I bow to Śiva, the lord of Umā, five-faced, blue-necked and three-eyed, calm and eager to bless the devotees;

21. The divine, adorned by all Devas, having moon on the crest, holding the bow Pināka in the hand, the lord of gods, the refuge of devotees;

22. Holding the trident, bearing the Ḍamaru and riding the bull, praised by the gaṇas with different kinds of fierce faces;

23. Mahākāla, the destoryer of Tripuras, the vanquisher of demons like Andhaka, wearing the elephant's skin and adorned with the tiger-skin;

24. Having as the *Upavita*, the serpent's body, holding the string of rudrākṣa, lord of all, though without a form assuming forms according to the devotees' desire;

25. Having the sun, moon and fire as the eyes, beyond the reach of words and mind, with prominent matted tresses and shoulders washed by Gaṅgā;

26. Having Kailāsa as abode and with hermitage in the Himālaya.

Praised thus, Lord Śiva spoke to Soma:

27. Seek a boon of me of what is in your mind, now that you have the rare opportunity of getting me before you.

Soma said:

28. O Lord, if you are pleased to give me a boon let it be that your presence is always there in this liṅga known after my name to grant the desires of devotees.

The great lord said:

29. I shall remain in this place for ever where the presence of Viṣṇu is also there, particularly in this Liṅga installed by you.

30. O moon, know that you are only a form of mine. I shall grant boons to all those that worship this Liṅga, even more than for the gods.

31. By the power of the penance of sage Sālaṅkāyana, I am here together with Viṣṇu.

32. The hill Śālagrāma is Viṣṇu and this Someśvara is myself. The stones here represent both Viṣṇu and Śiva.

33. Revā (the river Narmadā) once performed penance to propitiate Śiva that a son like him may be born to her.

34. I am not the son of any and shall not be of any. But the desire of Revā had to be fulfilled.

35. Thinking thus, I spoke to her with pleasant mind:

36. I shall be within you as son, but in the form of the liṅga and along with Gaṇeśa.

37. You are really myself in my form as water. We remain together as Śiva and Śakti.

38. Receiving the boon, Revā came to my presence here which came to be known as Revākhaṇḍa thereafter.

39. Gaṇḍakī (the river) also formerly performed penance for a thousand divine years, first living on fallen leaves and then on air alone, with a view to propitiate Viṣṇu.

40. Then Viṣṇu who always favours his devotees, appeared there and spoke:

41. O Gaṇḍakī, I am surprised and pleased at your penance and unflinching devotion.

42. Please ask what boon you desire. I am ready to grant it.

43. Seeing before her the Lord bearing the conch, disc and mace, she prostrated and began to praise.

44. O great god, I have seen you, difficult to be seen even by the Yogins. The entire world was created by you.

45. You then entered into it and hence you are known as Puruṣa. In this world which emanated as a result of your *līlā* (play) who is free?

46. O Viṣṇu, you are Brahman which is spoken of as without beginning or end and without limit. He who knows you is really the knower of the Vedas.

47. Your supreme power is the Universal Mother. She is called Yogamāyā, Prakṛti and Pradhāna.

48. Puruṣa is without qualities, is indistinct (*avyakta*), of the nature of knowledge, pure consciousness, actionless and unchanging.

49. By entering Yogamāyā you (Puruṣa) became the doer. It is Prakṛti that (really) creates and you who (simply) see it are called Sākṣī.

50-51. When Prakṛti by the three qualities is performing creation, you become its cause by your presence alone like the red colour in a clear colourless crystal by the presence of a shoe-flower nearby. Its light is because of your lustre. I bow to it.

52. How can I know that form of yours which cannot be known even by such seers like Brahmā?

53. I remain in this stupefied world without knowing anything. I do not know which has merit and which has not. I am simply held by you.

54. I attained a position in this world by your favour alone. now I ask you something out of my ignorance. All the same, it behoves you to give me that.

55. You are indeed very kind and so do not say 'No'.

56. Then the Lord said: Ask me whatever you like even if it is something which is not normally granted and is difficult for men to get.

57. Who has got his desire not fulfilled after seeing me?

58. O Soma, then that holy Gaṇḍakī spoke in sweet words with folded hands: If you are pleased to grant me the boon I ask, then may you enter my womb and be born as my son.

59. The Lord was pleased and he thought:

60. What is it that is asked by this river desirous of constant contact with me? Still, I shall grant boon for the emancipation of the world.

61. So thinking, he told Gaṇḍakī:

62. O goddess, listen to me. For the sake of devotees, I have already become your son, as I am lying within you in the form of Śālagrāma stones.

63. You will become the foremost among rivers because of my presence in you.

64. By seeing you, touching you, bathing in you or drinking your water, you remove all sins acquired through thought, word or deed.

65. He who bathes (in you) according to the prescribed rules and performs oblations to the manes, leads them all to heaven and himself goes to Brahmaloka.

66. And he who gives up life in you while remaining devoted to me, reaches my abode from where he never returns.

67. After giving these boons, he disappeared. From then onwards, O Soma, in this place I and Viṣṇu reside together in the form desired by the devotees.

68. So saying the lord (Śiva) blessed Soma and stroked his limbs making them free from all ills.

69. And while he was looking on, Śiva disappeared there.

70. To the south of Someśvara is the holy waterfall that arose as a result of Rāvaṇa splitting the mountain there by an arrow.

71. It is known as Bāṇagaṅgā and it is capable of removing all sins.

72. To the east of Someśvara is the penance-grove of Rāvaṇa. By spending three days there, one attains the result of penance.

73. This place is known as Nartanācala, because Rāvaṇa danced here, and pleased at it Śiva gave him boons.

74. He who bathes in the Bāṇagaṅgā and worships Bāṇeśvara attains the result of bathing in Gaṅgā and delights in heaven like the gods.

75. O Earth, I shall now tell you another secret.

76. Sālaṅkāyana was performing severe penance at Śālagrāma desirous of getting a son like Śiva.

77. Knowing this, Lord Śiva assumed the form of a beautiful boy (Nandī) through Yogamāyā and stood beside him as his son.

78. Although he was standing close on his right, the sage did not notice him.

79. Śiva (as Nandī) with the power of Māyā was there, beautiful, virtuous and shining like the sun, with the trident in hand. But the sage did not notice the son, being immersed in contemplating on me.

80. Then, at the command of Lord Śiva, Nandī told the sage laughing:

81. O great sage, rise up. Your desire has borne fruit. I am your son born of your right side. Tell me what I should do?

82. You started penance with the aim of getting a son like Śiva. None else is there like me. So I am myself now born to you.

83. Worshipping Lord Viṣṇu through penance, you have attained your desire, since I am here your son.

84. The sage was extremely glad to hear these words of Nandī.

85. But he was surprised and asked him: If my penance has borne fruit as you say, how is it that Lord Viṣṇu has not appeared before me?

86. As long as I am not able to see him, I don't think my penance can come to a close. So I shall continue to be here till I am able to see Viṣṇu.

87-88. My son, by the power of your yoga, quickly go to Mathurā and bring from there my disciple Āmuṣyāyaṇa from my hermitage and the wealth and cows there.

89. At this command, Nandī quickly went to Mathurā and reached the hermitage of the sage.

90. He saw Āmuṣyāyaṇa there and asked him about the well being of himself and about the wealth and cows.

91. Āmuṣyāyaṇa said: "Everything is all right because of the blessing of my guru. Tell me how he is and where.

92. Where are you coming from and what is the purpose of your coming ?

93. Tell me all this and receive this *arghya*.

94. So requested, he received the *arghya* and, after taking rest for a while, told him about his guru and the purpose with which he had been sent.

95. Then he started with him and the wealth and cows and, after a few days, reached the bank of Gaṇḍakī. And from there he reached Triveṇī and felt very happy there.

96. There is the river Devikā which arose as a result of the penance of Devas. This joins Gaṇḍakī.

97. Another flows by the hermitage of Pulastya and Pulaha and this too joins Gaṇḍakī. Thus Gaṇḍakī becomes Triveṇī (three-streamed).

98. This confluence is the great tīrtha called Kāmika, dear to the Pitṛs. There we get the great Liṅga called Trijaleśvara.

99. It gives both enjoyment and salvation at its very sight.

Earth said:

100. In Prayāga there is Triveṇī where Śiva remains with the name Śūlaṭaṅka and also as Someśvara;

101. Where Viṣṇu remains with the name Veṇīmādhava, and the rivers Gaṅgā, Yamunā and Sarasvatī meet;

102. Where, I have heard, is the presence of all Devas and Sages and all Tīrthas;

103. By bathing where one goes to heaven and, dying, gets salvation; which is the king of all tīrthas and is one liked by Viṣṇu most.

104. This is the well known Triveṇī. But now you speak of another and speak of it as a secret.

105. Therefore tell me this out of compassion for me and for the good of the world.

Varāha said:

106. Listen, O goddess, I shall tell you what you seek to know, also a story connected therewith.

107. In days of yore, Viṣṇu performed penance for the sake of the world in a beautiful mountain, the Himālayas, resorted to by the gods.

108. After a long lapse of time, a great effulgence emanated from him.

109. By its heat profuse sweat emanated in the cheeks, and this formed into a river capable of removing sins.

110. This caused wonder in all the worlds, but none could know its origin.

111. All the gods then went to Brahmā full of eagerness, and asked about the source of this.

112. Being affected by the Māyā of Viṣṇu, Brahmā too could not know. So he led the gods to Śiva.

113. Seeing him there with the gods, he asked them the cause of their visit.

114. Brahmā bowed to the great lord and said: O Maheśvara, there is a wonderful effulgence by which the whole world is affected.

115. But how it came and from where we are unable to know.

116. Śiva then meditated for a while and told Brahmā and others that he would show them its source.

117. He then, with Umā and Gaṇas, led Devas to the place where Viṣṇu was performing penance.

118. He then asked him: You are the creator of the worlds and their sustainer. With what purpose, then, do you perform this penance ?

119. You are the source of everything and the master of everything. What is there difficult for you to obtain ?

Lord Viṣṇu then bowed to him and said:

120. I undertook this presence for the sake of the world, to see you and to get boons from you.

121. Having seen you now, I am fully gratified, O lord of the worlds.

Śiva said:

122. This is Muktikṣetra where by the mere sight one gets salvation. Here flows the great river Gaṇḍakī which arose from the sweat of cheeks (*gaṇḍa*).

123. In future you will lodge yourself within it. And then because of your presence there,

124. Myself, Brahmā, gods, sages, sacrifices and Tīrthas will remain in the Gaṇḍakī for ever.

125. He who bathes in it during the whole month of Kārttika, becomes free from all sins and attains salvation.

126. This is the tīrtha of all tīrthas and the most auspicious.

127. By bathing here one gets the merit of bathing in Gaṅgā, and by its thought, sight or touch one gets free of all sins.

128. There is nothing comparable to it other than Gaṅgā. Gaṇḍakī is extremely holy and gives enjoyment and salvation.

129. Another by name Devikā mingles with Gaṇḍakī.

130. Pulastya and Pulaha formerly performed intense penance in separate hermitages for ordering creation and attained the skill therefore.

131. From there arose the holy river Brahmatanayā and it mingles with Gaṇḍakī.

132. There is thus, the Triveṇī which is very holy even for the gods.

133. There were Jaya and Vijaya, sons of sage Tṛṇabindu, a repository of the Vedas, who were engaged for a sacrifice by a king, but became sinful.

134. They were highly learned in the Vedas and clever in sacrifices.

135. They were worshipping Viṣṇu with full concentration of mind, and the Lord's presence was there every day before them being drawn by their intense devotion.

136. These two Brahmins were invited for a sacrifice by king Marutta.

137. At the end of the sacrifice, they were given handsome dakṣiṇās.

138. Reaching home, they thought of dividing daksiṇā between them and then arose a quarrel.

139. Jaya the elder, was for equal division, while Vijaya, the younger, was for each taking what he had got.

140. Jaya (who had got less) thereby became angry. He said: Since, having received you don't give me, may you become a crocodile.

141. Vijaya too said: Since you have become blind with the money, may you become an elephant which will be *madāndha* (blind with pride). Thus they became a crocodile and an elephant by mutual curse.

142. Vijaya became crocodile in Gaṇḍakī with memory of his past and in the place Triveṇī Jaya became elephant playing with female and young elephants.

143. Thousands of years passed for them and the curses were still working on.

144. Once the elephant got down into the stream Triveṇī along with his herd.

145. He enjoyed himself there playing with the rest, pouring water on the female elephants and drinking water offered by them.

146-147. While he was playing thus, the crocodile, remembering the former enmity, caught hold of his leg firmly by the teeth.

148. The elephant too dragged the crocodile and a fight ensued between them.

149. By the dragging of the elephant and biting of the crocodile in the course of the fight, many other creatures became wounded or dead.

150. Then the king Jaleśvara of the place made a request to the lord (to stop this fight).

151. Thereupon the lord, the protector of the devotees, smashed the mouth of the crocodile with the cakra Sudarśana.

152. While moving around again and again in the water, the cakra hit the stones, and, as a result, they became marked by it.

153. In that place the Vajra worms became abundant and they too made the marks.

154. Thus I have told you about the greatness of Triveṇīkṣetra. You need not have any doubt in this matter.

155. King Bharata worshipped Viṣṇu and Trijaleśvara near the hermitage of sage Pulastya.

156. And then he could give up his animal body and become himself again[1].

157. The worship of Jaleśvara generates the power of Yoga.

158. O Earth, aware of my presence in this place Śālagrāma, Jaleśa praised me.

159. Then due to my affection for the devotees, I threw my Sudarśana. The place which it hit first, became the holy Tīrtha.

160. By bathing there, one goes to the world of the sun and remains resplendent there, and by dying there, he goes to my world.

161. For protection of my devotee, I directed the Sudarśana. Wherever it rotated, the stones became marked by it.

162. Then spending there five nights according to the rules, he (Nandī) went with the cows and wealth to Harikṣetra (i.e. Śālagrāma).

163. Since lord Hari remains there, it became a place of worship.

164. From the time Nandī with the cows and the trident in hand stood there, the place came to be known as Hariharaprabha.

165. Since Devas frequent there, it also came to be known as Devāṭa. Who can adequately describe the greatness of this god ?

166. This god with trident in hand and protecting his devotees, is resorted to by sages, gods and Gandharvas.

167. It was in this place that the great god Śiva became son to Sālaṅkāyana in the form of Nandī.

168. He is a great yogin himself who bestows on others the power of yoga. And he remains in a high pedestal in this tīrtha Triveṇī.

169. Three streams fell down from the three streaks of Śiva's matted hair and these are Gaṅgā, Yamunā and Sarasvatī.

170-171. These three fell from his matted hair when he was sitting in yogic contemplation in the place Śālagrāma meditating on Viṣṇu and imparting knowledge to his devotees for release from *saṁsāra*.

172. He who bathes in this triple stream and performs oblations to the manes and worships the great yogin Śiva, never takes another life.

---

1. The reference is to the story of Jaḍabharata narrated in the Bhāgavatapurāṇa Skandha 5.

173. On the east of this place is the Haṁsatīrtha. I shall tell you something interesting about it.

174. Once, on a Śivarātrī day, devotees were performing worship to Śiva with many kinds of *naivedyas*.

175. Many crows came there with a view to eating these *naivedyas*. One crow snatched a bit of it and flew into the sky.

176. To snatch it away from this crow, another crow began to fight with it. Then both fell down into a pool below.

177. There they were transformed into *Haṁsas* (swans) lustrous like the moon. Seeing this wonder, the people present there called that pool Haṁsatīrtha.

178. From then onwards that came to be known as Haṁsatīrtha.

179. It was originally made by a Yakṣa and hence it was known then as Yakṣatīrtha.

180. He who bathes there gets purified and goes to the world of Yakṣas. And he who dies there with devotion to Śiva, crosses Yakṣaloka and reaches my world.

181. Of such effect is this tīrtha because of the prowess of Mahāyogī Śiva. Both I and Śiva are there blessing the world.

182. I have now told you all this secret, O Earth. This kṣetra extends over twelve yojanas commencing from Muktikṣetra and proceeding to Śālagrāma.

183. It gives supreme bliss to devotees.

184. This is the secret of all secrets. What else do you wish to know?

CHAPTER ONE HUNDRED AND FORTYFIVE

The Greatness of Sālagrāmakṣetra

Earth said:

1. O great Lord, what did sage Sālaṅkāyana do when he was performing penance at Muktikṣetra?

Varāha said:

2. When he was performing penance for a long time, he saw a fine Sāla tree before him.

3. It was of a nature that even the Devas could not get, being broad and big, unbroken anywhere, giving dense shade and bearing beautiful and fragrant flowers.

4. Seeing this wonder, the learned sage Sālaṅkāyana looked at this auspicious tree again and again.

5. Seeing the big tree, the wearied sage took rest under it, all the time desirous of seeing me.

6. He stood on the eastern side of the tree facing west, but under the influence of my māyā he was unable to see me.

7. Then on the Dvādaśī day of the month Vaiśākha he saw me on its eastern side.

8. Seeing me then, the sage in his penance repeatedly prostrated before me and extolled me with the hymns of the Ṛgveda.

9. Struck by my effulgence, he closed his eyes and when he opened them praising me still, I had gone to the southern side of the tree.

10. Giving up his original position, he moved opposite to me and began his praise again.

11. While he was praising me still with Ṛgvedic hymns, I moved to the western side.

12. He too then moved to the west and extolled me with the mantras of the Yajurveda.

13. While he was doing so, I moved to the northern side. He also moved and praised me with the mantras of *Sāmaveda*.

14. Pleased by his praise in this manner I told him:

15. O blessed Brahmin, sage Sālaṅkāyana, I am very much pleased by your penance and praise.

16. Seek of me a boon as your penance has fructified.

17. Thus told by me, Sālaṅkāyana stood close to the tree and spoke to me with a tranquil mind:

18. O Lord Hari, I performed this penance only by way of worshipping you, and I was wandering over the whole earth for this.

19. Now I have seen you, O great Lord. If you are pleased with me, then that very fact is fully gratifying to me.

20. And if you wish to give me a boon because of my worship, give me a son like Lord Śiva.

21. This is the boon you may be pleased to give me.

22. Such was the boon asked by that great Brahmin who was performing long penance for the sake of getting a son.

23. So hearing his words, I spoke to him in reply.

24. The aim of your long penance, you have achieved now.

25. Śiva in his form as Nandikeśvara is now born as your son from the right side of your body.

26. O sage, conclude your penance now and be happy in mind.

27. It is a long time since this has occurred, but you have not known the Nandikeśvara born.

28. By the power of Māyā, he was with me amidst the cows. He is now hẹre with your disciple Āmuṣyāyaṇa brought from Mathurā.

29. O great repository of penance, be happy in the hermitage there with your son in my kṣetra and become my equal.

30. O Śālaṅkāyana, listen to another secret which I now tell you. Because of my being pleased with you, know this place comes to be known as Śālagrāma.

31. The tree seen by you is none other than myself. This is not known to any one other than Maheśvara.

32. Because of Māyā I am not easily known. But I showed myself, being pleased with you.

33. Thus giving the boon to Śālaṅkāyana, I disappeared there as he was looking on.

34. After circumambulating the tree, the sage went to his hermitage.

35. The place Śālagrāma which liberates devotees from the bonds of *Saṁsāra*, is very dear to me.

36. O Earth, listen to secrets about this I am now telling you. They help people to cross the ocean of *saṁsāra*.

37. There are fourteen tīrthas there, which are not known to all.

38. There is the place called Bilvaprabha where there are four ponds within the distance of a krośa. It is very pleasing and beneficial to devotees.

39. The man who bathes there after fasting for one day and night, gets the merit of performing four Aśvamedha sacrifices.

40. And he who gives up life there, standing in my devotion, enjoys the fruit of Aśvamedha and goes to my world.

41. Another is known as Cakrasvāmī, where you get scattered many stones marked by cakras.

42. It extends over a length of three yojanas.

43. The man who bathes there after fasting for three nights, certainly gets the merit of three sacrifices.

44. And he who gives up life there with devotion to me, enjoys the fruit of Vājapeya sacrifice and goes to my world.

45. Then there is Viṣṇupada where three torrents of water fall from the peak of Himālayas.

46. The man who bathes there after fasting for three nights, gets the fruit of three Rātri Sacrifices.

47. And he who gives up life there free from all attachments, enjoys the fruit of Atirātra sacrifice and remains high in my world.

48. There is the place called Kālīhrada, where there is a pond and a stream arising from the Badari tree.

49. He who bathes there foregoing six meals, attains the fruit of Naramedha sacrifice.

50. And he who gives up life there free from all attachments, enjoys the fruit of Naramedha and delights in my world.

51-52. There is another important and wonderful place called Śaṅkhaprabha, where on Dvādaśī day the sound of conch is heard at midnight.

53. Then there is Gadākuṇḍa where the water on the southern side always vibrates.

54. He who bathes there after fasting for three nights, attains the same merit as is attained by the Brahmins who master Vedānta.

55. And he who gives up life there with full gratification, goes to my world with a big body and holding the mace in the hand.

56. There is the place called Agniprabha where a single torrent falls on the north-east.

57. He who bathes there after fasting for four nights, attains merit five times that of Agniṣṭoma sacrifice.

58. And he who gives up life there remaining in my devotion, enjoys the fruit of Agniṣṭoma and reaches my world.

59. A wonder here is that the water here feels hot in winter and cold in summer.

60. There is Sarvāyudha where seven torrents fall from Himavān.

61. He who bathes there after fasting for seven nights becomes a king with all weapons and arts.

62. And he who gives up life there remaining steady in my service, enjoys all royal pleasures and reaches my world.

63. There is Devaprabha where the water from the hill falls in five directions.

64. He who bathes there after foregoing eight meals, gets mastery of the four Vedas.

65. And he who gives up life there giving up all desires, gives up the result of Vedic actions too and remains high in my world.

66. Then there is Vidyādhara where also five torrents fall from the Himālayas.

67. He who bathes there after fasting for a night, goes to the world of Vidyādharas and becomes happy there.

68. And he who gives up life there free from all attachments, enjoys all pleasures in the world of Vidyādharas and goes to my world.

69. There is Puṇyanadī full of stones and bowers and resorted to by Gandharvas and Apsarases.

70. He who bathes there after fasting for eight days, moves at will in all the seven islands.

71. And he who gives up life there remaining in my devotion, gives up seven islands and reaches my world.

72. There is Gandharva where a single torrent falls on the western side.

73. He who bathes there after fasting for four days, delights himself with the devotees guarding quarters going freely wherever he likes.

74. And he who gives up life there remaining in my devotion, gives up the (company of) guardian deities and goes to my world.

75. O Earth, there is the place called Devahrada where the sacrifice of Bali was destroyed.

76. The pond here is cool and charming and deep and pleasant even for the gods.

77. In that pond, the fish have marks of the cakra and they move about here and there.

78. I shall tell you about another wonder that occurs there.

79-80. Thirtysix golden lotuses appear there at sunrise and these can be seen till noon.

81. He who bathes there after fasting for ten nights, attains the fruit of ten Aśvamedha sacrifices.

82. And he who gives up life there thinking of me, enjoys the fruit of Aśvamedha and then becomes my equal.

83. I shall now tell you about another place called Samastasukhavallabha at the confluence of two divine rivers.

84. Coming down from the celestial regions, the gods with their consorts remain in it, as also Gandharvas, Apsarases, Nāgas and Uragas.

85. So too the sages, seers, Siddhas and Kinnaras.

86-87. This abode of Śiva called Samastasukhavallabha in Nepal is more important than all other places of Śiva.

88. Here, along with Śvetagaṅgā that arose from the matted tresses of Śiva, mingle numerous other rivers visible and invisible.

89. And also Gaṇḍakī and Kṛṣṇā that arose from the body of Kṛṣṇa which mingle with the river Triśūlagaṅgā.

90. Such are the confluences of rivers in this place.

91. O Earth, know you that in that Kṣetra of mine there is a very holy place which is not easily accessible even to Devas.

92. That is Siddhāśrama, the most superior penance-grove of Śiva.

93. It is full of flowering and fruit-bearing trees like plantain, Nicula, Punnāga, Kesara,

94. Kharjūra, Aśoka, Bakula, Priyāla, Coconut, arecanut, Campaka and Jambu,

95. Lime, Pomegranate, Badarī, Ketakī, many varieties of Jasmine, Kurabaka and others.

96. Numerous couples of celestials play at the confluence there.

97. The man who bathes there gets the fruit of a hundred Aśvamedhas.

98. Bathing there in the month of Vaiśākha confers the result of (the gift of) a thousand cows, and the same in the month of Māgha confers the same result as of bathing in Prayāga.

99. He who bathes there according to rules in the month of Kārttika when the sun is in Tulā, doubtless attains salvation.

100. He who bathes there after fasting for three nights, attains the fruit of Rājasūya sacrifice and delights in heaven like the gods.

101. Sacrifices, penance, gift, śrāddha, worship of the favourite deity, whichever is done here, produces endless benefits.

102. I forgive also whatever offence committed in the course of these.

103. Just as it is rare for man to get at the confluence of Gaṅgā and Yamunā, so too the confluence of divine rivers here. This is the secret of this Kṣetra of mine.

104. In this great place Śālagrāma, I stand facing east, dear to the devotees.

105. I shall tell you another thing, O Earth, an inner secret which people under the influence of Māyā do not know.

106. That is that the great Śiva remains calm on my right side.

107. Those who know this Śiva really know me and those who know me really know Śiva too.

108. Where I am, Śiva too is there, and where Śiva is, I too am there. There is no difference between us.

109. He who worships Śiva, indeed worships me and he who knows this, attains immense good.

110. Such is this great place where both Viṣṇu and Śiva make their presence. People who die here attain salvation.

111. First Muktikṣetra, then Rurukhaṇḍa, then the confluence of divine rivers and afterwards Triveṇī.

112. The place where Gaṇḍakī flows is very holy, because Gaṇḍakī is the best of all rivers.

113. Then is the Harikṣetra where Gaṅgā mingles with Bhāgīrathī.

114. The sacredness of the place where Gaṇḍakī joins Gaṅgā cannot be fully known even by the gods.

115. I have thus told you, O fair goddess, about the greatness of Śālagrāma and of Gaṇḍakī which removes all sins, what you asked of me earlier and what is dear to all devotees.

116. This is the most important of all narratives, most brilliant among the brilliant, the foremost of merits and the best of penances.

117. This is the secret of all secrets and the best of all paths and the greatest of gains.

118. This should not be imparted to the wicked, the obstinate, the disobedient, the sinful, the ungrateful and the offenders of Brahmins.

119. This should not be imparted to a bad disciple, to one who condemns the scriptures, to the base or to one who does not know divine service.

120. It should be imparted to the disciple who is good and intellectually bright, free from greed and desirous of acquiring merit.

121. He who recites this, rising up early in the morning, liberates twentyone generations in his family.

122. And after death, he reaches my world.

123. I have thus told you about the greatness of Śālagrāmakṣetra. What else do you wish to hear ?

CHAPTER ONE HUNDRED AND FORTYSIX

Greatness of Rurukṣetra and Hṛṣikeśa

Sūta said:

1. On hearing about the greatness of Śālagrāma, Earth became wonderstruck and asked again.

Earth said:

2. How wonderful is the place about which you spoke to me ! I feel very much gratified to hear this.

3. You have said about a very sacred place called Ruruṣaṇḍa. Who was this Ruru and how could be that, O Hṛṣīkeśa you have chosen to remain there ?

4. Please tell me this if you consider me deserving of this favour.

Varāha said:

5. Once there lived a Brahmin by name Devadatta, a descendent of Bhṛgu, well versed in the Vedas and Vedāṅgas.

6. He was an expert in matters relating to sacrifice, highly ascetic, and fond of guests.

7. His penance-grove was full of sacred trees and creepers, was abundant in roots and fruits, and had herds of gentle beasts.

8. He performed penance there for a thousand years.

9. This made Indra restless in mind. He called the Gandharvas together with their associates and also the season spring and spoke to them in sweet words.

10. I badly need your help to overcome a serious trouble. Let me get peace of mind through you.

11. Then Kāmadeva and the Malaya wind replied to the lord of gods.

12. Command us as to what we may do for your pleasure. Which ascetic's mind, despite his control of senses, should we disturb ? Which man should we pull down from his severe penance ? Tell us quick.

13. Thus asked, Indra was pleased and he replied.

14. I was much worried till I saw you. I shall tell you everything in detail.

15. A sage named Devadatta is performing severe penance in the beautiful Hṛṣīkeśa in the Himālayas.

16. His aim is to attain my position. See that his penance is disturbed.

17. Receiving this command of Indra, Kāmadeva started with the spring season and the Malaya wind.

18. Then Indra called the celestial damsel named Pramlocā and spoke to her in endearing words.

19. I wish you success in what you do. Go to the hermitage of sage Devadatta and captivate him by your charm.

20. Accomplish this so well as to gain my special favour.

21. Taking this command of Indra, she went to the hermitage of Devadatta.

22. She stood there in the nearby grove which was beautiful with a variety of trees and creepers, sweet with the warblings of joyful cuckoos;

23. Delightful with the humming of swarms of bees that enjoy honey in the blossoms of the Rasāla trees;

24. With the music of Gandharvas spreading around and the Malaya wind blowing cool; with lotuses in bloom in the clear ponds;

25. With calm prevailing everywhere due to the prowess of the sage; captivating with the sweet odour spreading in every place;

26. And she began to sing there so well that the sage became attracted and he slowly stopped his penance.

27-28. The Gandharvas also began their music, and, seizing the occasion, Kāmadeva strung his flowery bow and aimed his arrows at the tranquil sage.

29. Hearing that music beautiful with the Pañcama svara the mind of the sage became perturbed.

30. Kāmadeva tirelessly shot his arrows again on him.

31. The sage, with perturbed mind, moved about all around and saw at a distance beautiful damsel playing with a ball.

32. Hit by the arrows of Kāmadeva, the great sage approched her with a smile.

33. She too looked at him amorously but with shyness.

34. Attracting the mind of the sage with her irresistible charms, she continued to play the ball unmindful of flowers falling from her dishevelling hair.

35. At that time the Malaya wind blew off her garment freeing it from its knot and the girdle holding it.

36. Kāmadeva lost no time in hitting him again. And the excited sage went close to her and said:

37. Who are you and whose, O lovely lady. What do you seek in this forest?

38. Do you wish to make people like me beasts to be drawn by your hands; and, catching us in this way, what do you propose to do?

39. Anyway, we are entirely under your control and we will do whatever you make us do.

40. Then he held that smiling damsel by the right hand. He embraced her and gave her delight.

41. Day and night he enjoyed with her every pleasure helped by the power he had acquired by his penance.

42. A long time elapsed like this. One day suddenly, as if waking from sleep, discrimination dawned upon him.

43. He felt aversion for everything and exclaimed with remorse.

44. How powerful is Māyā that deluded me in this way, that my dislodgement from penance was effected in spite of my awareness of it.

45. The saying that woman is like a pit of fire and man is

like a pot of ghee, is not of the wise because there is much difference when we think about it.

46. The ghee in the pot melts only in contact with the fire, but man melts at the very sight of woman, deluded by her.

47. So saying, he gave up the celestial lady, Pramlocā, and began to think.

48. There has been a great impediment to my penance here. So I shall leave this hermitage and go somewhere else where I can perform severe penance and emaciate my body.

49. So deciding in his mind, he went towards the hermitage of Bhṛgu.

50. He bathed at the confluence of the river Gaṇḍakī, performed ablutions there for the manes and gods, worshipped Viṣṇu and Śiva and then thought of the proper locality for penance.

51. Seeing the hermitage of Bhṛgu towards the north, he moved there on the eastern bank of Gaṇḍakī.

52. Resting for a while, he looked for a fit place there for penance.

53. He chose the spot known as Bhṛgutuṅga and engaged himself in meditating on Śiva.

54. After a long period Śiva became pleased and appeared before him in the form of a liṅga with water flowing from it at the bottom, top and the sides to give him peace.

55. He told the sage, "O sage, see me Śiva. Know me to be Viṣṇu too. Don't feel that there is any difference between us.

56. Formerly you took us to be different from each other. Therefore it was that impediment occurred to your penance and you were dislodged from it.

57. You will attain your aim if you look at us both with the same attitude.

58. This place where liṅgas have arisen due to the power of penance, will be known as Śubhāṅga.

59. He who bathes in the Gaṇḍakī tīrtha and worships these liṅgas, will attain the fruit of yoga. So saying Śiva disappeared.

60. The sage Devadatta obtaining supreme knowledge by the means suggested by Śiva, gained supreme beatitude.

61. Pramlocā, who became pregnant through the sage, gave birth to a daughter near the hermitage, but leaving the child

there, returned to heaven, considering herself as having taken a new birth.

62. The girl was brought up by the animals called Rurus. She, therefore, came to be known as Ruru and remained in her father's hermitage.

63. Although her hand was sought by many young men (when she came of age), she did not encourage any one.

64. She then resolved to perform penance meditating on lord Viṣṇu.

65. In the first month she took fruit on alternate days, in the second month once in three days.

66. In the third month once in five days and in the fourth once in seven. In the fifth month she took food once in nine days and in the sixth once in fifteen days.

67. In the seventh month she lived on fallen leaves and in the eighth on air alone.

68. A period of one hundred years was thus spent in meditating on Viṣṇu, and she became motionless like a stone.

69. She did not distinguish between opposites and attained the supreme stage of penance which gave a halo to her.

70. Seeing everything illumined by her halo, I was wonderstruck, O Earth, and I appeared before her.

71. But as she had withdrawn all her sense-organs, she did not see me.

72. Then I entered her sense-organs and stood before her heart. She saw me then.

73. Since I made myself visible thus by subduing the senses (*Hṛṣikās*), I came to be known as Hṛṣikeśa, and I continued to be there.

74. Soon after that, she could not see me. Then she opened her eyes and saw me standing before her. She then prostrated at my feet, with her whole body in horripilation, and was sobbing.

75. Seeing her in that condition, I spoke.

76. "O beautiful girl, I am pleased with your penance. Seek of me what you have in your mind. I shall grant you that even if it is one not normally granted to others."

77. Hearing these words of the lord, she bowed to him and said with folded hands.

78. "O great lord, if you are pleased to give me a boon, then let it be that you remain in this place in this very form."

79. (I then said): "Let it be so. I shall remain here. But seek another boon also, as I am pleased with you."

80. So asked, she prostrated at my feet again and said:

81. "If you are so pleased, O Lord, then make me holy and give this place my name".

82. Then, O Earth, I spoke to her again:

"Your body will become the holiest of all tīrthas.

83. This place also will be known by your name. He who takes bath in that tīrtha after fasting for three nights, will see me and become purified.

84. Even sins like killing the Brahmin, committed knowingly or unknowingly, will be removed immediately."

85. After giving her these boons, I again became invisible.

86. In due course, she became the tīrtha.

87. Thus have I told you about the greatness and secret of Rurukṣetra.

CHAPTER ONE HUNDRED AND FORTYSEVEN

Greatness of Goniṣkramaṇa

Earth said:

1. I have now known about the wonder of the Rurukṣetra and the greatness of Hṛṣīkeśa.

2. I now wish to know if there is any other place equally important.

Varāha said:

3. Now know about another place which is equally important at the top of the Himālayas.

4. It is called Goniṣkramaṇa, since a number of cows were released from there.

5. The Prajāpati Aurva performed penance there for seventy kalpas aided by my power of Māyā.

6. A long time elapsed for him in this way.

7. Then a doubt arose in the minds of the people as to why

he was doing penance since no boon was sought by him and no indication of his aim was available.

8. But he was performing penance unabated for quite a long time.

9. Then in that famous tīrtha known as Goniṣkramaṇa, lord Śiva came near him.

10. Aurva was then going to the river Gaṅgā to gather lotus flowers.

11. Knowing him thus out of the hermitage, Śiva entered it.

12. It was auspicious, beautiful and full of fruits and flowers.

13. But it was soon reduced to ashes by the heat of the halo of Śiva.

14. After burning that hermitage, Śiva quickly returned to (his abode in) the Himālayas.

15. Soon Aurva returned to his hermitage with the flower basket. He was calm, collected, patient and wedded to truth.

16. Still, when he saw his hermitage with its abundance of fruits and flowers burnt, anger set foot on his mind, and also sorrow.

17. He then said, his eyes red with anger. "He who burnt this hermitage full of fruits and flowers and water, shall also be afflicted with sorrow and wander about in all the worlds."

18. When this curse was pronounced by Aurva, the whole world began to fear.

19. From that moment Śiva, although he is the lord of the world, began to be tormented by great heat, and he told Pārvatī:

20. "Seeing the penance of Aurva, the gods were afraid and they told me: 'The heat of the penance of this Aurva affects the whole world.

21. But he does not desire anything. How can we remedy this ?"

22. When told thus, I cast my eye on his hermitage. In a moment it was burnt down, and we returned.

23. Being sorry and angry at this, Aurva cursed me, and that has resulted in this torment of mine."

24. Śiva wandered and wandered but could not free himself from the affliction. I too began to feel the torment of heat because of my identity with Śiva but I was unable to do anything.

25. Pārvatī then suggested: "We shall go to lord Nārāyaṇa and seek a solution for this."

26. They then went to Nārāyaṇa, and along with him to Aurva, and told him:

27. "Please withdraw the curse pronounced on Śiva. We are all tormented by it."

28. Aurva said: "What I uttered shall never be false. Let Śiva bring herds of cows and bathe them here. He will then be free from the curse, not otherwise."

29. At that time, I got down there seventyseven auspicious cows.

30. They were all bathed there and they became delighted as a result.

31. Such is the extremely holy tīrtha called Goniṣkramaṇa.

32. He who bathes there after fasting for a night, delights himself in Goloka (in heaven).

33. And he who dies there after performing all austerities, reaches my world and becomes endowed with conch and disc.

34. At the foot of the banyan tree called Pañcavaṭa there, fall five streams of water. He who bathes there after fasting for five nights, attains the fruit of five sacrifices (*Pañcayajñas*).

35. And he who gives up his life there after performing all austerities, enjoys the fruit of five sacrifices and then reaches my world.

36. There is the spot called Pañcapada there, where on my eastern side there are five big slabs.

37. Two of these form Brahmapada. Between them is a broad slab. Above it is the Viṣṇupada, which is mine.

38. He who bathes there after fasting for five nights, reaches those pure worlds dear to the devotees.

39. And he who gives up his life there, becomes free from all bondages, and reaches my world.

40. Then there is the place called Brahmapada where a single torrent falls on the western side.

41. He who bathes there after fasting for a night, reaches Brahmaloka and delights himself in the company of Brahmā.

42. If he does this on the Dvādaśī day in the bright half of the month Kaumuda, he attains the fruit of Vājapeya sacrifice.

43. And he who gives up life there remaining steadfast in my service, reaches my world after enjoying the fruit of Vājapeya sacrifice.

44. At a distance of five krośas from there on the north-western side is the place called Koṭivaṭa.

45. He who bathes there after foregoing six meals, gets the fruits of crores of sacrifices.

46. And he who gives up life in this Koṭivaṭa, reaches my place after enjoying the fruit of crores of sacrifices.

47. At a distance of five krośas on the north-east side there is Viṣṇusaras.

48. This lake is mine and it spreads for five krośas along a mountain.

49-50. He who walks there or circumambulates after fasting for three nights and performing all austerities, remains high in Brahmaloka for as many thousands of years as the number of steps he has trodden.

51. And he who gives up life there, after performing his duties well, leaves Brahmaloka and reaches my world.

52. Know you, O beautiful goddess, the wonder in this (Goniṣkramaṇa)kṣetra. A devotee of mine hears there the bellowing sound of the cows.

53. This will be heard very loud on the Dvādaśī day in the bright half of the month of Jyeṣṭha.

54. The devotee who performs pious deeds in Goniṣkramaṇa gets freed from all his sins.

55. In this manner was the effect of the curse got over by Śiva along with the gods.

56. I have thus told you in full about Gosthala which removes all ills.

57. This chapter bestows all auspiciousness on my devotees and it adds to my pleasure.

58. This is highly important, highly auspicious, highly beneficial and highly righteous.

59. Those of my devotees who read it, acquire effulgence, wealth and prosperity and attain their desires.

60. They remain esteemed in my world for as many thousands of years as there are syllables in this chapter.

61. Those who read it every day never face a fall. They

liberate seven generations of their ancestors and twentyone generations in his family.

62. This should not be imparted to the wicked, the foolish or the obstinate. It may be imparted to the son, the disciple and he who knows my service.

63. This should not be forgotten at the time of death by any one desirous of supreme bliss. A verse or even a foot of a verse may serve the purpose.

64. In that place which extends over five yojanas, I remain with pleasure on the eastern side.

65. Gaṅgā flows on the west for the sake of those who have no desire.

66. Such is the place where all actions generate well-being.

67. I have thus told you the great secret of this place about which you asked me.

CHAPTER ONE HUNDRED AND FORTYEIGHT

Greatness of Stutasvāmi

Sūta said:

1. Earth was very much wonder-struck on hearing the narration about Goniṣkramaṇa.

Earth said:

2. I am very much gratified to hear about the greatness of cows and the greatness of yourself, O Lord.

3. O Lord Nārāyaṇa, now tell me if there is any place even holier than this.

Varāha said :

4. I am lord Nārāyaṇa, the resort of all *dharma*. There is none to rival me and so I am the supreme lord.

5. I tell this śāstra to you in pleasure, assuming the form of the boar which is dear to all devotees.

Earth said :

6. "As you tell me more and more about *dharma* and its cause, I get more and more unbounded joy in my mind."

7. Hearing these words of Earth, the lord, who is the highest in *dharma*, and who had taken the form of the boar, told her.

Varāha said :

8. It is befitting of you to say this as you are devoted to me. I shall tell you what you ask for the happiness of the world.

9. There is my holy place called Stutasvāmi. My presence is there from the Dvāparayuga.

10. I will be born as the son of Vasudeva and Devakī to kill all demons.

11. I will have five disciples then who will be experts in *dharma* due to my favour. They will be establishing me as the embodiment of *dharma*.

12. These followers of mine will be Śāṇḍilya, Jājali, Kapila, Upasāyaka and Bhṛgu.

13. There will also be those of pure mind setting examples to others by themselves,

14. And upholding me by their power of knowledge, namely Saṅkarṣaṇa, Vāsudeva, Pradyumna and Aniruddha.

15. They will be devoted to me and propagate righteousness.

16. I will give them whatever boons they wish and they will speak to me in their knowledge of self.

17. Where dharma is firm, may there the science of self-knowledge become established. Let this be well known and let this never be false. May the world go on with your favour.

18. I will then be telling them : O dear disciples, let it be as you please, as you are dear to me.

19. What a good disciple desires will certainly be granted.

20. Then they will tell me dear to all desciples:

21. Just like butter churned out of curds, is the Varāha churned out of all śāstras. It is the cream of all knowledge.

22. They will thus proclaim as authoritative what I say and will attain supreme beatitude.

23. This is considered by the devotees as the greatest of all Śāstras leading to salvation of all.

24. Listen, O Earth, I shall tell you another thing, namely about the actions to be done.

25. Some people cross this world by knowledge while others engage themselves in actions for the same. Others do this by gifts.

26. Others resort to both knowledge and action, certain others realise me by the power of yoga and yet others by rituals.

27. But all follow *dharma* and do everything with concentration of mind.

28. This is the great śāstra for liberation from *saṁsāra* propounded for the sake of my devotees.

29. They will propagate this, each according to what appeals to him most and as the sages have demonstrated.

30. Those learned in śāstras along with their disciples will popularise what is suited for the particular yuga. And by my grace, they will all attain bliss.

31. Those among my disciples who have the fault of rivalry and those who find fault with my śāstra, will have rebirth.

32. For those who are caught in rivalry is not the world that is great beyond.

33. Listen, O Earth, I shall tell you another thing in regard to those that follow my path.

34. Even those who are learned, humble and free from many faults, come down if they have this fault of rivalry.

35. Rivalry destroys *dharma*, it destroys everything. He who has rivalry can never see me.

36-37. There may be those who do numerous good deeds, give gifts, learn Vedas, practice penance, attain knowledge and perform daily rituals. But if they have rivalry they do not see me, but are defiled by Māyā.

38. So none should have rivalry which destroys *dharma*, if salvation is wished for through what I have laid down.

39. Even wise people do not know about this, and many have brought ruin upon themselves by rivalry.

40. I have proclaimed this śāstra dear to all devotees in this boar form of mine.

41. Listen now to the wonder that happened at Bhūtagiri where there is an iron idol of mine.

42. Some consider it as of iron, others as of bronze, still others as of stone, yet others as of diamond,

43. Although they perform worship to me at the top or bottom and touch me in the middle of the head.

44-45. Those who have preceptors and worship me in Maṇipūragiri, derive virtues of the preceptors, get freed of all sins and attain beatitude.

46. In that place, on its north, is the tīrtha called Pañcadruma.

47. He who bathes there after foregoing food five times, delights in the Nandana garden with the Apsarā women.

48. And he who gives up life there fully gratified, gives up Nandana and reaches my world.

49. At a distance of half a yojana on the southern side is the tīrtha known as Bhṛgukuṇḍa.

50. My devotee who takes bath there subdues his senses and is never born again on earth.

51. He delights himself with the Apsarases in the peak of Meru where Dhruva remains.

52. And he who gives up life there, remaining in my service, gives up the world of Dhruva and reaches my world.

53. There is another spot called Maṇikuṇḍa where gems are seen in several places.

54. This is a deep pond and not easily accessible even to Devas.

55. He who bathes there after fasting five times, comes to possess gems and gets the marks of a king.

56. And he who gives up life there, remaining in my service, cuts asunder the bonds of *saṁsāra*.

57. There is Suguhya on the eastern side at a distance of three krośas. He who bathes there reaches my world.

58. Then there is Dhūtapāpa at a distance of five krośas on the Western side.

59. That is particularly dear to me and I have made it full of emeralds and glowing like gold.

60. He who bathes there after foregoing five meals,

61. Giving up all actions pertaining to the five elements, gets freed of all sins,

62. Reaches the world of Indra, O fair goddess, and delights himself there with Devas.

63. And he who gives up life there, remaining in my service, gives up the world of Indra and reaches my world.

64-65. Know you now about the wonder there. In that Maṇipūra hill the streak of water will not fall on the person who approaches it unless he is cleansed of all sins. When once the sins are removed, the streak begins to fall.

66. Similarly, there is an Aśvattha (Peepal) tree near which only a pure person is able to go and not one who is sinful.

67. On the western side, at a distance of half a yojana is an Āmalaka (Gooseberry) tree.

68. By my prowess it yields all desires, but this cannot be known by a sinful man.

69. The devotee who, with full control of the senses and concentration of mind, and fasting for three nights,

70. Goes there at sunrise and at noon or at sunset,

71. With undivided attention and full determination, and procures the Āmalaka fruit, gets (his desires fulfilled) in the course of five days in that Bhūtagiri.

72. Hearing these words of lord Nārāyaṇa, Earth asked again in all humility.

73-74. "Be pleased to tell me about Stutasvāmi, the holy spots there and how it got this name".

Varāha said:

75. O Earth, after killing the enemies of gods and cutting all bonds of *saṁsāra*, when I was remaining at Maṇipūra in Dvāparayuga,

76. Brahmā and other gods began to praise me with mantras.

77-78. Then, O goddess, Nārada, Asita, Devala and Parvata who were all deep in my devotion, gave me the name in the Maṇipūra hill as 'Stutasvāmī' (and then the place also got the name).

79. I have thus told you how and why the place got this name, what you asked for the good of the devotees.

80. I have told you about the greatness of Stutagiri where I will be from the beginning of the Dvāparayuga.

81. All these secrets about Bhūtagiri should be listened to by people with attention.

82. Thus have I told you about the greatness of Stuatasvāmi, What else do you wish to ask ?

CHAPTER ONE HUNDRED AND FORTYNINE

Greatness of Dvārakā

Sūta said :

1. Earth was very much pleased to hear the greatness of Stutasvāmi. She then said:

Earth said :

2. I have gained great tranquility of mind on listening to the account of importance (of Stutasvāmi).

3. This great śāstra has been imparted by the lord himself who bears the earth, kills the enemies of gods and holds bow and arrows, sword, conch, disc, mace and lotus.

4. Thus have I been told about the greatness of Sutasvāmi. If there is anything still greater, be pleased to tell me that.

Varāha said :

5. O you goddess wearing garland of lotus flowers, I shall tell you another secret aimed at removing sins.

6. In Dvāpara yuga my father will be born with the name Śauri in the Yādava clan.

7. There is a well-known city named Dvārakā there, built by Viśvakarmā and beautiful like the city of gods.

8. It is ten yojanas long and five yojanas broad. I will live there for five hundred years.

9. After removing the causes of trouble to Devas, I will return to the world of gods.

10. A sage by name Durvāsas with high spiritual powers, will curse my race.

11. As a result, the residents of Dvārakā, namely the Vṛṣṇis, Andhakas and Bhojas will all die.

12. Balabhadra, white like the moon and wearing the Vanamālā garland, will drag the city with his plough into the sea.

13. Hearing these words of Lord Nārāyaṇa, Earth desirous of *dharma*, held his feet and said:

Earth said :

14. You are the lord of the worlds and the custodian of Māyā. Tell me how Durvāsas can give such a curse.

Varāha said:

15. I will then get a wife called Jāmbavatī, beautiful and youthful.

16. A son by name Sāmba will be born to her who will be liked by me but who will be haughty because of his beauty and youth.

17. He will dress himself like a pregnant woman and ask the sage whether the child to be born will be a son, as such is the desire.

18. Knowing that he is really Sāmba, the sage will become very angry and say:

19. "From your pregnancy what will be born is a club which will eventually kill all Vṛṣṇis and Andhakas."

20. Hearing the words of curse uttered by Durvāsas, all the boys would be sorry. They would rush to me in fear.

21. I will then ask them why they have come and they will tell me what had happened.

22. I will tell them then that what Durvāsas said would certainly take place.

23. I have thus told you about the cause of the curse on the Vṛṣṇis and others. I shall tell you now about the holy places there.

24. In Dvārakā which gives delight to the Vaiṣṇavas, there is the great place called Pañcasara which is a little within the shore.

25. He who bathes there foregoing six meals, delights himself with the Apsarases in heaven.

26. And he who gives up life there, leaves the world of gods and remains high in my world.

27. In that place there is a big Plakṣa tree with numerous branches with a lot of good fruits shaped like pots.

28. Many people go there to get these fruits but none gets them other than my devotees.

29. Those who get the fruits become free from all sins and they attain beatitude remaining in my service.

30. There is the tīrtha called Prabhāsa which people with desire or greed are unable to see.

31. He who bathes there after foregoing five meals, delights himself in the seven islands and gets access to secret places there.

32. And he who gives up life there free from sins, gives up all attachment and reaches my world.

33. Know you now about the wonder there.

34. In the sea in Prabhāsa many big fish are seen moving about here and there.

35. They do not harm any one bathing there.

36. If Piṇḍas (balls of rice for the manes) are put there, they draw them towards them without themselves going near.

37. But they receive the piṇḍas of only those who are righteous and not of those who are sinful.

38. There is the tīrtha called Pañcapiṇḍa which is deep and spreads over one krośa.

39. He who bathes there after foregoing five meals, delights himself in the world of Indra.

40. And he who gives up life in this Pañcakuṇḍa[1], gives up the world of Indra and goes to my world.

41. Know you about the wonder there which can be seen only by the virtuous and not by the sinful.

42. At noon on the twentyfourth Dvādaśī day in the year, a golden lotus appears there.

43. There is the place called Saṅgamana where, in the Maṇipūra hill, four streaks of water fall.

44. He who bathes there after foregoing four meals, goes to the world of Vaikhānasas.

45. And he who gives up life there in full devotion gives up the world of Vaikhānasas and goes to my world.

46. Listen to the wonder that is there in the Maṇipūra hill. The streaks fall only before persons free from sin and not before others.

47. There is then Haṁsakuṇḍa where a single torrent falls from the Maṇipūra hill.

48. He who bathes there after foregoing six meals, becomes free from all attachments and delights himself in the world of Varuṇa.

---

1. Pañcapiṇḍa and Pañcakuṇḍa seem to be two different names for the same tīrtha.

49. And he who gives up life there, leaves the world of Varuṇa and becomes exalted in my world.

50. I shall tell you about the wonder in Haṁsakuṇḍa which is seen only by the pure persons and not by others.

51. On the twentyfourth Dvādaśī day in the year, at noon swans are seen there white like the moon.

52. Those who see these swans moving here and there, attain supreme bliss.

53. Then there is Kadamba where the Vṛṣṇis became purified and reached my world.

54. He who bathes there after foregoing four meals, delights himself in the world of sages.

55. And he who gives up life there, after performing all austerities, gives up the world of sages and reaches my world.

56. I shall tell you about the wonder there. There is a waterfall on its eastern side.

57. On the Dvādaśī day in the month of Māgha, flowers can be seen in it when the sun rises.

58. Those of my devotees who get these flowers attain supreme bliss.

59. There is Cakratīrtha where five streaks of water fall from Maṇipūra.

60. He who bathes there after foregoing five meals, delights in Svargaloka for ten thousand years.

61. And he who gives up life there, free from desire and delusion, gives up everything in Svarga and reaches my world.

62. I shall tell you about the wonder there which is known by none other than my devotees.

63. At midnight on the twentyfourth Dvādaśī in the year, a sound which is pleasant to the mind and ear is heard.

64. The wind wafts fragrance but this is perceptible only to the virtuous and not to others.

65. On its northern side there is a big Aśoka tree. It blossoms when the sun rises.

66. Those of my devotees who get this flower, attain supreme bliss.

67. There is the Raivataka (mount) in that place, which is known all over the world and where I had played.

68. It is full of thickets and bowers and abundant with flowers.

69. It has rows of slabs of variegated colours and caves everywhere and many lakes liked by even gods.

70. He who bathes there after foregoing six meals, goes to the world of Soma fully gratified.

71. And he who gives up life there remaining steadfast in my service, gives up the world of Soma and reaches my world.

72. Listen to the wonder there which people seeking *dharma* notice.

73. In the water numerous leaves from the trees standing around fall, but none can be seen within it and the water remains absolutely clear.

74. On the eastern side there is a gigantic tree and another by my side, spreading over an area of five krośas.

75. The water is full of lotuses, lilies and other fragrant flowers.

76. It has fish of various kinds. There are rocks in it with caves.

77. He who bathes there after foregoing eight meals, delights himself in the divine Nandana garden with the Apsarases.

78. Listen to the wonder there which, of course, is seen only by the seekers of *dharma*.

79. As in the sea, the water here rises at noon and falls at midnight.

80. On its western side is a big Bilva tree which flowers on the twentyfourth Dvādaśi day of the year.

81. This is seen by the virtuous when the sun sets, but not by others.

82. My devotees who get this flower attain, doubtless, supreme bliss.

83. In that place there is the spot known as Viṣṇusaṅkramaṇa where I was hit by the hunter and then attained my original form.

84. There is a small deep pond here by the side of Maṇipūra. A streak of water also falls here.

85. (He who bathes there) without any feeling of loss or gain, (goes to the world of the sun, and he who gives up life there) leaves the world of the sun and reaches my world.

86. I shall tell you about the wonder there, namely that Viṣṇu is easily visible there to the meritorious but not to others.

87. On its southern side is a big and beautiful Aśvattha tree which bears fruits at noon on the twentyfourth Dvādaśī day of the year.

88. Those of my devotees who get these fruits, get supreme bliss.

89. I remain in that shore facing north for the well-being of my devotees.

90. I am there together with Balarāma and the auspicious Ekādaśī.

91. All the three of us remain there in Dvārakā and the three delight there.

92. The place extends in all over thirty yojanas. Those who go there and see me in all devotion, soon get beatitude.

93. This is the best of all narratives, the best means for peace (of mind).

94. The greatest of all *dharmas*, the most lustrous, the best of all gains, the foremost of all actions,

95. The most sacred of scriptures, the best in penance.

96. This should never be forgotten at the time of death by one desirous of bliss. He then reaches my world.

97. He who recites this early in the morning, liberates seven generations of his ancestors and seven generations of his successors.

98. I have thus told you in detail about the greatness of Dvārakā. What else do you wish to ask?

CHAPTER ONE HUNDRED AND FIFTY

Greatness of Sānandūra

Sūta said :

1. Earth was very happy to listen to the greatness of Dvārakā and spoke to the Lord again, being desirous of knowing *dharma*.

Earth said :

2. "I am extremely delighted that you have been pleased to tell me all this.

3. If you are pleased to favour me further, tell me if there is any place even more important than this."

4. Hearing these words of Earth, Viṣṇu in the form of the boar, spoke to her.

Varāha said:

5. There is the holy place called Sānandūra to the north of sea and the south of Malaya mountain.

6. There I stand facing north in an idol which is neither very tall nor very short.

7. Some consider this idol to be of iron, others to be of copper, some others to be of bronze yet others to be of tin and still others to be of stone. Such is its wonder.

8. Now listen to the holy spots there which help people to cross the ocean of *saṁsāra*.

9. One wonder in Sānandūra is that a golden lotus appears there at noon.

10-11. In the spot called Rāmagṛha there, a big tree with a single creeper spread over it, stands in the sea, but it is not visible to any one (other than my devotees).

12. Another wonder I may tell you, O Earth, which also my devotees alone are able to see.

13-14. There are multitudes of fish there, but if a piṇḍa is thrown amidst them, none touches it until it is received by a big fish with the mark of disc on it.

15. There is the lake called Rāmasaras which is deep and broad and adorned with red lotuses.

16. He who bathes there after fasting for a night, goes to the abode of Budha and makes himself happy there.

17. And he who gives up life there, leaves the abode of Budha and goes to my world.

18. Now listen to the wonder in the Rāmasaras which people other than my devotees do not see.

19. This lake extends over one krośa and has around it numerous bushes and creepers.

20. It is attractive with numerous lotuses in every part of it and also with other water plants. There is amidst them one white lotus which is of silver.

21. On the northern side is the Brahmasaras where falls a single torrent shaped like a mace.

22. He who bathes there after foregoing six meals reaches the world of Brahmā and delights himself there.

23. And he who gives up life in this Brahmasaras, reaches my world being permitted by Brahmā.

24. Know you now the wonder in Brahmasaras which my devotees see.

25. The single torrent (about which I told you) falls on the earth at noon on the twentyfourth Dvādaśī day of the year.

26. Soon after noon, this ceases to fall on earth. Such is the wonder in this holy Brahmasaras.

27. There is the place called Saṅgamana where the sea and Rāma remain together.

28. There we get of a pond placid water with bushes and creepers all around and charming with birds.

29. It is just at a distance of one yojana from the sea and is full of fragrant lotuses and lilies.

30. He who bathes there after foregoing six meals, goes to the abode of (the lord of) sea and from there to my world.

31. I shall tell you about the wonder in that Saṅgama seeing which people move about happily free from all ailments.

32. The leaves falling in the water there are never seen in it.

33. The leaves (in the trees) in Rāmasaṅgama have no holes in them. No hole is seen in them even by my devotees.

34. At a distance of half a yojana in the east is the holy Śakrasaras.

35. Four streaks of clear water fall in the pond there.

36. He who bathes there after foregoing four meals, reaches the worlds of four (principal) guardian deities of the quarters.[1]

37. And he who gives up life there, gives up the worlds of guardian deities and reaches my world.

38. I shall tell you the wonder seen there by the pure devotees.

39. The four streaks fall on the four sides. They never increase or decrease in their flow.

40. And on the Dvādaśī day in the bright half of the month of Bhādrapada, highly pleasant music is heard there.

41. Then there is the place called Sūrpāraka where we get the hermitage of Paraśurāma.

---

1. These are Indra, Yama, Varuṇa and Soma.

42. There I take abode facing north with a Śālmalī (silk-cotton) tree in front on the shore of the sea.

43. He who takes bath there after foregoing food five times, goes to the world of sages and sees Arundhatī there.

44. And he who gives up life there, after performing all austerities, gives up the world of sages and reaches my world.

45. Those who prostrate there in reverence, get the benefit of prostrating for twelve years.

46. The Śālmalī tree is visible only to my devotees and not to those who are sinful;

47. And that too only on the twentyfourth Dvādaśī day in the year.

48. On the north-western side we get the lake called Jaṭākuṇḍa.

49. It spreads over ten yojanas and lies to the north of the sea and south of Malaya.

50. He who bathes there after fasting five times, goes to the abode of Agasti and delights himself there.

51. And he who gives up life there thinking of me, leaves the abode of agasti and reaches my world.

52. Nine streams fall into this lake and it is deep like the sea.

53. Know you the wonder there which is seen only by my devotees and not by others.

54. On the twentyfourth Dvādaśī day of the year when the sun rises, the water does not swell but remains steady.

55. I have thus told you about Sānandūra, its expanse and wonders which increase devotion.

56. This is the greatest secret and the holiest of all.

57. He who goes there remaining in the eight-fold path, attains the highest. I assure so,

58. He who reads this every day and he who listens to it, liberate six generations of ancestors and six generations of successors.

59. This should not be forgotten at the time of death, if easy passage to the world of Viṣṇu is desired.

60. I have thus told you what you asked me about for the sake of devotees. What else do you wish to ask ?

CHAPTER ONE HUNDRED AND FIFTYONE

Greatness of Lohārgala

Sūta said:

1. After listening to the greatness of Sānandūra, Earth asked Varāha again with folded hands.

Earth said:

2. "By knowing this secret, O lord, I have gained great peace of mind.

3. Are there places even greater than Sānandūra and more important,

4. O Lord of the worlds, best of Men, great hero, lotus-eyed and of the nature of Time."

5. Hearing these sobbing words of Earth, Lord Viṣṇu, the remover of all ills of the world, spoke in sweet tone.

Varāha said:

6. Listen, O goddess, I shall tell you what you ask.

7. My devotee may go to Lohārgala in the Himālaya, at a distance of thirty yojanas from Siddhavaṭa, (although it is) situated amidst (settlements of) Mlecchas.

8. It is fifteen yojanas long and five yojanas broad.

9. (Normally) it is inaccessible and intolerable being surrounded by the heinous (Mlecchas), but it can be reached by the virtuous who follow my path.

10. I stand there in a golden idol facing north.

11. The demons crept in there, but I stopped them with my Vaiṣṇavī māyā.

12. I shielded there Brahmā, Rudra, Skanda, Indra, Maruts, Ādityas, Vasus, Vāyu, Aśvins, Soma, Bṛhaspati and other celestials.

13. And with my effulgent cakra, quickly annihilated thousands of demons.

14. The gods thus became happy.

15. Thus was this place Lohārgala established by me after killing the valiant demons.

16. He who sees me there with all the effort necessary for it, establishes himself as a great devotee.

17-18. He who bathes there after fasting for three nights and performing all austerities, delights himself in thousands of heavens.

19. And he who gives up life there, gives up all these heavens and reaches my world.

20. I shall tell you about a great wonder there.

21. On the twentyfourth Dvādaśī day of the year, an offering is made to me there, which removes all desires.

22. I have installed there a horse, white in colour like the lily, jasmine and conch, and decorated with all kinds of gems.

23. Offerings of bow, arrow, rosary, spouted vessel and seat are made to me over this horse.

24. Climbing the white mountain and falling in the Kuru country, no injury is found sustained.

25. Making numerous forms fall from the sky, the horse remains in the sky calm and composed.

Sūta said:

26. Hearing these words of Earth, the great sage (Sanatkumāra), son of Brahmā became wonderstruck, being influenced by Viṣṇumāyā.

27. And in that state of wonder, he asked again.

Sanatkumāra said:

28. O goddess, you are extremely blessed that you got the sight of the lord of the worlds.

29. Tell me all that he told you in the course of your conversation with him, as that is conducive to the wellbeing of all.

30. My mind is full of eagerness to know the rare things told by the Lord for the sake of *dharma* and supported by reason.

31. What did that lotus-eyed god, fond of all devotees, say regarding the deeds prescribed ?

Sūta said:

32. Hearing these words of the great Sanatkumāra, (Earth) spoke to him in sweet words.

33. O dear son, I shall tell you what the Lord of worlds told me at my request.

Varāha said:

34. The performance there of the prescribed actions properly, removes all sins.

35. The horses of mine lead (such devotees and) those of theirs, but none else.

36. There is another important pond called Pañcasaras, where four white torrents fall in high speed.

37. He who bathes there after foregoing four meals, goes to the (Gandharva) world Caitrāṅgada and delights there in the company of Gandharvas.

38. And he who gives up life in that place, gives up the world of Gandharvas, and reaches my world.

39. Then there is Nāradakuṇḍa where five torrents fall, each like a palm tree.

40. He who bathes there after foregoing one meal, sees the divine sage Nārada and lives with him.

41. And he who gives up life there knowing the secret about me, leaves Nārada and reaches my world.

42. Then there is in that place Vasiṣṭhakuṇḍa where three torrents fall which are neither too big nor too small.

43. He who bathes there after fasting five times, goes to the world of Vasiṣṭha and enjoys there.

44. And he who gives up life there, remaining steadfast in my service, gives up the world of Vasiṣṭha and reaches my world.

45. Then there is the spot called Pañcakuṇḍa where five torrents fall from the Himalayan peak.

46. He who bathes there after fasting five times, goes to the world of Sage Pañcaśikha.

47. And he who gives up life there, after completely conquering the senses, gives it up and attains the highest bliss.

48. Then there is the famous Saptarṣikuṇḍa where seven torrents fall from Himavān.

49. He who bathes there after giving up seven meals, delights in the world of sages surrounded by their daughters.

50. And he who gives up life there, free from all attachment and desire, gives up the (company of) seven sages and reaches my world.

51. There is Śarabhaṅgakuṇḍa where a single torrent falls and flows as the river Śarabhaṅga.

52. He who bathes there after giving up six meals delights in the world (of Śarabhaṅga) in the company of daughters of sages.

53. And he who gives up life there, free from all attachment, leaves Śarabhaṅga and reaches my world.

54. Then there is the pond called Agnisaras where the water falling on the ground remains still.

55. He who bathes there after fasting eight times, reaches the world of Agnisaras[1] and derives great pleasure.

56. And he who gives up life there, remaining in my service, gives up the world of Agni and reaches my world.

57. Then there is the pond of Bṛhaspati full of waters of the Vedas, where a single torrent falls from the Himalayan peak.

58. He who bathes there after fasting six times, goes to the world of Bṛhaspati surrounded by the daughters of sages.

59. And he who gives up life there, gives up the world of Bṛhaspati and reaches my world.

60. There is the pond of Vaiśvānara where a single torrent falls from the Himalayan peak.

61. He who bathes there after foregoing six meals, delights himself in the world of Vaiśvānara.

62. And he who gives up life there, remaining in my service, gives up the world of Vaiśvānara and reaches my world.

63. There is the pond of Kārttikeya where fifteen torrents fall from the Himālayas.

64. He who bathes there after fasting six times, sees the auspicious six-faced Kumāra.

65. And he who gives up life there, after performing Cāndrāyaṇa, gives up Kārttikeya and delights in my regions.

66. Then there is the pond called Umākuṇḍa where arose Gaurī, the consort of Mahādeva.

67. He who bathes there after fasting during ten nights sees the goddess Gaurī and delights in her world.

68. And he who gives up life there, after fasting for ten nights, leaves the world of Umā and reaches my world.

69. There is Maheśvara Kuṇḍa which is full of Cakravākas, swans and cranes and where Umā was married (by Maheśvara).

---

1. The world of Agni is what seems to be meant here.

70. Three torrents fall there from the Himālaya mountain, which are big, beautiful and clear.

71. He who bathes there after fasting for twelve days, goes to the world of Rudra and is surrounded by women.

72. And he who gives up life there after performing all austerities, leaves the world of Rudra and reaches my world.

73. Then there is Brahmakuṇḍa from where the Vedas arose and where four torrents representing the four Vedas, fall from the Himālayas.

74. On the eastern side a uniform torrent falls which is high and beautiful and has whitish colour representing Sāma.

75. On the northern side is a torrent of clear water golden in colour and representing Ṛk.

76. On the western side is the torrent representing Yajus and on the southern side the one representing Atharva coloured like Indragopa.

77. He who bathes there after fasting for seven nights, reaches the world of Brahmā and remains in his company.

78. And he who gives up life there after subduing his ego, gives up the world of Brahmā and reaches my world.

79. The man who desires to attain bliss must, therefore, go to this Lohārgala of mine.

80. O goddess, this extends over twentyfive yojanas and he who goes there will not have any trace of his actions left in him.

81. This is the greatest of narratives, the highest of all *dharmas* and the purest of the pure.

82. Those of my devotees who read this or listen to this, liberate ten generations of ancestors and ten generations of successors.

83. Those who desire liberation from *saṁsāra* should never forget this at the time of death.

84. Thus have I told you about the greatness and secret of Lohārgala.

85. It is auspicious and holy and brings about happiness to the devotees.

CHAPTER ONE HUNDRED AND FIFTYTWO

Glory of Mathurā Tīrtha

Sūta said:

1. Listening to the greatness of the Lord of three worlds residing at Lohārgala, Earth became wonderstruck.

Earth said:

2. O lord of worlds, with eyes blooming like lotus petals, by your favour I have now heard the great Śāstra.

3. Being your disciple and servant, I have resorted to you. And you are the light of the worlds and their lord.

4. By your favour I have become resplendent like gold and endowed with all Śāstras.

5. For you everything is effortless. The entire world depends on you and nothing acts without your will.

6. Therefore, great pleasure resides in my heart (and curiosity too).

7. So be pleased to tell me whether there is any tīrtha which is even greater than Lohārgala.

Varāha said:

8. O dear Earth, there is no place equal to Mathurā in this world, the nether world or the upper world.

Sūta said:

9. On hearing this, Earth bowed to Varāha and asked again.

Earth said:

10. There are Puṣkara, Naimiṣa and Vārāṇasī. Leaving them out, why do you speak about Mathurā?

Varāha said:

11. Listen to me. I shall tell you in detail. There is nothing more dear to me than the wellknown Mathurā.

12. It is beautiful, famous and the place of my birth. Listen to its sanctity and glory.

13. People living there certainly get salvation. They get there the same result as accrues during Mahāmakha in Prayāga.

14. The same result is attained there as of (living in) Vārāṇasī for a thousand years.

15. The same result is attained in Mathurā in a moment as of the Kārttika festival in Puṣkara.

16. The same merit is acquired in Mathurā by one who has conquered his senses as is acquired in any other place he thinks of.

17. The foolish person it is that wanders in *saṁsāra* being deluded by my Māyā.

18. Even he who hears the name Mathurā uttered by another gets release from sins.

19. When Janārdana is asleep, all the tīrthas and sacred lakes in the world make their presence in Mathurā.

20. Through Śrāddha in the Mathurā region, the manes become propitiated as long as the great lord remains there.

21. Even those others (who are not my devotees) living in Mathurā attain beatitude by my favour.

22. In Kabjāmraka, Saukara and Mathurā, particularly in the last, salvation is obtained by my favour without Sāṁkhya or Yoga.

23. Those who live pure and devoted in the great city of Mathurā, making offerings and giving alms, are verily gods in human form.

24. In Dvāpara yuga, I will be born as a Kṣatriya in the family of king Yayāti in Mathurā.

25. In my four-fold form, I shall be there for a hundred years, praised by the sages and ready for battle.

26. These four forms[1] will have the colours of sandal paste, gold, Aśoka (flower) and blue lotus respectively.

27. I will then have numerous appellations, sacred and sanctifying and powerful enough to snap the bonds of *saṁsāra*.

28. I will then annihilate, O Earth, thirtytwo wicked demons like Kaṁsa who outrage *dharma*.

29. In that place, the river Yamunā, the daughter of the sun-god flows eternally.

30. Yamunā joins Gaṅgā at Prayāga known as Veṇī, but

---

1. The four vyūhas, namely Kṛṣṇa (Vāsudeva), Saṅkarṣaṇa, Pradyumna and Aniruddha.

Yamunā is hundred times more sacred at Mathurā. There need be no doubt in this regard.

31. There will be many tīrthas in that place, by bathing in which, people can reach my world.

32. And by giving up life there remaining in my service, one is never again born as a mortal, but attains four hands (and reaches my world).

33. By bathing in Avimukta, one gets salvation and by giving up life there, reaches my world.

34. He who bathes in the tīrtha named Viśrānti, reaches my world.

35. He gets the merit of bathing in all the tīrthas by seeing the Lord there.

36. The merit obtained by bathing in Viśrānti is not obtained by sacrifices, penance, meditation or subjugation of mind.

37. He sees with ease the past, present and future and by just two circumambulations, reaches the world of Viṣṇu.

38. There is another tīrtha by bathing in which one gets release from worldly existence and reaches my world.

39. That is the great Prayāga which is not easy to get at even for Devas.

40. He who bathes in this gets the merit of Agniṣṭoma sacrifice and goes to the world of Indra and delights there.

41. And he who gives up life there, reaches my world.

42. There is the tīrtha called Kanakhala, by the mere bath in which one gets enjoyment in heaven.

43. There is then the spot named Tinduka by bathing where, O goddess, one remains esteemed in my world.

Now listen to an old story connected with this tīrtha.

44. There is the city Kāmpilya in the Pāñcāla country with abundance of money and grain and ruled by Brahmadatta.

45. In that city lived a barber named Tinduka. Gradually his whole family became extinct.

46. Extremely grieved at this, he gave up every contact and went to Mathurā.

47. He lived there in a colony of Brahmins.

48. Steadfast in his austerities, he used to bathe in Yamunā every day and performed all religious rites for a long time.

49. In course of time he died, but by the prowess of this tīrtha he was born as a high Brahmin.

50. He became a great yogi with knowledge of his past life and a staunch devotee, and by the power of the tīrtha, attained liberation.

51-52. Then there is the Sūryatīrtha which removes all sins, where the sun was worshipped by Bali, son of Virocana, for acquiring wealth when he was banished from his kingdom.

53. He performed penance there for one full year with upraised arms and without food, and in the end attained his aim.

54. The Sun-god was pleased with him and asked him why he was performing such severe penance.

Bali said:

55. "O great god, banished from my kingdom, I am now living in the netherworld. And being penniless, how can I look after my family?"

56. The Sun-god then took out from his crown the Cintāmaṇi gem (which has the power of yielding all desires), and receiving it, Bali returned to the nether world.

57. He who bathes in that tīrtha gets free from all sins, and he who gives up life there, reaches my world.

58. The man who bathes there on Sundays, on the days of the Sun's transit and on the days of the solar and lunar eclipse, gets the benefit of Rājasūya sacrifice.

59. (There is the Dhruvatīrtha) where Dhruva performed penance on his own. He who bathes there becomes esteemed in the world of Dhruva and he who gives up life there reaches my world.

60. He who performs oblations to the manes in the Dhruvatīrtha, particularly in the fortnight when the anniversary of the manes falls, liberates them all.

61. To the south of Dhruvatīrtha is the Tīrtharāja by bathing in which, one attains my world.

62. Further south of it is the Ṛṣitīrtha, by bathing in which one reaches the world of Ṛṣis.

63. And he who gives up life there, becomes esteemed in my world.

64. To the south of the Ṛṣitīrtha is the Mokṣatīrtha by bathing in which one attains *mokṣa* (salvation).

65. There is then the Koṭitīrtha which is not easily reached even by Devas. He who bathes there or makes gifts, becomes exalted in my world.

66. The man who bathes in the Koṭitīrtha and propitiates the manes, liberates them all.

67. And he himself becomes esteemed in the world of Brahmā.

68. In the same place, there is the Vāyutīrtha which is not easily reached even by the manes. He who offers piṇḍa there reaches the world of the Pitṛs.

69. By offering piṇḍa there in the month of Jyeṣṭha one attains the same merit as of doing the same in Gayā.

70. Taking bath, giving gifts, practising *Japa* and performing *homa* in these twelve[1] tīrthas gives the benefit thousand-fold. All sins vanish by simply thinking of them and all wishes are attained by simply listening to the account of their greatness.

CHAPTER ONE HUNDRED AND FIFTYTHREE

Greatness of Mathurā Tīrtha

Varāha said:

1. To the north of Śivakuṇḍa are nine tīrthas. Never was there any greater tīrtha than these and never will be.

2. By merely bathing there, high prosperity is attained and residence in heaven in beautiful form is assured. And he who bathes there (after performing all austerities) goes to my world.

3. There is the tīrtha called Saṁyamana known in all the worlds and by bathing or dying there, one reaches my world.

4. I shall tell you what happened in days of yore in the Saṁyamana tīrtha.

5. A highly sinning and wicked hunter was living in the wellknown Naimiṣa forest.

6. Once he happened to go to Mathurā on the Caturdaśī day of the dark fortnight.

---

1. Actually only ten are given here. The other two are perhaps Śivakuṇḍa and Saṁyamana described in the next chapter.

7. He wanted to cross Yamunā and for that purpose he went to Saṁyamana.

8. As he was crossing the river there, he was drowned.

9-10. As soon as he lost his life thus, he was born as a king in the Saurāṣṭra country with the name Yakṣmadhanus.

11. He ruled the country very well observing his kingly duties. He married Pīvarī, the handsome daughter of the king of Kāśī.

12. Among his hundreds of wives, she was made the chief and he gave her pleasure in the gardens and woods, as also in fine palaces and attractive sands in the rivers.

13. He was protecting his subjects and giving gifts, but was also deeply immersed in enjoying pleasures.

14. Seventyseven years passed in this manner, and he had by then got seven sons and five daughters.

15. All the five daughters were beautiful and they were married to kings and the sons were settled in different places.

16. Once, when the king was sleeping with his queen Pīvarī, he rose up saying repeatedly 'Alas, alas !'

17. That was at the thought of Mathurā and Saṁyamana (tīrtha) there.

18. Then Pīvarī asked him why he was saying so and he replied:

19. "The intoxicated man, the sleeping man and the mad man sometimes blabber. So please don't ask about what I blabbered while asleep."

Pīvarī said:

20. "If I am your wife, please tell me the truth, and if you are going to hide it, I will give up my life."

21. At these words of his queen, the king replied: "If it is essential that I should tell you, let us go to the city of Mathurā. After going there, I shall tell you the truth.

22-23. (In the meantime) give liberal gifts to the Brahmins and instal our sons and grandsons in proper places taking into account the villages in our possession, the treasury and the jewels."

24. Then the citizens were summoned and told: This ancestral kingdom has to be ruled well.

25. I propose to entrust this duty to my sons with your approval.

26. Realising that people always wish for the kingdom, sons, wives and relations and never the world of Yama, and knowing what is really good for me,

27. I and my queen wish to undertake the trouble of going to Mathurā.

28. What a pity that so far I have been attached to my kingdom. I now understand that there is nothing more pleasurable than renunciation.

29. There is nothing more sorrowful than attachment and nothing more pleasurable than detachment.

30. It is indeed commendable to practically give up all desires.

31. Then crowning the eldest son as king and taking leave of citizens, he started for Mathurā followed by the four units of the army, and reached it after a long time.

32. There he saw the city beautiful like the city of Indra, with its twelve tīrthas, pure and sanctifying.

33. He also saw there the abode of Viṣṇu named Madhuvana by seeing which every one becomes gratified.

34. The man who bathes there on Ekādaśī day in the bright half of the Bhādrapada month, becomes fully gratified.

35. Then there is the third natural garden[1] called Kundavana by going where, O goddess, every one becomes equally gratified.

36. The man who bathes there on Ekādaśī day in the dark half of the Bhādrapada month becomes esteemed in the world of Rudra.

37. The fourth such garden is the Kāmyakavana by going where one becomes exalted in my world.

38. (Bathing) in the pond in Vimala[2] removes all sins, and giving up life there leads to my world.

39. The fifth is Bakulavana by going where one goes to the abode of Agni.

---

1. The account of the second appears to be lost.

2. This is perhaps the second garden and is presumably named Vimalavana.

40. At the other bank of Yamunā is Bhadravana, the sixth garden which is dear for gods also.

41. My devotee who goes there, goes to the world of Nāgas by the power of that garden.

42. The seventh is the Khadiravana well known in the world, by going where, O goddess, one goes to my world.

43. The eighth is a great garden named Mahāvana. This is very dear to me and one who goes there goes to the world of Indra.

44. The ninth is called Lohajaṅghavana being looked after by Lohajaṅgha. It is capable of removing all sins.

45. The tenth garden is named Bilvavana held sacred even by the gods. By going there, one attains the world of Brahmā.

46. The eleventh is Bhāṇḍīra which is particularly liked by Yogins. By its very sight one does not enter a womb any more.

47. By reaching this great garden Bhāṇḍīra and seeing lord Vāsudeva there, one gives an end to further births.

48. The twelfth is Bṛndāvana which is looked after by Bṛndā. It removes all sins and is particularly dear to me.

49. Those who see Bṛndāvana and Lord Govinda there, never go to the place of Yama, but go where the meritorious go.

CHAPTER ONE HUNDRED AND FIFTYFOUR

Power of the Tīrthas in Yamunā

Varāha said:

1. Both of them were very glad to see Mathurā of this description.

2. While living there, O Earth, the queen asked the king to tell her the truth as promised by him.

3. The king then asked her to tell him the truth about herself which she too had promised to reveal.

4. Then the virtuous Pīvarī laughed and told the king what he wished to know.

5. "I was living on the bank of river Gaṅgā. I came here to see this city on the Dvādaśī day in the month of Kumuda.

6. As I was crossing the river in a canoe, I fell down in the water and was drowned.

7. But by the power of that tīrtha, I was born as the daughter of the king of Kāśī and I was married by you. But the memory of my past life never left me.

8. All this was due to my losing life in the tīrtha called Dhārāpatanaka (in Yamunā)".

9. Hearing this the king narrated his own former life and of Saṁyamana where he lost his life.

10. Then they bathed in Yamunā and after worshipping me according to rules, died there.

11. And as they had given up all attachments, they reached my world.

12. Thus have I told you about the wonder that occurred there.

13. He who dies in the tīrtha called Dhārāpatanaka, gets all his sins removed and reaches heaven.

14. He who dies after worshipping Yamuneśvara, goes to the world of Viṣṇu and remains there in divine form with four hands, and he who gives up life there, reaches my world.

15. Then there is the very holy spot named Nāgatīrtha by bathing in which one goes to heaven and is never born again.

16. Then there is the tīrtha Ghaṇṭābharaṇaka which purifies everyone. By bathing in it one goes to the world of Sūrya.

17. By giving up life there one certainly goes to my world.

18. I shall tell you, O Earth, about another tīrtha which is known even in the world of Brahmā.

19. By bathing in this (Brahmatīrtha) and drinking the water there, one gets honoured by Brahmā and then reaches my world.

20. There is Somatīrtha in the holy Yamunā where Soma will see me in Dvāpara yuga.

21. He who bathes there remaining steadfast in his duties, delights himself in the world of Soma.

22. And he who gives up life there, reaches my world.

23. There is the Sarasvatī (tīrtha) which removes all sins. By bathing in this even an outcaste becomes a saint.

24. I shall tell you about another tīrtha in Mathurā.[1] He

1. The name of the tīrtha is not given.

who bathes there after fasting for three nights, gets even the sin of killing a Brahmin removed. And he who gives up life there, goes to my world.

25. Then there is Daśāśvamedha (tīrtha) which is resorted to by sages. A bath there makes entry into heaven easy.

26-27. On the western side of Mathurā is the tīrtha called Mānasa which was created by Brahmā from his mind and which is worshipped by sages.

28. Those who bathe there go to heaven and are never born again.

29. There is the Vighnarāja tīrtha by bathing in which one becomes immune from the troubles of Vighnarāja.

30. Those who bathe there particularly on Aṣṭamī, Caturdaśī and Caturthī days, are never troubled by Vighnarāja.

31. This son of Pārvatī wards off all impediments to them in education and in sacrifices and other ceremonies. He who gives up life there, reaches my world.

32. Then there is the holy Koṭitīrtha, by bathing in which one attains the merit of a crore of cows.

33. He who gives up life there without desire or delusion, transcends the world of Soma and reaches my world.

34. At a distance of half a Krośa from there is the temple of Śiva from where he protects Mathurā.

35. By bathing there and drinking the water, the same result as of doing them in Mathurā is obtained. And he who gives up life there, reaches my world.

CHAPTER ONE HUNDRED AND FIFTYFIVE

Power of Akrūratīrtha

Varāha said:

1. O goddess, I shall tell you about another important tīrtha named Ananta.

2. I remain there permanently for the good of the world, and people who see me there, attain salvation.

3. Those who go there during equinoxes, solstices and Viṣṇupadī, get freed from all sins.

4. We get then the tīrtha called Akrūra, by bathing in which during solar eclipse, one attains the fruit of Rājasūya and Aśvamedha sacrifices.

5. Akrūra is the king of all tirthas, and a bath there confers the same result as of a bath in Prayāga.

6. O Earth, listen to an old story in connection with this tīrtha.

7. There was a devotee of mine named Sudhana, a merchant affluent in money and grain.

8. He was happy with his wife, children and relatives and was highly devoted to me.

9. He was spending a lot of money for his family and in this way a long time passed.

10. Never did he commit any fraud either with the weighing balance or with the weights.

11. Every day at the proper time he performed the worship of Hari with flowers, lamps and fragrant sandalpaste, and also with incense and offering of food.

12. On the Ekādaśī days in both the (bright and dark) fortnights of the month he used to fast and keep awake in the night.

13. He once went to this Akrūra tīrtha and was dancing before me.

14. And when he was doing this keeping himself awake in the night, he was caught by a Brahmarākṣasa.

15. Who was huge in form, black in colour, fierce to look at and with hair vertical on the head.

16. He caught (Sudhana) by the feet and said:

17. "O merchant, I am a Rākṣasa living in this forest. I shall get high satisfaction by eating you up today."

Sudhana said:

18. "Please wait for a while. I shall offer you this fat body of mine nurtured by sumptuous food.

19. Let me complete this vow of keeping awake before Lord Hari.

20. After this is done, I shall come to you quickly when the sun starts rising.

21. You can devour my body when I return to you after this vow of keeping awake meant to propitiate Lord Viṣṇu.

22. Please don't obstruct the performance of this vow. You may eat me as you like soon after my return."

23. Hearing these words of Sudhana, the Brahmarākṣasa who was oppressed by severe hunger, spoke softly to him.

24. "O simple man, what you say is false. How will you come back ? Which man will come back when once he is let off from the clutches of the Rākṣasa ?"

25. At these words of the Rākṣasa, the merchant said:

26. "The whole world originates from truth and it is established in truth. The great sages well-versed in the Vedas attain their aim through truth.

27. As one who has never been defiled by any bad action in the past life and hence born as man, I swear before you that I will return.

28. After keeping awake and joyfully dancing (before the lord), I shall certainly come back to you. There is nothing false in what I say.

29. By truth is a girl given in marriage. The Brahmins speak truth. The kings remain in truth and the earth is held by truth.

30. Heaven is desired through truth, salvation is got by truth. The sun blazes by truth and the moon shines by truth.

31. Yama takes away (life) by truth, Indra sways by truth. That truth will be lost if I do not return to you.

32-33. If I do not return, I will be stained by the same sin as befalls a person who rapes the wife of another out of lust.

34. If I do not return, the same sin will fall on me as of taking away the gift of land once made.

35. If I do not return, the same sin will fall on me as of disowning a woman after enjoying her well and full.

36. If I do not return, the same sin will fall on me as of breaking a row of persons entitled to remain in the same row when eating.

37. If I do not return, the same sin will fall on me as of cohabiting with a woman after performing śrāddha on the new moon day.

38. If I do not return, I will go the way of those who do not bathe on the Ṣaṣṭhī, Aṣṭamī and Amāvāsyā days,

39. As also the sin similar to the one that accrues as a result of raping in lust the wife of the teacher, brother, son, uncle or friend, will fall upon me.

40. If I do not return, I will get the same sin as of cohabiting with the wife of a king, wife of a Brahmin or a widow.

41. If I do not return, the same sin will fall on me as of one, who having given a daughter once in marriage, gives her to another.

42. If I do not return, I will be stained by the same sin as is incurred by one doing sacrifice for the king or the villagers (for the sake of money).

43. If I do not return, my way will be the same as of those who kill Brahmins, drink liquor, steal (money) or obstruct a vow".

Varāha said:

44. Hearing the words of Sudhana, the Brahmarākṣasa was pleased and he allowed him to go.

45. Released by the Brahmarākṣasa thus, the merchant with a determination danced before me in devotion.

46. When day was dawning he danced more intensely and repeatedly uttered *namo nārāyaṇāya* (bow to Nārāyaṇa).

47. When the period of keeping awake was over, he bathed in Yamunā and after seeing my divine form, went to the city of Mathurā.

48. I then appeared before him as a celestial man and asked him where he was going in such haste.

49. Sudhana then said that he was going quickly to the Brahmarākṣasa.

50. I then forbade him pointing out that is for the living and, when once dead, there can be neither *dharma* nor fame.

51. The merchant then replied to the man "I shall tell you the truth. I have to go to the Brahmarākṣasa."

52. (He went to the Brahmarākṣasa accordingly and said) "I have now returned after happily dancing before Lord Viṣṇu and after keeping awake.

53. O Rakṣasa, you may eat up this body (of mine) as you like.

54. I have never uttered falsehood, O Brahmarākṣasa; you may, therefore, devour me now."

55. Hearing these words of the merchant, the Brahmarākṣasa said in soft tone:

56. "O merchant, I am glad that you have upheld both truth and righteousness. You have great knowledge and merit and that is why you are so.

57. Please transfer to me the whole merit of your having kept awake, and danced, so that I can liberate myself by it."

Sudhana said:

58. "I shall not give you the merit acquired by my dancing, O man-eater, full, half, quarter or even less."

59. Hearing these words of Sudhana, the Brahmarākṣasa said again: "Give me, O magnanimous merchant, the merit of a single dance."

Sudhana said:

60. "I shall not give you my merit. You may do what we have agreed upon.

61. By what fault did you attain this state of being a Bramarākṣasa? Tell me all that secret."

62. Hearing the words of Sudhana, the Rākṣasa laughed and said: "You may know that I was your neighbour, a Vedic Brahmin named Agnidatta.

63. I was stealing the bricks of others with a view to building a house for myself. And on my death, I became Rākṣasa.

64. You have now met me. Please do me this help. Give me the merit of a single respite in your service (to god).".

65. The merchant was full of pity, and he said: "O Rākṣasa, I give you the merit of a single dance."

66. By the power of the merit of that single dance, the Rākṣasa gained liberation.

Varāha said:

67. O Goddess, Sudhana then saw lord Janārdana of universal form standing in front of him.

68. The great lord Janārdana in his divine body holding the conch, disc and mace, spoke to him sweetly:

69. "Get into this splendid aerial car and arrive in my world." So saying, the lord disappeared there.

70. Sudhana, although he was in human form, got into the aerial car with his family, and reached the world of Viṣṇu.

71. O Earth, I have thus told you about the power of Akrūratīrtha, a greater one than which there never has been and never will be.

72. By the power of this tīrtha Sudhana got salvation.

73. He who bathes in it on the Dvādaśī day in the bright half of the month Kumuda, attains the fruit of Rājasūya sacrifice.

74. He who performs in this tīrtha in the month Kārttikī the Vṛṣotsarga ceremony (letting loose a bull), liberates all his manes.

75. He who performs Śrāddha there during Kārttikī, immediately liberates all forefathers.

CHAPTER ONE HUNDRED AND FIFTYSIX

The Appearance of Mathurā[1]

Varāha said:

1. I shall tell you about the tīrtha called Vatsakrīḍanaka., It is full of red stones and is beautified by red sandal.

2. By simply bathing there, one goes to the world of Vāyu, and he who gives up life there, goes to my world.

3. I shall tell you about another tīrtha, O Earth, namely Bhāṇḍīraka.

4. This is full of trees like Sāla, Tāla, Tamāla, Arjuna Iṅguda, Pīluka and Karīra.

5. He who bathes there observing the rules and fasting, goes to the world of Candra. And he who gives up life there, goes to my world.

6. I shall tell you about my place Bṛndāvana where I play with cows and cowherds.

7. It is a beautiful place and is not easily gained by gods and demons alike.

---

1. Although this is the title of the chapter what we get here is the account of some tirthas.

8. If one takes bath there in the particular spot covered by shrubs and creepers, after fasting for a night, one gets delight in the company of Gandharvas and Apsarases.

9. And he who gives up life there, goes to my world.

10. I shall tell you about another tīrtha in Bṛndāvana, namely the place where the (demon) Keśī was killed.

11. This tīrtha is a hundred times more holy than other tīrthas and a hundred times more holy than this is the spot here where lord Hari rests.

12. There is another speciality, O Earth, in the Keśītīrtha.

13. By offering piṇḍa to the manes there, the result of doing the same at Gayā is obtained. Bath, gifts and homa there, confer the fruit of Agniṣṭoma.

14. Then there are Sūryatīrthas pertaining to the twelve suns.

15. This is the place where the serpent Kāliya was moving about. Kāliya was vanquished by me and the twelve Ādityas installed. I asked the Ādityas to seek a boon.

Ādityas said:

16. "O Lord, if you consider us worthy of receiving a boon, be pleased to grant us bath in this tīrtha".

17. This request of the Ādityas, O Earth, was granted.

18. Mere bath there absolves one of all sins. He who gives life there, reaches my world.

19. Those who die in the strip between the Kāliya in the south and the place where I am installed in the north, are never born again.

CHAPTER ONE HUNDRED AND FIFTYSEVEN

Malayārjuna and other Tīrthas

Varāha said:

1. Beyond Yamunā, there is the tīrtha called Malayārjuna a pond near which (the demon in the form of the cart) Śakaṭa was smashed.

2. By fasting and bathing there, immense merit is derived.

3. By bathing and giving gifts there on Dvādaśī day in the bright half of the month Jyeṣṭha, one can get absolved of all sins.

4. He who takes bath there on this particular day and sees lord Hari in Mathurā, attains beatitude.

5. Bathing in Yamunā with full control of the mind and high purity and worshipping Lord Viṣṇu properly, brings about final liberation.

6. The manes in the other world always say: "How much we wish that some one born in our family bathes in Yamunā and worships Lord Viṣṇu in Mathurā after due fasting."

7. He indeed is a blessed man who worships Janārdana on the Dvādaśī day in the Jyeṣṭha month and offers piṇḍa to the manes in Yamunā.

8. He who bathes in the tīrtha called Bahula in the same Bṛndāvana, gets an exalted place in the world of Rudra.

9. He who bathes there on the Dvādaśī day in the bright half of the month Caitra, certainly goes to my world.

10. There is the pond called Bhāṇḍahrada where the auspicious Ādityas are seen every day.

11. He who bathes in the spot there called Arkasthala, gets freed from all sins and goes to the world of Sūrya.

12. And he who gives up life there, reaches my world.

13. Near Arkasthala there is a well of pure water called Saptasāmudrika which is dear even to the gods.

14. By bathing there, one gets the power to go wherever one likes to go. And he who gives up life there, goes to my world.

15. There is the place called Vīrasthala which is full of lotuses and lilies and where water is very near.

16. He who bathes there after fasting for one night, goes to the world of heroes (Vīraloka) by my grace, and he who gives up life there, goes to my world.

17. Then there is the holy Kuśasthala by bathing where one goes to the world of Brahmā.

18. And he who gives up life there, goes to my world.

19. Then there is Puṣpasthala where there is an important temple of Śiva. By bathing there one goes to the world of Śiva.

20. There is (a chain of five spots called) Pañcadeśa capable of removing all sins. By bathing there, O Earth, one enjoys the company of Brahmā.

21. There is Gopīśvara with capacity to dispel all sins. Sixteen thousand Gopīs were born there for Kṛṣṇa to play with.

22. There by the boy Kṛṣṇa was the pair of Arjuna trees crushed and the (demon in the form of) cart was smashed.

23. While playing with Kṛṣṇa, the Gopīs embraced him but the *dharma* in this was kept hidden.

24. Mātali came there at the behest of Devas and performed ceremonial bath to the lord in the form of the cowherd.

25. Water was brought in seven pots containing sacred herbs and gems, and was poured on him in the midst of Gopīs.

26. The Gopīs were then singing and dancing uttering repeatedly the name of Kṛṣṇa.

27. After consecrating Lord Gopīśvara, Mātali made a well also there with the (water in the) auspicious pots.

28. This is the well Saptasāmudrika with clean water. In front of the lord there are the cowherds.

29. The manes of one who performs Śrāddha in the well Saptasāmudrika with ablutions and piṇḍa, get propitiated.

30. He who offers piṇḍa there when the new moon falls on Monday, liberates seventyseven generations of his ancestors, and they become propitiated for a hundred crores of years.

31. He who dies in the place between the temples of Govinda and Gopīśvara, attains the world of Indra.

32. So too when death occurs in the place between the temples of Bahula, Śiva, and Govinda there, or between those of Gopīśa and Brahmā.

33. By bath, gift and piṇḍa in these places, ten generations of ancestors and ten of successors are liberated.

34. Bath in these leads one to the pleasure of the company of gods, and death there leads one to my world.

35. There is the great tīrtha Vasupatra, and on the southern side of Mathurā, the holy place Phālgunaka.

36. Bathing in them and drinking the water there, lead one to a place of esteem in the world beyond.

37. In Phālguna we get my temple named Vṛṣabhañjanaka.

38. He who bathes there, delights with Devas and he who gives up life there reaches my world.

39. At a distance of half a yojana from Mathurā on the western side, we see the place Tālavana held by the asura Dhenuka.

40. We get there a pond of clear water with lotuses and lilies. By bath and gifts there, one gets whatever is desired.

41. In that place there is the pond called Sampīṭhaka where we get a deep pit full of clear water.

42. He who bathes there after fasting for a night, gets the fruit of Agniṣṭoma, and he who gives up life there reaches my world.

43. When I took birth as the son of Devakī in the house of Vasudeva, I worshipped the sun.

44. As a result, I got a handsome, virtuous and intelligent son.

45. There I saw the sun-god holding lotus in the hand and effulgent with his rays in the month Bhādrapada.

46. On the Saptamī day in the dark half of the month the sun-god appears there.

47. He who takes bath in this pit on that day, finds nothing beyond his reach in this world by the favour of the sun-god.

48. If this is done when this day happens to be Sunday, the effect is absolutely sure for man as well as woman.

49. King Śantanu performed penance here installing the sun-god in front, and he got as his son the mighty Bhīṣma.

50. Getting that son, Śantanu went to Hastināpura. Bath and gift there, fulfils one's desires.

CHAPTER ONE HUNDRED AND FIFTYEIGHT

The Power of Mathurā-Tirtha

Varāha said:

1. The Mathurā region extends over twenty Yojanas. Bathing in the tīrthas there removes all sins.

2. In the Mathurā region, which is extremely holy, stay in the rainy season is particularly pleasant.

3. During the time of my sleep, the tīrthas and temples in the seven islands, make their appearance here.

4. O Earth, seeing me in Mathurā after I am awake, is to see me for all time.

5. To see my face after I am awake, is to bring about instantaneous cessation of all sins acquired in the course of seven lives.

6. Those who reside in Mathurā and see lord Keśava there, become fit for salvation.

7. He who bathes in Yamunā gets the fruit of Rājasūya and Aśvamedha and becomes esteemed in my world.

8. Circumambulating lord Keśava in Mathurā is equal to circumambulating the whole earth with its seven islands.

9-10. O Earth, by making the gift of a lamp before lord Keśava together with a vessel full of ghee and a cloth, one gets an aerial car five yojanas long and five broad and full of rows of lamps.

11. It is beautiful, full of pleasures, attended on by Apsarases and it fulfils all desires.

12. Devas, Gandharvas, Siddhas and Cāraṇas praise him for the merit acquired while on earth.

13. At the expiry of all the acquired merit, he is born in a meritorious family.

Earth said:

14-15. Who protects this place from beasts, goblins, demons and others that cause impediments, so that it may yield its proclaimed effects ?

Varāha said:

16. Due to my prowess they never even see this place of mine and they never do any harm to my devotees.

17. Moreover, I have entrusted the four guardian deities with the protection of this place.

18. Indra guards the east, Yama the south, Varuṇa the west holding the noose.

19. The valiant Kubera guards the north and Śiva, the husband of Umā, the middle.

20. He who constructs a temple in Mathurā, becomes forearmed and gets liberated even while living.

21. He continues to remain in his four-armed form always in the ponds of clear water in Mathurā.

22. He who gives up life there after taking bath, reaches the world of Viṣṇu and enjoys there.

23. I shall tell you about the wonder in the ponds of clear water there.

24. By my power, the water there will be warm in winter and cool like ice in summer.

25. The water does not increase during the rains or decrease during hot season.

26. In Mathurā at every step there is the merit of tīrthas, and bathing there removes all sins.

27. During the rainy season bath may be taken in the large tīrthas with effort, or in the wells, ponds and pits,

28. Or in the confluence of rivers, but one desirous of liberation should necessarily take bath.

29. There is the place called Mucukunda where sleeps Mucukunda, the Vanquisher of demons.

30. He who bathes there accomplishes all desires, and he who gives up life there reaches my world.

31. By extolling lord Keśava one gets rid of all sins acquired in this life as well as in the earlier ones.

32. What is the need for all the mantras if there is devotion for lord Janārdana, for He is the redeemer of all those who are tormented in hell.

33. He who circumambulates Lord Nārāyaṇa and rests near him acquires great merit.

34. O Earth, by seeing Hari in Mathurā after His waking, one becomes fourhanded and is never born again.

35. All sins disappear by circumambulating there on the Navamī day in the north of Kumuda.

36. He who has the sin of killing a Brahmin, drinking liquor, killing a cow or violating a vow, gets purified by wandering in Mathurā.

37-38. He who goes to Mathurā on the Aṣṭamī day and spending the night as a celibate, cleaning the teeth in the morning, washing the clothes and taking the bath, circumambulates there in silence, gets all his sins removed.

39. Even the touch of a person who so circumambulates, accomplishes all that is desired.

40. The same merit as of such circumambulation in attained also by seeing the lord in Mathurā.

41. The offering of piṇḍa and ablutions in the well of pure water in front of the lord there, propitiates the manes very much.

42. There is also the tīrtha called Catussāmudrika which is well known. He who bathes there enjoys himself in the company of gods.

43. He who gives up life there, reaches my world.

CHAPTER ONE HUNDRED AND FIFTYNINE

Circumambulation in Mathurā

Earth said:

1. By your favour, O Janārdana, I have now learnt a good deal about the numerous tīrthas and their efficacy.

2. The sort of merit we acquire by resorting to the tīrthas cannot be acquired by gifts, penance, sacrifices or circumambulation of the earth.

3. But it is difficult for people to go to all these tīrthas that lie scattered about in different parts of the earth.

4. So be pleased to tell me whether there is any easy means of doing this.

Varāha said:

5. Listen, O blessed one, I shall tell you the number of tīrthas calculated to be in this earth.

6. By going over the whole earth we can find sixty thousand and sixty hundred crores of tīrthas.

7. These tīrthas as well as devas and stars in the sky are counted by Vāyu who lives as long as the world exists.

8. All these have been visited by Brahmā, Lomaśa, Nārada, Dhruva, the son of Jāmbavatī, Rāvaṇa and Hanumān,

9. As also by Bali by wandering over the surface of the earth with its oceans and forests.

10. Sugrīva has gone to the interior places also. Formerly Indra did the same, so too the Pāṇḍavas.

11. Some sages like Mārkaṇḍeya also have done so by their yogic powers, but none else has done so or can do.

12. Ordinary people with their limited capacity, cannot even think of all these, then why say about their going there.

13. The merit of going to all tīrthas in the seven islands of the earth, is attained, and even more, by going to (the tīrthas) in Mathurā.

14. Circumambulation in Mathurā produces the same effect as circumabulation in the seven islands.

15. Therefore, circumambulation may be properly done in Mathurā by those desirous of accomplishing their desires.

Earth said:

16. Be pleased to tell me the rules of circumambulation at Mathurā.

Varāha said:

17. This was asked of Brahmā by the seven sages in yore and they were told about it.

18. Knowing the account about it in all the Purāṇas, he told them about this matter.

19-20. I tell you that hundred times the merit that accrues from all temples, all tīrthas, all gifts and all rituals for well-being in this world as well as in the world beyond, accrues by the circumambulation in Mathurā. This is the truth.

21. Hearing this the sages bowed to Brahmā and then went to Mathurā and put up their hermitages there.

22. Together with Dhruva they were waiting for the Navamī day in the bright half of the month Kumuda.

23. Circumambulating in Mathurā on that day removes all sins.

CHAPTER ONE HUNDRED AND SIXTY

The order of visits in the Tīrthas of Mathurā

Varāha said:

1. On the Aṣṭamī day in the bright half of the month Kārttika, one should bathe in the Viśrānti tīrtha with a view to worshipping the manes and gods.

2. By seeing Viśrānti and Viṣṇu reposing there, the effect of circumambulation is attained.

3. Fasting for the whole day or taking but a little food, the twig for cleaning teeth may be collected in the evening.

4. Spending the night in continence with the resolved mind, (the devotee) should bathe well, put on clean clothes and take the vow of silence.

5. Taking sesamum, rice and Kuśa grass and with a lamp in hand he shall go to the forest there for the worship of manes and gods.

6. He shall then start his visits in the order in which they were done by the sages like Dhruva.

7. By doing this full of devotion, he will attain all desires and the fruit of Aśvamedha.

8. He shall keep awake for the night and on the Navamī day, just before sunrise, start journey.

9. The first bath in the morning should be taken in the tīrtha Dakṣiṇakoṭi (at the southern end).

10. Then washing the feet and performing *Ācamana*, he shall worship Hanumān, the young Brahmacārin, who confers all auspiciousness.

11. He should be informed of the journey, as difficulties vanish by simply thinking of him and as he brings about success in the attempt.

12. (The prayer is) "You got great success in your journey on behalf of Rāma. May you grant me success in this undertaking of mine (to visit the tīrthas)."

13. After prayer to Hanumān, perform worship to Gaṇeśa with lamp, flowers and offerings of food.

14. Then Lord Viṣṇu, reposing there as Padmanābha, should be informed as he is the dispeller of all fear and the dispensor of all success. The mother goddesses also should be informed.

15. First there is the goddess Vasumatī, then Aparājitā installed in the armoury who removes all fears.

16. Then there are Kaṁsavāsanikā, Augrasenā, Carcikā and Vadhūṭī who annihilate demons.

17. There is also Jayadā. These are goddesses worshipped by the gods. These as well as the goddesses installed in the houses

and structures may be worshipped and their permission for the journey sought.

18. He shall go to Dakṣiṇakoṭi without speaking. After taking bath there, libations are to be given to the manes and Lord (Viṣṇu) should be saluted.

19. Then he is to go to Ikṣuvāsā worshipped by Lord Kṛṣṇa and where, as a boy, he played with the cowherds and where the tīrthas were established by the great sages.

20. Vaṣaṭputra is to be visited next where we get Arkasthala, Vīrasthala, Kuśasthala, Puṇyasthala and Mahāsthala.

21. These five spots take away all sins, and their mere sight gives one the company of Brahmā.

22. The result is got in full by seeing Śiva (installed as) Siddhamukha there.

23. Then Hayamukti should be visited where the sages speak about an old incident.

24. That a prince once went there riding on a horse, and then the horse got salvation and the prince alone remained there,

25. Which shows that one should not go there in any vehicle (but walking) if the result is to be achieved.

26. Seeing and touching him (the horse erected) in that tīrtha removes all sins. There is the Śivakuṇḍa by bathing in which one attains great results.

27. Seeing the Jasmine of Kṛṣṇa also produces success, so also by going to the Kadamba grove.

28. On the southern side is the Yoginī Carcikā surrounded by other Yoginīs, guarding Kṛṣṇa.

29. There are two mother goddesses named Aspṛśyā and Aspṛśā, whose sight gives great protection to children.

30. Then he should go to the holy Varṣaghāta, bathe there and offer libations to the manes. That removes all sins.

31. He should then go to the temple where Śiva is enshrined as the protector of the place. That makes the visit to Mathurā fruitful.

32. There is the Kṛṣṇakrīḍāsetubandha where the Lord made a dam for children to play.

33. He used to play with the cowherd boys there every day. He continues to visit it always.

34. There is Balihrada where the Lord used to play in water. Its very sight takes away all sins.

35. There is the place where Kṛṣṇa used to play with cocks. By the sight of this (Kukkuṭakrīḍana) even a heinous man gets salvation.

36. There is a group of pillars with good crests which were anointed with scents and worshipped by Kṛṣṇa.

37. To circumambulate it and offer it worship is to get absolved of all sins and go to the world of Viṣṇu.

38. (The visit to the place) where Vāsudeva lay alone for protecting the pregnancy of Devakī, removes all sins.

39. Then he should go to Nārāyaṇasthāna and go round Nārāyaṇa and other deities there for liberation.

40. He may then announce his visit to Vināyaka and also to Kubjikā and Vāmanā, the two Brāhmaṇīs protected by Kṛṣṇa.

41. Getting their approval, be may proceed to Garteśvara to see Śiva there so that the aim of his visit may be accomplished.

42. In that place there is also the goddess Mahāvidyeśvarī who protects it, protects the devotee and gives him success.

43. By seeing Prabhāmallī there, all desires are fulfilled. She remains there for guarding Kṛṣṇa.

44. There is another goddess who remains there always giving success.

45. She was installed there by Kṛṣṇa Balabhadra and Gopas when they thought of killing Kaṁsa and assembled there to consider the strategy.

46. She confers success as well as enjoyment. She is called Siddheśvarī (as she gives *siddhi* success) and Saṅketakeśvarī (as she was installed at the *Saṅketa* or the place of their meeting.)

47. There is a deep pit of holy placid water, where we can see Lord Śiva with the name Gokarṇeśvara, by whose mere sight one gets rid of all sins.

48. Seeing river Sarasvatī there, one derives everything auspicious.

49. Then Gaṇeśa, the remover of all impediments, may be worshipped. Much benefit is got by seeing him.

50. The highly purifying Gaṅgā is there, whose sight, touch or even thought bestows great benefits.

51. There is the place called Rudramahālaya having the appearance of Śiva's face. Seeing this confers the same benefit as by staying there.

52. At Uttarakoṭi (the northern end), there is again Gaṇeśa. Here Lord Kṛṣṇa was playing dice with the Gopīs.

53. Merrily playing with them, the Lord won all of them and their wealth in the game. He gave them all to the Gopas who commemorated the event there.

54. The visit to this place where Kṛṣṇa played in his boyhood, dispels all sins.

55. The sages contemplate on him in the exact form and in the exact deeds of his in his boyhood.

56. The devotee should go to this Rudramahālaya of pure water in Yamunā, bathe there and give libations to the manes.

57. Then he should go to Gārgyatīrtha, Bhadreśvaratīrtha and Somatīrtha.

58. After bathing in the Somatīrtha, he should worship Someśvara for the fulfilment of the aim of his visit.

59. At the confluence of Sarasvatī, he may do, according to rules, rites in propitiation of gods, manes, sages and men. That will give him merger in Lord Viṣṇu.

60. He should then go to tīrthas Ghaṇṭābharaṇaka, Garuḍa, Keśava, Vaikuṇṭha, Ghaṇḍavelaka, Saṁyamana, Asikuṇḍa,

61. Gopa, Muktikeśvara and Vailakṣagaruḍa, all of which are extremely holy.

62. They are as holy as Viśrāntitīrtha and the devotee may move about here with full control of the senses.

63. After propitiating gods and manes he may pray: "O Lord Avimukteśa, worshipped by seven sages, be pleased to make my perambulations in Mathurā fruitful."

64. After praying thus to Śiva, the protector of the place, he should go to Viśrānti (again) and perform libations to the manes.

65. Then, resting for a while, he should go to the temple of Sumaṅgalā and bow to her and pray for his success.

66. "O most auspicious goddess, the fulfiller of all desires, may this visit of mine be fruitful by your favour".

67. Then he is to go to Lord Pippalādeśvara, the Śiva consecrated by the sage Pippalāda, and anoint this deity's head.

68. The sage was saved by Śiva and so he consecrated him there with his own name.

69. Then, after seeing the serpent Kārkoṭaka, he may proceed to see the goddess installed by Kṛṣṇa.

70-71. On hearing about the wicked intentions of Kaṁsa at first, the cloth over the face of Kṛṣṇa was placed there for (good) omen.

72. On entering that place, an agreeable sound is heard, and there Kṛṣṇa has installed his auspicious sister.

73. Out of fear, Kṛṣṇa invoked the goddess Caṇḍikā also and installed her there with the name Ārtiharā.

74. By seeing this goddess, one becomes very happy.

75. She appeared in the north when Kṛṣṇa invoked her for good omen when he started for killing Kaṁsa. By seeing her all desires are accomplished.

76. In order to kill the wrestlers, Kṛṣṇa invoked Vajrānana, and after killing them, he installed him there.

77. And then Kṛṣṇa gave to every deity whatever was sought of him. Everything auspicious was bestowed on them.

78. The (memory of the) deeds of Kṛṣṇa in his boyhood, (it may be noted), takes away all sins.

79. Finally, after seeing Sūrya, the principal deity of the people of Mathurā, and giving gifts there, the visit may be concluded.

80. Visiting the different places in this manner on the Navamī day in the bright half of the month Kumuda, one goes to the world of Viṣṇu with the whole family.

81. As many people in his clan gain permanent abode in Sūrya as there are steps in his perambulation in Mathurā.

82. Even those who have committed the murder of Brahmin, taken liquor, stolen wealth, impeded vows, cohabited with prohibited women or carried away the wives of others, get absolved of their sins, if they visit Mathurā in this way.

83-84. Those who live in distant places get cleansed of their sins at the sight of the person who has returned after his ritualistic visit to Mathurā.

85. Even listening to the narration about this by one who has returned from Mathurā removes all evil and leads to heaven.

CHAPTER ONE HUNDRED AND SIXTYONE

The greatness of Devavana

Earth said:

1. O Kṛṣṇa, what is the way (for liberation) for those ignorant people who have no knowledge of righteous actions and (hence) are condemned to hell ?

2. Tell me by what means they can avoid the sorrows of hell ?

Varāha said:

3. For all those cursed people who never do righteous deeds it is goddess Mathurā (the Mathurā region with all its tīrthas) that removes all sins and sorrows of hell.

4-5. Those who live in Mathurā, those who resort to the tīrthas there, those who do perambulation there, those who see the woods there and those who do with might amidst them hundred and one[1], never go to hell but go to heaven.

6. (Among the woods), the first is Madhuvana, the second Tālavana, the third Kundavana,

7. The fourth Kāmyakavana, the fifth Bahuvana, the sixth Bhadravana,

8. The seventh Khādiravana well-known in the world, the eighth Mahāvana always dear to me,

9. The ninth is the holy Lohārgalavana, the tenth Bilvavana worshipped by gods,

10. The eleventh Bhāṇḍīravana and the twelfth Vṛṇḍakāvana. Those who see these will not have to go to hell.

11. Those who visit these worlds with full control of mind, go to the world of Indra.

---

1. What this refers to is not clear.

CHAPTER ONE HUNDRED AND SIXTYTWO

The greatness of Cakratīrtha

Varāha said:

1. Listen, O Earth, I shall tell you about another thing namely what occurred in days of yore in Cakratīrtha to the north of Mathurā.

2. There once lived a pious Brahmin in the city of Mahāgṛhodaya which is a jewel to the whole earth.

3. He went from there with his son to the holy Śāligrāma.

4. He lived there with full control of senses, bathing in the tīrthas and worshipping the deities.

5. There he got the acquaintance of a Siddha (with yogic powers)who belonged to Kalpagrāma and was living in Kānyakubja.

6. As days passed, he heard the Siddha describe the glory of Kalpagrāma.

7-8. The Brahmin then desired to go there and requested the Siddha to help him in this on account of their mutual friendship.

9. Hearing the words of the Brahmin, the Siddha said that only Siddhas could go there and not one like him.

10. But he offered to take him there with his son by his yogic power.

11-12. Then holding the Vaidic Brahmin in the right hand and his intelligent son in the left, he flew up and released them both at Kalpagrāma.

13. They lived there for a long time and then the Brahmin became afflicted by an ailment.

14-15. He then reached the last stage of his life and wishing to die in peace, he asked his son to take him without delay to the bank of Gaṅgā.

16. The son took the father to the bank of Gaṅgā, but he was crying, out of his affection for the father.

17. There a long time passed, and he was controlling himself out of devotion for the father.

18. In Kalpagrāma, the beautiful daughter of the Siddha was on the look-out for a suitable husband for her, but could get none.

19. There one day the Brahmin's son chanced to enter the house of the Siddha for food.

20. The Siddha asked about his whereabouts and he told him everything.

21. Then knowing his identity by his yogic power, he honoured him and gave him his daughter in marriage.

22. From then onwards he was taking food in the father-in-law's house and remaining near the father, attending on him.

23. As time passed, the father became extremely weak and the son asked the father-in-law about it.

24. "When will my father die?', he asked. The father-in-law laughed and told him.

25. "O Brahmin, your father has been eating Śūdra's food for a long time. Because of this, death stands away from him.

26. (The essence of) this food remains in his feet and not above the knees. When the effect of the Śūdra's food is over, he will die."

27. He reported to the father what the father-in-law said.

28. Hearing this the old man condemned himself very much.

29. At sunrise the next day the son went to the father-in-law's house, as usual.

30. When the son was gone, the father, being very much afflicted by his illness and wishing to die, stood up and looked around.

31. Seeing a stone near him he dragged it towards him by his foot and with it smashed both his feet. He then died.

32. When the son returned after his bath and food, he saw the father dead (and knew how).

33. He wept for long, but then he coolly thought of the Śāstra and came to the conclusion that the father did not deserve obsequies,

34. Because Āpastamba (the law-giver) has declared so regarding those that die by snake-bite, by wounds caused by animals with their horns, by the bite of carnivorous animals or by suicide,

35. And one who commits suicide is long tormented in hell; for him expiations may be done but not libation through usual obsequies.

36. Fate is powerful and valour is helpless there.

37. He then went to his father-in-law's house, only to be told by him in great sorrow.

38. "The sin of killing a Brahmin has come upon you. So you may go wherever you like".

39. He then said to the father-in-law: "I never committed the murder of a Brahmin at any time. Then how has this sin come upon me?"

40. Hearing these words of the son-in-law, the father-in-law said: "O dear man, the means of death was suggested to your father by you. And by that fault the effect of killing the Brahmin has come upon you.

41. By sleeping near such a condemned person, by eating with him and by talking to him, one gets condemned oneself in the course of one year.

42. Therefore, O great Brahmin, you can no more live in my house."

43. Hearing these words of the father-in-law, he requested him to direct him what he might do when thus rejected.

44. The ascetic Brahmin then asked him to leave Kalpagrāma and go to Mathurā, as nowhere else would it be possible for him to get himself purified.

45. He immediately left Kalpagrāma and in due course reached Mathurā.

46. There he began to live outside the settlement of the Brahmins.

47-48. He started feeding himself on the remnants of the food from the rest-house constructed in Mathurā by king Kuśika of Kanyāpura with provision to feed two thousand Brahmins every day.

49. He used to take bath in Cakratīrtha, but never begged alms for his food.

50. As days passed in this manner, the father-in-law began to think about him and knew by his yogic power what he was doing.

51. He persuaded his daughter to go to Mathurā and give her husband food.

52. By the spiritual power (of the father), she could go to Mathurā every day (from Kalpagrāma) with food for her husband.

53. At the close of the day, she used to go there with food and he used to eat what was given by his wife.

54. He used to keep his eating vessel in a hollow and live in the rest-house. In this way a full half-year passed.

55. Then the people there began to ask him as to where he was staying and from where he was taking food.

56. He then told them the whole matter. Then, O Earth, all those Brahmiṇs declared in one voice that he had become purified.

57. "You have already become purified by the power of Cakratīrtha. You have now become futher purified by this declaration of ours".

58. Hearing their words, the Brahmin became very happy and went from there to Cakratīrtha for bath.

59. Then the wife arrived with food and, delighted at heart, spoke to him.

60. "Take this food I have brought for you. I now see you free from sin that was in you".

61. Hearing this, he asked her to say again what she said.

62. She did so and added, "I have not been speaking to you before since you were possessed of the sin of killing a Brahmin.

63. Now you have become freed from it by the power of Cakratīrtha. O my lord, get up, let us go to the pleasant Kalpagrāma".

64. He then went with her to Kalpagrāma.

65. For Bhadreśvara the offering of money is commendable and before this deity there is a vessel for putting it. The full benefit of Cakratīrtha is got only by seeing Bhadreśvara.

66. O Earth, Cakratīrtha is hundred times more holy than Kalpagrāma. The sin of killing a Brahmin is removed there by fasting for a full day and night.

67. Of what need is Kalpagrāma or Vārāṇasī for one who goes to Mathurā and dies there ?

68. Even a bird, why a worm too, that dies there becomes four-armed (like Viṣṇu).

CHAPTER ONE HUNDRED AND SIXTYTHREE

The Greatness of Kapilavarāha

Varāha said:

1. I shall now tell you about another thing, namely what occurred in days of yore in Vaikuṇṭhatīrtha.

2. The city of Mithilā was ruled by king Janaka. The people of Mithilā, Brāhmaṇas, Kṣatriyas, Vaiśyas and Śūdras, started on a pilgrimage.

3. They bathed in the tīrtha Saukara and then reached Mathurā.

4. Great devotion to Mathurā arose in them and they all stood assembled in Vaikuṇṭhatīrtha.

5. A Brahmin among them had clear signs of the sin of killing a Brahmin, because blood was always oozing from his hand.

6. This was clearly perceptible and it never stopped although he had gone to many tīrthas.

7. But he had not gone to Vaikuṇṭhatīrtha before. And now that he went there, this oozing of blood ceased and all were surprised at this.

8. The Lord then appeared in the form of a Brahmin and asked them what had happened.

9. They told him about the sinful Brahmin and what had happened then.

10. The Lord said : "As the result of his bath in the Vaikuṇṭhatīrtha, the sin of killing a Brahmin has left him. So you need not be surprised at this. It is all due to the power of this tīrtha."

11. The Lord then disappeared there. O Earth, such is the greatness of this tīrtha.

12. He who bathes in Vaikuṇṭhatīrtha gets removed of his sins and he goes to the world of Viṣṇu.

13. I shall tell you about another, namely Gandharvakuṇḍa in the holy Asikuṇḍa.

14. He who bathes there, delights in the company of Gandharvas and he who gives up life there, reaches my world.

15. The Mathurā region extends over twenty yojanas and is like a lotus with Lord Keśava in its central part.

16. Those who die in this central part get liberation and become gods.

17. Those who see Lord Keśava on the western side will not get any sorrow.

18. Those who see the Lord on the northern side never fall into the cycle of births and deaths again.

19. Those who see the Lord in Viśrānti on the eastern side certainly gain liberation.

20. On the Southern side there is a divine image of mine.

21. It is long and beautiful and he who sees it delights himself in the company of Brahmā.

22. In the Kṛtayuga there was a king named Māndhātā. I was propitiated by him with a devout mind.

23. Pleased at this, I gave him this image and it was worshipped by him for his own salvation.

24. It was at the time of (Śatrughna's) killing Lavaṇa at Mathurā, it was installed there. It is holy, divine and resplendent.

25. There was a great sage by name Kapila who was devoted to me.

26. He made by his mind an image of (Viṣṇu in the form of) Varāha and was worshipping it every day.

27. The sage Kapila was propitiated by Indra, and pleased at this, he gave him this divine idol.

28. From then onwards, Indra was worshipping it with devotion and delight. As a result, he attained matchless divine knowledge.

29. Once the demon Rāvaṇa went to the world of Indra to conquer heaven by his might.

30. Severe fighting then followed between Rāvaṇa and Indra.

31. The gods together with Indra were defeated by Rāvaṇa and he then entered Indra's abode.

32. In that splendid house decorated with numerous jewels, he saw the idol of Kapilavarāha and prostrated before it.

33. But being deluded by it, he began to pray.

34. "O Lord Mādhava, Dāmodara, Hṛṣīkeśa, the holder of earth, the destroyer of Hiraṇyākṣa, be pleased to save me.

35. I bow to you, the essence of Vedas. I bow to you Vāsu-

deva. I bow to you in your form as the tortoise. I bow to you Nārāyaṇa.

36. I am not able to see you or ask anything, O abode of all virtues, the destroyer of Madhu and Kaiṭabha.

37. I bow to you, the Lord of Lords, the refuge of all devotees. I bow to you in all devotion. Be pleased with me."

38. At this prayer of Rāvaṇa, the Lord of the worlds adopted a gentle form.

39. Rāvaṇa then went near and attempted to raise the idol in order to put it in his Puṣpakavimāna, but he could not.

40. Surprised at this, he exclaimed: "O Lord, I was able to raise mount Kailāsa together with Śiva. You are here in such a small form, still I am unable to raise it.

41. I bow to you, god of gods, be pleased to enable me to take you to the great city of Laṅkā".

Varāha said:

42. Kapila (varāha) then told him that being a Rākṣasa he was not a Vaiṣṇava and he could not have the sort of devotion (necessary to achieve his aim).

43. Rāvaṇa said: "O great being, unflinching devotion has dawned on me by your sight. I bow to you. I wish to take you (to my city)".

44. The Lord then assumed a little form and so he was able to lift him and place him in his Puṣpakavimāna.

45. He installed me at Laṅkā and I stood there for a long time in his house worshipped by him.

46. Rāma, the Lord of Ayodhyā, then came there and killed Rāvaṇa in battle, and installed his brother Vibhīṣaṇa on the throne of Laṅkā.

47. Vibhīṣaṇa then offered everything to Rāma.

Rāma said:

48. "O Rākṣasa Vibhīṣaṇa, I shall not have anything to do with all this. You may give me that idol alone which was taken here from the city of Indra.

49. If you give me that, I shall take it to Ayodhyā and worship it every day".

50. He then gave Rāma the Kapila (Varāha) and Rāma carried it in the Puṣpaka.

51. He installed it at Ayodhyā and worshipped it there for hundred and ten years.

52. He then sent Śatrughna for killing Lavaṇa. Śatrughna bowed to him and started with an army with all its four divisions.

53. He then killed the terrific demon Lavaṇa and entered the city of Mathurā.

54. He settled there twenty-six thousand Vedic Brahmins who were all equal to me.

55. (Even) a non-Ṛgvedic Brahmin of Mathurā is equal to one who has mastered the four Vedas. To feed one of them is equivalent to feeding a crore of other Brahmins.

56. Thus have I told you about Lavaṇa's killing (by Śatrughna).

57. When Rāma came to know of the success of Śatrughna he asked him to seek of him any boon he wished.

58. Hearing this, Śatrughna said, "O Lord, if you are pleased with me and consider me worthy of receiving a boon, give me this (idol of Kapilavārāha)".

59. Hearing these words of Śatrughna, Rāma, said, "Take this (idol of) god in the form of Varāha.

60. That whole region is very much blessed, the city of Mathurā in particular. The people of Mathurā who worship this Kapila (Varāha) are highly blessed.

61. All sins disappear when he is seen, touched, contemplated upon, bathed or anointed.

62. When he is bathed or worshipped every day, he not only removes our sins but grants *mokṣa.*"

63. O Earth, so saying Rāma gave him the idol.

64. Receiving it, Śatrughna went to Mathurā.

65. He installed it in the middle of the city and worshipped it. In this way the Lord permanently came to be there.

66. By seeing this, the same result is obtained as by offering piṇḍa in Gayā during Puṣkara in the month of Jyeṣṭha.

67. The same result is also obtained in Viśrānti, Govinda, Hari, Keśava and Dīrghaviṣṇu.

68. My lustre is at Viśrānti in the morning, Dīrghviṣṇu at noon and Keśava in the evening.

69. This knowledge was kept a secret for a long time. Since you are my devotee and disciple, I imparted this to you.

CHAPTER ONE HUNDRED AND SIXTYFOUR

The greatness of Annakūṭa

Varāha said:

1. There is the highly holy place called Govardhana at a distance of two yojanas to the west of Mathurā.

2. There is a pond in it full of trees and creepers and there are four tīrthas in it.

3. In the east is the Indratīrtha, in the south Yamatīrtha, in the west Varuṇatīrtha and in the north Kaberatīrtha, and I remain playing in the middle.

4. He who bathes in the Indratīrtha with due austerities, gets over all opposites and delights in Indraloka.

5. He who bathes in the Yamatīrtha in the south after observing all the necessary rites, goes to the Yamaloka and delights there.

6. And he who gives up life there, without desire or delusion, leaves Yamaloka and goes to my world.

7. He who bathes in Varuṇatīrtha, goes to the abode of Varuṇa and becomes purified of all sins.

8. And he who gives up life there without desire or anger, leaves Varuṇaloka and goes to my world.[1]

9. He who bathes in the middle, delights with me, and he who gives up life there, goes to my world.

10. The devotee should then go to Annakūṭa and circumambulate it. He will then become free from further birth. This, I tell you, is true.

11. After bathing in Mānasagaṅgā, seeing Lord Hari in Govardhana and circumambulating Annakūṭa, one will have nothing to worry about.

12. By giving piṇḍa to the manes on new moon day falling on Monday, one gets the merit of Rājasūya sacrifice,

13. The same result as is obtained by giving piṇḍa in Gayā, is obtained here also, and no one need have any doubt regarding this.

---

1. After this there must be a verse relating to the Kuberatīrtha, but it is missing.

14-15. Going around Govardhana and seeing Hari there, confers the same result as of Rājasūya and Aśvamedha.

Earth said:

16. Please tell me about the power of Annakūṭá and the rules of its circumambulation.

Varāha said:

17. This should be done in Govardhana on the Ekādaśī day in the bright half of the month Bhādrapada, after fasting.

18. At sunrise, bath should be taken in Mānasagaṅgā and the mount Govardhana and Lord Hari at its top should be propitiated.

19. Then bath should be taken with the rites at Puṇḍarīka and worship should be made to Puṇḍarīka as well as to the gods and manes.

20. This removes all sins and leads one to the abode of Viṣṇu.

21. Then bath should be taken at the Apsarastīrtha, where bath and libations remove all sins and bring about the result of Rājasūya and Aśvamedha.

22. There is the tīrtha called Saṅkarṣaṇa guarded by Balabhadra. It removes the sin of killing a cow by merely bathing in it.

23. Near Annakūṭa is a tīrtha made by Indra. There a sacrifice meant for propitiating Indra was stopped by Kṛṣṇa.

24. The large quantity of food collected there for the worship of Indra was distributed among his own men.

25. The (enraged) Indra was pouring rain heavily and, to protect the cows from this, the big mount was raised and held over them (by the Lord).

26. This came to be known as Annakūṭa (literally, heap of food) and had to be worshipped by Indra himself.

27. Lord Viṣṇu satisfied here the gods, goddesses, cows and sages. By offering libations there, one attains the fruit of a thousand sacrifices.

28. Then there is the pool called Kadambakhaṇḍa with clean water. By bathing in it and offering libations, one attains the world of Brahmā.

29. The devotee should then go to Devagiri which extends over a distance of hundred cubits. By bathing and worshipping there, the merit of Vājapeya sacrifice is attained.

30. Seeing the great lord there also brings about great merit. By bathing there and offering libations, one goes to heaven with gratification.

31. A little to the north of (Mānasa) Gaṅgā, there took place the battle between lord Kṛṣṇa and the demon Ariṣṭa.

32. A tīrtha was formed at the place where Ariṣṭa, who had assumed the form of a bull, was angrily hit by the lord's fist.

33. Kṛṣṇa bathed at this wonderful tīrtha which appeared at the place of his killing the bull.

34. But he was sorry for having brought upon himself the sin of killing the bull although it was a demon.

35. Then Rādhā embraced Kṛṣṇa and told him about the pond which was known after her name and which was not far from there.

36. This Rādhākuṇḍa is capable of removing all sins (and Kṛṣṇa got rid of the sin there).

37. By bathing in Ariṣṭakuṇḍa and Rādhākuṇḍa, one gets the fruit of Rājasūya and Aśvamedha (respectively). There need be no doubt in this matter. The sin of killing a cow, man or Brahmin disappears there instantaneously.

38. There is the tīrtha called Mokṣarāja whose very sight dispels all sins and confers salvation.

39. On the eastern side is the tīrtha called Indradhvaja because of Indra's banner being raised there.

40. Those who bathe there go to heaven and those who die there are never born again.

41. Then by bathing in the spot called Cakratīrtha in the Pañcatīrtha, the devotee should dedicate the fruit of his pilgrimage to Hari.

42. Finishing thus the pilgrimage, he should keep awake at Govardhana for purification from sins.

43. Keeping thus awake on the night of the Ekādaśī day, he should bathe early morning on the Dvādaśī day and offer, according to his means, piṇḍa for the manes.

44. He who offers libation in this manner for the liberation of manes, gets freed from all sins and attains supreme Brahman.

45. I have thus told you about the circumambulation of Annakūṭa. This is laid down for the month of Āṣāḍha as well.

46. He who listens with attention to this account of the greatness of Govardhana gets the result of bathing in Gaṅgā.

CHAPTER ONE HUNDRED AND SIXTYFIVE

The Power of Catuḥsāmudrika well

Varāha said:

1. O Earth, now listen to what I say about what happened at Pratiṣṭhāna in the Deccan region.

2. In that city there lived a wealthy Vaiśya by name Suśīla with his wife and several children.

3. Always absorbed in the affairs of his family, he never turned his attention to religious matters like holy bath, gift, recitation of mantras, performance of homa or worship of god.

4. He was always engaged in trade and a long time passed like this. He never met any pious people.

5. He never listened to any discourse on dharma and he had no attachment towards Brahmins or gods.

6. He was incurring a lot of sin by his selfish deeds but he did not realise this.

7. It never occurred to him that gifts are necessary.

8. Though he was quite wealthy and was living in the great city of Pratiṣṭhāna, he never gave away anything to anyone. And not only that, he could not bear to see others giving.

9. Though deeply attached to his wife and children, in due course he died.

10. On death, he became a ghost and began to wander in places without water.

11. Full of thirst, he spent a long time like this in the desert.

12. A caravan of traders happened to pass by among whom were some from Mathurā.

13. When that moved away, he resorted to the foot of a tree and began to remain there.

14. He was fierce and terrific with long canines, short in arms, long in chin, big in eye, and cat-like in face.

15. After a long time, by his good luck, a merchant named Vibhu happened to pass by that place.

16. Seeing him even at a long distance, the ghost became glad. He danced towards him and said:

17. "You have now become the object of my food. Where do you wish to go ?" At these words of the ghost, the merchant was fear-stricken and he began to run.

18. The ghost caught hold of him and said: "You are the food for me come of its own accord. I shall eat your flesh and drink your blood".

19. Hearing this, the merchant said:

20. "I have reached this forest on my way to a place to seek something to maintain my family. I have an aged father in my house, and also my mother and virtuous wife.

21. If you are going to eat me, my family also will die".

22. Hearing his words, the ghost asked him to tell him from where he was coming.

Vibhu said:

23. Between mount Govardhana and river Yamunā, there is the beautiful city of Mathurā known all over the world. I live there in my ancestral house.

24. All the wealth I had accumulated there was stolen by thieves and I became penniless.

25. With the little that was left, I reached this desert.

26. I have thus come before you (by chance). You may do (with me) whatever you like.

The ghost said:

27. "I sympathise with you and I am not going to eat you. I shall release you on condition that you will do what I say.

28. You return to Mathurā for my sake I shall tell you what you should do there.

29. Take a ritualistic bath in the well called Catuḥsāmudrika, and offer piṇḍa there in my name. Then give me the fruit of this bath and go away as you please".

30. Hearing the words of the ghost, Vibhu said:

31. "I shall not go back to Mathurā without money. You may eat my body and satisfy yourself".

The ghost said:

32. There is a lot of money in your house. So go there and oblige me. Please don't delay.

Vibhu said:

33. "There is no money in my house as you say. All the wealth that is left is the house.

34. There is the fame of my ancestors, but that, of course, cannot be sold".

35. The ghost laughed and said: "There is certainly wealth in your house as I told you. A mass of gold is kept in a cavity in the house.

36. So return with pleasure. Retrace your path to Mathurā".

Sūta said:

37. The merchant was very much pleased and asked him how it was that he possessed the knowledge of such secrets when he was in that state.

38. Then he told him about his former life. "There is a great temple of Viṣṇu in the city of Pratiṣṭhāna.

39. From early morning Brāhmaṇas, Kṣatriyas, Vaiśyas and Śūdras gather there.

40. A reciter would read Purāṇic stories and a friend of mine always used to listen to this.

41. He once persuaded me very much to go there with him to this Viṣṇu temple.

42. I did so and seated myself near him. Then I heard (the reciter say) about the sacred well where all the four oceans meet.

43. I heard about the efficacy of this well and the merit it brings about.

44. All the people present there gave presents to the reciter, but I remained quiet although persuaded by the friend.

45. The friend asked me again to give whatever I liked, and, thus insisted, I gave a small gold coin.

46. In course of time, I died and by the decision of Vaivas-

vata (Death god), I became a ghost from which state it is difficult for me to redeem myself.

47. No gift was made by me, no offering made in fire, no bath was taken in a tīrtha and no libation was made to the manes. The result is this ghosthood.

48. I have told you now what you asked. Please do go to Mathurā".

49. Hearing these words of the ghost, Vibhu said:

50. "How do you maintain yourself at the foot of this tree ?"

The ghost said:

51. "I have told you about all that happened.

52. By the power of the gift of the gold coin I gave to the reciter I remain always satisfied.

53. As I had given it without any motive, my knowledge remains in me even though I have become a ghost."

54. The merchant then returned to Mathurā and did all that was requested of him by the ghost. And the ghost got liberation and went to heaven.

55. O Earth, I have thus told you about the greatness of Mathurā and how the offering of piṇḍa in the Catuḥsāmudrika well leads to liberation.

56. Those who die here in a tīrtha, house, temple or square, gain liberation but not elsewhere.

57. A sin incurred elsewhere is eradicated in a tīrtha, but a sin incurred in a tīrtha sticks on.

58. But a sin committed at Mathurā disappears there itself, but this city is so holy that there is no sin there.

59. The ungrateful, the drunkard, the thief and the vow-breaker all get cleansed of their sins in Mathurā.

60. A resident of Mathurā acquires more merit than one (performing penance) standing on one foot for a thousand years.

61. All residents of Mathurā are gods in human form even if they have no control of senses or are fond of others' wives.

62. Those who make offerings to gods, give alms, die without anger, inclined to take bath in tīrthas, are all gods in human form.

63. Honouring a single Brahmin of Mathurā is equivalent to honouring a thousand other Brahmins.

64. A Brahmin of Mathurā without knowledge of the Veda is equivalent to one with the knowledge of all Vedas elsewhere.

65. The very presence of a man from Mathurā in a tīrtha or temple makes it more auspicious.

66. Giving up four Vedas, honour a man of Mathurā. All beings and gods get pleased.

67. The celestials find the residents of Mathurā four-armed because they are Viṣṇu in human form.

68. But this is perceptible only to those with knowledge, not to others.

CHAPTER ONE HUNDRED AND SIXTYSIX

The power of Asikuṇḍa

Earth said:

1. I have been told, O great god, about various tīrthas. Be pleased to tell me now about the tīrtha named Asikuṇḍa.

Varāha said:

2. There was once a virtuous and renowned king named Sumati who went to heaven as a result of pilgrimage.

3. Then his son named Vimati began to rule the ancestral kingdom.

4. Nārada once went to him and the king duly honoured the sage with seat, *pādya* and *arghya*.

5. Receiving all this, Nārada said that the acquisition of *dharma* by a son depends on doing what he owes to the departed parents.

6. Nārada then went away and when he was gone, the king asked the ministers:

7. "What did Nārada say about the departed father. I have not understood what he meant by the words 'doing what he owes to the departed parents' ".

8. The ministers knew and they told him that what was meant was a pilgrimage and it is a debt that we owe to the manes.

9. The king immediately decided to undertake a pilgrimage.

10. He decided to go to Mathurā and spend there the four months of the rainy season.

11. When the king went there, all the different tīrthas began to consult one another.

12. "It is not possible for us to fight with this Vimati. Let us all go to Kalpagrāma where lord Varāha remains".

13. All the tīrthas, O Earth, went to Kalpagrāma where, by accident, I was in the form of the boar. All of them stood before me.

The tīrthas said:

14. Victory to you, O Lord Viṣṇu, victory to you, O Acyuta, victory to you, O Lord of the worlds, we all bow to you.

Varāha said:

15. Praised by the tīrthas, O Earth, I spoke to them; "Seek of me whatever boon you have in mind".

The tīrthas said:

16-17. O Lord Varāha, you should give us protection from this sinful Vimati who is a source of fear for us. Check him if you wish us happiness.

Varāha said:

18. "For the sake of all of you, tīrthas, I shall kill this great enemy". Then I went to the city of Mathurā for the purpose.

19. When the haughty king came there, I engaged him in battle and hit him down with the divine sword, and in that process the tip of the sword pierced the earth.

20. When the sword was drawn out from there, a clod of earth was removed, and there gods and sages made a tīrtha which came to be known as Asikuṇḍa (being the *kuṇḍa* 'pit', formed by *asi* 'sword').

21. I shall tell you about the wonder there pleasing to the mind and ear.

22. People who go there with full control of the senses on Dvādaśī or Caturdaśī never fail to get whatever they desire.

23. Having gone to Mathurā then, I remain there facing west.

24. Four golden images have also been installed in the Varāhatīrtha in Mathurā. They are all beautiful and he who sees them gets liberation.

25. One is Varāha, the other is Nārāyaṇa. The third is Vāmana and the fourth Rāghava.

26. He who bathes in the Asikuṇḍa and sees these four images gets the merit equivalent to going round the earth upto the four oceans.

27. He also gets the fruit of all tīrthas in Mathurā.

28. Asikuṇḍa is the most important of all tīrthas there. As regards the order of the tīrthas for the pilgrim told to you earlier, it is good to start it from Asikuṇḍa.

29. Even the man who bathes in Asikuṇḍa on Dvādaśī day after waking from sleep and sees the images there, becomes eligible for final liberation.

30. Even after a long lapse of time, he will not be born again.

CHAPTER ONE HUNDRED AND SIXTYSEVEN

The power of Viśrānti tīrtha

Varāha said:

1. O goddess, listen to me. I shall tell you what the Rākṣasa said about Viśrānti tīrtha to the Brahmin.

Earth said:

2. Tell me why the Rākṣasa spoke about Viśrānti tīrtha and why the Brahmin asked about it.

Varāha said:

3. In Ujjayinī there was a Brahmin who never cared for the rules of virtuous life. He never worshipped gods and never bowed to the saints.

4. He never bathed in any holy tīrtha. He knew neither the Vedas nor the Vedāṅgas. He was lustful and longed for the wives of others.

5. He used to sleep during dawn and dusk. He never gave the honour due to superior men and never did anything to propitiate the manes.

6. His mind was wicked, deeds sinful and his company bad. He was always immersed in the pleasures of conjugal life.

7. To discharge the duties of a householder is, of course, proclaimed to be a virtuous action and that all beings are sustained by that.

8. Just as all beings depend on the mother, so too they depend on wedded life.

9. So (when he felt the need for more money to maintain his family) he began to steal, and when once he was running in the night, he was caught by the king's sentinels.

10. He ran away from them, but while doing so, fell into a well and died. He then became a Rākṣasa of terrific form.

11. A caravan of traders happened to pass by that place.

12. Amidst them was a Brahmin who was protecting the entire group by uttering the Rakṣoghna mantra (meant to drive away Rākṣasas).

13. Then the Rākṣasa came to the Brahmin and told him:

14. "O Brahmin, I shall give you whatever you need. Don't deprive me of my food which I have got after a long time.

15. Get up from here and go and sleep somewhere else. Let me eat my food (these men) to my heart's content".

16. Hearing these words of the Rākṣasa, the Brahmin said: "I have come along with this group and I shall not forsake it.

17. This caravan is to be looked after by me like my wife. You may, therefore, go away from here. You will not be able to see it because of the power of my mantra."

The Rākṣasa said:

18. "By depriving me of my food you will be doing a great wrong. Please take pity on me and don't stand in the way of my food".

19. Then the Brahmin asked him about the particular misdeed as a result of which he had become the Rākṣasa.

20. Then he told him about his previous life and how by the violation of the rules of virtuous life he was turned into a Rākṣasa on death.

21. Then sympathising with him, the Brahmin said, "O Rākṣasa, you have become my friend now. So tell me what I may give you and what I may do to be helpful to you".

The Rākṣasa said:

22-23. If you are pleased to grant me my wish, then give me the fruit of your bath at Viśrānti tīrtha in Mathurā so that I may gain release from my present state.

The Brahmin said:

24. How do you know, O Rākṣasa, about the Viśrānti tīrtha. Tell me how it got the name.

The Rākṣasa said :

25. "I was living in the city named Ujjayinī and once I happened to go to the temple of Viṣṇu there.

26. There a Vaidika Brahmin was discoursing on the greatness of Viśrānti tīrtha.

27. By listening to it, devotion set in in my mind. I also came to know how it got the name.

28. Janārdana, the great lord of the worlds, reposes there. Hence it got the name Viśrānti".

29. Hearing these words of the Rākṣasa, the Brahmin said: "I give you the merit of one bath there".

30. As he was saying this, the Rākṣasa attained release.

CHAPTER ONE HUNDRED AND SIXTYEIGHT

The Tīrthas in Mathurā

Earth said:

1. Tell me who is this Kṣetrapāla who guards Mathurā and what merit is obtained by seeing him.

Varāha said:

2. By the very sight of this lord of beings in Mathurā, all sins disappear.

3. Śiva performed penance of a severe nature for thousand years, at the end of which I appeared before him and asked him to seek a boon.

4. "O Lord of gods, I know for certain that you are everywhere. Give me a place in Mathurā".

5. Hearing these words of the great god, Hari said:

6. "O god, you will be the Kṣetrapāla in Mathurā. To see you will beget the benefit of the whole kṣetra. Otherwise there will not be fulfilment.

7. Whatever good deed is done in this tīrtha, its full benefit will be derived through you.

8. The very entry into this place is capable of removing *saṁsāra.*"

9. This city is beautiful like Indra's Amarāvatī in heaven.

10. In this earth, Mathurā is most dear to me. The Mathurā region extends over twenty yojanas and at every step there, the fruit of Aśvamedha is obtained.

11. O Earth, I have not told this great truth to Brahmā or Śiva. I have been keeping it as a great secret.

12. In this region the city of Mathurā is splendid with gems and jewels, I shall tell you about the tīrthas there.

13. They are sixty crores and sixty hundreds in number. I shall give the names (of a few).

14. Govardhana, Akrūra, Dakṣiṇakoṭī, Uttarakoṭī,

15. Praskandana and Bhāṇḍīra. These six are equal to Kurukṣetra.

16. This most holy Viśrānti, Asikuṇḍa and Vaikuṇṭha are equal to Koṭitīrtha, Avimukta, Somatīrtha, Yamunā, Tinduka.

17. Cakratīrtha, Akrūra, Dvādaśāditya. All these are very holy and remove all sins. Mathurā is hundred times more holy than Kurukṣetra.

18. Those who read this account of the greatness of Mathurā or listen to it with attention, attain supreme bliss.

19. They liberate two hundred and forty generations.

20. He who calls this to mind at the time of death, snaps all *saṁsāra* and gets Supreme bliss.

21. I have thus told you about the greatness of these tīrthas. What else do you wish to know?

CHAPTER ONE HUNDRED AND SIXTYNINE

The Semicircular spot in Mathurā

Varāha said:

1. There is no place greater than Mathurā in all the three worlds. So I remain in Mathurā for ever.

2. Mathurā is the greatest of all tīrthas because Kṛṣṇa was playing in every spot there.

3. The whole place is circular and half of this circle is particularly important.

4. People who live between the northern and southern ends of this attain liberation.

5. This is Somacakra because of its appearance and it is efficacious for bath and gifts. Death there also is desirable.

6. He who bathes in this Ardhacandra (semicircular spot) reaches the world from which there is no return.

7. By simply following the law of the sacred thread, one may start from the south and go to its north.

Earth said:

8. O Lord, what is the law of the sacred thread. Tell me how it should be followed.

Varāha said:

9. O goddess, the law of the sacred thread is that the commencement should be in the south and conclusion in the north.

10. This is the law by which people are able to gain salvation.

11. One should start from home and silently go to the north and have bath there.

12. Then one may break silence and perform worship to Kṛṣṇa.

13. A milch cow may then be gifted and also gold and other things. Then Brahmins should be fed. This is that law.

14. One can also get these things done there for the sake of getting the results.

15. Such a person is never born again but remains esteemed in my world. He who dies there also goes to my world.

16. Those who die elsewhere also go to my world if they have done these things in Ardhacandra.

17. They remain in heaven as long as their bones remain in Ardhacandra.

18. In this Ardhacandra in Viśrāntitīrtha even a donkey becomes a four-armed person after it is cremated.

19. I remain as Garteśvara between the two ends of this place.

20. O Earth, I remain in the form of the people of Mathurā. I am satisfied when they are satisfied.

21. Listen, O goddess, to what happened to Garuḍa when he came to Mathurā to see Lord Kṛṣṇa.

22. He found all people there to be like Kṛṣṇa, and in order to know the real Lord Kṛṣṇa among them, he uttered this stotra:

Garuḍa said:

23. "Victory to the Lord of the universe, victory to Āditya, victory to Viṣṇu, victory to Acyuta, Victory to Kṛṣṇa, Victory to him who is beyond thought. I bow to you, O Lord."

24. When praised thus by the great Garuḍa, the lord appeared before him.

25. He consoled him and said to him pleasantly.

26. "Why have you uttered this praise? What do you desire? Why have you come to Mathurā? Tell me all this."

Garuḍa said:

27. "I came to Mathurā wishing to see you. But I was unable to see you.

28. I find here all of the same appearance and so I am stupefied. Hence I uttered this praise for your favour".

29. Hearing these words of Garuḍa, the lord laughed and told him in sweet words;

Kṛṣṇa said:

30. "The form of the people of Mathurā is my form. The sinful people never see them in that form".

31. So saying Kṛṣṇa disappeared there. Garuḍa also returned.

32. I have thus told you about the form of the people of Mathurā. Their propitiation is my propitiation.

33. Those who die in Mathurā attain salvation, and this will never be otherwise.

34. An animal, a bird or even a worm, all attain there the four-armed form.

35-36. He who fasts on the Ekādaśī day in the month of Āśvina, and on the Dvādaśī day bathes in the river Yamunā and sees Padmanābha and the deities Śiva and Viṣṇu united in a single form, ceases from rebirth.

37. He who bathes there on the Dvādaśī of the bright half, after fasting and keeping awake the previous day, and worships Viṣṇu, surely gets salvation.

38-39. He gets freed of the sin of killing a Brahmin by praising Yaśodā, Devakī and Vidyeśvarī.

40. Bath there removes all the evil effects of the planets, so too the prayer there to whatever deity.

41. Seeing the Lord as Dīrghaviṣṇu there is itself efficacious, and worshipping him yields all results.

42. This place itself is called Brahmā and doing all that Brahmā did there like japa, homa and dhyāna well, takes one to Visṇu.

CHAPTER ONE HUNDRED AND SEVENTY

The story of Gokarṇa

Varāha said:

1. O Earth, I shall now tell you an old story about Gokarṇa in Mathurā.

2. There was a wealthy Vaiśya named Vasukarṇa in Mathurā. He had a very virtuous life named Suśīlā.

3. She was very much devoted to her husband, but did not have a child even after many years.

4. Once seeing many women with children, she was wailing over her unfortunate lot at the confluence of the river Sarasvatī.

5. Seeing this, a sage who was sitting at the foot of a tree there, took pity on her and asked her who she was and why she was sad.

6. She told him that when she saw there numerous women playing with their children, she was feeling sorry that she alone had not that good fortune.

7. The sage then told her who was yearning for the blessing to get a child:

8. "By the blessing of God, you will get a son. Go to the Śiva temple known as Gokarṇa.

9. Worship there with your husband offering abhiṣeka, lamp and naivedya, reciting stotras and performing Japa".

10. Hearing this, she prostrated before him and went to her husband to tell him about the agreeable advice of the sage.

11. He told her that he very much liked the idea and felt that his long-felt desire was bearing fruit.

12-13. He went with her to the confluence of Sarasvatī and bathing there, worshipped Gokarṇa every day with flowers, lamp and naivedya.

14. Ten years passed like this. Then Lord Śiva became pleased with them and said:

15. "You will get a handsome and virtuous son and he will be getting many children by the blessing of God".

16. So said by the Lord, they bathed in the Sarasvatī early in the morning and made many offerings to the Lord.

17. They gave to the Brahmins a lot of food, clothes and liberal dakṣiṇā.

18. Signs of pregnancy could then be discerned in Suśīlā. The foetus was growing like the moon in the bright fortnight. In the tenth month was born a boy delightful like the moon.

19. To celebrate the birth of the son, the father gave numerous cows with gold and clothes to people of all castes.

20. He performed the Jātakarma ceremony of the new-born and also the Nāmakaraṇa naming the boy Gokarṇa after well thinking about it.

21. In due course, he performed for his son the other ceremonies like Annaprāśana, Cūḍākarma, Upanayana, Godāna and Vivāha at the appropriate times.

22. He gave numerous gifts, worshipped many deities and and performed several auspicious ceremonies.

23. But seeing him not getting children even in the prime of youth, he got more girls married to him making them four in all.

24. All of them were lovely, good-natured and in the bloom of youth, but none bore a child.

25. Gokarṇa started doing many things conducive to get a child like digging wells, making tanks, constructing temples,

26. Stalls for giving water and garlands, daily food, special feasts and such other things.

27. Considering the evanescent nature of human life, he always engaged himself in such activities.

28. Near Gokarṇa, on its western side, he constructed a temple of Viṣṇu in the Pañcāyatana.

29. He arranged for an extensive garden around it with all kinds of flowering plants and trees like mango, orange and pomegranate.

30. Around this he constructed a big wall with a moat and made provision for watering the plants and collecting flowers by women.

31. Every service in the temple including cleaning, was done by his wives.

32. All of them were devoted to him and faithfully carried out whatever he said.

33. A garland maker was appointed to water the trees and he was guarding the garden also.

34. In due time, the trees produced flowers and fruits and presented the appearance of an eternal festival of fruits. They were eaten by all and given to others also as in the garden of Indra.

35. While he was thus living in Mathurā making lavish gifts, his resources gradually began to dwindle.

36-37. He began to get worried as to what he could do with the little that was left with him to look after his parents, maintain his family and feed his servants.

38. So he started his trading business again and started with his employees to the eastern regions.

39. Purchasing things from there, he sold them in the northern regions with good profit.

40-41. He then bought from there fine gems, horses and clothes and brought them home in Mathurā. This business was continued.

42. Once during a trip like this, he and his people halted

for rest in a mountain valley with fine water and profuse growth of barley.

43. In a convenient place near a brook, they put up their tent, deposited their luggage there and let loose the horses for grazing.

44. He gave the necessary instructions to the followers, and with a few of them climbed up the mountain which was full of caves.

45. While he was strolling there for pleasure, he noticed a spot which was full of placid water amidst groves of oranges.

46. There were many trees laden with fruits and many plants full of flowers grown by the flowermakers therein between rocks.

47. As he went near and scanned it with his eyes, he heard words of welcome.

48. Surprised at this, he looked more carefully and saw there a parrot in a cage.

49. The parrot said: "Come here, let me accord you welcome and be hospitable to you, O wayfarer. Receive this water for pādya and take this honoured seat.

50. You and your people may partake of these sweet fruits, honey, meat and water as much as you like.

51. My parents will come and offer you further hospitality.

52. The ancestors of a householder, who is indifferent to duly receive guests, go to hell and those of one who respects them, go to heaven.

53. A guest who goes away disappointed, takes with him the merit acquired by the householder transferring to him all of his own sins.

54. So a guest should be attended upon in all seriousness irrespective of the fact whether the time of the visit is suitable or otherwise, for a guest is like Viṣṇu."

55. The merchant Gokarṇa was very happy to hear these words of *dharma* from the parrot, and he asked him.

56. "Which sage are you ? or are you a god or semi-divine that you appear superhuman and utter these words of wisdom ?

57. Please tell me who you are. You are enthusiastic and eloquent about guests. Surely blessed is the man near whom you are".

58. So requested, the parrot began to tell him about an improper action foolishly done by it.

59. "I happened to offend sage Śuka when he was performing penance on the northern side of mount Sumeru.

60. Śuka, the son of Vyāsa, was performing great penance and to hear the Purāṇas and Itihāsas from him, many sages came there.

61. There were among them the sages Asita, Devala Mārkaṇḍeya, Bharadvāja, Yavakrīta, Bhṛgu,

62. Aṅgiras, Taittirīya, Kaṇva, Medhātithi, Kṛta, Tantu, Sutantu, Āditya, Vasumān, Ekata, Dvita,

63. Vāmadeva, Aśvaśiras, Triśiras, Gautama and many Devas, Siddhas, Pannagas and Guhyakas.

64. They all sat before Śuka and asked him many questions relating to *dharma*. I was a disciple of sage Vāmadeva, by name Śukodara.

65. Curious to know things but not observing the necessary decorum, because of my being young, I went in front and repeatedly put questions of a hypothetical nature.

66-67. My master was stopping me every time saying that the objections are raised and the answers given by those who want to win a point over each other and it was not proper to interrupt them by my questions.

68. Thus chastised by my master, the other sages refused to speak to me.

69. And Śuka pronounced a curse on me: "As this boy blabbers like a parrot, let him become the parrot itself".

70. No sooner did he utter this, than this Śukodara was transformed into a Śuka (parrot).

71. The sages then sought the pardon of Śuka on my behalf, but he only said:

72. "What I said cannot but happen. But I shall give this parrot a boon to redeem himself after a lapse of time.

73. Because of your pleadings, I give him the power to be highly virtuous and get mastery of all Śāstras and get knowledge of the essence of Purāṇas even while remaining in the form of the parrot.

74. He will die in Mathurā and then go to the Brahmaloka".

75. Having incurred such a curse and getting the boon for redemption from it, I was living in despondency in a cave in the Himālayas.

76. I was then caught by a hunter and put in a cage, and he and his wife keep me as a plaything.

77. But by the grace of the sage, my knowledge does not leave me. I eat the fruit of my own bad action".

78. At these words of the parrot, Gokarṇa said: "O great soul, don't give yourself up to sorrow.

79. I belong to that holy Mathurā from where you are to gain redemption. I happened to come here on my way for trade.

80. I will be going back to Mathurā with all my merchandise soon. (I shall take you with me as my son)".

81. The parrot was happy to know that Gokarṇa was a resident of Mathurā and he agreed to the suggestion of the merchant that he would take him as his son.

82. When they were conversing thus, the huntress woke up and came out. She saw the handsome man sitting in the seat surrounded by his followers.

83. As she was looking at him again and again, the parrot said:

84. "Mother, here is a distinguished guest for us. He is named Gokarṇa and deserves to be well honoured".

85. As she was hesitating in spite of what the parrot said, the hunter returned home.

86. The parrot repeated the importance of honouring guests and the hunter agreed.

87. He offered him fruits, meat and sweet-smelling honey and then asked him what he might do for him.

88. But Gokarṇa said that what he desired was something else, and that may be given to him if he was willing.

89. He said: "Please give me the parrot in the cage as my son. I will take him to my parents at Mathurā".

90-91. Immediately the hunter said: "I shall give you the parrot if you are prepared to give us the fruit of the bath in Yamunā and in the confluence of Sarasvatī".

92. Gokarṇa replied: "Tell me, if you know, the result of the bath in the confluence of Sarasvatī".

The hunter said:

93. This parrot has told me about the merit that accrues in Mathurā, in the confluence and in performing Dvādaśīvrata.

94. He who performs this vrata, let him be a Rākṣasa or even an animal, attains final beatitude.

95. He who bathes in the confluence and sees Lord Gokarṇa there, never goes to the abode of Yama, but goes to the world of Viṣṇu.

96. Thus have I heard about the great merit that accrues in the confluence (Saṅgama).

CHAPTER ONE HUNDRED AND SEVENTYONE

The Story of Gokarṇa (continued)

Varāha said:

1. He took the parrot and went to Mathurā and presented him to his parents, telling them the whole story about him.

2. Many years passed happily in worship and discussions (of morals).

3. His resources again began to dwindle and he thought of starting trading again.

4. His idea was to collect gems from the sea through experts.

5. He then entered into an agreement with a troupe of sailors and started.

6. On an auspicious day together with the parrot and taking with him all the necessary food and drink.

7. Before entering the ship, he got the blessings of his parents and instructed his wives to do their duties in the temple and to look after the garden.

8. He asked them to attend well on the parents all the time without fail and to do for them what would be normally his duty.

9-10. Instructing them thus and getting their approval and propitiating God, he entered the ship together with the parrot and started voyage in the vast ocean.

11. The sailors moved the craft rapidly into the deep outer ocean.

12. Then an adverse wind began to blow which drifted it away and made the crew helpless and senseless.

13. "What a pity ! what can we do now", they exclaimed. Hearing their words, those on board began to accuse one another.

14. "Some sinful man who ought not to have entered the ship has got into it", they said. "Because of his sin we are all facing death now".

15. Four months passed and they observed the fruit of their adventure.

16. Listening to their mutual accusations, Gokarṇa asked Śuka who was in a self-disparaging mood.

17. "O my son, I am burning within myself because I am the sinner among us, as I have no (real) son and it is wellknown that the man without a son has no salvation.

18. Tell me out of your wisdom and proficiency in scripture what we may do in this predicament."

Śuka said:

19. "O father, be quiet. Don't have any fear and don't give yourself up to sorrow. Leave me to do what is appropriate in this situation."

20. Consoling his father thus, Śuka quickly flew in the northern direction to the region called Dhruva.

21. He crossed the expanse of water by flying low and reached the valley of a mountain spreading over one yojana.

22. He was thrilled to see the big mountain, and flying to its top, saw a fine temple.

23. It was a splendid temple of Viṣṇu, and after going around it, he hid himself within.

24. He thought, "I am the son, the father is now a wanderer. When will we be able to get over the present difficulty ?"

25. As he was thinking for a moment in this manner, the (chief) goddess entered there with a golden vessel in her hand and performed worship of the god.

26. She uttered 'Bow to Nārāyaṇa' and sat on a seat. In a moment there came numerous (other) goddesses similar to the chief goddess in age and beauty.

27. After delightfully presenting there vocal music, instrumental music and dance, they returned to their places.

28. On the southern side in the temple could be seen many flocks of Jaṭāyu birds.

29. Śuka, the parrot, entered into an understanding with them, as if in written form, and spoke in his language seeking their protection.

30. They consoled him and asked him how he came there crossing the expansive ocean full of all kinds of fish.

31. Śuka said; "My father remains in the craft drifted away to a difficult place by an unfavourable wind.

32. Desiring to seek protection for him I have come to this great mountain. Please see that he is safe and happy".

The birds said:

33. We shall see that this good desire of yours is accomplished. You will get your father as if by a canoe.

34. I will split the water with my feet (and make a shallow passage across the ocean) and your father will follow on my back.

35. The aquatic beings that come in the way will die by my beak pushing them down".

36. The plan was conveyed to the father, and he was made to cross the ocean on the back of Jaṭāyu.

37. While crossing, the water was in some places waist-deep, in others chest-deep and in yet others neck-deep.

38. He then reached that wonderful temple and saw there the tank full of gems and lotuses. He bathed there and offered libations to the gods and manes.

39. He collected flowers and worshipped Lord Keśava. After seeing the Pañcāyatana studded with gems, he sat in solitude with the approval of Śuka.

40. In a short time, the goddesses made their appearance as before, and after the dance, the seniormost among them spoke to the rest.

41-42. "To this Gokarṇa, the visitor who is great and spiritual, give the celestial fruit for eating and fine water for drinking so as to get him satisfaction for three months and his sorrow, sin and delusion disappear".

43. They did so and said, "Live in this heavenly place as long as you like, you will be free from fear and sorrow".

44. This continued and Gokarṇa was as happy as in Mathurā.

45. Meanwhile (as Gokarṇa was just leaving the craft),

a favourable wind blew and took it to a place of calm water full of gems.

46. His men collected a good deal of gems, and as they were taking them to him for his examination, they found him missing.

47. They were extremely sad and said, "Where has he gone? Is he dead or lost in water?

48. Or has he drowned himself out of shame? Any way we shall go to his father and move with him as if we are his sons.

49. We shall also give him the share in the gems due to him. This is the rule when we venture jointly as a group."

50. But Gokarṇa, who was in that island, was full of sorrow and he piteously spoke to Śuka about his parents.

51. Śuka, however, spoke to him, "I am but a bird with a frail little body, and, as such, I am unable to carry you.

52. I shall go to Mathurā across this sea and convey to them your words and convey back to you theirs. Give me your permission".

53-54. Gokarṇa then said to Śuka, "Let it be so. May you go to my parents and tell them about me. But return soon as I can't do without you."

55. The parrot said 'yes', and reaching Mathurā told everything to the parents (of Gokarṇa).

56. They heard all that but, however, presumed Gokarṇa as dead and wailed for a long time. Then they put affection on the parrot and said:

57. "O bird, you should narrate for our peace of mind stories up-holding *dharma*."

58. Distressed at the loss of the son, they were consoled by stories uttered by the parrot remaining in the cage.

59. Then the sailors (who had gone with Gokarṇa in voyage) returned with their collection of gems and gave to Vasukarṇa what was due to his son.

60. The mountain was worshipped by them by offering twenty gems each. They were all then duly honoured and sent to their homes.

61-62. They lived there attending to the needs of the old Vaiśya (Vasukarṇa) as if he was their own father.

CHAPTER ONE HUNDRED AND SEVENTYTWO

The Story of Gokarṇa (continued)

Varāha said:

1. Gokarṇa did in the temple for (the other) thirteen days (in the fortnight) what he did on the first day.

2. The goddesses, beautiful and well ornamented, used to visit there and happily perform their dance.

3. Gokarṇa soon forgot everything about his home. Then once he saw the goddesses coming there to be devoid of their usual lustre.

4. They were weak and pale, without their attractive garments and jewels, and with the hair on the head and eyelids reduced.

5. They were deformed and disfigured and had several bleeding wounds. He was very much pained to see them in that condition.

6. He felt that, being an issueless man, not only he himself will have no salvation, but by his association even these goddesses were reduced to that state.

7. Thinking so, he asked them to tell him how such a change occurred in their form.

The Goddesses said:

8. "O noble man, don't ask about this. Fate is the cause for everything. In the form of Time, it gives us the effects of our merits (as well as demerits).

9. Fate should be sought after for an answer. People who are very much distressed do not talk with one who is himself distressed."

10. Gokarṇa, however, out of a desire to know the truth, bowed to them and asked again.

11. "If you consider the cause of this disfigurement a secret and are not inclined to tell me about it, I shall put an end to my life."

12. When he told them thus, one among them said, "Let us tell him about our sorrow if that will give him relief.

13. I shall tell you how this disfigurement happened to us. Listen with attention.

14. There is the beautiful city of Mathurā which brings about salvation to people.

15. Once the king of Ayodhyā went there with all the four components of his army to worship in the tīrthas there for four months.

16. He chose there the temple of Viṣṇu with its five parts and having gardens and arbours around with wells and sweet-smelling flowers and trees bearing fruits in all seasons.

17. The king arranged his residence near this.

18. His followers destroyed the garden with its fruit-bearing trees and the surrounding walls were razed to the ground.

19. Although prevented from doing this, these sinful people did not listen. The king felt himself like a lion in a cage".

20. She then covered with the hands her face shedding tears on the breast and cried aloud, "Alas ! who will protect us".

21. Then all of them began to cry, and hearing their wailing sound resembling the cry of the Kurari birds, Gokarṇa became very sad.

22. He fell down at the feet of every one of them and slowly consoled them with soothing words.

23-24. He then told them that if he had been there, he would have prevented the king himself from being there, but unfortunately he was incapacitated.

25. When he said this, all of them became curious and asked him who he was and from where he came there.

Gokarṇa said:

26. "I am Gokarṇa. I told you I was happy to see you all formerly very beautiful.

27. But now you are all otherwise and that gives me grief. Tell me the cause of this transformation".

28. The eldest among them said, "We were well decorated with various flowers because we were in that garden protected by its owner.

29. Therefore you could see us beautiful with all those flowers. I shall tell you how the change occurred.

30. The king's men tormented us by their cutting and up-

rooting (the garden). We became miserable and hence the present appearance.[1]

31. We are without flowers, left but with the root and trunk. Thus are we reduced with loss of our identity.

32. The god who is shaped there in stone and clay, but who is really of the nature of Sattva, is the witness of all good deeds.

33. It is meritorious to water well the garden and to dig ponds and make them full of lotuses and swans.

34. The trees laden with fruits are (to be considered) golden To protect the garden is to provide pleasure to people. To destroy it is to do harm as the disfigurement of ours."

Gokarṇa said:

35. Tell me what kind of merit accrues to a person who makes a garden, digs wells and instals images of gods.

The eldest said:

36. For the twice-born, *iṣṭāpūrta* is the foremost means of *dharma*. Heaven is acquired by *iṣṭa* and liberation by *pūrta*.

37. He who renovates tanks, wells, ponds and temples gains the result of *pūrta*.

38. The same world as is ordained for those who make gifts of land or cows, is attained by one who grows trees.

39. He who plants a peepal, a margosa, a banyan, ten flowering plants, two pomegranates, two oranges and five mangoes never goes to hell.

40. Just as a dutiful son raises his family by hard effort and austere resolve, so do the trees with their flowers and fruits, raise up from hell their planter.[2]

41-42. The service of the trees in providing firewood, sticks for sacrifices like Agnihotra, shade for the travellers to rest, nests for birds and medicine for men through the leaves, root and bark is said to be its five sacrifices (*pañcayajña*).

43-44. The learned people declare a tree to be like a son because it provides materials for domestic life, provides shelter

1. This indicates that the goddesses were nymphs of the garden (*Udyānadevatās*).

2. The text has after this 'Gokarṇa said', but this seems to be wrong.

for small animals, twice in a year birds breed in it and it provides fruits to the originator throughout the year.

Varāha said:

45. When told thus by the goddess Mālatī, he swooned saying 'Alas, Alas !'

46. They brought him back to consciousness by sprinkling water on him and sought to know why he swooned.

Gokarṇa said:

47. "In Mathurā I have my aged parents and four wives. The garden and the temple you speak of are mine.

48. If I am able to go to my parents and see the king I shall tell them what has befallen you".

49. The eldest goddess said, "I shall take you wherever you like. We shall see Mathurā today itself.

50. You may get into this aerial vehicle. You may also take with you these celestial gems, jewels and fruits and present them to the king without *arghya*".

51. He agreed and, bowing to Lord Viṣṇu there, got into the vehicle and soon descended at the place where the king was camping.

52. He then presented to the king the numerous gems he had brought with him.

53. The king was very much pleased even at their sight. He welcomed Gokarṇa, showed him hospitality and honoured him by giving half his seat due to a donor of gems and money.

54. Gokarṇa then offered to show him a wonder and also explain about it.

55-56. He agreed and asked his commander-in-chief to get ready the army soon.

57. The commander-in-chief carried out the orders of the king[1]. The deformed goddesses attained their original celestial form.

---

1. After this the portion relating to what was done seems to be lost. Presumably it is about the king being taken to the deformed goddesses to convince him of the misdeeds of his men and then making him restore the garden and renovate the temple.

58. They praised Gokarṇa again and again. They gave him boons and bestowing benedictions went to heaven.

59. Gokarṇa then told the king all about himself and of the result of *Pūrta dharma*.

60. The king then bestowed on him some villages, cities, clothes, elephants, horses and abundant money.

61. Having known how great a dharma the making of a garden is and how wonderful its results are, the king did everything in that realm.

CHAPTER ONE HUNDRED AND SEVENTYTHREE

The story of Gokarṇa (continued)

Varāha said:

1. Remaining in that auspicious place, Gokarṇa honoured the parrot Śuka, his own parents and the four wives.

2. He then made the residents of Mathurā make gardens according to their capacity.

3. He himself then conducted a great sacrificial festival in which Brahmins were fed and gifts given every day.

4. He also provided for vocal song and instrumental music and did everything conducive to progeny.

5. He then prostrated separately at the feet of his father and mother.

6-7. Then looking at Śuka he shed tears and exclaimed: "It was because of your favour that I got my life, dharma and introduction to the path of salvation and the king gained profound merit".

8. Living happily with his family and friends, Gokarṇa constructed this temple of Śiva and named it Śuka.

9. He installed Śukeśvara (Śiva) there and then constructed the resthouse named 'Śukasatra' where two hundred Brahmins are sumptuously fed.

10. Śuka died there, and entering an aerial car went to heaven.

11. Gokarṇa had given to the hunter, in exchange for the parrot, the merit of his bath at the confluence and the Śrāddha and gift of gold and cows there.

12. (As a result) the hunter and his wife also entered the same aerial car as Śuka's and went to heaven.

13. Thus have I told you about the great merit that accrues at Mathurā, at the confluence of river Sarasvatī and Yamunā and at the temple of Śiva Gokarṇa.

14. The meditation on Gokarṇa confers great merits, enormous enjoyment and salvation in the end.

CHAPTER ONE HUNDRED AND SEVENTYFOUR

The greatness of the confluence of Yamunā

Varāha said:

1. I shall tell you another thing about the prowess of Saṅgama (confluence) which gains liberation even for the sinners.

2. An ascetic Brahmin by name Mahānāma was living in a forest there.

3. He had mastered yoga and was spending his time in reciting Veda, practising Japa and performing Homa.

4. In performing these with the idea of attaining Brahmaloka, many years passed.

5. He then thought of undertaking a pilgrimage and cleansing his body by the holy tīrthas.

6-7. His idea was to purify himself by starting early morning after the prescribed rites and first go to Asikuṇḍa, from there to Koṭitīrtha in the south and then proceed to the northern end bathing in all tīrthas including Mathurā and Puṣkara.

8. So he started from Mathurā and took the proposed route after performing worship and saluting the Lord.

9. Soon he came across five ghosts in the lonely forest full of thorns.

10. They were all terrific in appearance and so he became afraid for a moment and closed his eyes.

11. Soon he gave up his fear, and mustering courage, asked them:

12. "Who are you, O fierce beings? By what bad action have you become like this? Where have you come from and where do you go?"

The ghosts said:

13. We are full of misery and hunger and thirst overcome us. Our minds are bad and knowledge we have none.

14. We do not know the quarters or the subquarters, neither the sky nor the earth nor even the day.

15. We hope that this suffering of ours will ultimately lead to good and it is like darkness awaiting the rising of the sun.

16. I am by name Paryuṣita, this one is Sūcīmukha, these are Śīghraga and Rodhaka and the fifth is Lekhaka.

The Brāhmaṇa said:

17. How can the ghosts, who become so because of their own actions have names? Please tell me how you have got these names.

The ghost said:

18. O Brahmin, I used to eat well during the whole day and give what is left over (*paryuṣita*) to the Brahmins (the next day). Hence my name is Paryuṣita.

19. Many Brahmins who were seeking food were directed (*sūcita*) wrongly by this man. Hence he is Sūcīmukha.

20. This one used to go away quickly (*śighraṁ gacchati*) whenever a Brahmin made any request to him. Hence he is Śīghraga.

21. For fear of other Brahmins asking food, this one used to take food in the interior of the house. Hence he is Rodhaka (since he stopped others *rudhyati*).

22. This (last) one used to remain silent scratching the earth (likhan) in indifference. Hence he is Lekhaka.

23. Lekhaka moves about like an inebriate; Rodhaka has his head bent down.

24-25. Śīghraga is lame and Sūcīmukha (has a deformed face)[1] Paryuṣita has become one with thin limbs, long neck hanging big belly and stout testicles. I have thus told you all about us. You may ask if you want to know anything else.

1. The appearance of Sūcīmukha is not given.

The Brāhmaṇa said:

26. All beings in the earth need food. I wish to know what food you take.

The ghosts said:

27. O kind man, listen to what I say about our food, by knowing which you will despise us.

28. The ghosts eat phlegm, urine and faeces before women and in houses which are unclean.

29-30. The ghosts eat in such houses where there are no offerings to gods, no recitation of mantras and no gifts, where the elders are not respected, where women are dominant, where things are kept haphazard and where there is always quarrel.

31-32. We eat in homes where gifts are given to the undeserving or given without due rites, where contemptible Brahmins live, where bad and prohibited actions are done.

33. Such is the food for us who have done bad deeds. We are extremely dejected with this ghosthood. Please tell us how we can cease to be this.

The Brāhmaṇa said:

34. A man who undertakes vows like Kṛcchra and Cāndrāyaṇa for a single day or three days, gets purified and never becomes a ghost.

35. He who gives ample food and drink with due regard and honours ascetics, never becomes a ghost.

36. He who nurtures every day five, three or even one (being) with universal compassion, never becomes a ghost.

37. He who is inclined to worship gods and honour guests, elders and parents, never becomes a ghost.

38. He who has conquered anger, does not enter into rivalry, is free from avarice and attachment, is full of forbearance and is prone to give liberal gifts, never becomes a ghost.

39. He who fasts on the Ekādaśī, Saptamī and Caturdaśī days during the bright as well as dark halves of the month, never becomes a ghost.

40. He who bows to the gods, Brahmins, cows, tīrthas, mountains and rivers, never becomes a ghost.

The ghosts said:

41. We have now heard from you about the factors that are conducive to make one not to become a ghost. Please tell us what factors make one (necessarily) become a ghost.

The Brāhmaṇa said:

42. He who dies with the food given by a Śūdra within him, becomes a ghost.

43. By mere contact of, not to say sitting together or eating with, Nāgas (a naked sect), Kāpālikas or Pāṣaṇḍas, one becomes a ghost.

44. Such a person loses all his acquired merit and becomes condemned to be a ghost for ever.

45. He who remains in the abode of a Pāṣaṇḍa or is a drunkard, or cohabits with the wife of another, or is fond of flesh, becomes a ghost.

46. He who steals the wealth of gods, Brahmins or teachers or gives away his daughter for money, becomes a ghost.

47. He who gives up his mother, father, brother, sister, wife or son, when they are innocent, becomes certainly a ghost.

48. He who performs sacrifices for the sake of those who are not eligible for it and refuses to do the same for those who are eligible, and who is interested in serving Śūdras, becomes a ghost.

49. He who kills a Brahmin or cow or incurs the five great sins or is ungrateful, becomes a ghost.

50. He who does not heed the advice of an elder or preceptor meant for his well being, becomes a ghost.

51. He who receives gifts from bad people, particularly atheists, becomes a ghost without food or drink.

The ghost said:

52. Please tell us how those who do such prohibited deeds out of ignorance can redeem themselves.

The Brāhmaṇa said:

53-54. The only means of redemption for those who are ignorant and indifferent to *dharma* and do not have compassion or give gifts, is to perform worship and sacrifice to Lord Vāmana at the confluence at Mathurā when the star Śravaṇa is in combination with Dvādaśī in the month of Bhādrapada.

55. They should make gifts of gold, food, clothes, umbrella and sandals after bathing and giving libations to manes.

56. They not only do not become ghosts, but go to the world of Viṣṇu in an aerial car.

57. He who bathes in that tīrtha or thinks or speaks about it, gets the merit equivalent to bathing in river Gaṅgā.

58. I have heard it proclaimed that even he who, having become a ghost, listens to the narration of the prowess of this tīrtha, goes to the immortal world of Viṣṇu.

The ghosts said:

59. O auspicious man, tell us details of the rites of this vow so that we can do it and get redemption from this ghosthood.

The Brāhmaṇa said:

60. The details of this vow were formerly narrated to Māndhātā by Vasiṣṭha being asked about them.

61. I shall now tell the same to you since they are capable of securing your release.

62. Whatever bath, gift or sacrifice done in Bhādrapada when Śravaṇa falls on the Dvādaśī day, is a lakh of times more efficacious than at other times.

63. You may know the merit that accrues when the gift of a pot is made after bathing in the confluence and worshipping Vāmana.

64. It is the same as what is obtained by making gifts of a hundred cows with gold and all decorations.

65. By this Śravaṇadvādaśīvrata one not only never becomes a Rākṣasa, but takes abode in heaven for the duration of the period of fourteen Indras.

66. Then he is born as a Brahmin learned in the Vedas, proficient in Yoga, always following the path to *mokṣa* and conscious of his previous life. And by contemplation he becomes permanently liberated.

67. Gifts of gold, food, drink and jewels should be made there.

68. According to one's means a golden Vāmana may also be gifted along with umbrella and sandals according to rules.

69. After performing worship in the prescribed manner with mantras and also homa, the Brahmins may be propitiated.

(These are the items in worship:)

70. (Invocation): O lord of Lakṣmī, Eternal being, giver of gifts, although you are everywhere, be pleased to adorn this seat by your part for my favour.

71. (Reference to the star): I adore for the attainment of my desires that star in which form you shine in the sky on Dvādaśī day.

72. (Bath): I bow to you (and bathe you), O Keśava, you having lotus in the navel and forming the abode of Lakṣmī.

73. (Salutation): I salute you, O eternal and omniscient Lord Nārāyaṇa, the source of the whole world. (Worship): O Keśava, accept this worship of mine on this day when the asterism Śravaṇa is in conjunction with Dvādaśī day.

74. (Incense): O Lord of Lords, bearing the conch, disc and mace, here is the incense. I bow to you Vāsudeva, Acyuta, Ananta, Govinda.

75. (Lamp with flame): By this incandecense may all the eternal worlds be opened. O Janārdana, you are the lustre in everything and I bow to you.

76. (Food): You were born to Aditi as Vāmana for subduing the son of Virocana (Bali) and you then occupied the entire universe with three steps. I bow to you.

77. (Arghya): You are esteemed by the gods and you are the final resort of yogins. You repose in water and you are the source of the universe. Be pleased to accept this *arghya* (ceremonial water).

78. (Homa): You eat the sacrificial offering, you produce the sacrificial offering, you are the sacrificer and the sacrificial offering. O Keśava, I bow to you who are everywhere and permeate every being.

79. (Dakṣiṇā): O Lord, you are gold, food, water and cloth. (Umbrella and Sandals): O Janārdana, be pleased with this offering of sandals and umbrella.

80. (Praise): May the eternal Lord who is wind, water and fire, Varuṇa, Sūrya, Keśava, Śiva, Kubera, remove my sins.

81. (Gift of water pot): He who is Brahmā, Viṣṇu, Rudra, Candra, Sūrya, Indra, Tvaṣṭā, Yama and Agni, remove my sins.

82. (Reference to the worshipper): Vāmana is the giver of intelligence, Vāmana is the liberator. I bow to Vāmana.

83. (Receiver of gift): I give to Vāmana, Vāmana gives me. Vāmana is the liberator by both these means. I bow to Vāmana.

84. (Gift of cow): In the body of the cow remain the fourteen worlds. By giving a gift of the cow which yields all desires, people get gratification.

85. (Release): I offered worship to you, the dispeller of all my sins. I now release you after this worship to adorn any other place you like.

86. He who performs in this manner the worship on the Dvādaśī day in the Bhādrapada month, attains his aim.

87. He who performs like this in the Sarasvatī tīrtha at the confluence of Yamunā in particular, gets the merit a hundredfold.

88. Giving up everything, I have also been resorting to this tīrtha all this time with intense devotion. That was why you were not able to affect me.

89. The Vrata should be commenced when the tithi Dvādaśī actually starts combination with the star Śravaṇa and continues till one of the two is out of combination.

90. The prowess of the tīrtha is becoming manifest now itself. I find that your listening to this account has itself started gaining your liberation.

Varāha said:

91. As the Brahmin was saying this, the sound of Dundubhī could be heard in the sky and a shower of flowers from the sky on earth in hundreds.

92. Aerial cars descended there for the ghosts. A messenger of the gods then told them:

93. "By the narration of (the prowess of this tīrtha by) the Brahmin and his extollation of its efficacy and by your listening to all this, you are released from your ghosthood."

94. So conversation with a good man even with effort is a highly desirable thing, and in the mind there should always be the thought of the tīrtha and attitude of the Vrata.

95. This is evidenced by these ghosts getting their release and going to eternal heaven by their contact with the man who was always in the tīrtha at the confluence of Sarasvatī.

96. The result of their simply listening to the account of the greatness of the tīrtha was their release. So this which brought about the liberation of the five ghosts, is a great *dharma*.

97. He who devoutly recites this or listens with serious attention or performs what is ordained by this, never becomes a ghost.

98. The tīrtha named Piśāca is known in all the three worlds and simply to know about it is to safeguard against becoming a ghost.

CHAPTER ONE HUNDRED AND SEVENTYFIVE

The prowess of Kṛṣṇagaṅgā and Kāliñjara

Varāha said:

1. O fair one, now listen to the prowess of Kṛṣṇagaṅgā in river Yamunā.

2. Sage Kṛṣṇadvaipāyana (Vyāsa) used to bathe here thinking of Gaṅgā and do his daily routine.

3. Kṛṣṇagaṅgā is between the tīrthas Soma and Vaikuṇṭha. In this place in Mathurā, Vyāsa performed penance.

4-5. In this hermitage where there were many other great sages also, many sages used to go to perform Cāturmāsya and also many scholars deep in the knowledge of Vedas to clear their doubts.

6. Vyāsa used to clear their doubts by citing the relevant passages (from scripture).

7. In that place Śiva is installed with the name Kāliñjara, the very sight of whom confers the merit of Kṛṣṇagaṅgā.

8. Vyāsa lived there for twelve years free from all attachment, eating but once a fortnight and that too fruit in the new moon and full moon days.

9. He then went to Badarī in Himālaya and entered into dhyānayoga and became endowed with the knowledge of the past, present and future.

10. The greatness of this tīrtha was known through intuition by a Brahmin of the Pāñcāla country.

11-12. His name was Vasu, but being stricken by poverty, he proceeded with his wife to the south and settled in a town on the right bank of Śivanadī.

13. While living there pursuing his Brahmanic way of life, five sons and a daughter were born to him.

14. In due course, the daughter was given in marriage to a Brahmin with the necessary grain and wealth, but he passed away.

15. She then collected his bones and went to Mathurā, having known, by hearing the Purāṇas, that one whose bones are put in the Ardhacandra tīrtha gets a permanent place in heaven.

16. She went to Mathurā undertaking a pilgrimage and following a group of traders.

17. The youngest of the Brahmin's children thus became a young widow.

18. She was fair-complexioned, had wellformed limbs and curly black hair. Her thighs were stout and like the stem of the plantain.

19. Her fingers were close together and so too the toes and her nails rosy, her navel right-whirled and the belly had the three folds.

20. Her belly was small and even and breasts well rounded and raised. Her neck was conch-like, mouth tight, teeth sparkling and the lips and chin attractive.

21. Her eyes and brows were beautiful, speech extremely sweet. Her entire body was well proportioned. She bore the significant name Tilottamā.

22. Whoever was looked at by her, became dumbfounded by her beauty as if drawn in a picture.

23. As she was spending her days bathing in the tīrtha once she came to be seen by a group of courtesans.

24. The king of Kānyakubja, an upholder of Kṣatriya dharma, had constructed a permanent inn near the Śiva temple Devagarteśvara.

25. He had endowed it with a lot of wealth and entertainments with music and instruments as in Indra's abode.

26. Repeatedly induced by these courtesans attached to this

temple (for music and dancing), she took to music and dancing and gradually fell into their way of life.

27. In a short time, the virtuous woman became surrounded by the vicious.

28. As the consort of god, she began to enjoy with all those that came to her.

CHAPTER ONE HUNDRED AND SEVENTYSIX

The Prowess of Kṛṣṇagaṅgā and Kāliñjara

Varāha said:

1-2. The youngest of the five sons of the Pāñcāla Brahmin was rich and handsome and he started with his men and merchandise for trade in different countries.

3. After trading in various places, crossing different kingdoms, mountains and rivers, he came to the city of Mathurā and put up his tent in a place where food and fuel were plentiful.

4. He took bath early in the morning in that tīrtha together with his men and dressing and decking himself well, proudly drove in his cart.

5. He saluted the deities and gave many gifts..

6. Then out of curiosity he visited the temple of Garteśvara and, seeing there the supremely charming Tilottamā, fell a prey to passion.

7. To her matron he respectfully gave many clothes and hundreds of beautifully designed bangles.

8. He gave her also many jewelled chains and the essence of Agaru with camphor and sandal.

9. In that house (where Tilottamā was living) he was spending his time every day and used to go to his camp only after the sun had risen high in the horizon.

10. But everyday he would bathe in the tīrtha in Kṛṣṇagaṅgā. Out of the pride of wealth he was continuing in this way and six months passed.

11-12. Once when he went there to bathe, he was seen by sage Sumantu, who was in his hermitage nearby, to be full of worms all over his body.

13. These worms used to fall in plenty till he took bath, but the moment the bath was taken, they disappeared and he became handsome again.

14. This wonder was noticed by Sumantu for many days and he wanted to know who this youth was.

15. He then boldly asked him who he was, who his father was and what he was engaged in day and night.

Pāñcāla said:

16. I belong to Pāñcāla. I am the son of a Brahmin. I have taken to trading business.

17. I have come from Dekkan to this Mathurā and spending the night in my camp, I come to this tīrtha in the morning.

18. After bath, I worship this Lord Śiva named Trigarteśvara and also Kāliñjara and your feet and then return to my camp.

Sumantu said:

19. "I see a wonder in your body everyday. I find it full of worms before bath but clean after bath.

20. You have unknowingly incurred some great sin which is kept afar by the power of this tīrtha.

21. And by the contact of Kāliñjara, the body becomes pure also.

22. Think well and tell me what can possibly be the cause of this sin now unknown to you. Seeing the power of this tīrtha, I am asking this for your good".

23. Hearing these words of the sage who knew the past, present and future, he could not say anything and simply went away.

24. When he was alone with Tilottamā, he asked her:

25. "O dear, please tell me who you are, whose daughter, to which place you belong and why you are living here like this, though happily".

26. Although he pressed for an answer, she did not speak a word. He repeated the request several times but she was mum.

27. A few days passed and then he threatened to give up his life if she still refused to say the truth.

28. Compelled thus, she told him about her parents, brothers, native place, relations and the family (of her husband) to which she belonged.

29. "There is the beautiful city of Pāñcāla on the northern bank of river Gaṅgā. My parents were living there.

30. During a famine which caught hold of the entire country, they moved to Dekkan and settled on the southern bank of Narmadā in a town full of Brahmins.

31. Five sons were born to them there and a daughter as the sixth. That daughter is myself and I became a widow.

32. The youngest of the five brothers, but elder to me, left home even while he was a baby with a view to earn and make himself rich.

33. When he was gone, the parents died. I came here with a group of traders to put the bones in this tīrtha.

34. I used to spend my time here bathing in this tīrtha and worshipping the gods and Brahmins. Then I was lured by these (courtesans) and transformed to my present state.

35. By resorting to prostitution I have traduced my family. By this sin of mine I have brought to hell twentyone persons in both the families".

36. Telling him all this, Tilottamā cried for long thinking of her once high family.

37. She cried in the night thinking of her own doings.

38. Hearing her cry, the other women there came to her and asked her why she was crying and spoke words of consolation.

39. By then, hearing her story, the Pāñcāla too fell down unconscious and the women stood around and consoled him too and brought him back to consciousness by their efforts.

40. Seeing him revive, they asked him why he fell down unconscious.

41. He then said all about himself and his great family in detail before those associates of Tilottamā.

42. He became much dejected at his having committed inadvertent incest and thought seriously about the expiation for it.

43. If a Brahmin incurs the sin of killing a Brahmin or drink-

ing liquor, the expiation ordained by the sages is the destruction of the body.

44. The only purification for the guilt of incest with mother, teacher's wife, daughter, sister or daughter-in-law is immolation of the offender in fire.

45. He who cohabits with a prohibited person falls into the same category as the killer of the Brahmin, drinker of liquor, the murderer of women and the offender of the chastity of the teacher's wife.

46. Knowing her paramour to be her own elder brother, that woman from Pāñcāla (feeling herself guilty) gave away all her ornaments to Brahmins.

47. She gave them also all her jewels, clothes and grain. She gave these also for adorning Kāliñjara and for (the maintenance of) the garden.

48. Then at the tīrtha in Kṛṣṇagaṅgā she arranged a pyre in the prescribed manner and blazed the fire for her own purification.

49. The Pāñcāla too decided to do similarly for himself.

50. He took his bath, bowed to the gods and saluted sage Sumantu. He then sat before him and performed rites relating to his death.

51. He called the people of Mathurā and gave them gifts liberally.

52. He purchased villages then and there and made them over to Brahmins. He asked them to recite the divine Īśāvāsya (upaniṣad).

53. He entrusted with them money for the maintenance of the rest-house and for conducting his obsequies.

54. Then bathing in that tīrtha of Kṛṣṇa and bowing to the Lord, he endowed funds for the worship of Kāliñjara, for the rest-house and for the temple and gave the necessary instructions in the matter to his own people.

55. Then he held the feet of the great Sumantu and said: "O sage, your knowledge is wonderfully divine and exhilarating.

56. My sin has been now proved to be the consequence of incest.

57. From the time I came to Mathurā, I was having sexual contact with my sister and I have thus done great harm to my family.

58. By your pure sight, O sage, you were able to see worms falling from my body but the body becoming clean again by the power of Kṛṣṇagaṅgā.

59. All this was seen by you and I was asked about it again and again.

60. The sin of incest suspected has now been confirmed and for purification from that sin I am now giving up this body. I bow to your feet. Please give me approval."

61. When he was about to enter the pyre blazing with the ghee poured on it, an aerial voice was heard to say:

62. "Don't do this rash deed since you both have become free from the sin, for redemption from which you have decided to immolate yourselves.

63. This place where Lord Kṛṣṇa had played and walked about with his feet marked by the disc is pure and equal to Brahman.

64. A sin committed elsewhere disappears in a tīrtha, but a sin committed in a tīrtha sticks close like *vajralepa* (cement concrete).

65. Since both of you were bathing in Gaṅgā saṅgama (you are freed from your sins). By bathing here even once, a man becomes free even from the sin of killing a Brahmin.

66. The same merit as is acquired by bathing in all other tīrthas on earth, is acquired surely by bathing in five tīrthas.

67-68. Bathing in Viśrānti on Ekādaśī day, Saukara on Dvādaśī, Naimiṣa on Trayodaśī, Prayāga on Caturdaśī and Puṣkara on the new moon and full moon days in the month of Kārttika removes all sins.

69. Among these five tīrthas in Mathurā, Viśrānti is the most important.

70. But the same result as is obtained by bathing in these tīrthas or in Asikuṇḍa in the river Sarasvatī or in Kāliñjara, is obtained tenfold by bathing in Kṛṣṇagaṅgā.

71. Whatever sin is incurred knowingly or unknowingly disappears in Mathurā, so too all merits and demerits."

72. This narration of the greatness of tīrthas made by Varāha to Earth is capable of removing all sins.

73. Varāha combines in himself all gods and Vedas. He has no end and he cannot be fully known.

74. How can we speak fully of this god in whom the entire space is covered by but a part of his ear?

75. The entire heat (as well as light) in the world is covered by the corners of his eyes.

76. The whole of Air is covered by his breath and the seven oceans by the tips of his hoofs and look like particles of sweat there.

77. The whole Earth that was lost is seen clinging with the mountains and forests in the roots of his hair. Who is greater than this god?

78. In order to protect tīrthas he has taken his form himself.

79. And this is the Purāṇa narrated by him for clearing the doubts of Earth.

80. There need be no doubt that the moment he is seen, every sin disappears.

81-82. By bathing in (Kṛṣṇagaṅgā) on Navamī day in the bright half of the month Jyeṣṭha and in Sūkara for three days and then giving a lamp according to capacity, one gets rid of all sins.

83. By bathing in Kāliñjara on Dvādaśī day and worshipping god, one ascends an aerial car bright like twelve suns, and accepted by Viṣṇu, remains esteemed in Viṣṇu-loka.

Varāha said:

84. Thus comforted by the divine voice, the Pāñcāla asked Sumantu:

85. "O sage, you are my preceptor and father. Tell me what I may do, to enter this fire or resort to this tīrtha.

86. May I perform for three days expiatory rites like Kṛcchra and Cāndrāyaṇa in this place rendered more holy by your feet and get salvation?

Sumantu said:

87. The aerial voice we heard is true. It can never be false.

88. I was able to perceive the sin in your body before bath every day and its recession after bath.

89. You remain in this hermitage free from sin for the rest of your life. This sister of yours, who has also been freed from her sin, will surely attain salvation.

Varāha said:

90. O Earth, such is the prowess of this tīrtha in Mathurā.

91. The greatness of the tīrtha in Kṛṣṇagaṅgā, Kāliñjara and Sūkara is as I narrated to you.

92. He who listens to this with attention or recites it in the morning, will never be touched by sin.

93. The sin committed in seven lives disappears and the merit of giving a hundred cows is acquired.

94. Heaven is reached and immortality attained.

CHAPTER ONE HUNDRED AND SEVENTY-SEVEN

Consecration of Sūrya by Sāmba

Varāha said:

1. O fair goddess, now listen to another deed of Lord Kṛṣṇa, when while living in Dvārakā, (his son) Sāmba got a curse.

2. When Kṛṣṇa was living there with his wives and sons, once Nārada stepped in.

3. Kṛṣṇa offered him pādya, arghya, āsana, madhuparka and cow according to the usual etiquette (in receiving a distinguished guest) and began to converse with him.

4. But Nārada took Kṛṣṇa aside and spoke to him in private.

5. "I have to tell you something in secret. Please listen. Your son Sāmba is young, eloquent and handsome and is longed by all the women here.

6. The Supreme God gave you these sixteen hundred divine women for your pleasure.

7. Their minds get agitated (with love) when they see Sāmba, and this (scandal) has spread even in Brahmaloka.

8. O great god, I have come here to apprise you of this. Dvaipāyana (Vyāsa) has a significant verse relevant here, namely,

9-10. "By (proper) deeds one gets residence in heaven, and by its reverse residence in hell; the result of meritorious actions spreads all over the earth and the doer becomes the Puruṣa indestructible, unchanging and eternal and the opposite of this puts him in hell, so say the wise."

11-12. By calling Sāmba and all this multitude of women and seating them here, I shall show you whether what I say is true or false.

13. Then seats were spread for all of them and they were called and seated in groups.

14. Then Sāmba entered with folded hands and waited to know the command (of Kṛṣṇa).

15. Seeing the exceptionally handsome Sāmba, all those noble women felt agitated in mind even when Kṛṣṇa was watching them.

16. Then Kṛṣṇa asked these beloved women of his to get up and go to their homes and they did so.

17. Sāmba stood there shivering with folded hands. Looking at Nārada, Kṛṣṇa bent down his face in shame.

18. He then told Nārada in detail about the nature of women and their conduct leading to sin.

19. "They have no consideration of time, of secrecy of what they do. Still they pass to be virtuous.

20-21. Women irrespective of their age, whether they be girls, teenagers, middle-aged or advanced in age, get their passion excited at the sight of a handsome man. O great sage, this is natural to them.

22. As for Sāmba, he is dignified, bright, virtuous and good. His excitement is only because of his beauty."

23. Nārada fully agreed with Kṛṣṇa in what he said, but knowing more about the working of the mind, made a remark that led to the curse of Sāmba.

24. "A chariot does not move," (he said), "with a single wheel alone. It is only with the response of men do women get excited with passion. They get gratified by the looks of men.

25. Seeing (your other son) Pradyumna, they become highly shy.

26. But by seeing Sāmba, they become stricken with passion and the sandal paste and such other things (on his body) act as additional excitants.

27. So Sāmba must be held responsible for ruining your women and you cannot obliterate the scandal that has reached even Satyaloka.

28. I hear again and again from the people and the sages (the opinion) that you should give up Sāmba to save you from the ignominy affecting your family.

29. O great Lord, I have told you what is good for you". After saying so, Nārada remained quiet.

30. Kṛṣṇa then cursed Sāmba to become ugly and immediately he became a leper.

31. Foul-smelling blood began to ooze from his body which became full of wounds.

32. Then Nārada spoke of the means of redemption from the curse also namely the worship of the Sun.

33-34. "O Sāmba, son of Jāmbavatī, listen to me. Prostrate before the Sun uttering Vedas, Upaniṣads and the like when he rises in the eastern mountain. The Sun will be pleased in this way (and get you out of this curse), not otherwise."

Sāmba said:

35. "O sage, how can the Sun-god become pleased with a person who has committed a prohibited sexual contact ?"

Nārada said:

36. By your discussion of this, there will arise a Purāṇa by name Bhaviṣya. I will read this in Brahmaloka before Brahmā himself, and Sumantu will impart it to Manu in the world of mortals.

Sāmba said:

37. You have suggested a remedy for my present distress, but how can I go to the eastern mountain when I am reduced to the state of a mere mass of flesh ?

Nārada said:

38. The result that is obtained by worshipping the Sun-god at the eastern mountain is obtained by worshipping him at Ṣaṭsūrya in Mathurā.

39-40. Worshipping him there in the noon and evening confers even a kingdom.

41. Reciting the mantras of the Sun in the morning, noon and evening at Mathurā, one gets all sins removed.

42. By worshipping the Sun after bathing in Kṛṣṇagaṅgā, all sins disappear and so also all diseases like leprosy.

Varāha said:

43. Then at the bidding of Kṛṣṇa, Sāmba went to the city of Mathurā which brings about salvation, for worshipping the Sun.

44. He worshipped the rising sun at Ṣaṭsūrya according to the rules given by Nārada.

45. Then, by yogic power, the Sun appeared before Sāmba and asked him to seek a boon for his good and for the establishment of the Sūryavrata.

46. "Recite before me the fifty ślokas strung with expressions from the Vedas with which I was propitiated by Nārada. I am pleased by your worshipping me".

47. He was then touched by the Sun-god and soon he regained his wellshaped form and appeared like another Sun-god.

48. The Sun then taught Sāmba the sacrifice of Yājñavalkya called 'Mādhyandinīyaka' to be performed at noon whence he is Madhyandina.

49. There is the tīrtha Mādhyandinīyaka on the western side of Vaikuṇṭha (tīrtha). To bathe there and see Mādhyandina is to get free from all sins.

50. The all-pervading Sun remained with Sāmba in the morning and evening, and in the evening he stood on the southern side of Kṛṣṇagaṅgā.

51. To see the Sun there in the morning and evening is to get removed of all sins and to attain Brahman.

52. Thus appearing before Sāmba by splitting himself by the power of yoga from the sky, the Sun removed leprosy which was afflicting him.

53-54. Sāmba disappeared in the tīrtha, but was riding with the Sun in his chariot day and night and asking him about the Purāṇa spoken by him.

55. He then propagated this Purāṇa known as Bhaviṣya.

56. He then consecrated Sūrya in the rising form at Udayācala to the south of Yamunā, in the fully brilliant form at noon at Kālapriya and in the setting form at Astamanācala in Mūlasthāna.

57. Thus he consecrated Sūrya in his three forms pertaining to morning, noon and evening.

58. O Earth, in Mathurā too he established a place known after his name as Sāmbapura, according to Purāṇic rites.

59. He arranged there (the festival of) Rathayātrā as suggested by the Sun.

60. On the Saptamī day in the month of Māgha people conduct Rathayātrā there, giving up all opposites in their nature.

61. They go to the abode of peace in the regions of the Sun.

62. I have thus told you the sacred story relating to Sāmba's curse and release, which removes all sins.

CHAPTER ONE HUNDRED AND SEVENTYEIGHT

Śatrughnalavaṇa

Varāha said:

1. The fierce Lavaṇa was killed by Śatrughna (in Mathurā) for the protection of Brahmins.

2. O fair one, he who recites the account of Śatrughna, fasting on the Dvādaśī day in the month of Mārgaśīrṣa, and propitiates Brahmins with sumptuous food (gets his desires fulfilled).

3. By Śatrughna's killing of Lavaṇa, the great Rāma was extremely pleased.

4. To celebrate this victory Rāma came there from Ayodhyā with his retinue.

5-6. And Śatrughna at Mathurā fasting on the Ekādaśī day in the bright half of the month Āgrahāyaṇī, bathed in the Viśrānti tīrtha and performed the festival together with the whole family and propitiated the Brahmins with food.

7-8. He who performs this festival on the same day in the year, gets rid of all his sins and delights for long with his forefathers in heaven.

CHAPTER ONE HUNDRED AND SEVENTYNINE

Expiations for Offences

Earth said:

1. O great Lord, by committing offence to you, one becomes guilty even if otherwise not so, and is despised by Vaiṣṇavas.

2. Tell me by what acts of expiation he can get the fruits of his worship.

Varāha said:

3. "People who are sinful in thought, word and deed (commit offences). Eating the tooth-stick, eating the king's food,

4. Sexual intercourse, touching a dead body, passing motion, passing urine, sight of a woman recently delivered or during her monthly course and touch of such a woman.

5. Obscenity in speech, eating oilcake, wearing red garment, another's cloth, soiled cloth, or coloured blue with indigo,

6. False compulsions on elders, eating the food of an outcaste, eating prohibited items of food, boiled rice or myrobalan,

7. Keeping good food for oneself, eating the goose or crane, entering the temple wearing sandals,

8. Using prohibited flowers during worship, performing worship without removing the previous day's flowers or in dim light or darkness,

9. Drinking liquor, rousing the Lord in darkness, non-prostration before the Lord at the close of worship.

10. These are the thirtythree offences (connected with worship), O Earth. He who is guilty of these will never see Lord Viṣṇu.

11. The prostration should not be performed from a long distance, because then it will be like the worship by the Rākṣasa.

Taking in *pañcagavya* for one day, two days or three days, bathing along with the dress worn are the expiations in order for the offences commencing with wearing soiled cloth.

12. For the offence of using indigo, rubbing with cowdung is to be done. The offence of wearing cloth dyed with indigo is removed by the rite Prājāpatya.

13. The offence to an elder (or preceptor) can be removed

by performing Cāndrāyaṇa twice. If the food of the outcaste is eaten, both Cāndrāyaṇa and Parāka should be performed.

14. If prohibited food is eaten, Cāndrāyaṇa, Parāka and Prājāpatya should be performed and the gift of cow and food should be made in addition.

15. He who enters the place of worship wearing sandals, gets purified after fasting for five days and taking in *pañcagavya.*

16. One-fourth of a Kṛcchra and fasting for two days will be the atonement for bathing the deity and doing other items of worship without the prescribed flowers. For the offence of performing worship without removing the previous day's flowers is bath in *pañcāmṛta.*

17. For the offence of drinking liquor by the twice-born, the expiation is four Cāndrāyaṇas and three Prājāpatyas for twelve years.

18. Purification is also obtained by Brahmakūrca, gifting of three cows on a single day and by taking in *pañcāmṛta.*

19. By reciting the hymns of Viṣṇu also, one gets free from the effect of offences. I have thus told you about this important matter. What else do you wish to know ?"

20. Lord Janārdana said this again and again, but Earth seemed to be falling into a swoon.

21-22. She soon recovered and said: "Knowing about the offences starting from the sight of the recently delivered woman and the numerous expiations to be done by people, I was really lost in sorrow and stupor.

23. Is there any means by which you get propitiated in the same manner as by these rites of expiation ?"

Varāha said:

24. Bathing after due fasting in the Śaṅkara tīrtha in Gaṅgā in the middle of the year, removes the effect of offences, similarly in Mathurā.

25. He who resorts to these two tīrthas gets rid of the effect of offences he has done in a thousand lives.

26. The sins disappear by bathing there, by drinking the water there, by carrying it, by speaking about it or thinking about it, also by hearing about it and seeing it.

Earth said:

27. Both Mathurā and Śaṅkara are dear to you. Of these two, tell me which is the greater.

Varāha said:

28. Among the tīrthas of the world extending upto the ocean, Kubjāmraka is considered the most important by my devotees.

29. The Saukaratīrtha is a crore times more efficacious than that.

30. There is Sītātīrtha which is sacred to the Vaiṣṇavas on Dvādaśī day in the month of Mārgaśīrṣa. In Purāṇas this is known as Gaṅgāsāgara.

31. Even more important is the Mathurā region which is half a parārdha more efficacious than Sītātīrtha.

32. Whatever sin remains even after visiting tīrthas like Kubjāmraka, disappears quickly on reaching Mathurā.

33. The name Viśrānti (rest) is significant because the pilgrimage comes to a close there.

34. The best place for those who seek release is Mathurā.

35. Release is obtained without Sāṅkhya or Yoga in Kubjāmraka, Saukara and in Mathurā in particular. The same effect as the one obtained by a Brahmin practising yoga is obtained by dying in Mathurā.

36. I have thus told you the truth in essence. There is no tīrtha greater than Mathurā and no god greater than Keśava.

CHAPTER ONE HUNDRED AND EIGHTY

Greatness of Dhruvatīrtha in Mathurā

Varāha said:

1. I shall now tell you a story about Dhruvatīrtha which propitiates the manes.

2. In this city there was a valiant, virtuous and magnanimous king named Candrasena.

3. He had two hundred young and noble wives among whom was one, Candraprabhā of an ascetic turn of mind, although the mother of valiant sons.

4. Among her hundred attendants, there was one named Prabhāvatī. The manes for whom obsequial rites were due from her (servant) had not got the Ekoddiṣṭa ceremony done.

5. Their number exceeded a hundred and they all fell into hell because of this.

6. And it is well known that this sort of mixture leads to hell as it violates the rules of the family.

7. Then thrown out from there, all of them came to Dhruvatīrtha as a cluster of minute beings, black in colour and resembling mosquitoes.

8. They were seen there by the sage Trikālajña who was mainly living on water and taking food only once in three days.

9. He was observing the vow of silence and was following the course of the sun, but at that moment he was stupefied and did not perform japa.

10. While he was looking at them with compassion and curiosity, three quarters of the day passed.

11. Some manes came to the earth from the sky, others from the north, east, south and west.

12. Some were happy by themselves, some were made happy by their sons and they all went upwards with nourished bodies, pleased and satisfied.

13. They had all small bodies and they were interested in bath and penance. They had good dress and decorations and were moving about in groups in delight.

14. There were others who were naked but nourished.

15. Still others returned as they came and came back again. Some came in various kinds of vehicles and others came on birds.

16. Some returned after pronouncing benedictions and others pronouncing curses in anger.

17. Some who came famished returned well-fed in Śrāddha.

18. The sage rose up after seeing all this as if it was a festival and when the manes were gone, their sons returned home with their wives.

19. Soon Dhruvatīrtha became desolate. But in one remote corner there was a puny being, very much famished and unable to move.

20. It was shivering, its eyes had gone low and belly much depressed. Its feet were mere skeleton. Its voice was feeble like that of a tiny bird.

The sage asked:

21. Who are you that look so mutilated and surrounded by these mosquitoes?

22. Having come here you don't attempt to return. Tell me about what you have done.

23. My daily routine in this tīrtha is badly affected as I was stupefied at the sight of these numerous beings of various sorts here.

24. Seeing you in this form, my attention was turned towards you. Tell me with confidence all about you. I shall do you good.

The being said:

25. "The greatest means of propitiation for the manes is the performance of Śrāddha in Dhruvatīrtha and offering of water with sesamum.

26. Manes who have sons go to heaven being propitiated with sesamum. I am famished for want of such a thing.

27. Due to the guilt of mixture of caste, I fell into hell and have been there for a hundred years hoping against hope.

28. I have no means to go from here. Those who were propitiated with śrāddha and libations by their sons went to heaven. What way is there out for one like me?

29. Those who have a line of progeny, get propitiation from their sons and attain liberation.

30. The manes of King Candrasena were propitiated today, and, O Trikālajña, you saw them going to heaven with your divine eye.

31-32. You saw here what happened to the manes of Brāhmaṇas, Kṣatriyas, Vaiśyas, and Śūdras and the performance of Śrāddha by Śūdras, the progeny of *hypergamous* and *hypergampous* marriages."

33. Thus he said to the Brahmin the cause of his remaining there. The sage then spoke to him in curiosity.

34. "Due to fate you have no proper progeny. If I can do

anything to help you to get out of your present state, please tell me".

35. Remaining in that despicable condition surrounded by the manes, he said:

36. "The emaciated mosquitoes that cover my body remain so due to the lack of progeny. I am the slender thread for them to hold on.

37. In the palace of Candrasena at the centre of the city, there is the servant of the queen by name Prabhāvatī.

38. She too has a servant by name Virūpanidhi.

39. She is the continuing thread in our progeny and we are eagerly awaiting for the śrāddha to be performed by her for us.

40. All this long time we have been spending in this water and now we have to return to hell because of our own deeds".

41. Hearing this Trikālajña was baffled and said: "How can the libation offered by a lowborn woman be of any use to you ? By what rule can she be your proper issue?"

42. Hearing this, he told the learned and merciful Trikālajña:

43. "People desire to have sons because even when they fall down (in hell), they are raised up and sent upwards by (the proper actions of) the son.

44. The manes have the service of the son done, if they perform śrāddha, libation of piṇḍa and gifts on normal as well as special occasions. They have no other way.

45. Howmuch do we wish that at least one among our progeny gives us libation !

46. Standing in waist-deep water in rivers full of cool water, and particularly at the middle of the tīrtha spot, he should offer handfuls of water together with sesamum.

47. He should do this with darbha in his hand and three times each for the manes uttering the gotra and name of each of them and saying 'svadhā' and 'may my manes be pleased'.

48. It should be known that in propitiating the gods, sages and manes (Devas, Ṛṣis and Pitṛs) the number of handfuls of water is to be respectively one, two and three.

49. In the end should be uttered the mantra *tṛpyadhvam* (may you all be pleased').

50. First should be given the three libations to the father reciting the mantras *Udiratām* etc, *Aṅgiraso* etc, and *Āyantu naḥ* etc, in order, and then to the mother uttering the gotra and name and also *svadhā* and *tṛpyatu*.

51. Then for the mother's father with gotra and name, and similarly for father's father.

52. For these the mantras *ūrdhvam pitṛbhyaḥ* etc, *Ye ceha te pitaraḥ* etc, and *Madhu vātā* etc, should be used.

53. Then it should be done for father's mother and grandmother as in the case of the mother and then for mother's father and grandfather each three times separately uttering the mantra *Namo vaḥ pitaraḥ* etc.

54. In each case utter the gotra and *Asūryān nāśayāmahe*. Offer āsana (seat) uttering the gotra and the particular Pitṛ by his name.

55. In the case of the female Pitṛs also utter the gotra and the particular pitṛ (*mātā, mātāmahi*) by name (*devi*) for āsana. Similarly for *pitāmaha* (grand-father).

56. In the saṅkalpa for *arghya*, in *piṇḍa* and in *avanejana* (pouring water over the piṇḍa) the form should be (genitive) as *gotrasya, piturṁahasya* and *śarmaṇaḥ*, for females (dative) as *gotrāyai, māturmahyai, devyai*.

57. In *āvāhana* (invocation) the form should be accusative, in worship dative and in benediction nominative.

58. In śrāddha it should be genitive for *ādāna* and *akṣaya* (praying for their eternal abode in heaven). At the times prescribed for *akṣaya*, the *datta* rite should be performed for the manes.

59. The twice-born son who does this devotedly or offers even water with full devotion, leads them to eternality.

60. When the Brahmin performs Śrāddha with due attention and in the prescribed manner, the manes become happy.

61. O Trikālajña, remain quiet. We now go to Naraka (hell) to live there long because of the result of our former deeds".

Trikālajña said:

62. Among the manes I saw there in this tīrtha many were happy and many unhappy too.

63. Some received Śrāddha offered by the sons in great anxiety and some returned mum. Please tell me why this was so.

Agastya said :

64. The śrāddha performed by the son sometimes goes in vain and sometimes even leads to hell. I shall tell you, please listen.

65. What is given at the wrong place and time, given without proper rites or dakṣiṇā, or given to the unsuitable person and is impure, produces great sin.

66. The śrāddha done without the necessary attention, not in the proper form, seen by the bad, or without sesamum, mantra or kuśa grass, becomes *āsura* (demoniac).

67. It is well known that Lord Vāmana gave the fruit of the śrāddha of Śūdras to Vairocana (Mahābali).

68-69. Similarly, Rāma, son of Daśaratha, after killing Rāvaṇa, the chief of the Rākṣasas, with all army, became pleased to hear about the devotion of Rākṣaṣī Trijaṭā, and gave her a boon.

70-71. "O Trijaṭā, I give to you all the Śrāddha offerings done in unclean houses, those done without pādya, without oil, without food or without dakṣiṇā and the gifts given with anger although to the proper persons."

72. Similarly, Śrāddha was given to Vāsuki, the king of serpents, by Śiva who was pleased with him. I shall tell you about this, please listen.

73. "The annual śrāddha done by the twice-born without proper dakṣiṇā even if all the rituals are observed,

74. Done by one who takes false resolve in the presence of gods and Brahmins, done without the proper rites and mantras,

75. Done by one who bathes at night with the dress worn, who does not respect the teacher who imparts knowledge,

76. Done by one who propagates primitive ideals—I give to you". (So said Śiva).

77. We hear about such things from the Purāṇas and Itihāsas.

78. Śrāddha, dāna and vrata done without sincerity, never produce their results. Hence the nakedness etc., of these manes.

79. Due to such defects in the conduct of śrāddha, the manes who are invoked, do not get result and they return as they came.

80. Having come to receive, they return silently. This I say in reply to what you ask.

Trikālajña said:

81. "I have been taking food only once in three days. But even that I don't wish to take till you are satisfied. Be cheerful and await my return.

82-83. Out of compassion for you, I am giving up my routine austerities here to hasten to bring that woman here.

84. I shall see that she performs śrāddha here according to the prescribed rules."

85. So saying, the sage quickly left the place (and went to the king).

86. Seeing the sage suddenly there, the king fell down at his feet and said: "I feel honoured and favoured indeed by your coming to my home. I shall arrange for all sacrificial rites due therefore. My life is made fruitful by your presence here.

87. Here is the *pādya*, here is the *arghya*, here is *madhuparka* and here the cow. Receive them, O sage, so that my mind may rest satisfied."

88. Receiving the hearty welcome, the sage said:

89. "O king, great is the purpose with which I have come here. Do now what I ask you to do so that I may be happy".

90. Thus asked, the saintly king replied: "Please tell me that purpose so that I can see it accomplished."

Trikālajña said:

91. "Call your queen and also her beautiful attendant Prabhāvatī before me here."

92. Then came there from the harem the queen with the attendant and prostrated at the feet of the sage.

93. When they were seated, the sage said to them: "I shall tell you about something strange that happened in Dhruvatīrtha.

94. The manes from all the worlds came there and, propitiated by their sons by performing śrāddha, went to heaven.

95. There was, however, a very old one among them extremely emaciated and fatigued by thirst and hunger and surrounded by numerous minute beings.

96. He was very much disappointed and was preparing to return to hell. Then out of pity I asked him who he was and what his wish.

97. Then he told me what had come upon him as a result of his own deeds. I sympathised with him and came here.

98. Your servant's servant by name Virūpanidhi is his progeny. Please call her here."

99. The queen then sent many persons to find her out and bring her there.

100. She was found fully intoxicated and still taking meat and drink and seated on the bed with a man.

101. The queen's man caught hold of her and brought her before the sage.

102. Although she was in that drunken state, the sage told her about what she was to do.

103. "You have not made for your manes any gift libation or other ablutions. Nor have you done for them the propitiatory offering of water".

104. She said that she had not done any of these and that she did not know who her manes were and what rites she was to do.

105. When she said so, Trikālajña said, "May the king of Mathurā, with his queen and all good people in this city witness the wonder of what progeny can do to the manes".

106-107. Then all those curious people and the virtuous Brahmins were called together and the king proceeded with them accompanied by the sage to Dhruvatīrtha.

108. There, that being was seen extremely fatigued and surrounded by the mosquitoes.

109. The sage then told him, "Your descendant has been brought here for your propitiation. Do what you please".

Agastya said:

110. Let her bathe in the Dhruvatīrtha and offer libation according to the rules enunciated.

111. Let her then perform Śrāddha with dakṣiṇā, cloth and sandal-paste and give piṇḍa in veneration.

112. By making her do this śrāddha you can see me here made happy".

113. Hearing this, the queen made that servant perform śrāddha with abundant dakṣiṇā,

114. And fine cloth and good incense and camphor and sandal followed by sesamum, many kinds of food and piṇḍa.

115-116. When Śrāddha was thus done and piṇḍa offered, he attained a divine form, so too those surrounding him. He looked like a sacrificer after the concluding bath. Those in the mosquito form were transformed into handsome persons.

117. The sky was covered with aerial cars from heaven, and as he was preparing to get into it, he spoke to the sage and the king:

118. "Be pleased to listen to what I say regarding the propitiation of the manes.

119. There are many sacred tīrthas, rivers, mountains and ponds and places like Kurukṣetra and Gayā and many temples.

120. But a place like this for the propitiation of the manes, there never was and never will be.

121. From the first day in the month of Aṣāḍha till the first day in the bright half of the month Āśvina, the manes remain here enjoying the śrāddha and the piṇḍa.

122. In fact, during this period, the city of the god of death, heaven and the netherworld become practically empty since the manes flock here desiring the offerings of their son or any other descendant or brother.

123. He who performs śrāddha and tarpaṇa in Dhruvatīrtha when the sun enters the Kanyā rāśi (Virgo), propitiates sixteen generations of his manes very much.

124. We are now fully propitiated and we are all liberated. Such is the greatness of Dhruvatīrtha.

125. You have now seen the wonder of what has happened to us. By your kindness, O sage, we have become absolved of all sins".

126. Telling thus to the king, the sage, the people assembled, the queen, the servant and his own daughter, he bade them all well.

127. He then got into the aerial car and ascended to heaven surrounded by gods.

Varāha said:

128. Astonished at the greatness of that tīrtha, the king bowed to the sage and returned to his palace with his people and attendants, always thinking of Lord Viṣṇu.

129. I have thus told you, O auspicious one, about the great-

ness of Mathurā, the very thought of which removes even the sins acquired in former lives.

130. He who recites this with attention before Brahmins, propitiates all his forefathers.

131. This should not be narrated to any one who does not undertake vows, who does not listen with attention or one who does not worship Hari.

132. This is the greatest of all tīrthas, the highest of all dharmas, the most exalted of all knowledge and the best of all gains.

133. O blessed one, this should always be narrated to the meritorious devotees of the Lord.

Sūta said:

134. Earth was full of wonder hearing these words of the Lord and asked him in joy about the erection of idols.

CHAPTER ONE HUNDRED AND EIGHTYONE

Consecration of Wooden Images

Sūta said:

1. Having heard about this place of supreme importance, Earth asked again out of curiosity.

Earth said:

2. "How great is the prowess of this place about which you have so kindly told me ! Hearing this, I have really become free from all uneasiness.

3. But I have long been wishing to know about one secret. Be pleased to tell me that for my enlightenment.

4. That is this: How do you remain (in idols of) wood, stone or clay,

5. (In idols of) copper, bronze, silver or gold?

6. How do you remain in (idols of) ivory.

7. O Janārdana, how do you remain in a wall (in picture) and how on earth (in pictures drawn with powers) ?"

8. Hearing these words of Earth, the Primeval Boar replied.

Varāha said:

9. First of all, the material in which the idol is to be made should be brought and the idol moulded or carved according to the rules.

10. The purification of the idol should then be made and then it should be consecrated. Worship for release from saṁsāra may be started thereafter.

11. The Madhūka tree may be used for cutting wooden idols. After consecration, it may be worshipped with the kind of sandal paste mentioned before,

12. As also with camphor, saffron, Agaru, benzoin and powder of fragrant roots.

13. The idol may be smeared with these. Svastika and Vardhamāna hymns are to be recited and Śrīvatsa and Kaustubha are to be offered.

14. The auspicious pāyasa should be offered (in naivedya). Scented wicks are to be lighted and sesamum and fruits to be offered.

15. With cleanliness, purity and devotion the worship is to be made with all that is prescribed.

16. Prāṇāyāma (control of breath) should then be made and the following mantras uttered:

17. "Be pleased to remain in this (idol made of) wood, you with the power of yoga pervading the whole world".

18. Thus consecrating the Lord in the wooden idol, it should be circumambulated together with other devotees.

19-20. A lamp should be then lit facing the idol and, without looking upwards or sideways and free from desire and anger, *Namo nārāyaṇāya* (Bow to Nārāyaṇa) should be uttered, and then reciting the following mantra, the ritual is to be performed.

21. The Mantra: "You, the most heroic of all, remain as the unfailing lord and refuge of all. O Lord of the worlds, Vāsudeva, may you by this mantra remain consecrated in this."

22. After completing the rite of my consecration, all the devotees assembled there should be honoured.

23. They should be honoured according to the prescribed rules with sandal, garlands, unguents and food.

24. O fair one, this is the way to consecrate the wooden idol. I have told this to you for the sake of *dharma*.

25. He who consecrates the wooden idol in this way never returns to *saṁsāra* but goes to my world.

CHAPTER ONE HUNDRED AND EIGHTYTWO

Consecration of Stone Images

Varāha said:

1. I shall tell you now how I am to be consecrated in stone images.

2. A beautiful, flawless stone should be selected after careful examination and a quick and clever artisan should be engaged to carve out the image. The outline may be made with a white brush.

3. After circumambulation, worship should be made with rice grains and the like.

4. Lamp should then be offered and then rice with curd. Then *Namo nārāyaṇāya* (Bow to Nārāyaṇa) should be uttered and the following mantra recited.

5. The mantra: "You are the most heroic of all, the foremost among the intelligent and effulgent like the sun, the moon and the fire. May you be consecrated here by this mantra and may fame increase. Hail, hail, great Varāha".

6. Whatever is necessary should be done with this mantra. Consecrating Lord Nārāyaṇa in this form, he should be installed facing east.

7-8. Fasting for a whole day and night, wearing white dress and white Yajñopavīta, and after cleaning the teeth, the following mantra should be uttered taking sandal water.

9. The mantra: "O Lord of the worlds, you who are the entire world with all forms, remain worshipped in this. You are always held in the mind, you are the supreme example of indestructibility, you are never defeated, you have no old age or death. Being worshipped, fix yourself here by this mantra *Om namo Vāsudevāya*.

10. After this consecration, the stone idol should be given *adhivāsana* (rest on a substratum) in the asterism Proṣṭapada.

11. He who instals me in this manner, goes to the world of Viṣṇu. There need be no doubt about this.

12. The whole day and night should be spent thus eating only wheat cooked in milk. (The next day) during the evening sandhyā four lamps should be offered.

13. At the foot of the deity four small pots containing water mixed with *pañcagavya* and sandal should be placed.

14. A festival should be conducted with vocal and instrumental music and recitation of Sāmaveda by Brahmins should be arranged.

15. I make my presence there when thousands of Vedic syllables are uttered in proper tone and tune, because, O goddess, the recitation of Vedic mantras is dear to me.

16. The idol should then be installed in the company of devotees and invocation should be made with the following mantra:

17. "Come here, O lord, with the mantras, the five sense organs and the mind. You, the dispenser, remain in all these beings".

18. With the same mantra, hundred and eight *āhutis* (offerings in fire) should be made using twigs, sesamum clarified butter and honey.

19. When all this is done, I voluntarily make my presence in the idol.

20. When the night is over and the day dawns, *pañcagavya* should be offered with mantra as prescribed.

21. Sandal, fried rice and water with *pañcagavya* should then be given and the idol installed in the temple with vocal and instrumental music and recitation of auspicious hymns.

22-23. Taking different kinds of sandal paste, the mantra should be recited: "O Primeval being, may you who have been here according to the prescribed rules, be pleased to enter this temple with all effulgence together with Lakṣmī. Bow to you again and again."

24. With this mantra the idol should be taken into the temple and placed there in the exact centre, not on the side.

25. The idol should then be erected. Sandal, saffron etc., should be applied and the following mantra should be recited:

26. "O Lord of the world, you are the foremost in the world, worshipped by Brahmā and Bṛhaspati. Remain here welcomed and saluted with mantras".

27. After installation in this manner, worship should be made with sandal and garlands. White cloth should then be offered with the following mantra:

28. The mantra: "O Lord, accept these garments given by me with devotion and put them on. Be pleased with me. Bow to you again and again".

29. Clothes should be offered to me in this way following the rules. Incense should then be offered with Agaru and saffron. While giving this *dhūpa* the following is the mantra:

30. "You are the most ancient Man, the foremost in the world and without a beginning. Accept this sandal, garlands, incense and lamp, O Lord. Bow to you again and again."

31. After this food should be offered as before.

32. For this the same mantras as before may be used. Then should be given water for cleaning.

33. Śāntijapa should then be conducted, which accomplishes all desires, with the mantra: "O Lord of the worlds, bestow peace on the king and the kingdom and on the Brahmins. Bestow peace on the infants and the aged, on herds of cows, virgins and chaste women.

34. May ailments vanish everywhere, may the farmers always get good yield. May the world be prosperous and peaceful with the rains falling in time."

35-36. After performing worship to the Lord in this manner with all the rites, Brahmins should be feasted and the poor fed according to capacity.

37. He who instals me in this way remains in my world for as many thousands of years as there are waterdrops in my body.

38. O Earth, he who does all this without any ego liberates seven, seven and seventy in his clan.

39. Thus have I told you about the installation of stone idols for the sake of *dharma* and for the good of devotees.

CHAPTER ONE HUNDRED AND EIGHTYTHREE

Consecration of Clay images

Varāha said:

1. I shall now tell you another thing, namely my presence in idols made of clay. Please listen.

2. The idol in clay should not have any defect or crack. It should be neither too big nor too short nor having any bend.

3. With such an idol my devotee can perform worship as he likes.

4. The clay idol may be used when one in wood or stone is not available.

5. Idols are also made in copper, bronze, silver and gold by experts for auspicious purposes.

6. My worship in the pedestal is done by some out of devotion, by others to avoid censure and by still others for publicity.

7. I am also worshipped for domestic prosperity. Even the disc which has arisen out of my effulgence may be worshipped.

8. O Earth, know that when I am installed like this and worshipped, I give all wealth.

9. With whatever aim a man worships me in proper form with mantras, I give that with pleasure.

10. He attains beatitude by my grace.

11. My devotee who is full of things to do, may please me by mental worship.

12. I will be pleased by his mere giving me a handful of water. Why should he bother about flowers, Japa and rules?

13. I grant all desires and give divine enjoyment to him who meditates well on me.

14. I have told you all this secret incidentally.

15. My devotee who takes the clay image may perform its *adhivāsa* in the asterism Śravaṇa and then consecrate it according to the rites mentioned before.

16. Bath may be then done to the idol with water mixed with *pañcagavya* and sandal with the following mantra:

17. "O Great Lord, master of all worlds, the worlds arise out of your grace. O Acyuta, extend to me your grace and remain in the idols of clay. Bow to you again and again, the cause of all causes, the great Man beaming with great lustre."

18. By this mantra, it may be taken into the house and installed and then, as before, four pots may be placed and the following mantra uttered:

19. The mantra: "Om, the ocean having got Varuṇa was honoured with self-satisfaction. By this mantra I perform the bath and always bow with raised hands Him from whom arise fire, earth and all tastes."

20. After this bathing ritual, the devotee should worship with sandal and garlands as before.

21. He may offer incense with Agaru, camphor and saffron uttering *Namo nārāyaṇāya* (Bow to Nārāyaṇa).

22. After incense, yellow garment is to be offered uttering *Namo nārāyaṇāya* and the following mantra should be recited:

23. "The lord becomes pleased by the yellow garment, and when he becomes pleased, the whole world becomes happy. May the lord accept this garment and protect me from the bondage of worldly existence."

24. Having offered the garment with this mantra, incense and lamp should be given and then food.

25. The offering of food should be as stated before and then water should be given with the mantra.

26. (Peace should be prayed for with) the mantra: "Let there be peace for the gods, Brahmins, Kṣatriyas and Vaiśyas. May the rain god shower rain and make the earth full of vegetation."

27. After Śānti with this mantra, the other devotees should be honoured and the Brahmins fed.

28. The devotee should prostrate before them and give them dakṣiṇās.

29. Words of maṅgala should then be recited and the deity should be released.

30. After the release, those assembled there should be honoured with clothes and decorations. The preceptor should then be honoured if union with me is desired.

31. I tell you the truth, O goddess, that if the Guru is properly worshipped, I become worshipped.

32. The king, when pleased, may grant but a village; but when the Guru is pleased, he leads one easily upto the state of becoming Brahman.

33. Therefore, in all Śāstras, the worship of the Guru is ordained in my own words.

34. He who performs my consecration in this way liberates three, thirty and seventy in his clan.

35. He remains in my world for as many thousands of years as there are drops of water falling in worship.

36. Thus have I told you, O Earth, about the consecration of clay idols. I shall tell you now another thing dear to my devotees.

CHAPTER ONE HUNDRED AND EIGHTYFOUR

Consecration of Copper Images

Varāha said:

1. Getting a beautiful image made of copper, it should be brought to the middle of the abode with due rites.

2. It should be placed facing north and the *adhivāsana* should be done in the asterism Citrā.

3. Bath should then be conducted with water mixed with *pañcagavya* and sandal and with the following mantras:

4. The Mantra: "You, the essence of everything, remain in copper as the eye. O, the abode of all worlds, come to this idol with the five elements."

5. After consecrating with this mantra, *adhivāsana* and worship should be done as before.

6. When the night is over and the sun rises, purification should be done with mantras of the Ṛgveda and bath should be performed with mantras.

7. The Brahmins assembled may recite the Vedas. Auspicious materials may be placed in the Maṇḍapa.

8. The devotee should then bring scented water and bathe me with the following mantra:

9. The mantra: "O Lord of worlds, you are the greatest of all with power of *māyā* and *yoga*. Be pleased to come quick for my sake and remain in this copper image. O Lord, the best of Men, fire, Sun and air, be here yourself, Om".

10. Then I should be led into the sanctum and installed on a pedestal and worship done.

11. The installation should be done with the following mantra and with sandal, flowers and lamps.

12. The mantra for installation: "Om, the light of all light, the light of the world, the embodiment of knowledge, embodiment of bliss, the lord of the universe, be pleased to come and remain here, O the best of Men, and protect me".

13. After installation in this way, white cloth should be offered with the mantra: "Om, O lord of the celestials, the pure soul, the most ancient Man, the truth of the worlds, accept these clothes. Bow to Puruṣottama."

14. After dressing me with the clothes, the devotee should perform *arcana* (with flowers).

15. After *arcana* and offering of sandal, incense etc, the offering of food should be made.

16. When the *naivedya* with delicious food is over, *Śāntipāṭha* (invocation of peace) should be made.

17. The mantra: "Let there be peace for the gods, peace for the Brahmins, peace for the kings and their kingdoms, peace for Vaiśyas, peace for boys and pregnant women. Let there be peace everywhere by your grace, O Lord".

18. After uttering this *Śānti*, the Brahmins should be honoured.

19. Then the Guru should be honoured and the Brahmins should be fed according to capacity.

20. Particularly when the Guru is honoured with clothes, decorations and food, I am worshipped and this is the truth, I tell you.

21. I am far away from him whose Guru is not pleased.

22. He who performs my installation in this way, liberates thirtysix generations in his family.

23. Thus have I told you about the installation of idols. He who does this remains in my world for as many thousands of years as there are drops in the water during the bath given to me.

CHAPTER ONE HUNDRED AND EIGHTYFIVE

Consecration of bronze images

Varāha said:

1-2. Getting a well-made, complete and beautiful idol in bronze, the devotee may take it into the temple to the accompaniment of song and drums and all that is auspicious.

3. Then taking *arghya* in the proper manner, the following mantra should be uttered:

4. "O Lord of the worlds, worshipped in all sacrifices, contemplated upon, the desire of the whole universe, the great soul, the master benign, may you be pleased with me and remain for worship here".

5. After this *arghya*, the idol should be placed facing north and *adhivāsana* done in the prescribed manner.

6. Then four pots should be got ready for my bath containing *pañcagavya*, sandal paste, fried rice and honey.

7-8. When the sun has set, the worshipper may perform consecration holding pots and in the company of other devotees.

9. He should utter *Namo Nārāyaṇāya* and recite the following mantra:

10. "O lord of the worlds, you are the primeval being remaining through all aeons and the dispenser for all time. You are one, you have no second. Please come and take your abode here. You are all the transformations, but you yourself have no transformation. You are the letters A, S, Ś, Ṣ. You take forms at will. The decaying, the undecaying, the sustaining, the formless are all you. Bow to you, O Puruṣottama".

11. When the night is over and the sun is rising and when the latter part of asterism Mūla is reached,

12. According to the rites mentioned before, the idol may be placed at the door-way of the Sanctum.

13. Then taking the sacred water, sandal and fruits, the devotee should utter *Namo nārāyaṇāya* and recite the following mantra:

14. "Om, You are Indra, yourself (Viṣṇu), Yama, Kubera, Varuṇa, Soma, Bṛhaspati, Śukra, Śani, Budha, Rāhu, Ketu, Sūrya and Kuja.

15. Your are herbs, waters, air, earth, fire, Nāgas, Yakṣas and quarters. Bow to you, O Puruṣottama."

16. Doing well all the rituals with this mantra, the idol may be taken into the sanctum.

17. It may then be bathed with the water with sandal kept in the pots.

18. During the bath, the following mantra may be recited:

19. "For you, Puruṣottama, may the lakes, oceans, rivers, tīrthas and wells, make their presence here by your grace for this bath".

20. I may be installed in this manner and then worshipped with sandal, incense etc, according to the materials available.

21. Then clothes should be offered as also decorations for pleasure.

22. Placing the clothes before me and prostrating at my feet, the following mantra may be recited.

23. "O lord of the worlds, I have brought here for you nice and beautiful clothes pleasant to put on. Be pleased to receive them. O Veda, Upaveda, Ṛgveda, Yajurveda, Sāmaveda, Atharvaveda, I extol you. Bow to you, O most supreme".

24. After decoration in the manner stated before, food is to be offered as prescribed.

25. After food, water should be given, and then *śāntipāṭha* should be recited in the form of the following mantra:

26. "May all knowledge, Brahman, Brahmins, planets, rivers and oceans, Indra and other guardian deities of the quarters bring about peace. *Āyāma, Yama, Kāmadama, Vāma Om namaḥ puruṣottamāya.*"

27. When all these *upacāras* (services) are over, circumambulation should be made and then *abhivādana* and *stuti* (praise).

28. Then the pure devotees should be honoured and the Brahmins fed with *pāyasa* and other materials.

29. Sacred water should be received from the Brahmins and sprinkled on me. Then after sending them off, worship of the Guru should be performed.

30. There is no doubt that I become worshipped when the preceptor is honoured with ring, garments and other gifts.

31. It is also true that I see to the extinction of those that condemn the Brahmins, my devotees and the preceptors.

32. He who instals me in this manner remains in my world for as many thousands of years as there are drops of water in my body.

33. He liberates every one in his paternal and maternal lines.

34. I have thus told you about the consecration of bronze images.

35. I shall tell you now about the consecration of silver images.

CHAPTER ONE HUNDRED AND EIGHTYSIX

Consecration of silver and golden Images

Varāha said:

1. Getting a pure, well-shaped and well-proportioned silver image, free from all defects,

2. White like the moon and radiating lustre in all directions,

3. The devotee may take it to the temple to the accompaniment of music and the sound of the conch and drums and praises and benedictions.

4. Then taking water for *arghya* and *pādya*, the following mantra is to be recited:

5. The mantra: "O lord of worlds, you who are the *arghya* in all worlds, worshipped by all and honoured by the celestials, the master of my Agnihotra done at Sunrise, be pleased to come here and receive this *arghya*. The glow residing in the middle of the sun".

6. After giving *arghya* with this mantra, the idol should be placed facing north.

7. On the day when the asterism Āśleṣā is in the Zodiacal house Karkaṭaka, when the sun has set, the *adhivāsana* should be done with mantras and in the prescribed manner.

8. Four pots filled with sandal water should be placed there with all herbs and decorated with mango twigs.

9. Then the devotees should do the rituals as instructed by the preceptor.

10. *Namo Nārāyaṇāya* should be uttered and the following mantra recited:

11. The mantra: "O lord the creator of all worlds, the ruler of all, the form of all forms, worshipped by Dhruva and the deities guarding the quarters, be pleased to make your presence in this idol . Bow to Ananta."

12. When the night is over and the sun rises and the quarters are clear, it should be taken to the doorway of the sanctum.

13. Then my devotees should perform the bathing ceremony there.

14. He may perform this bath in the prescribed manner uttering *Namo nārāyaṇāya* and reciting the following mantra:

15. "This water I have brought, O lord, from rivers like Gaṅgā and the Oceans and scented with camphor for your bath".

16. The idol should be taken to the interior and installed there with the following mantra:

17. "O lord of the worlds, known through the Vedas, worshipped by those who know the Vedas, having the form of sacrifice, the giver of the fruit of sacrifice, I invoke you here for sacrifice. Be pleased to remain in this idol. Wealth, people, silver, gold, bow to Ananta."

18. After installation in this manner with a pleasant mind, *arcanā* should be done in the manner stated before.

19. Then blue garments may be offered, as they are dear to me.

20. Taking clothes and kneeling down, *Namo Nārāyaṇāya* should be uttered and the following mantra recited.

21. The mantra: "O lord, resplendent like moonbeams, resembling the conch, jasmine and milk, may you be pleased to accept these garments for my sake : Dress, good dress, O lord, endless, imperishable, causing death, Cause, easy to obtain, difficult to attain, the supreme".

22. After giving me clothes with this mantra, food is to be given with all reverence, uttering *Namo nārāyaṇāya* and reciting the following mantra:

23. "O lord Puruṣottama, may you be pleased to receive this food containing cooked rice and *pāyasa* with sugar and ghee".

24. After this *naivedya,* water should be given.

25. For the welfare of the world, *Śāntipāṭha* should be recited.

26. "Om, peace is brought about by Brahmā, Rudra, Viṣṇu, Sūrya, Rātrī, Sandhyā, Nakṣatras and Diks. Motionless, vibrating, moving, moving in the sky, rapidly moving, having the hue of lotus, Bow to Vāsudeva."

27. After the *Śāntipāṭha* which removes sins, the devotees should be honoured.

28. The Brahmins should then be fed according to capacity and water taken from them should be sprinkled on me.

29. Then Brahmins and relatives should be sent off with folded hands.

30. The preceptor should be worshipped with gifts. When he is worshipped, I am worshipped.

31. He who does this remains in my world for as many thousands of years as there are drops of water falling at the end of the meal.

32. He who worships in this manner liberates his paternal and maternal lines.

33. This is the way to instal silver images. I shall now tell you about the installation of golden images.

34. The golden image may be made in the same manner as the silver image and invocation etc., may be made similarly.

35. The benefit of erecting idols in wood, stone, bronze etc., becomes a crore times more with golden images.

36. Twentyone generations are liberated (by one installing golden idols) and he is finally merged in me without being born again.

37. O Earth, I have thus told you what you desired to know. What else am I to tell you?

Earth said:

38. You have now told me about the idols made of gold and other metals. You remain in all these, no doubt, but you remain in Sālagrāmas too.

39. O Mādhava, be pleased to tell me the number (of these Sālagrāmas) to be worshipped in homes and the general and special benefits arising therefrom, as also the number in worshipping Śiva and other deities.

Varāha said:

40. In the house two (Śiva)liṅgas should not be worshipped, so also three Sālagrāmas.

41. Two Cakras from Dvārakā should not be worshipped, so also two Sūryas. Three Gaṇeśas should not be worshipped, so also three Śaktis (Ambikās)."

42. A Pair of Śālagrāmas should be worshipped, but not two pairs. Odd number should not be worshipped because this amounts to a single one.

43. Burnt or broken (Sālagrāmas) should not be worshipped at home, as this may bring about calamities.

44. But even if broken, if the Cakra is clear, then it is good enough.

45. I shall tell you, O Earth, the merit of worshipping twelve Sālagrāmas.

46. The same result is attained in a single day as of worshipping twelve crores of liṅgas worshipped with golden lotuses for twelve aeons.

47. The merit that accrues to a man worshipping a hundred Sālagrāmas, I am unable to recount even for hundred years.

48. All deities can be worshipped in idols by people of all castes. Crystal liṅgas can also be done similarly.

49. But a Sālagrāma should not be touched by men of inferior caste or by women and Śūdras.

50. If a woman or Śūdra touches it even out of curiosity, the result will be torment in hell till deluge.

51. But if a woman or Śūdra has devotion (for me through the Śālagrāma), then worship may be got performed by others without oneself touching it. The drinking of that water (used for worship) removes all sins.

52. The offerings made to Śiva like leaf, flower, fruit and water, are prohibited from use. But they get purified by association with Śālagrāma.

53. I shall tell you the merit that accrues to a person who makes gift of a Śālagrāma together with some gold to a devotee.

54. It is equivalent to making gift to a worthy person of the whole earth with its gold, mountains, forests and oceans.

55. Sale of a Śālagrāma leads to hell both the seller and the buyer.

56. I will be unable to say in full about the good results o this worship even if I take a hundred years.

57. I have thus told you about the installation of idols and the specialities relating to the Śālagramas and the Liṅgas.

58. I have also told you about the rules in worship. What else do you wish to know ?

CHAPTER ONE HUNDRED AND EIGHTYSEVEN

The origin of Śrāddha

Sūta s aid:

1. Hearing all this from Lord Nārāyaṇa, the ascetic Earth asked Him again with folded hands.

Earth said:

2. I have now heard this great narration and the great merit that results from the place. But I wish to know another secret and it behoves you to tell me that.

3. You told me about Pitṛyajña (rites to propitiate the manes) in connection with the hunting adventure of King Somadatta.

4. What is the merit of Pitṛyajña and how is it to be done ? Who conceived of this Śrāddha, for what purpose and of what nature is it ?

5. I wish to know all this. Please tell me in detail.

Varāha said:

It is quite proper that you ask me this.

6. Because of the weight you have to bear, you have become stupefied. But I shall give you divine intelligence to enable you, O fair one, to grasp the significance.

7. I shall tell you about the origin of Śrāddha, but before that I shall tell you about the origin of heaven and Devas.

8. When there was no light and darkness was spreading everywhere, the idea dawned upon me to create the three worlds with all their moving and non-moving beings.

9. I was then all alone, sleeping on the bed formed by the serpent Śeṣa and not inclined to activity.

10. I keep awake and fall asleep due to my power of Māyā, and this Viṣṇumāyā, O Earth, you are unable to know.

11. Thousands of aeons have passed and thousands will be coming. Still māyā is unintelligible to you.

12. I have held you with this boar form of mine for five hundred divine years. Still you have not known this.

13. That is why you ask me this question. (I shall tell you). My single form became transformed into three, namely Brahmā, Viṣṇu and Hara.

14. Because of anger I created Īśvara (Hara), the destroyer of Asuras. From my navel appeared a lotus and Brahmā was within it.

15. Thus by Vaiṣṇavī māyā this world came into being and we three gods remain in it in great pleasure.

16. But there was only water everywhere and nothing could be discerned except a banyan tree, the tree of Viṣṇu's fame.

17. In this banyan tree I remained as a little boy with my māyā, seeing in entirety the three worlds that I created. I am holding you, O fair Earth, and you know this.

18. After some time, O goddess, I produced Baḍavāmukha (the marine fire) by my māyā, to dry up the water.

19. When the deluge was thus over, Brahmā, the grandfather of the worlds, was told by me after meditating for a while.

20. "O Brahmā, create quickly the gods, demons and men."

21-22. Thus told, Brahmā took his vessel of water, cleansed himself with the water, and then created Devas—Ādityas, Vasus, Rudras, Aśvins, and the group of Martus and also, for the liberation of all Brāhmaṇas who are the gods on earth.

23. From the hands arose the Kṣatriyas, from the thighs Vaiśyas, and from the feet Śūdras for the service of all.

24. Devas and Asuras who were thus born of Brahmā had the power of penance, heroism and strength.

25. To Aditi were born Ādityas, Vasus, Rudras, Aśvins and the groups of Maruts, all together constituting thirtythree divinities.

26. To Diti were born Asuras, the enemies of gods.

27. Brahmā then created Ṛṣis full of penance and resplendent like the sun, and all of them Brahmins well-versed in the

śāstras. The sons of Brahmā then created their sons and grandsons.

28. To Nimi was born Śrīmān renowned as Ātreya, (being a descendant of Atri) who became great and full of penance even at the time of his birth.

29. He performed penance with full concentration of mind and steadiness of body, in the midst of five fires, standing on one foot, with hands thrown upwards,

30. Feeding himself on fallen leaves and water, remaining in the water in winter, and performing Kṛcchra and Cāndrāyaṇa.

31. He performed penance like this for a thousand years O Earth, and then died.

32. Seeing the son dead, Nimi became griefstricken and was brooding over what had happened day and night.

33. Immersed in this sorrow and thinking deeply what he might do, an idea occurred to him at the end of three days.

34. It was the Dvādaśī day in the month of Māgha and he had become particularly pure. His mind had given up all worldly objects and his intellect had become expansive.

35. Then with concentration of mind, he began to think of Śrāddhakalpa (the rules relating to the conduct of Śrāddha).

36. What can be the sort of food, roots and fruits, what items will be fresh and tasty, what will be particularly suitable and so on.

37. The sage then made himself pure (by bath etc), and inviting (seven) Brahmins, propitiated them with everything (that occurred to him to be duly done).

38. Each was separately honoured and then all were seated together and fed with meat, vegetables, roots and fruits.

39. With great attention he then placed Kuśa grass with their tips facing south, and gave *piṇḍa* to Śrīmān uttering his name and gotra.

40. Having done this, the sage felt (relieved) that he had discharged the dictates of *dharma* (with regard to his departed son).

41. When the day came to a close and the sun had set, he performed the ritual that is to be done with meditation and which is conducive to the attainment of Brahman (namely, the worship of Sandhyā).

42. He did it alone, in seclusion, with full control of mind, free from desire and declining even what is offered, sitting steadfast in a clean place,

43. In a seat that is neither very high nor very low and arranged with Kuśa grass, (deer)skin and cloth in successive layers, with control of senses, mind drawn inward and fixed on a single object,

44. And practised this Yoga for the purification of self, sitting steady and erect with the chest, neck and head in line,

45. Directing the eyes to the tip of the nose and not looking anywhere else, free from fear and radiant in self. Thus did he do in contemplation of Brahman.

46. My devotees, without anything else in mind, should remain in this manner with full control and direct the mind always towards me.

47. He thus performed the worship of Sandhyā. Then the night set in. He began to think again and his mind became afflicted with sorrow.

48. He began to repent for having done the rite of piṇḍa (for his son), because what he did was never done (or sanctioned) by the sages.

49. "Libation done for a son is improper. Alas, I have foolishly done it out of my love (for him).

50. How will the sages spare me from burning me with their curse? What will Devas, Asuras, Gandharvas, Piśācas, Uragas and Rākṣasas, as also my own manes, say about this?"

51. He was thinking in this manner, O Earth, till the whole night passed.

52. When the day dawned and the sun rose, he worshipped Sandhyā and performed rites to be done in fire.

53. He then became again immersed in his earlier thought and was extremely sad. With his mind thus full of grief, he said to himself:

54. "Fie upon my age, fie upon my action, fie upon my strength, fie upon my very life. I do not find in my life the son with all pleasures.

55. The wise say that the sorrow in the mind (because of this) leads to hell called Pūtikā. It is the son that saves one from this (sorrow) in this world and (from the hell) in the other world.

56-57. (Even) by worshipping gods, giving munificent gifts and making offerings in fire, scrupulously observing the prescribed rules, a man attains heaven (only) through the son, a grandfather through the grandson and a great-grandfather through the great-grandson. Now that I am without my son Śrīmān, I don't wish to live."

58-59. At that time the great sage Nārada came to that penance-grove, which was full of hermitages of sages, beautiful with plenty of flowers, fruits and water.

60. Seeing him enter his hermitage beaming with effulgence, (Nimi) honoured him with welcome.

61. He gave him *pādya* and *arghya* and seated him properly. Taking the seat, Nārada spoke to him.

Nārada said:

62. "O you highly intelligent Nimi, cast off your sorrow and listen to me.

63. You are now grieving over one who is not really an object for grief, and though you are intelligent, you also not realise this fact. Those of true learning never grieve over the dead or the living.

64. Grieving over one that is dead, lost or gone, simply makes glad those that are not friends; the departed person never returns.

65. I do not find immortality for any moving or non-moving being in any of the three worlds. Gods, demons, Gandharvas, men, beasts and birds, all have death; only they wait for their time.

66. Every being that is born is bound to die at the destined time, and it has to respond to the call of death.

67-68. Your son, the great Śrīmān, the repository of all opulence, performed extremely difficult penance for a full thousand years, and when it was time for him to die, attained supreme divine beatitude. Knowing all this, you should not give yourself up to sorrow."

69-70. Thus told by Nārada, the great Brahmin Nimi, who was perturbed in mind, prostrated at his feet, and spoke to him with fear and shyness, in a pitiable voice, sobbing and heaving frequently.

71. "O great sage, the foremost among those who know *dharma*, I am greatly consoled by your sweet and kind words.

72. Be pleased to listen, whether it be due to affection or friendship, what I say with reverence. What I did out of love for my (departed) son, instils sorrow incessantly in my mind.

73. I propitiated seven Brahmins with food, fruits, and the rest and then released piṇḍa over darbha grass spread on the floor.

74. I performed libation also in *apasavya* (with Yajñopavīta on the left).

75. All this I did because of my sorrow. But it is not something approved by the good, not conducive to the attainment of heaven and not favourable to renown.

76. Being deluded by ignorance, I had lost then my common sense, memory and stamina. I had never heard of it and the gods or sages had never done it.

77. All that I have now is the great fear of the fierce curse that the sages may pronounce on me."

Nārada said:

78. "O great Brahmin, don't be afraid. Go to your father and seek refuge in him. I don't find here anything wrong. What you have done is *dharma*, no doubt."

79. Thus said by Nārada, Nimi entered into meditation and resorted to his father through thought, word and dead. He alone was in his mind who was the originator of his line.

80. When thus meditated upon, the father came to the ascetic son who was tormented by the grief at the loss of his son.

81. He then comforted him in agreeable words "O ascetic Nimi, you performed Pitṛyajña (sacrifice for the manes).

82. The Pitṛyajña (is a ceremony) declared by Brahmā himself as *dharma*.

83. A *dharma* greater than this is Śrāddha, which was first done by Brahmā himself."

84. I shall tell you, O fair one, what he heard from Nārada, the foremost among those who know the rules, about the Śrāddha ceremony and what is to be done to the dead.

85. I give to the person concerned the necessary mental power for this.

86. To every being that is born, the time for death will certainly occur. Everyone will have to leave (this world) by the order of the lord of death. There is no immortality even for small beings like the ant.

87. Liberation is, of course, there, but that is through the (necessary) actions and by the expiations.

88. There are three (qualities) in the body,—Sattva, Rajas and Tamas. People become short-lived at the close of the aeon.

89. He in whom Tamas predominates does not understand the Sāttvika because of the defects in his actions. It is hell, animalhood and demoniac nature that pertains to Tamas.

90. Those who know the Veda resort to the Sāttvika to enter the path of liberation. Knowledge of *dharma*, godliness and renunciation from Sāttvika,

91. Cruelty, cowardice, despondency, aggressiveness, shamelessness, ignorance and ghostliness are the Tāmasa qualities.

92. The Tāmasic person never understands what is told to him. He is always haughty and heedless.

93. Strength, good speech, fickleness of mind, perseverance, valour and ego are the qualities of the Rājasa person.

94. Forbearance, composure, purity of mind, undivided attention, penance and study of scripture are the Sāttvika qualities.

95. Considering all this, sorrow should be given up, because it leads to the ruin of everything.

96. Sorrow consumes the body, intelligence is lost through sorrow, so too humility, courage, righteousness, prosperity, fame, memory and tactfulness.

97. All the *dharmas* leave the man who is hit by sorrow. Thus the father asked the son to give up his sorrow.

98. O Earth, he who commits injury or speaks falsehood due to the power of love, is tormented in hell because of his own wrong actions.

99. Controlling affection (and attachment) in everything, one should direct the intellect in matters of *dharma* for the welfare of the world. This is the truth I tell you.

100. I say this for all the four castes, what Svāyambhuva[1] said to Nimi and others with regard to srāddha.

---

1. Svāyambhuvamanu of whom Nimi was the descendant.

101. When (to a dying person) the life-breath has reached the throat and he is full of fear and anxiety, he should be quickly taken out of the house.

102. He should be laid over a layer of Kuśa grass. He may not be able to see anything even when he gets momentary consciousness.

103. Then Brahmins should be asked to recite the scriptures and gifts of gold and money should be made.

104. For welfare in the other world, gift of a cow is particularly efficacious.

105. Cows are brought into being by the creator in this world as the embodiment of all gods. They move about yielding nectar (milk). By making gifts of them, all sins are removed.

106. Then should be uttered into the ear, as the life-breath is leaving, the divine scripture.

107. To my devotee who is in this struggling condition, the mantra should be recited in the prescribed manner, and by this means liberation from *saṁsāra* should be procured.

108. Madhuparka should be quickly brought and administered with the following mantra.

109. The mantra: "Receive this pure madhuparka, which is equivalent to ambrosia, which is the foremost among the means for getting rid of *saṁsāra*, which is prescribed by Lord Nārāyaṇa, which is honoured by all the gods and which gives relief to the devotees when their bodies are cremated."

110. With this mantra, madhuparka should be given at the time of death, as it brings about pleasure in the other world. If life departs in this manner, the man does not return to this world.

111-112. When a man is unconscious as he is nearing death, he should be taken to the foot of a big tree and his body should be smeared with ghee, oil and sandalpaste, considering them all as giving him effulgence and eternality.

113. He should then be placed in water, with the head on the southern side and bathed invoking all the tīrthas in the water.

114-115. Tīrthas like Gayā, the holy rocks, Kurukṣetra, the holy rivers Gaṅgā and Yamunā, Kauśikī, the purifying Payoṣṇī,

116. The auspicious Gaṇḍakī, the strength-giving Sarayū, the nine gardens in the Varāha tīrtha in Piṇḍāraka,

117. All other tīrthas on earth, the four oceans, all these should be mentally invoked in the water before he is bathed in it.

118. When he is actually dead, the pyre should be duly arranged and the body should be placed on it with the head on the southern side.

119. Meditating on gods like Agni and taking the fire (pot) in the hand, fire should be blazed up and the following mantra uttered:

120. "After doing all difficult actions, knowingly or unknowingly, the man died (*lit.* reduced to the five elements) when the time for death came.

121. (O fire), consume this body of his which was the seat for all that was righteous and otherwise, and for all desire and stupefaction, so that he may go to the celestial world."

122. Then a circumambulation should be quickly done and the fire placed on the head.

123. This is the sort of cremation for all the four castes.

124. Bath should then be taken and the clothes well washed, and returning, piṇḍa should be offered on the ground for the departed. There is *Śauca* (pollution) from that time onwards and so one should (during that period) keep aloof from service to god (like worship, etc).

CHAPTER ONE HUNDRED AND EIGHTYEIGHT

The rituals of Śrāddha[1]

Earth said:

1. O Mādhava, lord of the gods, lord of the worlds, I wish to know from you the rites to be done during the period of āśauca.

Varāha said:

2. Listen, O auspicious one. I shall tell you about āśauca and how people are purified after it.

3. On the third day after the death (of the relative), bath should be taken in the river and piṇḍa should be given together with three handfuls of water.

1. This is on the basis of contents. The title actually given is *Piṇḍakalpaśrāddhotpattiprakaraṇam* based on the statement at the close of the chapter.

4. On the fourth, fifth and sixth days, there should be piṇḍa and one handful of water. On the seventh day this should be in a different place. This should be continued upto the tenth day.

5. On the tenth day, all those belonging to the gotra of the departed should bathe taking oil of sesamum and myrobalan and wash the clothes with cleaning materials.

6. After giving piṇḍa, they should get themselves shaven, bathe again according to rites, and return home along with the relatives.

7. On the eleventh day, the Ekoddiṣṭa ceremony should be done and after bath the (soul of) the dead person should be united in Brahmins.

8. This Ekoddiṣṭa is to be done by all the four castes and Brahmin should be fed with all the materials prescribed.

9. After bath, the departed soul should be united with the departed.[1]

10. Brahmā has laid down that for the first three castes and also for Śūdras who were really doing service, cooked food should be used and for others uncooked food.

11. On the thirteenth day Brahmins should be fed with well-cooked food.

12-13. Having in mind the name of the dead and with conviction that its aim is to make him go to heaven, the Brahmin should be sought in his house, and invited in all humility, uttering mentally the following mantra:

14. "You have gone to the celestial world and ordained by the god of death. Your mind has become the wind. So enter this Brahmin."

15. The Brahmin should be approached soon after sunset, and after giving *pādya*, should be prostrated before and his feet caressed, all for the sake of the departed.

16-17. So long as the Brahmin is having in his body the soul of the departed thus invoked, he shall not, O Earth, touch my images.

18. In the morning, soon after sunrise, proper shaving should be got done for the invited Brahmin.

19. An oil bath should then be given for him which gives pleasure to the departed.

---

2. Perhaps there is some confusion here. In verse 7 we get *pretaṁ vipreṣu yojayet* and here *pretam preteṣu yojayet.*

20. A small earthen pedestal by a heap of clods on a low clean place near a river or a pond, should be made as the place for the departed.

21-22. This may be marked into sixtyfour parts. Then on the south-east in the shade or under a tree on the river bank, the rites for the departed are to be done in a place free from Caṇḍālas and other outcastes and creatures like the fowl, dogs and pigs.

23-24. If Śrāddha is done in a place, where the dog blocks (the people) by its moan, the pig by its grunt, the fowl by the wind wafted by its wings and the Caṇḍāla (by his very presence), it brings about bondage to the departed (and not release). The wise should avoid such places for these rites.

25-26. O goddess, Devas, Asuras, Gandharvas, Piśācas, Uragas, Rākṣasas, Sacrifices and all beings moving and non-moving are set on your surface.

27. And I hold this universe full of Viṣṇu-māyā and with the Caṇḍāla upwards and all the good and evil of the people.

28. Therefore, let the libation be made in the clods on the pedestal.

29. Those who do libation without these earthen clods, make what remains impure.

30. Neither gods nor manes accept such offerings and that leads only to the ghastly hell.

31. The offering for the departed should be made in the earthen pedestal in the forenoon uttering the name and gotra and saying that the piṇḍa is offered.

32. After this, all in the family and those in the same gotra are to partake of the remains (after the offering). This food should not be given to those belonging to other gotras for whom it is not permissible to take it.

33. This is what is ordained for all the four castes and those that are departed get propitiated by this.

34. He who eats it before offering to the departed, shall go to a great river and bathe there along with the clothes he wears (as expiation).

35. (Then for feeding the Brahmins), first calling to mind all the tīrthas, water should be thrice sprinkled on the floor, and thus getting the place purified, the Brahmins should be quickly brought there and, when they have come, the ritual of welcome should be made for them.

36. *Arghya and pādya* should then be given and then *Āsana* (seat) with the following mantra:

37. The mantra: "O great Brahmin, please take this seat offered and rest in it; also be pleased to favour me."

38. After seating the Brahmin thus in the seat, umbrella should be given for keeping out beings moving in the sky like Devas, Gandharvas, Siddhas and Asuras.

39. The umbrella is meant for the effulgent to hold in the sky.

40. For the sake of the departed, the umbrella may be given when the Brahmin is pleased with earlier offerings.

41. The Brahmin may be made to hold it over his head.

42. In the sky, Devas, Siddhas, Gandharvas, Asuras and Rākṣasas will see the departed, and this will produce shyness in him.

43. When he (the departed) is thus shy, the Asuras and Rākṣasas may laugh at him. To avoid this, the umbrella was devised by Āditya long ago for all those who go to such regions and for the sages.

44. There may be shower of fire, shower of stones, shower of hot water and shower of ashes day and night.

45. The umbrella is to be given to the Brahmin for warding off all this.

46. Then foot-wear should be given to enable comfortable walking. I shall tell you the purpose of this.

47. The feet should not be injured in the region of Yama which is dark and difficult to traverse.

48. The departed is led alone through that difficult part day and night by the god of death and his associates.

49. Therefore the Brahmin should be given footwear for the protection of the feet.

50. (The departed has to move along) places of hot sand and those full of thorns. The foot-wear helps to cross them (unhurt).

51. Then *Dhūpa* (incense) and *Dīpa* (lamp) should be given with mantra in order that they may go to the departed.

52. The departed should then be invoked in a stretch of darbha on the ground uttering the name and gotra.

53. (Sandal paste should be offered saying:)

"You have left this world and got liberated. Receive this sandal paste given with reverence, O you departed".

54. "O Brahmin, accept this sandal paste, flowers, incense and lamp and give liberation to the departed".

55. Similarly, clothes and ornaments should be given to the Brahmin and then cooked food again and again.

56. Such materials as can be used by the departed should be given. Then (the performer of these rites) should wash his feet thrice. This is common for all castes.

57. But in the case of Śūdras all this should be without mantra. What the Śūdra gives without mantra, the Brahmin receives with mantra.

58. After doing all this, the Brahmin should be fed with cooked food.

59. When the Brahmin, purified by knowledge, is eating, the offering with all its accessories to the departed should be given.

60. It may be known by the wise that godhood and Brahminhood are given through the piṇḍa for the departed and manhood through libation.

61. For the manes the offering should be accompanied by mantra:

62. After washing hands, the cooked food along with its accessories is accepted by the Brahmin with mantra.

63. After the Brahmin eats for the departed, (what is left) should be shared by all the relatives of him for whom it is done.

64. None should prevent anything being given to the Brahmin. He who prevents, incurs the sin of killing the preceptor.

65. In such a case what is offered is not accepted by gods, fires or manes, thus resulting in the loss of *dharma*. Then the departed does not get propitiation.

66. With all this consideration in mind for guarding dharma, should the food for the departed be given in the midst of relations.

67-68. When the Brahmin is pleased, particularly with the offering for the departed, the departed soul gets free from sins.

69. When he is fully satisfied with the cooked food, water should be poured into his palm.

70. The remnants of the food (left by the Brahmin in the

eating vessel) should not be thrown away. With his permission it should be disposed of in a blemishless manner.

71. After purification with sacred waters sanctified by śāntimantras, the performer should go to the place of libation and bow to the earth.

72. He should utter mantras and praises full of devotion for the earth.

73. "I bow to you again and again, O Earth, mother of the world, holding big mountains. I bow again and again to you in whom the whole universe rests."

74. Then uttering the name and gotra of the departed, water with sesamum should be poured.

75. Kneeling down and prostrating before the Brahmins, they should be raised up holding their hands with mantra.

76. A bed should then be given and also ornaments and collyrium. The Brahmin should receive them and occupy the bed.

77. After a while, going to the place of libation, a cow should be given to the Brahmin by holding its tail.

78. The vessel made of Udumbara wood containing water and black sesamum should be taken and mantras relating to the cow should be recited.

79. The cow should be gifted holding its tail and sprinkling it with this water sanctified by the mantras and capable of removing sins.

80. Then the departed (who was invoked earlier) should be released and gifts given to Brahmins. The balls of rice offered to the manes should be given to the crows, because of their impurity after the offering.

81. Then the performer should go to his house with other Brahmins and feed them all with cooked food.

82. Food should be scattered also for tiny beings like the ants for propitiating the departed.

83. When all these are thus made happy, happiness accrues to him who has departed to the world of the dead.

84. All the food thus distributed becomes an inexhaustible store for him. These are the rites to be done for the departed to enable change from that state (to become manes).

85. This will be adopted by all the four castes since it is something revealed to Svayambhū.

86. Now you need not have any fear, O son, for having done the obsequial rites to your son.

87. I have now told you everything in detail and in the presence of Nārada.

88. You have now set the precedent for the sacrifice for the departed son. Hereafter, this Pitṛyajña will be established in the world.

89. The rules of the rites for the manes were thus told by Ātreya (the father)[1].

90. The oblations should be done in the third, seventh, ninth and eleventh months after death, and at the end of one full year the annual rites should be performed.

91. Getting pure in body and mind and with concentration of mind, the departed should be invoked and cooked food offered according to the rules.

92. This should be done with mantra for all the castes, except the Śūdras for whom it should be without mantra.

93. When the rites for the departed are over at the end of the year, some get full release and some return (to be re-born in the world).

94. Although there may be the grandfather, daughter-in-law, wife, and relatives close and distant, we should realise that this world is like a dream.

95. All of them mourn for a while, but soon turn themselves away. The bond of affection and attachment is there for a moment, but that is broken soon.

96. Whose is the mother, whose is the father, whose the wife and whose the sons ? In life after life they are there and have attachment by bond of delusion.

97. But the rites for the dead should be done with a feeling of attachment, though it is true that we are having thousands of parents and hundreds of wives and sons in the numerous cycles of birth and death.

98. (What I told you) is the rules of obsequies laid down by Svayambhū.

99. When the rites relating to the departed (*pretakārya*) are over, the status of manes (*pitṛtva*) is attained, and so libation for manes (*pitṛtarpaṇa*) should be performed on the new moon day every month.

---

1. This is possibly an interpolated passage.

100. The father, grand-father and great-grand-father (should be given libation), and if the Brahmin is fed on that day, they get permanently propitiated.

101. After describing the rites of Pitṛyajña in this manner, Ātreya (the father) meditated for a while and soon disappeared.

Nārada said:

102. "Having heard about the obsequies narrated by Ātreya for all the four castes, (you should now be convinced that) you have (really) established *dharma*.

103. The sages also perform Pitṛyajña as part of *śrāddha* on a particular day every month. The Brahmins do it in this way and the Śūdras without mantra.

104. The Śrāddha performed by Nimi is followed by the twiceborn and it has come to be known as 'Nimiśrāddha'.

105. O great sage, let good befall you. I take leave of You."

106. So saying, the great sage Nārada returned to heaven spreading his lustre everywhere.

107. O Earth, this is the conception of piṇḍa and the origin of Śrāddha and they are established among the Brāhmaṇas by the sage Ātreya himself.

CHAPTER ONE HUNDRED AND EIGHTYNINE

The qualities of the Brahmin to be fed in Śrāddha[1]

Earth said:

1. "I have now heard in full about the Śrāddha, the purities and impurities connected with it and also about the feeding for the departed relating to the four castes.

2. I have a doubt and it behoves you to clear it. (You said that) for all the four castes, the gifts should be given to the Brahmins.

1. The title actually given is *Piṇḍakalpotpatti* (origin of the instructions for piṇḍa).

3. Those who receive them, particularly the food for the departed, really do a contemptible thing namely eating with the departed (ghost).

4. By what means does such a Brahmin free himself from such a position and how does he help the donor? I ask this, O Janārdana, because of your affection for me and my nature as a woman (who always has doubts)."

5. Asked thus by Earth, the Lord in the form of the boar replied to her in a tone resembling the sound of the conch and Dundubhi.

Varāha said:

6. It is quite proper that you ask me this. I shall tell you how the Brahmin helps himself and the donor.

7. After eating what is offered through him to the departed (*pretabhojya*), the Brahmin wanes in his knowledge.

8. To purify his body, he should undertake fasting. By fasting for one full day and night, he regains his power of knowledge.

9. Then after performing the worship of the morning Sandhyā and making the routine offerings in the fire, he shall perform Homa with sesamum reciting the Śāntimantras.

10. Then he shall go to a river flowing in the eastern direction and bathe there with due rites and drink *pañcagavya* together with *madhuparka*.

11. Taking water sanctified with Śāntimantras in a vessel made of the wood of Udumbara, he shall sprinkle it all over in his residence.

12. After performing propitiatory rites for gods like Agni, he shall perform Bhūtabali and feed Brahmins.

13. The gift of a cow also should be made for the removal of sins. If all this is done, he enters the supreme path (of liberation).

14. If one dies with the food offered through him to the departed in his stomach, he has to remain in the fierce hell till the end of the aeon.

15. Then he becomes a Rākṣasa before he is freed of the sin. So the proper expiation should be done for the welfare of the donor and the recipient.

16. The Brahmin who, after receiving gifts of cow, elephant,

horse, money and the like with mantra and in the prescribed manner, performs the prescribed expiations, surely enables the donor to cross (saṁsāra).

17. The Brahmin who is rich in knowledge and is ever devoted to learning the Vedas, surely enables himself as well as the donor to cross (saṁsāra).

18. O Earth, the Brahmin should not be offended by any person belonging to the three castes.

19. The Brahmin invited for food during a ceremony for gods, birthday, Śrāddha, new moon day or rites connected with the departed, should be carefully chosen.

20. The Brahmin who has mastered the Vedas, who is highly righteous, goodnatured, contented, virtuous, truthful,

21. Forbearing, learned in Śāstras, and wedded to non-violence—should be called.

22. And the gifts should be given to him, because such a person alone is capable of enabling the donor to gain his aim (of crossing *saṁsāra*).

23. But a gift of this sort should never be given to a Kuṇḍa or Gola[1], for then it will be in vain. They pull the donor down.

24. Seeing a Kuṇḍa or Gola in a ceremony for them, the manes get disappointed and fall into hell. In the ceremony for gods also what is given to them goes in vain.

25. Therefore, a gift should never be given to any one not eligible to receive it. In this connection, I shall tell you what once happened in yore. Please listen.

26. In the Avanti country there was a highly righteous king named Medhātithi, a descendant of Manu.

27. He had as his priest one Candraśarmā, a virtuous Brahmin belonging to the Ātreya gotra and very much devoted to the Vedas.

28. The king used to give hundred cows to the Brahmins every day before taking food.

29. Once on the anniversary day of his father in the month of Vaiśākha, Medhātithi invited many Brahmins for Śrāddha.

30. When all of them had come, Medhātithi with pure mind bowed to them all and also to his preceptor and started performing the Śrāddha.

---

1. Kuṇḍa and Gola are both bastards, the one born to woman by her paramour when her husband is alive, and the other after he is dead.

31. Doing the rites of Śrāddha in the prescribed manner, offering piṇḍa and libation, he gave food to Brahmins sumptuously.

32. Among them was a Gola and to him too the food was given with due rites.

33. Because of this sin, the manes of the king fell from heaven into a forest full of thorns, and they repeatedly began to cry being oppressed by hunger and thirst.

34. Medhātithi chanced to go there for hunting with two or three attendants.

35-36. Seeing them wandering there, he asked them who they were and due to what wrong action they were in that sorrowful state.

The Pitṛs said:

37. "We are the ancestors of king Medhātithi and we are on our way to hell."

38. Hearing these words of theirs, the king felt very sorry and told them in a consoling voice.

Medhātithi said:

39. I am Medhātithi and you are my ancestors. What is the sin committed, as a result of which you are now forced to hell?

The Pitṛs said:

40. "The food in the Śrāddha for us was given to a Gola and, as a result of that misdeed, we got to hell.

41. After suffering there much, we will return to heaven. O son, you are a liberal giver and see to the welfare of the world.

42. You have gifted numerous cows with munificent dakṣiṇā. By the merit of that we will return to the pleasant heaven.

43. But there will not be food there to satisfy us. So you have to perform the Śrāddha again for our satisfaction."

44. Hearing these words, Medhātithi returned home and, calling his preceptor Candraśarmā, told him.

Medhātithi said:

45. "O Candraśarmā, I am going to perform the Śrāddha again. Call the Brahmins but see that there is no Kuṇḍa or Gola among them."

46-47. Immediately, the priest Candraśarmā called Brahmins who were always learning the Vedas, who were good-natured, forbearing, of good family, free from anger and of fine conduct, and the king conducted Śrāddha.

48. After Śrāddha, piṇḍas were offered and libation given and the Brahmins were fed and honoured with dakṣiṇā.

49. They were then released and the king took his food. Soon he went to the forest and saw the manes.

50. Seeing them now well-nourished, strong and happy, he was very much delighted.

51. The manes spoke to him with modesty and pleasure: "May good befall you. We are now proceeding to heaven.

52. For our sake you should be careful about one thing that anything meant for the gods or manes should never be given to a Gola (or Kuṇḍa). The wise declare it to be in vain what is offered through them.

53. If in a ceremony meant for the propitiation of gods or manes, a suitable Brahmin is not found available, the offering may be given to a cow, keeping in mind the aim always.

54. If even a cow is not available, it may be thrown in a river.

55. But it should never be given to an ineligible person, an unbeliever or one who is against his own teacher, and surely not to a Gola and never to a Kuṇḍa."

56. So saying the manes went to heaven and Medhātithi returned to his city together with the Brahmins. Thereafter, he carefully observed what the manes had said.

57. Therefore it is said, O goddess, that a single virtuous Brahmin enables us to tide over even the worst difficulties.

58. A single one is capable of taking us across. Therefore, O Earth, gifts should be given to the true Brahmin.

59. Śrāddha is approved by all gods, demons, men, Gandharvas and others.

60. Sages like Nimi began to do it every month in the fortnight of the manes.

CHAPTER ONE HUNDRED AND NINETY

Other details about Śrāddha[1]

Earth said:

1. "O Lord, when men or animals die, some go to hell while others go to heaven.

2. This world is like a dream. Here the good and bad are the result of one's own actions. It is sustained by the power of your māyā.

3. O Lord, who are the manes that eat the essence of Śrāddha? They have existence in the fire according to the actions done.

4. How are the rules of piṇḍa to be observed month after month? Who are those that eat in Śrāddha and what are the rituals for the manes? I very much desire to know this for certain."

5. Asked thus by Earth, Lord Nārāyaṇa in the form of the boar replied.

Varāha said:

6. Well have you asked, O Earth, in your eagerness to see the establishment of *dharma*. I shall tell you what you seek to know.

7. The enjoyers in Pitṛyajña are the father, grand-father and great-grand-father.

8-9. The saṅkalpa for the Piṇḍa should be made on the particular day in the month in the particular fortnight and on the day in which the nakṣatra is in combination with the particular tithi. The Śrāddha done then yields great result.

10. O fair one, listen. I shall tell you all about Śrāddha which the learned do with great attention.

11. Some of the twice-born perform the rite called Brahmayajña, some perform Devayajña in fire.

12. Others perform Bhūtayajña and yet others Manuṣyayajña when they live the life of a householder.

13. I shall tell you about the Pitṛyajña. Those who perform

---

1. The title given is *Śrāddhapitṛyajñaniścayaprakaraṇam* (determination of *śrāddha* and *pitṛyajña*).

a single one or a hundred of this, remain in me. This, I tell you, is the truth.

14. O Mādhavi, in *havya* as well as *kavya*[1], Agni (fire) is the mouth of Devas,

15. In all sacrifices I am the Uttarāgni, I am the Dakṣiṇāgni and I am the Āhavanīyāgni.[2]

16. I am the fire and the purifier in all matters relating to sacrifices for gods.

17. For Vaiśvadeva may be engaged a pure Brahmacārin, a mendicant in holy tīrthas and an anchorite in the Vānaprastha stage.

18. These are to be worshipped for the sake of gods, but should not be chosen for ritualistic feeding in Śrāddha. I shall tell you who are the twice-born that are to be engaged in Śrāddha.

19-20. O Mādhavi, the sort of people that are to be fed in Pitṛyajñas are those that are superior, contented, forbearing, calm, having full control of the senses, taking pleasure and sorrow alike, truthful, propounding dharma, well versed in Vedic knowledge and eating well.

21. The offering should first be made in fire in tīrthas sacred for Devas and then to the Brahmin.

22. In the Pitṛyajñas the rules for different castes relating to Śrāddha should be observed.

23-24. During Śrāddha in Pitṛyajña, the food should not be seen by dogs, fowls or pigs. The performer should not see those Brahmins who are forbidden eating in his company, who have not undergone sacred rituals, who apply themselves to all kinds of work and who eat anything without discrimination.

25. The Śrāddha that is seen by the prohibited persons is considered 'Rākṣasa'. I have ordained already the offering in such śrāddha to Bali when he overpowered the three worlds.

26. Such a Śrāddha is taken to be one without mantras and rituals. Therefore, the wise should avoid such people in Śrāddha.

27. One should keep oneself pure during Śrāddha and, making the Brahmin pleased, he should be fed free from the sight of others.

1. *Havya* is the offering for gods and *Kavya* the offering for manes.
2. These are the three forms of fire laid down for various ceremonies.

28. The manes should then be invoked with mantra according to the prescribed rules. Three piṇḍas should then be offered, together with condiments, for the father, grand-father and great-grand-father.

29-30. Water with sesamum should be given every month after bowing to the goddesses who are the carriers of such water, namely Vaiṣṇavī, Kāśyapī and Ajayā. When done in this way, the manes doubtless become propitiated.

31-32. I have made the supreme soul reside in the bodies of gods. From the body of gods, O beautiful goddess, three beings came out. They are the Pitṛdevas (manes-gods) who enjoy piṇḍas given for the manes.

33. The Devas, Asuras, Gandharvas, Yakṣas, Rākṣasas and Pannagas, all in airy form, watch the pitfalls during performance of Śrāddha.

34. Upon those who perform Pitṛyajña with due attention, the manes bestow long life, fame, strength, effulgence, wealth, sons, kine, women and health.

35. Such men, by their actions, go to the auspicious world beyond. After death, they will never have to be born as animals.

36. The householder who worships the manes, gods becomes the saviour of those (of his ancestors) who are tormented in hell.

37. He who fully propitiates the Brahmin according to rules in Śrāddha makes the manes propitiated and enables them to go to the world of eternity.

38. Those who worship the manes attain supreme beatitude and, being thus blessed, reach the Sāttvic white path.

39. I shall tell you another thing in brief, O fair one, please listen.

40. Those who are engulfed in the darkness of ignorance and are obstinate, are tormented in hell, bound by their own hundreds of strings of attachment.

41-42. For such people who thus suffer endless torment, if their sons or grandsons offer libation in any pool of water on new-moon day, propitiation is obtained (and they are able to leave the hell).

43-44. Those who perform Śrāddha duly propitiating the Brahmins and offer in solemnity to the manes piṇḍas and water with sesamum, also are freed (from the fear) of hell and get permanent satisfaction.

45. Water with sesamum should be in a vessel of Udumbara wood. Calling the Brahmins in reverence, dakṣiṇā should be given to them according to the means for the salvation of manes.

46. The gift of a blue bull avoids the torments of hell. When water is poured on the tail of such a bull (while making the gift), the manes become propitiated for sixty thousand years.

47-48. If the blue bull, when released by its horn, digs up a clod of mud by the horn, then the manes of the donor that have fallen in hell, get released, and together with them, the donor goes to the world of Soma.

49-50. By the merit of releasing a blue bull in this manner, they delight themselves in the Somaloka for sixty thousand and sixty hundred years free from hunger and thirst.

51. This is the duty of the householder with his sons and grandsons. They, thus, save their fallen manes and themselves remain in happiness.

52. O fair one, the householder is the source moving animals and flying birds.

53. Thus the state of being the householder is the base wherein *dharma* gets firmly established.

54. The householder who performs Śrāddha every month in the proper tithi in the particular fortnight, liberates all his ancestors.

55. The sacrifices, gifts, learning of scripture, fasts, baths in holy waters, agnihotra, however carefully done following the rules, do not generate the merit in magnitude that the performance of Śrāddha generates for a householder.

56. The manes emanated from the bodies of Brahmā and Viṣṇu[1]. They are the father, grand-father and great-grandfather. These are, O Earth, the manes-gods.

57. Since these devatās invoked in Śrāddhas are the creations of Kaśyapa, gods like Indra and others do not know them.

58. Īśvara (Rudra) does not know this although they came out of his body. Similarly, Brahmā too does not know. This is because of my māyā.

59. Thus are Brahmā and Rudra kept out by my māyā.

60. I shall now tell you another thing relating to Pitṛyajña. Do not give food in Śrāddha to the Brahmin before offering it to Fire.

1. From later stanzas, it appears that Rudra also should be added here.

61. (I shall narrate to you a story). O Earth, after taking *saṅkalpa*, darbha grass was strewn on the floor and piṇḍa was placed on it.

62. But the manes-gods became afflicted by indigestion and could not eat any more. They went to Soma to report their sorrow.

63. Soma saw them suffering from indigestion. Still he extended to them welcome.

Soma said:

64. "Who are you, O gods ? Wherefrom did you arise ? Why are you in grief now ?"

They replied to Soma:

65. "O Soma, please listen to us. The three of us are manes-gods. We arose from Brahmā, Viṣṇu and Hara respectively.

66. We are the gods for Śrāddha. The piṇḍas for the manes were offered to us. But we developed indigestion and hence our sorrow."

Soma said:

67. "I shall be your friend and be the fourth with you three. We shall seek the means for our well being."

68. So said by Soma, they went with him in pursuit of the means for their relief.

69. They went to Brahmā who was resting in the peak of Meru surrounded by great sages.

70. Soma, the son of Atri, prostrated before Brahmā and told him.

71. "These manes-gods are afflicted by indigestion. They have come here with me seeking your favour. Be pleased to rid them of their ailment."

72. Brahmā meditated for a while and soon saw before him Īśvara.

73. Brahmā then spoke to the great lord of Yoga.

74. "O lord, these manes who are suffering from indigestion, have come to me with Soma seeking my help. It will be good of you to tell me how these have come into being."

75. Thus asked by Brahmā, Īśvara meditated for a while entering into his divine Yoga, and saw there Lord (Viṣṇu) in his Yogic form.

76. He was wonder-struck at this and then spoke to Brahmā.

77. "These are the creations of Viṣṇu by his māyā. They are the exalted manes-gods.

78. The father is the god from Brahmā as he arose out of you. The grandfather is the god from Viṣṇu as he arose out of Viṣṇu. The great-grand-father is the god from Rudra as he arose out of myself.

79. They are assigned as manes-gods in Śrāddha performed by men. They are created by the māyā of Viṣṇu for the sake of Brahmins.

80-81. If it is that they have come to you with Soma, having developed indigestion when they were propitiated in Pitṛyajña, I shall tell you how their indigestion can be cured and they can be made happy. Please listen, O Brahmā, grandfather of the whole world.

82-83. There is the resplendent Fire with his tawny banner, the son of Śāṇḍilya. When men perform Śrāddha, they should first make offering to him. The piṇḍa should be eaten along with him."

84. When Īśvara said like this, Brahmā called in his mind Fire, and he immediately appeared before him.

85. The all-consuming Fire with all his effulgence was associated with the five Yajñas by Brahmā by the power of my māyā.

86. Brahmā then spoke to Fire. "O you consumer of all offerings, the first piṇḍa offered should be eaten by you.

87. What is left after that will be partaken by the gods and the Maruts. Then should be eaten the wholesome food of the Śrāddha (by the Brahmins).

88. The piṇḍa after that is eaten along with Soma."

89. Thus told by Brahmā, O Earth the manes-gods departed with Soma. In the Pitṛyajña (therefore), food is eaten together.

90. So, O Earth, in Śrāddha the first offering is for Agni, after honouring Brahmins for the sake of manes.

91. Then is the piṇḍa on the floor overstrewn darbha grass. There, the first piṇḍa is for father who arose from Brahmā.

92. The middle one is for grand-father who arose from Rudra and the third is for great-grand-father who arose from Viṣṇu.[1]

93. Those who perform Śrāddha with mantras according to the rules laid down, get blessings of the manes. The twice-born perform Śrāddha by the strength of my māyā.

94. I shall now tell you who are the Brahmins that are ineligible to be fed in Śrāddha.

95. Eunuchs, artists, those who condemn the king, those with bad nails or irregular teeth, or are blind or pot-bellied,

96. Dancers, singers, those dependent on the dramatic stage, those who teach Veda for money, those who perform sacrifice for anybody,

97. Those in the service of the king, traders, those of a mixed origin though born to a Brahmin woman, those who have fallen into depravity,

98. Those who have not undergone the saṁskāras, those who do the deeds of Śūdras for their living, those who serve Śūdras, astrologers, those who perform sacrifice for the public,

99. Those under initiation (for some ceremony), usurers, those who sell mercury, those living upon Vaiśyas,

100. Thieves, inscribers, beggars, platform-builders, those that live in hills and mountains, dissemblers,

101. Those that do any kind of action, those that offer for sale everything—these should not be called for eating in Śrāddha.

102. Those who have gone far away and earn their living there, those engaged in the sale of mercury or of sesamum, and actors are considered *Rājasa* in Śrāddha by the wise (and may be called in the absence of others).

103. But the rest in the list should be considered *Rākṣasa* in the form of the Brahmin. They should not be seen in Śrāddha.

104. If such prohibited persons are found eating in Śrāddha, the manes become subjected to serious sorrow for a period of six months.

105. For this expiation should be done quickly.

106. Clarified butter should be poured in fire and the sun should be looked at.

107. The grand-father, father and great-grand-father should be invoked again and sandal paste, flowers, incense and water

1. This is at variance with the earlier statement that the grand-father arose from Viṣṇu and the great-grand-father from Rudra.

with sesamum should be offered and then the Brahmin fed according to rules.

108. I shall tell you another thing briefly, please listen. The Brahmin who is purified by knowledge is purified by mantra.

109. One who never partakes of the food for the dead, should not be insisted upon taking food in Śrāddha but may be given food in Vaiśvadeva.

110. If such persons are given the food for the dead, then one has to do expiation.

111. He goes to hell, but I shall tell you what expiation he has to do.

112. On Dvādaśī day in the month of Māgha he should take rice cooked in milk together with ghee, after propitiating Brahmins with meat and honey.

113. In order to make himself pure, he should make the gift of a cow with calf and then perform Śrāddha again calling Brahmins and giving them unguents.

114. The Brahmacārin should purify himself by giving up the twig for cleaning teeth.

115. It should not be used at all on newmoon days.

116. If one uses the twig for cleaning teeth on newmoon day, he causes torment for Soma and the manes.

117-118. When the day dawns and the sun is rising, one should perform morning duties and invite Brahmin and see to his shaving and pairing of nails. He should then be given oil for bathing and unguents.

119. Rice should then be cooked well with all purity and the Śrāddha should be commenced at noon.

120. The Brahmin should be welcomed and water given for *pādya*. He should be led into the house.

121. Seat should then be given and the manes should be invoked in him. *Arghya* should be given then and the sandalpaste and the garland.

122. Incense and lamp should follow, as also cloth and water with sesamum. The plate for eating should be placed before him.

123. The place should then be marked off by a streak of ashes. The rites in fire should then be done and a circle of water made round the rice.

124. No separate saṅkalpa need be made then regarding the manes. The Brahmin should be requested to eat at ease.

125. The Rakṣoghna mantra should be recited. When the Brahmin is fully satisfied with the food served, *Vikira*[1] should be done.

126. The ritual of offering piṇḍa should then be done laying darbha grass on the floor and facing south.

127. Piṇḍa should be offered for the three manes, father and others. The piṇḍas should be worshipped for the sake of progeny.

128. The Brahmin should be given akṣata in the hand, and after making him pleased with dakṣiṇā, his words of blessing should be obtained, and then released.

129. As long as the piṇḍas remain on the floor, so long do the manes remain in the house.

130. Becoming clean after washing hands, *śāntyudaka* (water for peace) should be offered to the three deities that carry the libation to the manes, namely Vaiṣṇavī, Kāśyapī and Akṣayā,[2] after prostrating in the floor.

131. One should eat the first piṇḍa oneself, the second should be given to the wife and the third thrown into water. This is the rule in Śrāddha.

132. The manes-gods should then be released and obeisance made to them.

133. Done in this way, the manes-gods become pleased and they bless with long life, wealth and progeny.

134. The Śrāddha should be performed with Brahmins of high knowledge; otherwise it will be in vain.

135. He who performs Śrāddha without mantra or ritual, gives part of the merit to my Asura devotee.

136. The moment the Brahmin without knowledge takes the plate for eating in Śrāddha, it is snatched away by the Rākṣasas.

137. O fair one, I have now told you about the rites relating to the manes, its origin, the gifts to be made and merit that accrues from it.

138. O Earth, what else do you now wish to know?

---

1. *Vikira* is scattering of cooked rice in a streak outside the plate in which the Brahmin invoked as manes eats.

2. The name given earlier is Ajayā.

CHAPTER ONE HUNDRED AND NINETYONE

Madhuparka

Sūta said:

1. After knowing so much about dharma, Earth asked again the Lord in the form of the boar.

Earth said:

2. I have now known so much Śāstra from your own mouth. Still I don't feel that I have known all that I should know.

3. It, therefore, behoves you to tell me as to what is the nature of *madhuparka*, who is its devatā and what merit arises from it.

4. And also what are its ingredients and to whom it should be given.

5. Hearing these words of Earth, the great Lord in the form of the boar replied.

Varāha said:

6. Listen, O Earth, I shall tell you how *madhuparka* is made, what is its origin and how it should be gifted.

7. When I, Brahmā and Rudra caused dissolution of the world, all beings remained in an indistinct form.

8. Then from my right side came out Man, beautiful, lustrous, auspicious, humble and famous.

9. Then Brahmā asked me: "O Viṣṇu, who is this person that has came out of your body to be a fourth among us three. He is small and has come out in secret. This is not proper on your part."

10. Hearing these words of Brahmā, I said:

11. "The being that has come out of me is known as Madhuparka, necessary in all ceremonies and capable of bringing about the release of devotees from *saṁsāra*. This, in brief, is what I have to tell you and Rudra."

12. (Brahmā said:) "Good it is that he has come out as your part." The origin of Madhuparka is thus decided.

13. Then Brahmā asked me as to what should be done with madhuparka.

14. "Please tell me what is the way to utilise madhuparka so that it may not go in vain."

15. Hearing the words of Brahmā, I said: Madhuparka is to be made and gifted. If madhuparka is given after performing my worship one goes to the exalted place where there will be no sorrow.

16. I shall now say how its gift should be made by which one attains divine path.

17-18. When in my worship, the upacāras are over, madhuparka should be taken and this mantra uttered:

19. "This, O Lord, is what arose from your body. It is by name madhuparka and it is capable of granting release from saṁsāra, I offer it to you with great devotion. Be pleased to receive it. I bow to you."

20. O Earth, now listen to what I say about the nature of madhuparka and how it is to be offered.

21. It should be made with equal parts of honey, curds and ghee reciting the prescribed mantras if the full benefit should be attained.

22. It may then be offered to me in the proper manner. I have thus told you what you wanted to know.

CHAPTER ONE HUNDRED AND NINETYTWO

Peace for all

Sūta said:

1-2. Having heard about the origin, gift, merit, result, making and holding of madhuparka, the saintly Earth was wonderstruck, and holding the feet of Lord Janārdana, said:

3. "O Lord, it is dear to you to offer madhuparka after the upacāras in your worship and it should be done then. But tell me how to do it in the best form."

Varāha said:

4. You have asked me well. I shall tell you all that since it is capable of gaining release from the sorrowful saṁsāra.

5. After doing all the rituals which you referred to, Śānti

should be performed for me for the well-being of the whole country.

6. At the close of the rituals, one should kneel down on the floor.

7. Then *Namo nārāyaṇāya* should be uttered and the following mantra recited:

8. I resort to you, O Lord, saviour from the ocean of saṁsāra. O handsome one, you have come to me again.

9. Look at the directions, look below, protect me from all ills.

10. Be pleased to bestow always peace and happiness to this country with the king and his army, to pregnant women, to old men, to Brahmins and cows and to the cereals.

11. Give abundance of food, bring plentiful rain, prosperity and freedom from fear. Let the nation progress, O Lord, let there be peace for ever.

12. For gods, Brahmins, devotees, maidens, animals and other beings, let there be peace for ever.

13. After reciting this Śānti, my devotee shall offer a handful of water and recite the following mantra:

14. "O Vāsudeva, may you who are the originator of all the worlds, the witness in all sacrifices and the spirit in all the gods, give us peace and release from saṁsāra."

15. This is the best attainment, the best fame, the best energy, the best gain and the best path.

16. He who recites this auspicious Śānti in all seriousness, gets merged in me without rebirth.

17. After reciting this Śānti, is the occasion for madhuparka. *Namo nārāyaṇāya* should be uttered and the following mantra recited:

18. "O Lord, the greatest of all gods, the venerable one with the name Madhuparka, be pleased to come here and remain in this vessel for my deliverance."

19. (The madhuparka should be) in a vessel made of Udumbara wood and should consist of equal parts of honey, curds and ghee. If honey is not available, gur may be used.

20. If ghee is liberally available, it may be mixed with fried rice. If curd is not available, milk may be substituted.

21. Thus curds, honey and ghee may be mixed in equal

qualities uttering 'O Lord, I am offering you curd, honey and ghee."

22. For the benefit of all, my devotee may take it in his hand and recite the following mantra:

23. "You who created from the navel, you who are to be invoked by mantras in all sacrifices, receive this offering named madhuparka meant for you."

24. He who offers it to me in this manner, attains the merit of all sacrifices and goes to my world.

25. I shall now tell you another thing about this, O Earth, Please listen.

26. This should be administered in proper form with mantra to a dying devotee of mine.

27. This reliever from saṁsāra may be given to my devotee who is dying after doing good deeds all his life.

28. Seeing such a person in the throes of death, a devotee should take madhuparka in his hand and recite the following mantra:

29. "May you, O Nārāyaṇa, the most important in all the worlds, who remain in everybody, be pleased to accept this madhuparka brought by the devotee".

30. Madhuparka should be given to him with this mantra. Given at the time of death, it gives release from saṁsāra.

31. O fortunate one, I have told you thus about madhuparka which no one else knows.

32. Madhuparka should be given by those desirous of accomplishments. Given after worshipping the great Lord, it brings about release from saṁsāra.

33. One who gives madhuparka attains beatituds, because it is pure and removes all desires.

34. It should be given to a holy preceptor by the devoted pupil. Never should it be given to the ignorant or immodest.

35. He who listens to this purifying account of madhuparka, also attains beatitude.

36. I have told you thus everything about madhuparka for the sake of release from saṁsāra for those that wish for it.

37. Those who recite this Śānti in the king's gateway, the cremation ground, or when in fear or sorrow, get relief.

38. The man without son gets one, the man without a wife

gets one, the woman without a husband gets one, and the person who is bound gets release.

39. O Earth, I have told you about this great Śānti, which is of a highly secret nature and gets release, from saṁsāra.

40. He who performs Śānti in this manner, gives up all attachments and goes to my world.

CHAPTER ONE HUNDRED AND NINETYTHREE

Departure of Naciketas

Lomaharṣaṇa said:

1-5. King Janamejaya, the last of the Kuru line, after completing the twelve-year-long expiation for his killing a Brahmin after the performance of Aśvamedha sacrifice, impelled by his own action and very much worried, approached Vaiśampāyana, the great sage, disciple of Vyāsa, living on the bank of Gaṅgā, soon after he had finished his morning rites, and spoke to him in great repentance.

Janamejaya said:

6. O sage, when I think more and more about the deeds of man, I feel convinced how we have to face their results unavoidably.

7. I therefore, wish to know, of what kind is the abode of Yama, how extensive it is and how one sees it on going there.

8. Also how I can avoid going to that place of the king of the dead, the king of dharma who directs the whole world.

Sūta said:

9. Asked thus by the king, the sage replied in sweet voice.

Vaiśampāyana said:

10-11. O king, listen to this old story, which is auspicious, conducive to dharma and famè, purifying, bringing about good, the favourite of the learned and narrated in Itihāsas and Purāṇas.

12. In days of yore, there was a great sage by name Uddālaka who had mastered the Veda with all its accessories.

13. He had a son by name Naciketas who was a yogi, very intelligent and virtuous and a master of Vedic lore.

14. But he was cursed by the angry father to quickly go to Yama and see him.

15. The brilliant son said 'yes', meditated for a while and entered into yoga.

16. Soon he became invisible and told his father in great humility:

17-18. "O virtuous father, your words can never go false. I am, therefore, leaving for the glorious abode of Yama, the lord of dharma. But, doubtless, I shall return here".

The father said:

19. You are my only son and I have no other relative. So let it be false, against dharma or affecting your fame. (Please do not go).

20. You will be able to save me although I have said something wrong in my anger, and it is true that he who utters something unbecoming mercilessly in anger defiles his entire family.

21. I who cursed you, the virtuous boy thus, have become so defiled as not to be deserving of being spoken to.

22. I have become one who does not say the proper thing, but I don't wish any outrage on dharma.

23. O you good son, you have always been obedient, composed, forbearing and devoted to dharma. You have been sincerely attending on me and you alone are capable of enabling me to gain liberation.

24. I, therefore, earnestly request you not to go there.

25. If lord Yama happens to see you there even accidentally, he will never release you in his anger.

26. Know, then, that I will perish as one who has cut off the family line, condemned by all as a base sinner.

27. Hell is horrible and it is known as 'put'. The son is 'putra' because he saves the father from this.

28. Whatever penance the son performs, whatever he gifts and whatever he offers in fire, all that nourish his ancestors. To one without a son this is not there.

29. One may be a Śūdra engaged in service (prescribed for him), a Vaiśya engaged in cultivation, a Kṣatriya engaged in protection of the produce, or a Brāhmaṇa doing his deeds.

30. He may perform intense penance and make munificent gifts. But if he is without a son, he never attains heaven. So have I heard.

31. A father gets gratification through his son, a grandfather through his grandson and a great-grand-father through the son of the grandson.

32. I shall not let you go, the potential continuer of our family line. So I implore you in all earnestness not to go there.

Vaiśampāyana said:

33. The virtuous son spoke with composure and pleasure to the wailing father.

The son said:

34. "Don't be sorrowful, O father, you will see me return here. After seeing that god (Yama) who is revered by all, I shall certainly return to you, for I have no fear of the god of death.

35. That king (of the dead) will honour me because of your compassion.

36. You remain in truth and uphold truth. Truth is the ladder to heaven as the boat is the means of crossing the ocean.

37. The sun shines by truth, the fire blazes by truth and the earth remains firm by truth.

38. The sea does not advance over the shore because of truth; the mantra produces its wholesome effect over the world because of truth.

39. The sacrifices with their purifying mantras and honoured worship rest in truth. The Vedas sound by truth. The whole world is set in truth.

40. The Sāman sings by truth. Everything is established in truth. Heaven is truth, so too dharma. There is nothing outside truth.

41. O father, I have learnt that everything is got by truth. There is nothing that transcends truth.

42. It is well known that Brahmā, the very repository of the

Vedas, was banished by Rudra remaining in truth and Brahmā remains in austerity controlled by him.

43. Similarly, Agni was thrown into the mouth of the submarine horse by Aurva remaining in truth.

44. O father, all the worlds and gods were held by the valiant Saṁvarta out of compassion for gods.

45. Bali remains in the netherworld, protecting truth.

46. The great mountain Vindhya with hundreds of its rising peaks, does not grow because of truth. The whole world, with all its moving and statonary beings, goes on in truth.

47. All the duties of the householder, those of the Vānaprastha and the rules of all austerities are based on truth.

48. If a thousand Aśvamedhas and truth are weighed against each other, it is truth that weighs more.

49. Dharma is ruled by truth, and dharma protects when itself is protected. Therefore, follow truth and save yourself by your own self."

50-51. Having said this cheerfully, the effulgent and truthful son of the sage, resorted to his power of yoga attained by penance and reached the place of king Yama.

CHAPTER ONE HUNDRED AND NINETYFOUR

The return of Naciketas

Vaiśampāyana said:

1. On reaching the place of that inaccessible king (Yama), Naciketas was duly honoured and let off.

2. O king, when the sage saw his son returned, he was extremely delighted. He embraced him, smelt his head and filled the earth and sky with his shouts of joy.

3. Then he called the other sages and told them.

4. "O great sages with divine lustre, see the greatness of my son. He has gone to the abode of Yama and quickly returned here.

5. I am seeing him alive because of good luck, filial affection and service to elders.

6. There is none in this world as blessed as I am, because my son has returned here after falling into the jaws of death.

7. (Then he asked the son). You were not beaten or bound in the abode of Yama ? Your path was unhampered when you were going there ?

8. The horrible diseases did not pursue you there ? What strange things did you see there ? Were you happy ?

9. Did you see the king of the dead ? Did he see you with his eyes ?

10. Was he glad that you went there on your own accord ? And did he let you return so soon ?

11. You didn't have to face the harassment by the fierce doorkeepers there ? And even though released by the king, the others there didn't do you any harm ?

12. You found it possible to get a way to enter there and also to get out of it ? (He then turned to sages again and said:) My son has now come back to me. The gods are pleased.

13. So also the venerable sages and the pious Brahmins, in that my son has returned from the world of Yama".

14. Hearing him say like this, the sages there flocked to him giving up their vows and observances.

15-17. Those performing Japa or worshipping deities, others standing with thrown-up arms, yet others remaining on one foot and gazing the sun, still others worshipping fire, all of them hastily gathered to see Naciketas.

18-19. Naked sages, those remaining within heaps of stones, those in vow of silence, those eating the fallen leaves and water, those that torment themselves in fire, all these stood around him.

20. Some sat down, some remained standing, but all wanted to ask him many things.

21-22. Seeing Naciketas who had returned from Yama's world, some were afraid, some were glad, some were inquisitive, some were indifferent and others were full of doubts. But they all together asked him:

The sages said:

23. O Naciketas, the intelligent son observing dharma, the truthful boy devoted to serving the elders,

24. Tell us in truth what you have seen or heard (in Yama-

loka). All of us are eager to know it, particularly your father.

25. Even if it is a secret, you should tell us when asked, because you can see how full of fear all of us are.

26. By the māyā of Kāla the dead are never seen again. Man gets the result of whatever action he does.

27. Whatever action, good or bad, one does here, the result of it accrues in the other world.

28. We see the working of māyā of Kāla in that beings become dead and also become born.

29. Those who think about it do not find a solution since the whole world is engulfed in the darkness of desire and stupefaction. What is necessary is not thought upon, what is pleasurable is gone after.

30. What does Citragupta do there and what does he blabber ?

31. What is the appearance of Dharmarāja and what is Kāla like ? What form do the diseases have there and how do they act ?

32. By what action is one released from there and what are the deeds to be done ? That is the final resort of the whole world and nothing can be transgressed there.

33. People who know about (good and bad) actions speak of angry bindings, torments, draggings and cuttings there.

34. What befalls pure souls there and what befalls sinners ?

35. We ask all this out of affection and friendliness. Tell us in detail what actually you have seen, heard or understood.

Vaiśampāyana said:

36. O Janamejaya, listen now to what Naciketas said in reply to what the sages asked him.

CHAPTER ONE HUNDRED AND NINETYFIVE

The sinners in Yamaloka

Naciketas said:

1. O ascetic Brahmins, I shall tell you what you seek to know. Listen. Bow to Lord Dharmarāja.

2. I tell you briefly and according to my ability. Liars, molesters of animals, women and children,

3. Killers of Brahmins, deceivers, the obstinate, the ungrateful, those fond of the wives of others,

4. Those who outrage the modesty of maidens, defilers of Veda, those who harass the people following Vaidik path,

5. Sacrificers on behalf of Śūdras, condemned Brahmins, performers of sacrifices for those who are ineligible, those afflicted by leprosy,

6. Those who drink liquor, the Brahmins who kill other Brahmins or warriors, those that live on usury, those crooked in sight,

7. Those who give up their mother, father or wife, those that have ill-will towards their preceptors, those of bad conduct, messengers who speak indistinct,

8. Encroachers upon houses and fields, destroyers of bridges, people without children, without wife, those without the necessary attention in their deeds,

9. The unclean, the merciless, harassers, vow-breakers, sellers of soma, the henpecked, those that sell everything,

10. Speakers of falsehood, teachers of Veda for money, teachers of out-castes, the astrologers, the fortune-tellers,

11. Cohabiters of all including those prohibited, magicians, balance-holders,

12. Doers of actions without the idea of sin, those that harbour strong enmity, those that do not stake their life for the master, those averse to battle,

13. Those that steal others' wealth, assassinators, those justifying sinful actions, those earning their living by fire,

14. Those that do not serve others as prescribed, anchorites committing sin, makers of vessels,

15. Those selling things in temples, inns and tīrthas, those who speak against vows, those that speak untruth,

16. Those who grow hair and nails simply to appear as sannyāsins, crooked persons, those who make false documents,

17. Those who do not observe austerities though out of ignorance, those banished from hermitages, those who receive every offering, those who defile sacred places,

18. The quarrelsome, the cruel and thousands of others were there.

19. Now hear what women and men do on going to Yama's place.

Vaiśampāyana said:

20. Hearing these words of Naciketas, the sages were wonderstruck and they asked him again.

The sages said:

21. O you, the best among the learned, tell us about everything there as seen by you.

22. Of what nature is Kāla because of whom the whole world continues.

23. The selfish person who performs actions in this world is not allowed entry in the world of Brahmā.

24. Although tormented and burnt till the end of the aeon, there is no loss to the body in that place,

25. Torture is applied again and again according to the nature of the action, and one has to suffer it. No Brahmin will dare to go there because of fear.

26. One avoids going there by giving gifts and performing austerities.

27. What is the nature of Vaitaraṇī ? What is the sort of water that flows in it ? How is the hell Raurava and how is the deceptive Śālmalī tree ? How are the messengers there and what do they do ?

28. What should a person do to shield himself from all this by his merit acquired previously ?

29. Being under the influence of sin, courage is lost, and even those that are sinless get stupefied.

30. What should be known is not known nor what is virtue and what is not. The thinking faculty is lost because of sin.

31. Due to illusion what is the supreme is not known and many toil there having committed sin.

32. Please tell us about all this as you have seen with your own eyes.

CHAPTER ONE HUNDRED AND NINETYSIX

The city of Yama

Vaiśampāyana said:

1. Hearing these words of the great sages, he began to tell them everything in detail.

Naciketas said:

2. O great sages, listen to me. The city of the god of death is one thousand yojanas in breadth, double that in length and double that in perimeter.

3. It is full of mansions, golden spires and beautiful rows of buildings.

4. It has got a golden fort also of great height.

5. The houses there shine like the Kailāsa mountain. Rivers flow there full of spotless water.

6. There are beautiful lakes, lotus-ponds and pools; also tanks and wells.

7. It is full of men and women and elephants and horses of different kinds and from different places.

8. We find there every kind of living being. Here and there battles and single combats are also seen.

9-10. Hundreds of thousands of people are there, some singing, some laughing, some sorrowing, some playing, some eating, some sleeping, some dancing, some standing and some remaining bound.

11. In accordance with their actions, some are found big and some small.

12. My limbs become languid and the mind becomes disturbed when I think further. Still, a divine feeling comes upon me. So I shall tell you what I have seen and heard.

13. There is an important river named Puṣpodakā (flowery water) full of all sorts of trees on the bank, but it is (alternately) seen and not seen.

14. There are golden flights of steps in it and it is full of golden sand.

15. Its water is placid, cool and sweet-smelling. On its banks are groves of flowering and fruit-bearing trees with numerous birds on them.

16. That great river flows there removing all sins. I saw thousands of trees on its sides.

17. The gods play in its water. The Gandharvas seem to be singing Sāman there with their wives.

18. The Nāga and Kinnara women sing and play there.

19. Thousands of divine damsels play in this manner in the water and in the mansions.

20. There are many trees whose branches bear fruits and flowers at all times, and birds flock there to get what they need.

21. Beautiful women with lovely girdles provide delight to men there to their heart's content.

22. They splash the water with their lovers and sweetly sing with inebriation.

23. With the splashing of water and jingling of jewels, the river appears to be decked with divine gems.

24. The great and auspicious river named Vaivasvatī beautifully flows in the middle of the city, protecting it like a mother her son.

25. Swans, white like the jasmine and the moon, gracefully move about in its sands in the midst of the charming water.

26. With fine Cakravākas and lotuses with golden carpets and with attractive golden flights of steps, it is very resplendent.

27. Its water is clear, pure, sweet-smelling and very tasty like ambrosia. The trees in the forests on the banks are full of flowers and fruits.

28. Inebriated beautiful women play in it as much as they like but they never get weary.

29. It is worshipped by gods and sages. With its plentiful water, it is like the weighty words of poets pregnant with meaning.

30. There is an image of the river erected there, on which numerous people pour water (in reverence). The lofty rows of buildings on the bank inspire wonder.

31. In the fine groves there women gather in large numbers and sing playing instruments and beating tāla.

32. They provide great pleasure to the gods in heaven with their fine voice mixed with the sound of the drum, the lute and the flute.

33. They never get satisfied with playing in the balconies from where the wind wafts the scent of Agaru and sandal.

34. In some places the scent spreads in such an intense manner as to block entry there, in some other places people engage themselves with playthings, and in yet other places the music of women fills the air.

35. Some play with their beloveds in golden pedestals. Some play in the water with great delight.

36. The different items of beauty there cannot be recounted even if we take a number of days for it.

CHAPTER ONE HUNDRED AND NINTYSEVEN

Yama and his associates

The sage's son (Naciketas) said:

1-2. There is a hundred-tiered gateway in the north, ten yojanas in breadth and double that in length, with a fort on the sides, shining prominently and so tall as to appear as a scraping the sky.

3. It is highly lustrous and provided with several contrivances. This is the entrance for gods, sages and others (of their category) who do good and virtuous deeds.

4. There is another gateway (on the east), white like a heap of autumn clouds. It is the entrance for (ordinary) human beings who have acquired merit.

5-6. Built of iron and highly hot is the gateway in the south, terrific in appearance.

7. The son of the Sun (Yama) has assigned this entrance for all sinners and killers.

8. Made of Udumbara and very much uneven is the gateway in the west.

9. It always glows with fire and is difficult to look at. It is meant for those that do bad and prohibited deeds.

10-11. In that beautiful city, there is a jewelled assembly hall constructed by Yama.

12. Therein is the seat of justice occupied by saints who are truthful and virtuous and free from anger, desire and attachment.

13. That is the assembly where justice is dispensed for the righteous as well as sinful, for good as well as bad, according to the store of result of the actions performed.

14. These judges decide the merit of actions according to Śāstra, taking their stand on *dharma* and without doubt, fear or favour.

15. They consider matters from a universal point of view according to Śāstra and their observation.

16. All of them think well on the matter with full restraint and in all seriousness.

17. (The judges are) Manu, Prajāpati, Pārāśarya (Vyāsa), Atri, Auddālaki, Āpastamba, Bṛhaspati, Śukra, Gautama,

18. Śaṅkha, Likhita, Aṅgiras, Bhṛgu, Pulastya, Pulaha and other law-givers.

19. Along with Yama they think of the justice to be dispensed. The divine as well as human among them are dispassionate.

20. One among them stands out with kuṇḍala (on the ears), aṅgada (on the wrists) and mukuṭa (on the head) and he is the effulgent Brahmadatta.

21. He is so brilliant in his appearance and speech that he appears like the single embodiment of all the rest.

22. By his side stand the great divine sages steeped in Veda and Vedāṅga.

23. They discuss the meaning of Veda, truth and dharma, and also about Śikṣā, Chandas and other Śāstras.

24. They also discuss Nirukta, the Sāman music, alchemy and everything else pertaining to Veda.

25. I saw there in the palace of Dharmarāja sages and manes reciting auspicious stories.

26. Near there, I saw one black in colour, with projecting cheek, erect hair and uncouth form,

27. With face ugly, canines protruding, full of anger and generating fear, holding a big cane in the left hand.

28. He is the eternal Kāla who listens to Dharmarāja whenever ordered to execute punishment. There are others also there to carry out such orders.

29. I saw there a resplendent female form worshipped by Yama with celestial sandal and other unguents.

30. She is the destroyer of the worlds and there is nothing beyond her.

31. None has ever suggested any means to go beyond her. The Asuras and even the sages are afraid of her.

32. She is worshipped by gods and demons and also by yogins.

33. It is from her body that the oppressing ailments arise, as also the dreadful diseases brought about by time.

34. I then saw the god of death who is full of valour, but cruel and angry.

35. He is full of strength and lustre. Age and death do not affect him,

36. Along with the god of death are many that sing and laugh and excite life.

37. Some there glow with divine ornaments, chowries and umbrellas.

38. Some I saw there installed in seats and worshipped.

39. In many places there I saw serious fevers and severe pains in the form of men and women.

40. There were fierce women, the embodiments of desire and anger, consuming life.

41. The sound of their conversation near Dharmarāja seemed to break the earth.

42. (I saw there) Rākṣasas big and small who eat flesh, some having both feet, but some single-footed, some with three feet, some with many feet;

43. Some with both hands, but some with a single hand, some with three hands and some with many hands; so too some with small ears, and some with ears as big as elephants.

44. Some people were wearing many kinds of ornaments like keyūra and mukuṭa.

45. Some had garlands and some anklets. Some were holding axe, some mace, some disc, some trident.

46. Some had spear, some javelin, some bow, some sword and some club.

47. Some were holding curd in hand, some sandal, some varieties of food and some clothes.

48. Some were holding incense and some different kinds of garments.

49. There were palanquins and various vehicles to which were yoked horses, elephants and swans.

50. There were śarabhas, bulls, elephants, peacocks, cranes, cakravākas and horses. I saw all this. But there were fearful things also.

51. While some were well dressed, some were shabbily dressed. Some wore fresh silk and while some wore torn cloth. Some spoke well while others were dumb. Some were out to kill others.

52. Some were tawny and some black. Some were for dharma and some for fame. These were in attendance on Yama.

53. So if the Brahmin performs the sacrifices, he will not have any disappointment.

54. Those who deserve honour should be duly honoured. When they get pleased, all good results.

CHAPTER ONE HUNDRED AND NINETYEIGHT

Torments in Hell

Naciketas said:

1. Yama, the god of the dead, gave me audience in his assembly.

2. He duly honoured me with seat, *pādya* and *arghya* according to Vedic rites.

3. He then asked me to sit in a golden seat on which were strewn darbha grass and flowers.

4. His face which is always terrific, became calm as I was looking at it.

5. Due to his kindness for me, his reddish eyes soon became gentle like lotus petals.

6. His attitude created confidence in me and I became glad.

7. Then issued from my mouth a hymn in his praise which removes all sins, brings about all desires, confers fame and is commended even by gods.

8. Yama, the great upholder of dharma, was pleased at this.

The sage's son (Naciketas) said:

9. O four-footed lord, the god of the manes, you are the ordainer and sustainer of Śrāddha. I bow to you.

10. O Dharmarāja, the great god of the dead, you are the

knower of time, the knower of whatever that is done, and one wedded to truth. I bow to you.

11. You are action and the actuator of action. You are the lord of past, present and future. You are the purifier as well as the stupefier. You are the essence as well as elaboration. O uneven-eyed holder of rod and noose, I bow to you.

12. O you resplendent like the sun, the observer of the life of all, black in complexion, indomitable, having the form of sesamum oil, I bow to you.

13. You are lustrous like the sun, you are the carrier of offerings to gods as well as to the manes. You are a mighty lord. I bow to you.

14. You are destroyer of sins, you stand in austerity, you are ever the guardian of Śrāddha, you are a great ascetic. With one eye transformed into many you are Kāla and Death. I bow to you.

15. Sometimes you appear with a rod, sometimes with a fully shaven head, sometimes as the fearful Kāla, sometimes as a boy, sometimes as an old man, sometimes in a form that strikes terror, I bow to you.

16. The world is controlled by you through dharma. You see to this directly and, without you, dharma cannot be accomplished.

17. You are the god of gods, the penance among penances and the japa among japas. In this I don't find anyone other than you.

18-19. You never attempt to push down from here sages without any relations or friends and chaste women in distress engaged in penance.

20. So, among all gods, you are the greatest upholder of dharma.

Vaiśampāyana said:

21. Listening to this hymn uttered by the son of sage Uddālaka, Yama was extremely pleased.

Yama said:

22. I am delighted at your sweet hymn. May good befall you. Tell me frankly what I may do for you.

23. O Brahmin, ask of me any boon you like, whether it be prosperity or health or longevity.

The sage's son (Naciketas) said:

24. "O great lord, I desire neither death nor life. If you, who look after the welfare of all, are pleased with me and wish to grant me a boon, then let me see this entire region of yours as it is.

25. If you are inclined to give me a boon, then show me the whole thing so as to know what befalls the good people and what befalls the sinners.

26-27. Show me also, O lord, Citragupta who considers on your behalf what is to be meted out to whom according to the particular action done by each."

28. When I said thus, he called the man at the door and said "Take this Brahmin safely to Citragupta.

29. Tell him that he should treat him in a fitting manner and do what he desires."

30. I was then quickly led by that attendant to the presence of Citragupta.

31. He rose up and, thinking for a while, welcomed me saying 'O great sage, make yourself quite at ease here'.

32. Telling me thus, he gave instructions to his fierce-looking servants who were remaining there with folded hands.

Citragupta said:

33. "Listen to me, O my devoted and dutiful servants,

34. With my permission, this Brahmin is going to the place where the dead reside. He should be well concealed and carefully guarded.

35. He should not have anything to feel unhappy. He should not have fatigue either from heat or from cold; nor should he suffer for food or drink. I command you so.

36. This Brahmin who is full of compassion for all beings and is following the wish of his father, has been granted such a boon by me.

37. Let him see this city of Dharmarāja as much as he likes." So saying he asked me to go and see it.

38. The attendants were asked to lead me there. (Going

there I saw) mighty beings running and chasing people and beating, binding and burning them.

39. They break their bones by beating them again and again with bamboo sticks and often with more heavy objects.

40. With broken bones and bruised heads, the people piteously cry aloud, but find none to help them.

41. In deep and dark abysses, many are scorched in fire and also used as fuel for the fire.

42. Some fall in boiling oil, some in molten lime as the result of their own evil deeds.

43. They are severely tortured again and again.

44. Some are put into machines and crushed like sesamum and blood flows out profusely from them.

45. There is the horrible river Vaitaraṇī with eddy and foam, difficult to cross for sinful persons.

46. Hundreds of people are held by the feet, thrown over the trident and then thrown into Vaitaraṇī.

47. Hundreds of people in their curdled blood are bitten by numerous snakes.

48. When they sink in the river unable to cross it, whirlpools and ripples arise there in abundance.

49. The sinful people get parched there, sinking and vomitting, but find none to save them.

50. Many are thrown over the deceptive Śālmalī tree, full of metallic nails and severely beaten again and again with swords and spears.

51. I saw in its branches, a large number of goblins and demons furiously hanging down.

52. Those thrown over the tree move to the branches, being unable to bear the pain of piercing nails.

53-54. The demons in the branches then pounce upon them swiftly like monkeys in big trees and eat them up.

55. I could hear the crushing sound like that of a mleccha eating fowl.

56-57. They eat them in their fierce mouths as if these were ripe mango fruits and after sipping the marrow also, throw down on the ground their skeletal form.

58. Those in the forests also are similarly handled.

59-60. The sinners standing below in large numbers implore

the servants of Yama to leave them in mercy, but they are only further tortured.

61. Hit by showers of stones and choked by clouds of dust, many rush to the shade of the tree, only to find there scorching fire.

62. They are then beaten up and thrown in blazing fire.

63. Many request these attendants to be pleased to give them a pot of cold water.

64. But what is given to them is boiling water by drinking which they get scalded and cry aloud.

65. In their agony they fall down clasping one another. So do many others becoming unconscious due to hunger.

66. But there is also sumptuous sweet-smelling food in heaps.

67. There is curd and milk, sesamum cakes and milky soup, also honey and liquor.

68. There is fruit juice of various kinds and cool and fragrant drinks.

69. There are also drinks mixed with milk, ghee or curd. All these await the good souls going there.

70. We find there for them incense and fine sandal paste. Everything is inviting and abundant.

71. For serving food for these souls there are handsome women well ornamented.

72. They hold basketful of fruits in their hands and keep flowers and water for *pādya*. They are graceful with jingling anklets.

73. They serve food for thousands of them.

74. While these women honour the virtuous in this way, the servants of Yama beat the sinners under their control, laugh at them and say:

75. "O you ungrateful, avaricious, adulterous wretches,

76. Evil in mind, bad in action, reluctant to gifts, active to speak ill of others, conversing only with sinners,

77. Shamelessly ready to ask from others. When you were affluent on earth, you never gave anything, food, drink or fuel.

78. Therefore it is that all these torments are imposed on you.

79. When the effects of your misdeeds are over, you will be released from here to be born again on earth in misery.

80. The sinners are born in poor families in human world with the sins adhering in them.

81. But those that have lived an irreproachable life, particularly those belonging to the four castes, being truthful, peaceful compassionate and virtuous,

82. Rest here for sometime with their followers, and then go to the supreme abode or are born on earth again in a high family,

83. Affluent, well ordered, full of beautiful women and then attain supreme bliss."

CHAPTER ONE HUNDRED AND NINETYNINE

Torments in Hell (Contd.)

The Sage's son Naciketas said:

1. The entire ground there is strewn with iron nails and is rugged and dark.

2. The sinners with their hands, feet and head bruised, are not able to leave that place for long.

3. But only the sinners are thrown there. Those who are devoted to dharma and have control of self, remain there as in their homes.

4. Beautiful women wait upon them with sumptuous food and cool drinks.

5. The sinners are thrown on hard and burning rocks.

6. They are shown places with trees and as they run to go there with feet and waist scorched,

7. The servants of Yama rush there and harass them. There is none to save them from the torment.

8. Then there are others who are bitten by ferocious dogs from head to foot and they cry aloud again and again.

9-10. In another place fierce beings with projecting canines, pierce the sinful souls with needles and leave them without food and water, when they are hungry and thirsty, for the sin incurred by them in refusing these essentials to those in need.

11. A cruel woman of a body of brandished steel embraces a man and chases him when he runs away.

12. She tells him: "I am (the combined form of) your sister, daughter-in-law,

13. Maternal aunt, paternal aunt, uncle's wife, preceptor's wife, friend's wife, brother's wife, king's wife,

14. The wives of Vaidikas and Brahmins, all of whom you have molested. You cannot escape from me even if you go to the nether world.

15. For the wrong you have done, I am going to thrash you. O shameless man, why do you try to run away?"

16. She chases him again and tells him repeatedly:

17. "Even if born among thousands of learned men, a sinner is tormented in this manner,

18. I, therefore, a low woman, embrace you. Why do you cry?

19. When I lead you like this, don't you feel ashamed to entreat me with folded hands?

20. Why do you try to get away? wherever you go in this abode of Yama, I will pursue you, as you have outraged the modesty of another's wife."

21. (In another place) people are beaten with iron rods like cowherds beating the kine with sticks.

22. Some are bitten by tigers, lions, jackals, donkeys and dogs and some pecked by crows.

23. There is a grove of palms of swords enveloped by flames and fumes, resembling a conflagration and glowing all around.

24. The sinners are thrown there by Yama's men and scorched.

25. When they run from there to the trees in the grove of palms of swords, they are cut again and again.

26. Thus dragged and burnt and mutilated, they cry aloud.

27. The noble souls that stand at the entrance to the grove of palms of swords, chastise the sinners.

28. "O you sinners who have destroyed the bridge of dharma for that very reason you have to undergo torments in thousands.

29. After all this, if at all you are born as human beings, it will be in extremely poor families and you will always be in misery."

30. (In another place) there are birds resembling tongues of fire and raising loud cries. Their beaks are of iron.

31. These as well as carnivorous animals like tigers and wild dogs angrily bite the sinners.

32-33. I saw the mighty servants of Yama throwing many persons in this grove of palms of swords which is full of tigers and bears and innumerable worms and ants.

34. Some were bruised by swords and others pierced by tridents.

35. There were thousands of wells, pools, ponds, lakes and rivers, all of blood.

36. O great sages, I saw also places full of marrow, flesh and faeces.

37. In them were put numerous sinners who have not only to put up with their foul smell, but also to dip themselves in them again and again.

38. Cranes from above make showers of blood, bones and stones upon them.

39. I could hear the pitiable cries of those who were floating in them or running out of them and they were bound and beaten again.

40. Their wailings filled the entire place.

41. Bound in some places, blocked in others, struck in yet others and thrown up in still others, their pitiable cries could be heard everywhere.

42. I saw certain other things in certain other places, the very thought of which will make one shudder.

CHAPTER TWO HUNDRED

Torments in Hell (*Contd.*)

The Sage's son (*Naciketas*) *said*:

1-2. There are eight hells where the sinners are tormented, namely, Tapta, Mahātapta, Raurava, Mahāraurava, Saptatāla, Kālasūtra, Andhakāra and Andhakāravara.

3-4. They are first taken to the first, then to the second where the duration is twice, from there to the third where the duration is thrice, from there to the fourth where the duration is four times, then to the fifth where the duration is five times, then to the sixth where the duration is six times, then to the seventh where the duration is seven times and then to the eighth where the duration is eight times.

5. The dead go there in the course of a single day and night and for those of them afflicted by sin, there is only misery and more misery.

6. There is only misery there and no pleasure. The misery goes on increasing. There is no means at all there to get even a little happiness.

7. Man, after death, is left there. There are no killers there, but he never gets pleasure through any of the senses—sound, touch, colour, taste or smell.

8. He never gets pleasure, physical or mental. All that is there is sorrow lone.

9. The earth there is full of hot and sharp iron nails and the sky is covered with flocks of birds with fiery tongues.

10. Hunger is there much, so too thirst. But what is hot is too hot and what is cold is too cold (to eat or drink).

11. When one wishes to drink water, one is taken by the Rākṣasas to a pond having lotus and lilies and swans and cranes.

12. But on reaching there in all eagerness, one finds the water boiling hot.

13. The Rākṣasas then bring cooked meat, but throw it in a pond of brackish water.

14. (When one enters the pond for taking it) one is bitten by the numerous fish there.

15. At the end of the assigned period, when one tries to run away, one gets the body fleshy for being tormented again.

16. Whether sitting at the top or leaving or running, serious torment is absolutely certain.

17. There is the abominable Kumbhīpāka which is a deep pit of dung shaped like a lotus leaf.

18. The Rākṣasas thrash the sinners there biting their lips in anger and exclaiming aloud.

19. There is a forest of swords and another of red lead. The latter is strewn with red hot sand.

20. There the sinners are burnt, cut, struck, hit, thrashed, dragged and dismembered.

21. Black and spotted dogs bite them, so too do serpents and scorpions.

22. There is the deceptive Śālmalī tree with its numerous projecting thorns. They are dragged there till the body is left with bones alone.

23. All the torment and adversity for the sinner arise soon.

24. When he wants coolness, he gets heat and when he wants warmth he gets coldness. When he desires pleasure, what he gets is sorrow. Pleasure he never can have.

25. He always receives injuries in thousands all over his body and at all times.

26. A furious river full of ferocious animals, has to be crossed.

27. This is named Karambhavālukā. It is a hundred yojanas in length and is like blazing fire.

28. Then there is the big river Vaitaraṇī of bitter water, fifty yojanas long and five yojanas deep.

29. It is deep in mud and is full of skin, flesh and bones. There are in it big scorpions with sharp teeth.

30. There are owls as big as bows and ferocious and poisonous with tongues sharp enough to break bones.

31. Somehow crossing this river of deep mud, some manage to reach the empty and supportless abodes there,

32. Where, however, they are devoured by numerous rats leaving but the skeleton.

33. But in the morning the body gets flesh again as soon as the wind wafts over it.

34. Then there is a mango-grove where ferocious birds feed on the man eating up all his skin and flesh and veins, eyes and years.

35. On the south, at a distance of three yojanas, is a banyan tree which glows always like an evening cloud.

36. There is a big fire-place ca'led Yamacullī, ten yojanas deep.

37. It always burns and is ever blinding with its smoke.

38. Thousands of dead are thrown into it incessantly by the Rākṣasas, servants of Yama. In this fire-place they are to remain for a month.

39. Then there is the river called Śakunikā which is full of fat and morrow.

40. This proceeds from the interior of the Yamacullī. On crossing this, there are seven kinds of torments to be undergone.

41. Every one of these is extremely painful, but the sinner has to go through them in their order.

42. There are ten Śūlas and thirteen Kumbhīpākas where one whole day and night should be spent.

43. The merciless and fearful Rākṣasas hold the sinners in tridents and bake them over glowing cinders.

44. They are then held head down-wards over clouds of choking smoke and then fried in hot oil in big vessels.

45. They are then held over the fire of burning marrow in a pit of dried cowdung. This is done for ten days in each.

46. When these seven kinds of torments are over, they are taken to the river 'Yama' at a distance of three yojanas wherein flows molten lead.

47. Crossing it with burnt body and completely unconscious, they get rest there for a while.

48. They see a beautiful pond with cool water and shady trees around. They get there whatever they want, because this is the sister of Yama.

49. All the sinners get food and drink there, but all this is forgotten after spending three days there.

50. Then there is the mountain called Śūlagraha which extends over a hundred yojanas. It is constituted of a single rock and no being lives in it.

51. The clouds shower hot water on it and people traverse it with difficulty in the course of a day.

52. There is the Śṛṅgāṭaka forest which is full of biting black flies.

53. The bite of these flies transforms one into a worm. One has to face there showers of flesh and blood.

54-55. Traversing this, the sinner goes to another place of torment where he sees his sons, mother, father, wife and other dear ones. But he is bound and can only helplessly cry.

56. "O son, save me, save me," he cries, but what he gets then is beatings with clubs, rods and bamboo sticks, knocks with the fist, blows with whips and bitings by snakes.

57. Unable to bear all this pain, he swoons.

58. The sinners get here this sort of treatment again and again.

59. Those who commit the five heinous sins, necessarily reach this place.

60. When the punishments for these sins are undergone, one becomes a stationary being.

61. After a period in that form, the dead man is born as an animal.

62. But this is after his life in hell for sixty thousand and sixty hundred years.

63. When the effects of his actions are over, he becomes a being born of sweat and undergoes all its life-process.

64. He then takes birth as a bird, then as a cow and afterwards as a man.

65. Among men he is first born as a Śūdra and after a proper life as a Śūdra, takes birth as a Vaiśya endowed with the result of all actions.

66. After his life as a Vaiśya, he is born as a Kṣatriya and after that as a Brāhmaṇa.

67. If, after taking birth as a Brāhmaṇa, he commits sins again and debases himself with evil mind and self-ruinous actions, he gets afflictions physical and mental.

68. As a result of his actions, he develops a tendency to Brāhminicide, becomes a leper, squint-eyed and crow-voiced.

69. He gets protruding teeth, develops foul odour in his body and gets a bent of mind to drink liquor, kill the parents and murder the king.

70. He also becomes a stealer of gold, and, in short, one similar to a killer of Brahmin.

71. In another place in hell, I could see sinners badly mutilated as a result of their own actions, and blood flowing everywhere.

72. The whole place is full of such people who groan again and again.

73. There frequently arise cries of those who are bound in various ways and beaten.

74. They are tormented by beatings with iron rods and pricking weapons.

75. This is done till those engaged in this get tired.

76. When they are thus tired, they make a report to Citragupta.

CHAPTER TWO HUNDRED AND ONE

Fight between Rākṣasas and Yama's men

The Sage's son (Naciketas) said:

1. Then Yama's men of different forms gathered together and went to Citragupta with folded hands.

The men said:

2. "We have become weak and tired (by this work in which we are now engaged). So please entrust this work to others. We shall do some other work, however difficult it may be.

3. Save us, O Lord. Please see how much wearied we are. Others will do this work to your satisfaction."

4. Enraged at these words, Citragupta heaved a sigh like a serpent and looked all around with eyes red with anger.

5. His eyes fell on an uncouth figure standing not far from him and immediately that person came near him.

6. The angry Citragupta sent him on an errand. He was the Rākṣasa named Mandeha[1] and he departed immediately.

7. He went to the giant Rākṣasas who were in various forms, wearing many ornaments and standing ready to bring about any kind of destruction.

8. They were the persons meant to be brought there by Citragupta who looks at all beings alike.

9. Then those cannibalic Rākṣasas having numerous forms mounted elephants and horses,

10. Donned armour and gloves, took their weapons and led by their servants, bowed at his feet.

11. Awaiting his order in great joy, they said, "O Lord, tell us what we should do. We are here to carry out your orders. Whose life should we cut ?"

12. Hearing their words, Citragupta said choked with anger, heaving again and again.

13. "O you warriors, Mandehas, who always do what I wish, bind these (my men) and bring them here.

14. You are all highly valiant and you are the annihilators of all beings. Bring these that disobey me, wounded or bound."

---

1. The chief of the group of demons called Mandehas.

15. Hearing these words, they said:

The Rākṣasas said:

16. "Wearied, hungry or sorrowful sages, should be considered as ministers, so too the thousands of servants.

17. They are ordered to be killed by your great self. It is not proper that they should become the source of our destruction.

18. Just as they have arisen thinking of *dharma*, so too are we. You are also for the same purpose.

19. Let there be no false resolve for one remaining in *dharma*. If you are pleased, give up this idea of our fight.

20. Protect us from those mighty servants who will be struck by us Rākṣasas in the battle-field."

21. Then fierce diseases with forms at their will soon came ready there.

22. Some came on elephants, some on horses, some in chariots, some on swans and some on lions.

23. Others came on deer, jackals, buffaloes, tigers, asses and goats, also on vultures, eagles, peacocks, cocks and serpents.

24. In vehicles in this manner, armed with numerous weapons and mutually challenging, they all appeared there.

25. The warriors on either side, in their eagerness to gain victory, brandished their weapons and raised shouts which seemed to make the earth shudder.

26-27. Then started the battle, and in its darkness shone the crowns, bangles and ear-rings all over the place.

28-29. The battle became exciting and frightful with clashing tridents, spears, swords, clubs and other weapons.

30. Hand to hand fight was followed by each dragging the other by the hair and thus swelled the battle.

31. The Rākṣasas were vanquished by the valiant men of Yama and Loud utterances like 'give, give', 'strike', 'hold', 'stand' etc. could be heard.

32. Those who were fleeing were caught hold of and challenged by their opposites with eyes red with rage.

33. "Wait, Wait, where do you go?" "I am not going, be assured." "I have released this weapon to destroy your body".

34. "O fool, you have not released any weapon to injure me." "I have aimed these arrows. Receive them. Why do you run ?"

35. "What do you say, O wicked man ? I am an adept in battle. Tell me whether you can live facing this weapon which I release."

36. The Mandeha Rākṣasas soon came to be caught in their thousands.

37. Then they resorted to magical means as they could assume any form at will.

38. Their army became covered with darkness and they could be visible as well as invisible. Then Yama's men resorted to Jvara, the fierce fever, for help.

39. He was uneven-eyed, held the trident in his hand and was the destroyer of all beings.

40. "Ordered by Citragupta, the Rākṣasas called Mandehas are killing and eating us. They are in the form of a thousand ailments and we are as ourselves. O Lord of the worlds, protect us."

41. Hearing these words of Yama's men, the black, squint-eyed Jvara holding the iron rod in his hand, became angry.

42. He then called a large number of his mighty soldiers who were shining like fire. They stood before him with folded hands. He commanded them:

43. "Burn these Rākṣasas by your physical strength as well as yogic power".

44. At this command of Jvara, they rushed to the place of these Rākṣasas shouting like thunder.

45. They struck with their numerous weapons the haughty Rākṣasas in large number.

46. They became seriously wounded and drenched in blood.

47. Yama himself then interceded, stopped the battle and saved the Rākṣasas who were being thus killed.

48. He then went to Jvara in all humility, honoured him holding his hand and pacified him.

49. He led him into his house and wiped off the sweat on his face.

50. After he had calmed down, Yama said, "O lord, you are full of penance and you pervade everywhere. But what have you done ?

51. You are worshipped by the whole world. O lord, you and I control this whole world as we should, as we have seen and heard.

52-53. I am to be received by you when my end comes, although I am the annihilator of all beings. So be pleased to go to your abode and to put an end to this battle.

54. The six crores of Rākṣasas will be revived and they will become decayless but will not go to you."

55. Thus bringing the war to a close, Yama restored friendship between Citragupta and his men.

56. They then requested Citragupta to allot them their duties as before regarding the good and the bad the mortals acquire.

57. Then they went to Rudra by the side of Citragupta and bowing to him, said:

58-59. "As the worlds, as the king and as Death, O lord, rise-up. Forgive us, forgive us."

CHAPTER TWO HUNDRED AND TWO

Punishment according to deeds

The sage (Naciketas) said:

1. I was wonderstruck at the instructions given by the wise Yama to Citragupta.

2. Those who have swerved from the righteous path have to take the consequences. Some are scorched in fire and some severely bound. They are tortured as the result of their own deeds.

3-4. (Yama says): "Take him away soon, this sinner who has done bad deeds, who is ungrateful and who is of wicked mind. Let him be devoured by pouncing dogs.

5. Take him who has the sin of killing the father, mother or cow, to the deceptive Śālmalī tree and let the sharp thorns in it pierce him.

1. This shows that the Jvara was the manifestation of Rudra.

6. Fry him in oil or in decomposed ghee and then from the hot vessel throw him in a hot copper plate.

7. Then throw him in burning fire. He will be then born as a man and will face the torments of debts.

8. Throw the man, who has stolen a bed or seat or set fire, quickly into Vaitaraṇī.

9. For the man who defiled holy places for bath is this pike fresh from fire.

10. Pierce the ears of him who has given false evidence or uttered falsehood otherwise.

11. Bind the Brahmin who has performed sacrifice for the village, who has been unsteady in mind or boastful or obstinate, and give him nothing.

12. Cut off the tongue of the man who has offended any one by his words.

13. Cut off the generative organ of the man who has committed adultery whether without knowing it or deliberately out of lust, and then apply lime and also heat.

14. Yoke him to the mortar who has ruined his coparceners out of selfishness.

15. Thrash this usurer all over his body for the great sin he has committed.

16. The stealer of gold and the ungrateful man should be equated with the person who has killed a Brahmin.

17. Cut his bones and apply lime and fire. Let five ferocious tigers tear him with their sharp teeth.

18. Put him in boiling slime who has failed to maintain fire or given it up altogether.

19. Give him to the fierce scorpions for he has incurred the sin of killing a hero.

20. Throw him who performed sacrifices for all into the deep pond. Let him carry water to all kinds of beasts.

21. Let there be none to help him or give him anything.

22. Let those who performed vows without gifts, those who sold Veda and those that did all kinds of ritual not be given anything.

23. Let him who took away the water-vessel and prohibited any one from food, be beaten with strong rods.

24. He should be beaten with bamboo sticks, whips and iron rods. He should not be given food or water.

25. Burn him in fire who failed to keep the confidence reposed in him.

26. Put him in fire for thousands of years who has committed theft of a Brahmin's wealth.

27. Afterwards send him to be born as an animal. Let his minute body then enter different kinds of worms and birds.

28. After thousands of such lives, let him be born as a man again and again in various families, but always as a wicked person.

29. The man who has killed a Brahmin should be oppressed to the maximum; so too the murderer of the king, the stealer of gold and the drinker of alcohol.

30. Then he should be afflicted with consumption.

31. Let this man who has killed a cow be made to climb up the deceptive Śālmalī tree. Let him be dragged by the Rākṣasas.

32. Let him be then put in the hell Pūtīpāka and bitten by beasts. To a period one-fourth of that for Brahminicide, he should remain born as a beast.

33. He should be condemned wherever he goes and he is to be born again and again doing sinful things.

34. This man is wicked. He has incurred the sin of killing his father. Let him be bitten by the beasts for a hundred years.

35. Let him then be put in different hells. Let him become a human being again, but die even while in womb.

36. Let him be thus in ten wombs and then released to be born as a man but full of misery. Let him suffer due to hunger and diseases.

37-38. Let him who has betrayed his friend be quickly crushed in machine and put in fire for two hundred years.

39. Let him be born as a dog and afterwards as a man full of misery, discarded by all and suffering ailments.

40. This man has stolen salt and also what belonged to the Brahmin.

41. Let him be put here for five hundred years. Then he will be born as a worm in faeces. He will then take birth as a bird and afterwards as a pig.

42. Let this man who used to set fire (to useful things) be put in this fire of burning wood.

43. When the effect of his actions is over, he will be born as an animal and then as a man full of misery.

44-45. Those who jointly persuade one for bad deeds and those that steal the wealth of others, are to be put in the hell Raurava.

46. And he who does bad instigated thus is to be tortured in Kumbhīpāka. He is to be born as an ass and later as a pig eating filth.

47. He who commits theft of wealth should undergo severe suffering. He will be born as an ass ten times.

48. Then taking birth as a human being, he will be a thief and incur all sorts of sins harassing others. Then he will be born as a being hanging head downwards from a tree.

49. Let the greedy miser be burnt in fire.

50. He is to be released only after a hundred years.

51. He will be born as a pig and then as an ichneumon and finally as a human being again.

52. The man who gives false evidence and is wedded to falsehood, never gets peace anywhere, being condemned by his own actions.

53. Let this liar who has appropriated for himself the field of another, suffer here as long as the result of his actions persists in him.

54. Let him suffer for his actions one after another. That will be, no doubt, for a lakh of years.

55. Let him then be born as various animals and later as a man without anything to appease his hunger.

56. He will be full of sins and his desires will never be fulfilled. He will be born blind or deaf.

57. He will be born sometimes dumb, sometimes blind and sometimes full of diseases. He will, thus, have only suffering and never happiness.

58. He who misappropriates the field, even after a thousand lives as various beings, never attains peace.

59. Let him who takes for himself another's land, although distressed by his own mental anguish, be bound well and burnt in fire.

60. After a long period in that manner in my world, let him be born as a cat.

61. Let his hunger be never appeased and let him continue to be kept bound. Let him be born as fifty kinds of animals.

62. Let this man who is guilty of killing birds, be bitten by dogs and vultures.

63. Let him then become a cock eating filth and afterwards as a fly and mosquito. After a thousand of such lives, let him become a man again.

64. Let this sinner who has killed pigs be hit by buffaloes.

65. Let him be thus hit and smashed by the hoofs and horns for a thousand years.

66. Released from there, let him become a pig, then a buffalo and later a cock, a hare and a jackal.

67. In all these lives he will be a prey. There is no other way to mitigate his actions.

68. Then he will become a man, but as a hunter. There is no other way even after a hundred lives.

69. Put in glowing cinders for three hundred years this man who has given to others food left after his eating.

70. Let this bad adulterous woman, who was unfaithful to her husband, embrace these seven men of iron.

71. She will then become a dog, afterwards a pig and, when the result of her actions is over, a distressed woman. She will never attain happiness.

72. This man made his servants toil very much and then sent them away without giving them any food or drink.

73. He was only fond of his own glorification.

74. Let him, therefore, be put in the terrific hell Raurava.

75. Beat the man who performs all sorts of actions for thousands of years.

76. Let him then be born as a robber and afterwards as a serpent.

77. Let him then be a pig, and then a goat, then an elephant, a horse, a jackal and crane.

78. After a very long time, let him become a man.

79. He is to be born dead in five lives and die as a boy in five others.

80. Only afterwards does he become a man.

81. Whatever good or bad a being has done, the result of that necessarily accrues to it.

82. So it is that the great Lord has laid down the results of all actions."

CHAPTER TWO HUNDRED AND THREE

Sins and punishment for them

The Sage's son (Naciketas) said:

1. Citragupta (himself) spoke about other miscellaneous sins (and their punishments). Listen to them.

2. Those who do not have good conduct and self-control and have great sins in them, and who die (as a consequence) in the dark half of the month, face punishment.

3. Those who incur the displeasure of the king or the teacher are all condemned. They care only for their sustenance and they are not dependable or affable.

4. Those who delight in injuring others, who are cruel, deceitful, obstruct others in their work, kill the gayal, buffalo and goat,

5. Those that set fire to the forest and those that trade on pigs are tormented in hell for a long time.

6. When this period is over, they are born again, but will be short-lived and disease-stricken.

7. Sometimes they are dead even when in womb, sometimes in boyhood or a little later.

8. They may die by accident like the fall of a log of wood or by weapon or may be blown away by a stormy wind or burnt by fire. They may meet with death also by drowning or being caught in a net or by a fall or by poison.

9. Those who have the sin of killing mother, father, friend or relation, repeatedly face punishment as long as life-breath remains in them.

10. Dishonest traders in metals and jewels, those who bring about abortions, magicians, dealers in poison, those who indulge in arson,

11. Makers of cages, hitters with the trident, tale-bearers, those who pick up quarrels, or make baseless allegations against others,

12. Dealers in the flesh and hides of cattle, elephants, asses and camels and those that unnecessarily provoke others are all harassed in hells.

13. After these terrible torments, they take birth as human beings again,

14. But with mutilated limbs and immersed in misery.

15. Because of their actions, they meet with injuries in the ear, nose, hands and feet.

16. They get physical ailments as well as mental. They suffer pain in the neck, severe headache and serious stomach disorders.

17. They become stupid, blind, deaf, dumb and lame, often creeping with their legs.

18. They may become paralytic, dwarfish, limping, pot-bellied and disfigured.

19. Their bad actions bring upon them leprosy of various kinds, hernia, hydrocele and diabetes,

20. Ophthalmic disorders, venereal diseases, asthma, heart-trouble and diseases of stomach and spleen.

21. They become, thus, afflicted by numerous diseases. These people who have committed cruelty are asked to be severely beaten.

22. Messengers who deliver the false message are ordered to be duly dealt with.

23. Those who are harsh towards women, whose talk is of four kinds, namely, false, offensive, ironical and treacherous,

24. Or provocative, stinging, contemptible, unfriendly, harsh, inconsistent,

25. Or trifling like the pith of the plantain, or wounding,

26. Grating, meaningless, ceaselessly chattering, incoherent,

27. Who speak false and defamatory words obstinately, shameless even when condemned and still utter words stinging to the quick,

28. Who do not tolerate the virtues of others being extolled, all such base persons are ordered to be well bound and punished.

29. They are then born several times as beasts, worms and birds.

30. People who have done harm to others or caused harm by others are also punished for their sins for a long time.

31. When the effects of their deeds are over, they again become born as men but without proper knowledge or ability and are insulted by their own kith and kin.

32. They will be given up even by their friends and relations as they have done harm to the world and are disliked by the world.

33. Even the sins of others fall on their heads in the form of lightning, weapon, poison or physical clash with another. Such is the punishment for blabberers.

34. Those who are corrupt with regard to matters of theft, violence and justice,

35. Who steal or rob, who live upon taxes and pretending to be rulers,

36. Who harass the poor in the villages, who cheat people of gold, gems or pearls,

37. Who do not honour agreements, who oppress people, who are clever in accomplishing selfish aims,

38. Who engage themselves in unnecessary litigation, who destroy minerals to make silver,

39. Who appropriate for themselves what is deposited with them, or perform sorcery, all these are tortured in various hells.

40. These sinners are ordered to be put in these hells for a long time.

41. At the expiry of the result of their actions, they are born as human beings again,

42. But in places which always instil great fear, fear from thieves, kings, dangers, diseases and hunger,

43. Where there will be natural calamities and the people ever greedy.

44. They will be full of sorrow even while in womb and, when born, they may be deformed, single-handed or potbellied,

45. With veins protruding all over the body and rheumatic. Their wives will always shed tears and never associate with them.

46. Their children will never be well-formed. They will be dwarfish and deformed and with unsteady eyes.

47. In their miserable life they may raise horrible cries, but in vain. They will get only food that is left by others.

48. Being inferior in appearance, strength and conduct, they may become royal servants of the lowest category.

49. But they will be homeless, full of misery.

50. They are cared not even for a straw even by friends and relations in the same caste. They incur royal punishment every day.

51. They are simply disappointed even when big ceremonies are performed.

52. If they turn to farming, cattle rearing or trade, whatever they do results in failure, and they fail to know why it is so.

53. Whatever bad befalls that place, these sufferers will be the most affected.

54. Their fields will not get rainfall, even when there is heavy rain everywhere else; on the contrary they may be damaged by lightning fall.

55. These people never get happiness, but always great misery. Only a series of sorrows comes upon these who have the sin of stealing.

56. Now listen to the torments for people who set their minds on the wives of others.

57. They will be born as animals and will be of unsteady mind.

58. Those who do adultery will be caught firm and suitably dealt with.

59-60. Know now what happens to those who outrage the modesty of noble women, either by force or otherwise, by sorcery or in a political turmoil, as also to those who defile rules of Classes and bring about contamination of castes, or molest virtuous persons.

61. They are put in the terrible hell for thousands of years.

62. Then they are born as human beings but low in families of contaminated castes.

63. Those who resort to prostitutes, sorcerers or dealers in liquor and have sexual alliance with bad and outcaste women, although shamelessly wearing the caste-mark and pretending gentlemanliness,

64. Those who kidnap women and ruin them, those who sport with them, put on their dress,

65. Those who live upon women, depend on their earnings, worshipping their deities, following their rules, wearing their garments and speaking like them,

66. Adopting their ways and always speaking about them.

67. Becoming addicted to pleasures and having a repulsive look,

68. Get physical and mental distress in abundance.

69. They are bathed in boiling oil and are fed upon by worms. They are burnt in fire, soaked in lime and thrown in the river.

70. This is what happens to those who have their minds on the wives of others. I have thus told you all this.

CHAPTER TWO HUNDRED AND FOUR

Instructions to Messengers

The Sage's son (Naciketas) said:

1. O great Brahmins, I also heard these instructions given by Citragupta to his men.

2. "Do you say that this one is far away, and his actions have not come to a close ? Why do you take pity on him ? Bring him here. Don't be sorry.

3. Why do you remain indifferent with a shy face ? Why don't you hasten ? What have you been doing all this time ?

4. Go, go, bring him here soon. That you are weak should not make you insolent.

5. Do you say that his marriage is going on, or that he is an ascetic ?

6. Do you say that we should wait for some time, or that he is remaining with his wife ?

7. Do you say that she is a chaste and good woman ? Do you say that he is a boy and has returned home only last night ?

8. Do you say that the man is sitting for his food, or is lying in water, or is giving a gift ?

9. O you are all virtuous and I alone am cruel ! Go, go, do your duty without any loss of time.

10. You soon become a snake, you become a tiger, you a python, you a crocodile and you a poisonous worm.

11. You become a disease and hold him who is to go to hell. You become diarrhoea and you vomitting.

12. You become ear-ache, you cholera, you high fever.

13. You become rheumatism, you dropsy, you epilepsy, you insanity,

14. You become vertigo and you paralysis and do your work.

15. You remain like this as long as necessary. At the end

of the period or when good befalls otherwise, you will be relieved from this.

16. So go away quickly. Don't tarry.

17. What I have told you is the order of Yama. May be that you have to spend only one day like this, may be it is two.

18. May be it is three, four, six, ten or a fortnight, a month, even many months.

19. After due time, you will get relief. It is true that this is difficult.

20. But as long as I have to discharge my duty, you too have to discharge yours.

21. I have instructed you according to my direction. You have to obey my orders irrespective of whether the person concerned is alert or deluded.

22. I shall give you protection from Brahmins. So don't hesitate to do your duty, let it be a sage, a woman or a mighty man.

23. Don't be afraid of any trouble. It is my command.

24. Do as I have asked you without any delay."

25. The great Citragupta ordered them thus.

26. His command was like that of Rudra, Indra and Brahmā.

CHAPTER TWO HUNDRED AND FIVE

Good and bad results

The sage's son (Naciketas) said:

1. O great Brahmins, I shall now tell you what Yama and Citragupta spoke. Listen.

2. "Let this man return to worldly life, let this one go to the heaven of kings. Let this one become a tree, this one an animal and let this one get final release.

3. Let this one become a serpent and let this one attain supreme beatitude.

4. Let this man see his ancestors who are suffering, crying

and asking for help again and again, but condemned to eternal hell because of their own sins.

5. Let this man who was unrighteous, gave up his wife and is without sons and grandsons, be put in the Raurava hell and smashed by mighty hands.

6. Release these who have been brought here and those who are being brought, because they are all sinless.

7. In prosperity as well as in adversity these people have upheld *dharma*.

8. Let them remain happy in heaven for many *kalpas* and, after enjoying there very beautiful women, be born again as men in Kali age.

9. Let this man have permanent residence in heaven as he died fighting an enemy in battle.

10. Any one who has staked his life for the sake of a Brahmin, a cow or for the nation, should be immediately taken to Amarāvatī, the city of Indra. He will remain there for one *kalpa* riding in the aerial car.

11. This man was a highly righteous person always steeped in *dharma*, giving numerous gifts and compassionate to all.

12. Honour him quickly with sandalpaste and garlands.

13. Let him be thus honoured and fanned with chowries and then given a chariot,

14. So that he can leave this place of the dead and go to heaven where he will have a place even above Indra.

15. He will be received there with the sound of conchs and words of welcome.

16. Let this one also go to Indra's world, since the whole world is full of his fame.

17. Indra awaits him there for his hundreds of virtues. He will remain in heaven like Indra himself.

18. He enjoys the pleasures of heaven till the expiry of his *dharma* and then he takes birth as a man and enjoys all pleasures.

19. Take this virtuous man, who is full of dharma and who has made gifts of even gems, to the world of Aśvinīdevas full of pleasure.

20. Let this great man go to the great lord Rudra, as he has given numerous milch cows to Brahmins,

21. And given to them good food in abundance.

22. He remains there for one *kalpa* injoying the beautiful Rudra women.

23. By this person were given to Brahmins honey with sugar-candy and tasty food with good flavour,

24. And good milch cows together with calves, gold and golden garments.

25. I have seen three crore entries for him in heaven. And after his life in heaven, he will be born in a family of sages.

26. Let him who has made gifts of gold be reported to Devas, and after their approval, betaken to Lord Rudra.

27. Let him in all effulgence enjoy there as he likes.

28. Let him who propitiates his ancestors be with them and let those who are liberal givers go to heaven.

29. This man was compassionate to all and fulfilling the desires of all and he should be honoured here by granting him whatever he desires.

30. Let this man who has made gifts of land to Brahmins go to heaven. Let him remain with his followers in the world of Brahmā.

31. Let him with all his desires fulfilled, get the unaging and eternal place, honoured by sages."

CHAPTER TWO HUNDRED AND SIX

The Result of good actions

The Ṛṣi (Naciketas) said:

1. O great ascetic Brahmins, I shall tell you about the instructions given by Citragupta, as I heard them. Please listen.

2. "This is a highly compassionate and forbearing man who takes all as his guests and gives all of them alike good food and eats only what is left after that.

3. Leave him, leave him. That is the dictate of Dharma.

4. I stand here with Kāla and Mṛtyu and I am flanked by the disfigured sinners.

5. But this man is sung in the sky by Gandharvas and Apsa-

rases. So give him a divine seat and a vehicle and whatever else he may wish.

6. And all this should be given without any delay. Such is the command of Yama because he has given numerous gifts without any ostentation.

7. See to it that this person is fed well with his followers because he is a hero.

8. Let him remain here till the aerial cars arrive from heaven. He may then board them with his retinue and go to the abode of gods and receive their honour.

9. Let him remain happy there as long as the worlds last.

10. One who goes there like this is really gratified and remains there in all purity.

11. Honour him with carrying out all that he wishes, who has given several girls in marriage or performed several sacrifices and let him attain the abode of Viṣṇu.

12. Let him remain there for a hundred thousand years and then be born in a high family in the human world.

13. Honour this man who is full of compassion for all. Let him remain like a god for a million years. He will then be born as a highly honoured man in the world.

14. Honour him well who has made gifts of sandals, umbrellas and vessels for water several times.

15. Let him extend his soft and cool hand in assemblies where thousands gather,

16. And be an ever happy Vidyādhara attended on by four Mahāpadmas.[1]

17. At the end of this period, let him be born in the world in a family full of beautiful women.

18. Let him who has given milk, curd and ghee to Brahmins be honoured when he comes here.

19-20. Get for him without fail vessels in thousands of milk and its products so that he may enjoy them together with his relatives.

21-22. Let him then go to the enviable Goloka and enjoy there for hundreds of years as a god attended on by several beautiful women."

---

1. These are embodiments of treasures.

23-24. Citragupta said this also, "(The cows) move about in the world bearing ambrosia (in the form of milk). They combine in them all gods and goddesses and also the Vedas. They are the best of all tīrthas.

25. They are the holiest of holy and the most nourishing among nourishments. Therefore the gift of cows should be made for getting purity.

26. By offering once curds, all the gods are pleased; by milk, Śiva is pleased; by ghee, Agni is pleased; by milk-pudding Brahmā is pleased.

27. By offering this for thirteen years and by taking them oneself, satisfaction and purity are obtained.

28. By drinking Pañcagavya, the result of performing the Vājimedha sacrifice is obtained. The products got from cow are the most pure. There is none else like them.

29. In the teeth of the cow remain gods Maruts, in its tongue Sarasvatī. In the middle of the hoofs are Gandharvas and in their ends serpents.

30. In its joints Sādhyas, in the eyes the sun and the moon, in the back all Kṣatriyas and in the tail *dharma*.

31. In its excretory organ are the tīrthas and in the urine the river Gaṅgā. In the feet the four oceans.

32. In the roots of hair the sages and in the dung Lakṣmī. In the hair remains all knowledge and in the skin the two Ayanas (northern and southern).

33-34. Because of the cow, one is endowed with courage, determination, tranquility, prosperity, progress, memory, intelligence, humility, health, fame, knowledge and progeny.

35. Where there are cows, there is the universe with the god of gods foremost. Where there are cows, there is Lakṣmī and eternal *dharma*."

36. I saw the cows honoured everywhere, in the houses and in the broad streets.

37. Men and women with great restraint were found in thousands sitting, eating and sleeping.

38. They were also engaged in sports and other entertainments in thousands. Many were found decorated with flowers and garlands in drinking houses.

---

1. These are milk, curd and ghee and cow's urine and cowdung.

39. There was abundant food of great variety and beds, seats and drinks, and also horses and elephants.

40. I saw there beautiful women of various kinds, some of them engaged in sports in water, some playing in the gardens and others in their happy homes.

41. There is none like this and none other than this.

42. What a fine structure and what a fine decoration in house after house there.

43. Seeing all this wonderful place well, I came to Yama again.

CHAPTER TWO HUNDRED AND SEVEN

Good results

The Sage's son (Naciketas) said:

1. O great sages, there is another thing which I heard from Nārada in the assembly of Yama.

2. As he was asking him about the doings of the great, he narrated a story as told by Citrabhānu.

3. That was about King Janaka attaining all his great desires.[1] I shall tell you that. Please listen.

4. The resplendent sage Nārada arrived at the assembly of Yama.

5. Seeing him arrive there at his own accord, king Yama quickly received him with due honour, circumambulated him and said:

6. "O great Brahmin Nārada, welcome to you. By my good luck have you come here.

7. You know everything, see everything and you are the foremost among those knowing *dharma*. O sage, You know well the legends about the Gandharvas.

8. We have become extremely purified at your sight. The whole of this place has also become sanctified.

9. Please tell me without any hesitation whatever you have

---

1. This story, however, is not found narrated.

in mind, whether anything is to be done by me or got done by any one else.

10. There is nothing in this world which cannot be got by great ascetics and Brahmins like you."

11. Hearing these words of Yama, Nārada, the knower of *dharma*, began to speak.

Nārada said:

12. I shall tell you since you have asked. You are always the protector, keeper and the leader of *dharma*, doubtless by your truth, penance, forbearance and courage.

13. There is none like you who can read the minds of others and know what is done. I have a great doubt and that has to be cleared by you.

14. How is immortality obtained by practising vows, following rules, making gifts or performing penance?

15. How is high prosperity attained in the world and how great fame, and how the eternal abode free from all troubles?

16. What leads one to the despicable hell?

Tell me all this",

Yama said:

17. O sage, people who do unrighteous deeds undergo numerous torments in hell.

18. I shall tell you all that in detail. Please listen and then think about it.

19. Those who maintain (the sacrificial) fire, who have sons, who make gifts of land, who are valiant, who live for a hundred years, who are well-versed in Vedas never go to hell.

20. Chaste women, truthful men, those who never face defeat, are not obstinate, ever faithful to the master never go to hell.

21. Those who abstain from injury, follow the rules of celibacy, observe chastity, make gifts and are devoted to Brahmins, also do not go to hell.

22-23. Those people of composure who look after their own wives and avoid the wives of others, are fully compassionate to all, never go to this infernum full of darkness and wailings, the place for torture.

24. Men of great knowledge, who are indifferent (to you and sorrow alike), those that stake their lives for the sake of the

master, those that are liberal givers and kind to all beings, also do not go there.

25. Those who look after the comforts of their parents also do not go there.

26. These who make gifts of sesamum, cows, gold and land to Brahmins do not go there.

27. Those who perform sacrifices, observe Cāturmāsya and maintain the sacrificial fire,

28. Who carry out the wishes of preceptors, who are calm and collected, who recite the Vedas every day and who are always cultured, never see me, having realised the self themselves.

29. Those who have full control of the senses and who avoid sexual acts in prohibited times, also never go to hell.

30. Those Brahmins who have given up all desires and have control of senses become gods.

31. They do not go to this terrific hell which is for sinners.

Nārada said:

32. Is it the gift that is conducive to well-being or the worthiness of the person to whom it is given ? By what kind of action is the honour of the heaven attained ?

33. By what kind of gift do we get good physique, wealth, grain, longevity and good family. Please tell me.

34. It is impossible to detail even in the course of a hundred years what befalls the good and what the bad.

35. I shall tell you, therefore, briefly about it. The well-being is mainly the result of virtues.

36. Listen to this secret, O sage, as to who obtains what after death.

37. It is by penance that heaven is attained, by penance fame, and by penance again longevity and prosperity.

38. Learning, knowledge, health, beauty, wealth and happiness are all acquired by penance and not by the mere desire for them.

39. O sage, in this way, by silent order everything is got due to merit, enjoyments by gifts and the very life by celibacy.

40. By non-violence is got handsome form and by vows birth in good family. By austerities like eating only roots and fruits a kingdom is obtained and by feeding on leaves heaven.

41. By feeding on milk one attains heaven and by attending on the preceptor acquires abundant wealth. Progeny is got by performing Śrāddha.

42. By gifts of cow in proper time and with the necessary ritual, by austerities like sleeping on grass and by drinking water in Triṣvana ceremony, one attains the world one desires.

43. The performer of sacrifice goes to heaven, particularly if he lives on water alone for ten years.

44. One attains splendour by giving up tasty food and gets long-lived children by giving up meat.

45. By giving up sandal and garlands, the body becomes well-formed. By gifts of food, one attains intelligence and power of memory.

46. By the gift of umbrella is obtained a good house, by the gift of a pair offootwear a vehicle, by the gift of cloths handsome body, wealth and children.

47. By giving drinks, eternal satisfaction is gained, by food and drinks, all desires are accomplished.

48. He who offers to a Brahmin a tree full of fragrant flowers and fruits, gets a house full of women and gems.

49. By gifts of food, drink and dress, one attains the same. By gifts of garlands, incense, sandal, flowers and fine house-hold items to a Brahmin, one gets a handsome body and becomes free from diseases.

50. By gift of a house beautiful with beds and full of grains to a Brahmin, is acquired a lofty residence full of women, horses and elephants.

51. By gifts of incense and cows, one attains the world of Vasus.

52. Eternal bliss in heaven is attained by gifts of elephants, cows and bulls. Lustre is obtained by the gift of ghee and gracefulness by the gift of oil.

53. By the gift of honey, satisfaction in all tastes is obtained, and by the gift of lamp, effulgence is acquired.

54. By milk-pudding is acquired the nourishment of the body, by the mixture of sesamum and sugar suppleness, by fruits children and by flowers all happiness.

55. By vehicles one gets palanquin and aerial car and also prosperity.

56. By giving shelter, one attains all that is desired.

CHAPTER TWO HUNDRED AND EIGHT

The story of chaste woman

The Sage's son (Naciketas) said:

1-2. In a short while there could be seen many Brahmins with high spiritual attainments proceeding to heaven in aerial cars resplendent like the sun, accompanied by their wives and relations.

3. At this sight, Yama became pale in face and reduced in lustre. He soon became angry and sorrowful.

4. Seeing him lose his lustre and knowing his mind, Nārada asked him.

5. "You were beaming all along as if you were another lord of beasts (Śiva). How is it that your happy face has become so very pale all of a sudden ?

6. O king, what is your anguish that you heave like a serpent ? I wish to know what causes you fear."

Yama said:

7. "True that my face gets discoloured and mouth parched. I shall tell you why. Please listen.

8. Eminent Brahmins who depend on alms received, who are steadfast in learning Vedas and performing penance, who are humble and free from jealousy,

9. Who have control of senses, honour guests and contemplate on the supreme and know self, by-pass me.

10. They never come near me and I have no control over them. They pass over my head together with their wives and followers.

11. They have fine sandal smeared all over the body and are dressed well and adorned with garlands and they offer garlands to me. I am, therefore, distressed.

12. (They make fun of me saying) 'O Death, whom are you awaiting here,' 'How can death occur ?' 'Why don't you speak. O Death', 'Have you become unwanted in the world ?'

13. I strike at sinners who give up *dharma* and are greedy. But with regard to these who have earned the merit of penance, I am nobody.

14. For these great souls, I have no powers of benediction or

destruction nor of injunction or prohibition. I am, therefore, distressed, O Sage."

15. Just then there arrived a chaste woman with her husband and followers in an aerial car ushered in with the sound of musical instruments.

16-17. Seated in that car, she spoke to Yama in pleasant words.

The chaste woman said:

18. "O great lord of *dharma* honoured by all, don't have any ill-will towards these Brahmins who are full of penance.

19. The greatness and power of their penance, none can estimate. The Brahmins are steeped in Vedic lore.

20. They are always to be honoured by all. They have all gods in themselves. Jealousy or anger should not be shown to them.

21. Without considering what they do is good or bad, you should respect them. Impelled by desire or delusion, the virtuous should never be made the object of rage."

22-23. Seeing that chaste woman pass in the sky like a lightning, after being honoured by Yama, Nārada asked him.

Nārada said:

24. Who is this beautiful and virtuous woman who spoke to you for your good and departed receiving your honour.

25. I am very much eager to know this. So tell me in brief.

Yama said:

26. I shall tell you in full the auspicious story about this lady whom I honoured here.

27. In Kṛtayuga there was a very famous, effulgent and truthful king named Nimi.

28. He had a son named Mithi who had a wife named Rūpavatī very much devoted to him.

29. She always followed her husband's words, was pleased with him and performed auspicious deeds.

30. He was very virtuous, compassionate to all, highly truthful and full of penance.

31. When he was ruling the earth with all *dharma*, there was no disease, decay or death.

32. There was always rain in the country. His kingdom became endowed with all that is good.

33. Not a single man was there who was suffering from disease or distress.

34. After a long time, the queen spoke in all humility to this king of Mithilā.

The queen said:

35. Whatever money that was with you in this house, with our servants and followers and with the Brahmins in this earth, has been now fully spent.

36. O king, you are not aware that there is not necessary food.

37. We have no kine, dress or even flowers and roots.

38. I do not find now even the necessary vessels.

39. Please tell me what I should do. I am ever prepared to obey you.

The King said:

40. I am unable to tell you anything unpleasant. At the same time, I do not find anything to please you or the people.

41. Therefore, if you are pleased, I shall tell you what we may do in our present condition.

42. A hundred years have passed in our sacrificial austerities. We will now build a temple with the wood of Kuddāla and perform rituals there. You will then get the food and drink we need.

43. Told thus, the queen replied to the king.

The queen said:

44. O king, here we have thousands of servants, horses, elephants, camels, bulls, buffaloes and asses.

45. How will they fail to carry out your wish?

The king said:

46. "Our servants do whatever duty we allot to them. I have engaged them in annual as well as other functions.

47. The bulls, asses, horses, elephants and camels are assigned to the discharge of various other duties.

48. All the iron, tin, copper, silver and gold have been given for various purposes.

49. O queen, I do not find now any iron or gold for the temple to be made with Kuddāla.'

50. Told thus by the king, the queen spoke to him joyfully.

51. "O king, proceed as you like, I shall certainly follow you.' Thus agreed, the king started with queen.

52. Then the king and queen set out searching for a suitable place and traversed a long distance. Then the king said:

53. "This I find to be a good place. Let us remain here. I shall cut off bushes and thorns and you may clear them from here.

54. This will be your service and we will accomplish our aim".

55. Said thus by the king, the queen spoke to him sweetly with a smile.

56. "The tree we want stands close by and a golden bush too. But nowhere near do I find water.

57. How will we be able to build a temple here? It will result only in disease of the heart.

58. Here is the tree in this fertile land. But how can our action be useful here?'

59. Hearing this, the king spoke in endearing words:

60. "Let us begin with the preliminaries. We may be able to get water near or a little away. There is no obstacle of any kind here."

61. Then he began to clear the place together with his wife.

62. It was the summer season and the sun was blazing high up in the sky.

63. The heat was severe and the gentle queen became hungry and thirsty.

64. Her tender rosy feet turned red with heat.

65. The rays of the sun were like fire at noon. Then the tormented queen told her husband:

66. "Oppressed by this sweltering heat, I am extremely thirsty. Be pleased to give me some water quickly".

67. So saying she fell down being very much fatigued but as she was falling down, she looked at the sun.

68. As her look was in anger, the sun in the sky became fear-stricken and fell down on the earth.

69. Seeing this strange thing, the king asked:

70. "O great luminary, why have you come here leaving your orb ? Tell me what I can do for you. You are worshipped by the entire world".

71. To the king who was asking thus, the Sun said apologetically: "This chaste lady got very much angry with me. As a result I fell down. I am now here to do you whatever service you require.

72. There is none equal to her in all the three worlds. Certainly there is none like her in this world.

73. What a prowess is hers, what a penance and what a courage ?

74. She is a nice match for you, very obedient and pure with penance.

75. She is chaste and good and always looks after your comforts.

76. She is as suitable to you as Śacī is to Indra. The good has joined the good due to merit as can be seen from the perfect harmony.

77. Your desire will never go in vain. Put up here the temple as you wish.

78. There is none else who deserves the fruit of all this.

79-80. So saying the Sun gave the king a Vessel of water, a pair of sandals and a well-decorated umbrella, being very much pleased with him.

81. He gave all this for his pleasure and use for meritorious purposes.

82. The (Sun) gave this for the sake of the king's beloved.

83. The queen was sprinkled with the water. She regained consciousness and asked the king wondering what had happened.

84. "O king, who gave you this pleasant water and these fine sandals and umbrella ?"

The king said:

85. "O queen, this god Sun came down here from the sky out of compassion for you."

86. Thus told by the king, she said to him: "What can I do for him ? Please ascertain his desire."

87. Then the king fell at his feet with folded hands and said, "O god, please tell us what we may do for you ?"

88. Thus requested by the king, the Sun said, "O king, let me have protection from women."

89. Hearing these words of the Sun, the king communicated them to his wife.

90. Knowing thus from the king, the queen said with great pleasure:

91-92. "Since you have given this umbrella for warding off your rays, a water-pot (for keeping water) and the sandals for soothing feet, I give you protection you seek."

93. Therefore, O sage, I bow to the chaste woman and honour her.

CHAPTER TWO HUNDRED AND NINE

The greatness of the chaste women

Nārada said:

1. "O great king clad in black, please tell me by what virtuous deeds or penance do the saintly women attain the supreme path."

2. Asked thus by Nārada, the lord of *dharma* said:

Yama said :

3. It is not the observance of rules nor penance, fasting or gifts nor worship of god, but the conduct about which I shall tell you in brief.

4. She who sleeps after the husband sleeps, wakes up before he wakes up and eats after he has eaten, certainly overcomes death.

5. She who remains silent when he is silent and stands when he stands, overcomes death.

6. I am afraid of her who has the same outlook and mind

as the husband's and carries out what he says. She becomes honoured even by gods.

7-8. She who never retorts to whatever the husband says, remains calm even when chastised by him and never considers anyone other than him as god, never goes to the mouth of death.

9-10. She who always attends to the comforts of her husband and follows him closely, never enters the mouth of death.

11. She who attends on the husband considering him the mother, the father, the relation and god, overcomes me. In fact, I bow to her.

12. She who always thinks of her husband, follows the husband and shares the woes of the husband, never sees the door of death.

13. She who never turns her attention to music or dance or similar other attractions, never sees the door of death.

14. She who does not think of any one other than the husband when bathing, standing or decorating, never sees the door of death.

15. She who has her husband in mind when worshipping god or feeding the Brahmin, never sees the door of death.

16. She who wakes up before sunrise and cleans the house, never sees the door of death.

17. She who keeps well covered the eyes, body and the feelings and always observes the rules of cleanliness, never sees the door of death.

18. She who looks at the face of the husband with a view to carry out his desire and is always ready to do anything for his good, never sees the door of death.

19. Such virtuous wives of men in this world will be seen as goddesses in heaven.

20. All this was said by god Sun regarding the chaste woman.

21. Knowing all this, I honour the chaste woman.

CHAPTER TWO HUNDRED AND TEN

Means to destroy sin

Nārada said:

1. "You have now told me about the duties and greatness of chaste women as propounded by god Sun.

2. I now wish to know about something which relates to all beings.

3-4. There are people who stricken with sorrow perform penance, undertake vows with steadfast mind and without consideration of pain and pleasure. Why do they meet with impediments ?

5. It is always said that all our virtuous actions lead to welfare. Then how is it that the mind sometimes turns to sinful actions ?

6. Whose doing is this ? Who is the doer and who is that makes him do so ? Who is it that restrains this world of the four kinds of beings ?

7. Why does the mind act with anger ? How is there the horrible mixture of joy and sorrow in the world ?

8. If I can be told this secret which cannot be known even by gods, please do so."

9. Requested thus by the sage, the great lord of *dharma* spoke to him in all humility.

Yama said:

10. O Sage, I shall tell you what you wish to know. Please listen.

11. Everything is established in supreme *dharma*. I don't find really any doer or actuator of action other than that.

12. It is this that is applauded, it is this that orders, it is this that speaks, it is this that does.

13. I shall tell you what I have seen and heard about this in this celestial assembly full of great sages.

14. One gets the cumulative result of one's own actions. It is the self that brings down itself by the wrong action it does.

15. The air gives it consciousness and it is made firm in

worldly life and here the being gets the fruit of actions according as they are good or bad.

16. Overpowered by obstructions, one should redeem one's own self. One's own self is one's friend as well as foe. The self has nothing other than itself.

17. The nature and extent of the bondage is determined by the previous actions and the soul undergoes it in hundreds of lives.

18. It is wrong to say that everything is wrought by the world. Whatever action one does, it is all one's own.

19. The more and more the bad effect gets reduced, the more and more the thought for good works in man.

20. The soul that takes birth in the world because of its evil, can redeem itself when the effect of the evil is over.

21. One gets the mind to do good or bad according to one's action, good or bad, in the previous lives. When good actions are done, the sin and suffering are removed.

22. Good or bad, is thus acquired according as the action is proper or improper. When once the good actions alone are there, one becomes exalted among gods.

23. Heaven is the result of good actions and hell that of bad ones. There is no giver or remover of this.

Nārada said:

24. It is one's own actions that bring about good or bad results; good action paves the way for progress and bad one for downfall,

25. It behoves you to tell me how by thought, action, penance and conduct one can attain the birthless state.

Yama said:

26. I shall tell you about this sacred matter, how the sins can be dissolved and how even the bad can be made to yield good.

27-28. I first of all make obeisance to the creator of the world, who dispenses the good and the evil, who is without a beginning or end, and who is difficult to be known by gods as well as demons.

29. The man of knowledge, who knows the whole Vedas, who is calm in mind and has control of the senses and looks at all beings alike, gets absolved of all sins.

30. He who knows the truth about Puruṣa and Prakṛti and, having known it, is never deluded, attains the eternal abode.

31. He who has the capacity to discriminate between virtue and vice and between the eternal and ephemeral, and is able to get over delusion by contemplation, gets absolved of all sins.

32. He who always inquires about the pleasure and pain in oneself as well as in others, gets absolved of all sins.

33. He who never injures anything, is free from desire and anger, and is always just, gets absolved of all sins.

34. He who holds his breath by proper *prāṇāyāma* and keeps the mind steady as a result, gets absolved of all sins.

35. He who remains free from desire for everything, including such things as are naturally liked, and gives up life in tranquility, gets absolved of all sins.

36. He who is ever attentive, free from anger, free from desire for another's wealth, and free from jealousy, gets absolved of all sins.

37. He who always attends on elders, is sworn to non-violence and is never mean in his conduct, gets absolved of all sins.

38. He who performs only praiseworthy deeds and never what is not so, and always considers only the auspicious, gets absolved of all sins.

39. He who resorts to the tīrthas with purity in mind and does not commit anything bad, gets absolved of all sins.

40. He who greets a Brahmin with reverence by going towards him, gets absolved of all sins.

Nārada said:

41. What you have said is suitable, convincing, and conducive to the good of all.

42. Seeing discerning people resorting to various means, I had a doubt and that has been now cleared by you.

43. O great knower of Yoga, be pleased to tell me if there is any means still more simple for the destruction of sin.

44. The difficult practice of yoga you have already explained. What I wish to know is whether there is anything easier to practice,

45. What will be simple and pleasant and capable of removing every kind of sin,

46. What can be practised by oneself, is not very elaborate, and fully favourable for this world as well as the world beyond.

47. What is capable of exploding the effect of all bad actions that leads to birth of various kinds.

Yama said:

48. Bowing to the creator, I shall tell you about the *dharma* he has expounded in this connection.

49. Listen to this course of action which is meant for the benefit of the world and for the removal of sin.

50. He who is desirous of attaining Absoluteness, should do with a steady mind what is ordained by *dharma*.

51. He who does so with pure mind gets free from all sins and attains all desires.

52. He who makes the form of the creator in the form of the constellation Śiśumāra and bows to it with concentration of mind, gets absolved of all sins.

53. He who sees with intensity the moon in its body, gets absolved even of great sins.

54. If he sees it in the forehead, then also he is absolved of all sins, so also when he sees it in the neck or chest.

55. Seeing it in the abdomen removes all sins committed through thought, word or deed.

56. Seeing the sun in its Lāṅgala form also brings about removal of all sins committed through thought, word or deed.

57. He who performs circumambulation on seeing Jupiter in it, gets free from every kind of sin.

58. He who contemplates on him as the one without dissolution, becomes free from al sins.

59. He who performs circumambulation considering him as Mercury, Venus, Saturn, Mars and the benign Moon and contemplates on him with pure mind, becomes pure like the moon in autumn.

60. One gets absolved of all sins by a hundred prāṇāyāmas also.

61. O sage, seeing the moon in the best of form and bowing to him in reverence, removes all sins.

62-63. He who contemplates on him (by the mantra of) hundred and eight syllables and alternately sees the sun and moon in their full effulgence and purity, gets free from all sins.

64. Seeing there the Brahmin Vāmana, Varāha that arose from water holding Earth, and the Lion and bowing to them in austerity, consuming only milk, he gets absolved of all sins.

65. He who performs Prāṇāyāma also gets free from all sins.

CHAPTER TWO HUNDRED AND ELEVEN

Means to destroy sin (contd.)

The sage's son (Naciketas) said:

1. Hearing these words of the lord of *dharma*, Nārada spoke again in reverence.

Nārada said:

2. O great Dharmarāja, you look alike on all beings, stationary or moving.

3. I have now heard from you about the circumambulation which is particularly favourable to the welfare of Brahmins.

4. Three castes participate in sacrifices and share their benefits in general. The Śūdras are kept out by Brahmins from those that are purified by Vedas.

5. Since you look upon all beings as equals, you should tell me what leads to their welfare also, what action the Śūdra may do.

Yama said:

6. I shall tell you what is favourable to all the four castes as sanctioned by *dharma*.

7. I shall tell you that by listening to which with attention and following it in action, one gets free from sin. Please listen.

8. The cow is sacred, auspicious and fit to be worshipped even by gods. He who tends it with devotion, gets absolved of all sins.

9. He who drinks *Pañcagavya* at the auspicious time, immediately gets absolved of all sins acquired from birth.

10. He who receives on his head the water scattered by the

cow by its tail, acquires the merit of bathing in all tīrthas and gets free from all sins.

11. He who bathes in cow's urine on Rohiṇī day, gets all his sins burnt away.

12. He who receives on his head the milk from the cow's udder, gets cleansed of all sins.

13-14. The Brahmin, who soon after his bath bows to the rising sun with devotion, gets free from all sins.

15-16. He who worships the sun with purity and holding curd and raw rice in hand thrice a day, gets all his acquired sins dispelled.

17. A similar offering to the moon on full moon day, removes all sins.

18-19. He who makes such offering with concentration of mind and according to Vedic rules to Arundhatī, Budha and all sages, gets his sins instantaneously removed.

20. He who propitiates Brahmin, attending on him with great devotion, becomes free from all sins.

21. He who makes gifts of milk during solstices gets immediate destruction of his sins.

22. Worshipping along with Brahmins a bull over a streak of Kuśa grass strewn with tips facing east, brings about removal of all sins.

23. Bathing according to rules in an east-flowing river where it bends in a right hand direction, removes all sins.

24-25. Taking water in a right-spiralled conch and pouring it over the head with purity and pleasure, destroys all sins.

26-27. Bathing in an east-flowing river at a spot where the water is waist-deep and offering seven times handfuls of water mixed with black sesamum and performing *Prāṇāyāma* thrice with control of senses, brings about immediate destruction of all sins.

28. He who bathes thrice in water taken in untorn lotus leaves in which different gems are placed, gets free from all sins.

29. I shall tell you about another great secret. The Ekādaśī day in the dark fortnight of the Kārttika month is known as Prabodhinī. It gives both enjoyment and liberation.

30. The body of Viṣṇu with its numerous indistinct forms, O sage, became Dvādaśī in the mortal world.

31. Those who fast in the proper form with full devotion to

Lord Nārāyaṇa, get absolved of all sins acquired in numerous lives.

32. The great lord in the form of Varāha was once asked by Earth about Ekādaśī for the good of the world.

Earth said:

33. O Lord, in this fierce Kaliyuga we find people inclined to do sinful deeds like stealing the property of the Brahmin and also killing him.

34. They are inclined to do harm to the preceptor, the friend and the master and outrage the modesty of the wives of others.

35. They are drawn to steal the wealth of others, eat prohibited food and to denounce the Vedas and the Brahmins.

36. They are found to be dissemblers, not respecting decorum, proclaiming atheism, eager to receive anything even from the bad and interested in sexual relations with the prohibited.

37. Be pleased to tell me, O lord, how people who incur these and other sins can redeem themselves.

Varāha said:

38. It is good that you asked me about this. I shall tell you this secret for the sake of the world.

39. What I have ordained for those who have acquired no merit but a lot of demerit due to their great sins, I shall now tell you. Please listen.

40. The supreme power of Viṣṇu with its numerous indistinct forms, has assumed the form of Dvādaśī in the mortal world.

41. By fasting on that day, O fair one, even those who have committed serious sins go to the eternal abode, free from the effect of merits and demerits.

42. There is no means other than observing Ekādaśī for the dissolution of all sins.

43. The Ekādaśī in the bright fortnight as well as in the dark fortnight of the month should be observed. The first gives devotion and the second liberation.

44. Therefore, O Earth, every effort should be made to observe Ekādaśī always if the world of Viṣṇu is desired to attain.

45. The observance of Ekādaśī burns away all sins committed through thought, word or deed in the course of a month.

46-47. Even sins acquired earlier are dispelled. Therefore, one should not take food at all during Ekādaśī, if one wishes to go to the supreme abode of Viṣṇu.

48. With raised up hands I cry aloud that Viṣṇu, the lord of the universe, should be worshipped on Ekādaśī day without any slackness.

49. During Ekādaśī on both fortnights, water from the conch should not be drunk and fish and pig should not be killed.

50. He who takes food on either Ekādaśī in the month, incurs the same sin as of killing a Brahmin, drinking wine, stealing gold and committing adultery on the teacher's wife.

51. What sin is not incurred by the man who follows the suicidal practice of knowingly eating on Ekādaśī day?

52. He who finds it unable to fast on the Ekādaśī of the bright fortnight may eat at night whatever he gets unasked.

53. The Dvādaśī should be observed by eating once and giving gifts. He who does not observe this or does not give gifts incurs great sin and does not get liberation anywhere.

54. O fair one, those who are unable to fast at other times may do so, at least, on that Dvādaśī which is known as Prabodhinī.

55. He who worships the lord of the universe on that day, gets the merit of twelve Dvādaśīs.

56. The Dvādaśī which occurs in conjunction with the asterism Pūrvabhādrapada is great and its observance produces endless merit.

57-58. The Ekādaśī which occurs in conjunction with the asterism Uttarabhādrapada brings in a crore times the merit of others if the lord is worshipped once on that day.

59. Just like Prabodhinī (in which the lord wakes up) is the Śayanī in which the lord goes to sleep. Fasting on that day too produces abundant merit.

60. Śayana, Bodhana and Parivartana (Dvādaśīs on which the lord goes to sleep, wakes up and turns his side) bring about purity to man when he fasts.

61. Therefore, whoever desires permanent liberation should by all means observe fast on Dvādaśī.

62. Ekādaśī falling on Monday in conjunction with Uttarabhādrapada in the month of Kārttika gives endless merit.

63. If that is observed, it yields great results.

64. The same falling on Tuesday confers supreme merit to one who bathes and worships the lord on that day. He gets the benefit of twelve Dvādaśīs.

65. The devotee shall place at a pure spot a pot filled with water, over it a vessel of ghee containing the five gems, and

66. Over that lord Janārdana in the form of the fish made with gold weighing one niṣka.

67. He shall then bathe him with Pañcāmṛta, decorate with saffron, dress with a pair of yellow cloths and provide with umbrella and a pair of sandals.

68. He shall then worship him with lotuses keeping the senses in full control.

69. He shall worship him as the ten incarnations namely the fish, tortoise, boar, man-lion, dwarf, (Paraśu)Rāma, Rāma, Kṛṣṇa, Buddha and Kalkī.

70. He shall do worship with every kind of decoration and offering flowers, incense, lamp and food of various kinds.

71. The lord should be released at night. When the day dawns, the devotee shall take his bath and worship him in all earnestness with flowers, incense, lamp and different kinds of fruits.

72. He shall then worship the preceptor, according to his means, with food, clothes and decorations.

73. Then the image should be gifted to him with due rites and with the mantra:

74. 'May lord Janārdana who is the source of the universe, who is in the form of the universe and who is the first in the universe, be pleased with me'.

75. The Ekādaśī is to be observed in this way. I shall tell you now, O Earth, about the merit that accrues from it.

76. The merit of Prabodhinī cannot be fully uttered even with a thousand tongues. Still, I shall tell you about it briefly.

77. The man who observes this, enters with all his dependents the celestial aerial car splendid like the sun, the moon and the stars and goes to my world.

78. At the end of a thousand *kalpas* he becomes the lord of all the seven islands constituting the earth and enjoys full health and happiness. He then becomes free from birth.

79-80. The sin of killing the Brahmin, drinking wine, stealing (gold) and committing adultery on the teacher's wife, disappears by hearing the very name of this.

81. Even he who is unable to do the rites for want of money, may get himself purified and attain heaven, if he touches with devotion the man who performs them and renders him service.

82. Even by reading this account about the efficacy of this, all bad dreams disappear and all fear from worldly existence vanishes. Should we then say about the effect when the Prabodhinī is actually observed?

83. They who worship me in the proper time are indeed blessed. They are happy. A really virtuous deed has been done by them and the essence of life has indeed been earned by them.

84. He who always takes the name of Nārāyaṇa, Acyuta, Ananta or Vāsudeva, O Earth, would merge into myself.

85. What to say of those who worship with undivided attention devotedly in accordance with the manner advised by the preceptor. They would undoubtedly be merged into myself.

86. Those who bow down to that boar-shaped Viṣṇu, possessed of unlimited energy, are always adorable even by the gods.

87. Hence, the station of Viṣṇu is to be carefully aspired by the seekers. The state of being the devotee of Viṣṇu, O pretty madam, is rarely attainable in the three worlds.

88. By virtue of propitiating lord Śiva during thousands of births, a man may attain the state of a devotee of Viṣṇu on the decay of his sins.

89. The decay of the sin is effected by the worship of lord Śiva. Rudra, the supreme lord, has to be worshipped by a person who seeks after knowledge.

90. While worshipping me, one would attain the highest station of Viṣṇu. The Vaiṣṇavites, O propitious madam, do purify the entire universe.

91. If a devotee of Viṣṇu, even though he be a Cāṇḍāla, is recollected, named, seen or touched accidentally by any body, O dear madam, the former purifies them.

92. Knowing it therefore, the learned and the wise should worship lord Viṣṇu in accordance with the Vedic rites or scriptural injunctions.

Yama said :

93-94. Having heard all this, the fortunate Earth who had her vows fulfilled, worshipped the lord of the Universe according to regulations and got merged into him. Hence, the wise man should seek for the state of a devotee of Viṣṇu with all effort.

95. Those who observe even once this Dvādaśī called Prabodhanī with due fasting, go to the supreme abode.

96. Such souls never see Yama or his messengers or the travails in hell. What I say is simply the truth.

97. I have thus told you what I have seen and heard in reply to what you asked me.

98-99. O great sage desirous of knowing *dharma*, I have now told you in brief what was said to me about this by the creator.[1]

CHAPTER TWO HUNDRED AND TWELVE

The Awakening

Nārada said:

1. "Well, well, O great king, the great knower of all *dharma*, you have now told me about this important matter of *dharma*.

2. Remaining in the path of *dharma* spoken of by you, I am very much satisfied on hearing what you have said.

3. I feel particularly honoured by you. I shall now go to whichever world I wish to go.

4. May good befall you, O great king, be free from fear."

5. So saying, the great sage Nārada left, illumining the sky with his lustre like the sun and freely moved about in the celestial region.

---

1. There is some confusion in this chapter because of the use of 'Ekādaśī' and 'Dvādaśī' as apparently relating to the same.

6-7. When he was gone, that king (Yama), turned towards me, honoured me with his sweet words and let me off very much pleased.

8. Thus have I told you, O Brahmins, about what I saw and heard in that city of Yama and how I have returned here.

Vaiśampāyana said:

9. Hearing his words, the sages became very much delighted. Some jumped up from their seats.

10. The eyes of some were filled with wonder and they gave out exclamations in appreciation.

11. Even old ascetics and those living in forest and those among them living on scattered grain, proclaimed the greatness of compassion for all beings.

12. Those lying on rocks, those lying on wood, those eating uncooked food or partly cooked food,

13. Those following prescribed rules, those who had overcome themselves, those observing full silence, those lying in water,

14. Those who were lying high up, those moving like animals, those sitting in the midst of five fires, those feeding on fallen leaves and fruits,

15. Those living on water, those living on air, those living on vegetables, all these began to do severe penance, being convinced that there is nothing greater than penance.

16. Some bold sages, being not afraid of birth or death, gave up *dharma* and *adharma* (merit and demerit) and resorted to continuous concentration of mind.

17. Hearing the narration (of Naciketas), the divine sages resorted to follow such of the rules as are commended.

18. (The father of) Naciketas, seeing his ascetic son, was immensely pleased and began to think of *dharma* alone.

19. Remaining in penance, he always contemplated on the great lord Viṣṇu extolled by the Vedas.

20-21. He who listens to this great narrative which generates devotion to the Lord, or makes others listen to it, attains his desires.

CHAPTER TWO HUNDRED AND THIRTEEN

The greatness of Gokarṇeśvara

Sūta said:

1. In days of yore, when the manace in the form of demon Tāraka had been completely crushed in battle, and the army of the demons routed,

2. Indra had been restored to his position, the enemy being annihilated, and the world of animate and inanimate beings had become fully productive,

3. And in the golden peak of the Meru full of gems,

4. Brahmā was sitting in comfort with full concentration effulgent like the sun and fire,

5. Sanatkumāra approached him with great humility, prostrated at his feet in reverence, and asked him.

Sanatkumāra said:

6. "O lord, I wish to know from you about an old thing which the sages cherish, namely,

7. How is the northern Gokarṇa, how the southern, how is it placed at the top of the peak,

8. Of what dimension is that place, what is the merit of the tīrtha there, how is there Lord Śiva in the form of an animal,

9. How did gods led by you reach there, where is the animal form of his consecrated, and

10. What are the special rules to be observed there. Be pleased to tell me all this."

11. Thus asked by the son, lord Brahmā told him about his old and secret matter.

Brahmā said:

12. O sage, my son, I shall tell you this secret truth, as I have heard it.

13. On the northern side of the great mountain Mandara, there is a peak called Muñjavān, beautiful like the Nandana garden.

14. It has pebbles shining, stones resembling coral and slabs like sapphire and many caves and waterfalls.

15. With its rising rocks covered with creepers bearing a variety of blossoms, it seems to scrape the sky.

16. The caves in it are beautiful with numerous flowing minerals and flowers of mushrooms.

17. The streaks of forests in it shine with the flowers of Jasmine and Ketakī.

18. In that mount washed by streams of pure water blue like sapphire, having stretches of slabs covered with many kinds of flowers.

19. Displaying a variety of colours as in the rainbow and so appearing like the abode of Kubera,

20. With celestial couples playing, groups of Apsarases dancing and inebriated peacocks cooing,

21. With ponds full of clear water and having full-blown flowers of lotus and Kalhāra and resorted to by swans and cranes,

22. With numerous brooks flocked by herds of elephants, dear, birds and many sages,

23. With groves enjoyed by Devas, Gandharvas and Vidyādharas, where the cuckoos warble and the hollows resound with the music of Kinnaras,

24. With numerous waterfalls and green meadows illumined by natural glow,

25. Natural gardens full of flowers blossoming in all seasons and resorted to by Kiṁpuruṣas and Guhyakas,

26. With very attractive and auspicious penance-groves of sages and Siddhas,

27. There remains always lord Maheśvara as Sthāṇu, the preceptor of all gods, granting boons.

28. He remains there accompanied by Pārvatī, Guha and attendants, full of grace for the devotees.

29. The gods used to go there in their aerial cars to pay homage to that great lord. The demigods also used to go there for his worship.

30. Once in Tretāyuga, a great sage named Nandī began to perform severe penance in order to propitiate Śiva.

31-32. Sitting in the midst of five fires in summer, standing in cold water in winter, with hands raised and remaining without support, feeding on water and air alone, and observing numerous vows and restraints,

33. And with Japa and offerings of flowers from time to time, he worshipped Śiva with great devotion.

34. He fully engaged himself in severe penance, as a result of which he became much emaciated and almost looked like a piece of wood.

35. He became very lean and dark in complexion. Thus worshipped, Śiva was pleased.

36-37. Śiva then appeared before the sage and told him, "I am pleased with you and I give you divine eyes with which to see my form which is visible only to those with the highest knowledge."

38. Seeing the great lord Mahādeva shedding lustre like a thousand suns, with a blazing halo around him,

39. With prominent matted hair adorned by the moon, surveying the whole universe with his three shining eyes,

40. Very attractive with hundred heads, hundred bellies, thousand hands and feet, thousand eyes and mouths,

41. Smaller than the smallest, bigger than the biggest, wearing the rosary and holding the water-vessel in hand,

42. Wearing the skin of lion and serpent for Yajñopavīta, the sage became thrilled.

43. He prostrated before him with folded hands and uttered a hymn in praise.

"Bow to the creator, dispenser, granter of boons, Śambhu,

44. The enjoyer of the world, three-eyed, Śaṅkara, Śiva, Bhava, the protector from worldly existence, sage, wearer of elephant's skin,

45. Blue-necked, Bhīma, the combiner of the past, present and future, with hanging brows, ferocious, auspicious,

46. With broad, matted and tawny hair, the wise, holding the trident, lord of beasts, omnipresent, Sthāṇu,

47. Lord of Gaṇas, the creator, condenser and frightener, who is calm and benign,

48. The resident of the cemetery, Rudra, the benevolent, wearing a garland of skulls and tawny moustache,

49. Lover of devotees, I bow to you the supreme soul."

50. Thus praising Śiva, he bowed to him again and again.

51. Śiva was very much pleased with him and spoke to him.

52. "O great sage, seek from me whatever boons you wish. I shall grant you all of them, even if they are such as are not normally granted.

53. Tell me soon what you desire, whether it is lordship, the status of Devas, Indra or Brahmā, the position of the guardian deities, liberation, eight-fold power or leadership of Gaṇas.

54. Asked thus, the sage replied with great delight.

55-56. "I don't desire lordship, the status of Devas, Indra or Brahmā, the position of the Guardian deities, liberation, the eight-fold power or leadership of Gaṇas.

57. O great god Śaṅkara, if you are pleased with me and wish to favour me,

58. Please give me that kind of devotion which will make me worship you alone and none else.

59. I wish to have devotion for you who dwell in the minds of all. Let there be no impediment in this. I wish to worship you with the *Rudra mantra* a crore times."

60. Hearing these words of Nandin, lord Maheśvara laughed and then spoke in sweet words.

61. "O sage, I am pleased with you. Rise from your penance. I am fully propitiated by your pure mind and constant devotion.

62. Enough of this penance. You have been deeply devoted to my feet.

63. You have already recited three crores of *Rudra mantra* before me.

64. You have completed, O sage, thousand years of severe penance, the like of which neither Devas nor Asuras nor sages have ever done.

65. You have done something difficult and wonderful as a result of which the three worlds are awed.

66. All Devas led by Indra will come to see you. You have become eternal and fully knowable by Devas or Asuras.

67. With your divine body and divine ornaments you have become equal to me.

68. You will get a form and splendour like mine, three-eyed and endowed with all virtues and worshipped by Devas and Asuras.

69. With this body which will be free from age and death, you will also be the lord of Gaṇas.

70. O Brahmin, you will be the foremost among my attendants and will be known as Nandīśvara.

71. O sage, you have attained the eightfold power and Devas will bow to you as my second form.

72. Hereafter, O sage, by my blessing you will be the chief in all matters relating to Devas.

73. As the chief of my attendants, you will be worshipped by all beings that desire my favour.

74. You will be the dispenser of boons in this world and the refuge for the fear-stricken.

75. He who hates you hates me, he who worships you worships me. There is no difference between us just as there is none between the sky and air.

76. O lord of Gaṇas, you should stand on the right of my door-way and Mahākāla on the left.

77. You will be the principal doorkeeper. You are to guard me and Mahākāla is to guard the Gaṇas.

78. None will be able to injure you in the three worlds whether by the Vajra, Cakra, fire or Cane.

79. Devas, Asuras, Gandharvas, Yakṣas, Rākṣasas, and Pannagas will resort to you, so too men who are my devotees.

80. When you are pleased, I will be pleased and when you are angry, I too. There is none more dear to me than you."

81. Being thus pleased with him and after giving him these boons, Śiva spoke to him again in clear tone which filled the air.

82. "See gods together with the Maruts come here to see you. You have now become fully gratified.

83. If the words I spoke giving you the boons have not yet entered into your ear, see these gods in the sky here.

84. The gods and Maruts led by lord Viṣṇu come here out of love and regard for you. Sages will come here to get boons.

85-86. Yakṣas, Vidyādharas, Siddhas, Gandharvas, Pannagas and sages who are already immersed in penance, knowing about what you have accomplished by penance, engage themselves in various kinds of severe penance with a desire to gain similar boons.

87-88. Before they come here knowing me to be present in this peak Muñjavān, I shall go away from here.

89. I have to see Brahmā and other gods who are waiting for my blessing. I know what they have in mind."

90. Thus blessing him and giving him boons, he disappeared from there.

CHAPTER TWO HUNDRED AND FOURTEEN

Boons to Nandikeśvara

Brahmā said :

1. When Śiva, the lord of beings, disappeared, Nandī became the leader of Gaṇas and divine in form,

2. With four arms, three eyes, divine demeanour, divine complexion and divine Agaru-like odour,

3. Having trident, spear, club, the bow pināka and girdle of Muñja grass and full of lustre like another Śiva.

4. With his raised foot he seemed to be aiming at pervading the whole universe like Trivikrama.

5. Seeing him, the gods became afraid and they rushed in great hurry to inform Indra.

6. Hearing this, Indra and others in his city became perturbed and began to think about what they might do.

7. "Here is some one who has got a boon from Maheśvara, and with his grĕat might he is sure to get control over all the worlds.

8. His enthusiasm, effulgence and strength will enable him to snatch away the place of celestials.

9. Before he sets foot on this celestial world for the purpose through his power, let us go and propitiate the benign Śiva himself who has given him the boon."

10. So saying, they went with me to mount Muñjavān made by the gods.

11. Myself, Viṣṇu, Indra and others rushed there in anxiety.

12. The gods and sages began looking for him. Then Viṣṇu, along with them, went to the spot where Nandī was remaining like a god.

Nandī said:

13. My life has become fruitful as also all my efforts since I see before me Indra, the lord of gods, and Viṣṇu, the lord of the worlds.

14. This is enough for me and I am fully gratified.

15. The great lord Hara became pleased with me, gave me a place among his attendants and blessed me with boons.

16. This is a greater blessing for me and I have become extremely purified.

17. What Brahmā told gods about me is absolutely true. Now the gods and sages have come here and speak sweet words to me. This shows Brahmā's affection for me.

Devas said:

18. "We wish to see the benevolent god Śiva who appeared before you pleased by your penance".

19. They asked him again, "Where can we find lord Śiva ?"

Nandī said:

20. "After blessing me, the lord disappeared there itself. I do not know where he is. A search may be made".

Sanatkumāra said:

21. Please tell me what the Lord had told Nandī since he did not disclose where he was. Was there any secret for Śiva in this matter ?

Brahmā said:

22. I shall tell you what Maheśvara said to Nandī regarding why the gods should not be told as to where he could be seen. Please listen.

Śiva said:

23. "Beyond Himālaya there is a nice and holy place with numerous hermitages. There a great serpent by name Śleṣmātaka lives.

24. He has now freed himself of all sins by penance and so I have now to go there urgently to bless him.

25. The place around him there is very beautiful and (strangely) there are no monkeys there.[1]

26. Due to the long penance he performed there, it has now come to be known as Śleṣmātaka forest and even the rocks there have become sacred.

27. I will be moving there in the form of a deer and I will see then the gods who finally come there wearied after a long search.

28. You should not tell this to Devas or Apsarases". Saying so and blessing him he disappeared from there.

29-30. Indra reached that table-land in his chariot which moves at will, beautiful like the crescent moon and sprinkled with divine drops, accompanied by the Maruts and followed by the gods, shedding lustre all around.

31. The benevolent Varuṇa, the lord of aquatic animals came in an aerial car splendid with crystals and diamonds, together with his followers.

32. Kubera came there in another beautiful golden car.

33. In numerous such cars shining like the sun came in crores of Yakṣas and Rākṣasas.

1. This seems to be an interpolated verse. In the next chaper we find the mention of monkey here.

34. Yama came there along with the good souls. The sun, moon, planets and the entire group of stars arrived there in aerial cars shining like fire.

35. The eleven Rudras, twelve Ādityas and Aśvins came to that great mountain Muñjavān.

36. The Viśvedevas, Sādhyas and the ascetic Bṛhaspati came there covering the milky way.

37. Skanda and Vināyaka came to the great peak full of cooings of numerous peacocks.

38-39. At the command of Indra came there also in aerial cars Gandharva leaders like Viśvāvasu, Parāvasu, Hāhā and Hūhū and also sages like Nārada and Tumburu.

40. Vāyu, Agni, Dharma, Dhruva, the divine sages, Siddhas, Yakṣas, Vidyādharas, Guhyakas all arrived there.

41-42. Celestial women like Gandhakālī, Ghṛtācī, Buddha, Gaurī, Tilottamā, Urvaśī, Menakā and Rambhā flocked there.

43-45. At my bidding and also at the bidding of Viṣṇu and Indra, came the sages Pulastya, Atri, Marīci, Vasiṣṭha, Bhṛgu, Kaśyapa, Pulaha, Viśvāmitra, Gautama, Bharadvāja, Agniveśya, Parāśara, Mārkaṇḍeya, Aṅgiras, Garga, Saṁvarta, Kratu, Jamadagni, Bhārgava and Cyavana.

46-49. Also came there great rivers like Sindhu, Puruṣa, Sarayū, Tāmrā, Aruṇā, Cārubhāgā, Vitasthā, Kauśikī, Sarasvatī, Kokā, Narmadā, Bāhudā, Śatadrū, Vipāśā, Gaṇḍakī, Godāvarī, Veṇī, Tāpī, Karatoyā, Śītā, Cīravatī, Nandā, Paranandā, Carmaṇvatī, Parṇāśā, and Daivikā.

50-52. At Indra's instance came there in large numbers tīrthas like Gaṅgā, Prabhāsa; Puruṣa. Soma and Lohita and even the ocean, all in their own forms.

53-55. All the mountains also presented themselves, Meru, Kailāsa, Gandhamādana, Himavān, Hemakūṭa, Niṣadha, Vindhya, Mahendra, Sahya, Malaya, Dardura, Mālyavān, Citrakūṭa, Droṇa, Śrīparvata, Pāriyātra and others.

56. So too all sacrifices, all kinds of knowledge, all the Vedas, Righteousness, Truth, Forbearance, Heaven and the great sage Kapila.

57-63. There came the great Vāsukī, the serpent (Rāhu) who drank nectar, Ananta, the holder of earth with his thousand hoods, Dhṛtarāṣṭra, Kirmīraṅga, Ambodhara, the mighty Arbuda, Vidyujjihva, Śaṅkhavarcas, Nahuṣa known in the three worlds, Satya, the son of Virocana with numerous brilliant spots, Rūpī like a mountain having numerous peaks, Arimejaya, Vinata, Kambala, Aśvatara, Elāpatra, Karkoṭaka, Dhanañjaya and several other lords of serpents.

64. Arrived there Day and Night, Fortnight, Month, Year, Heaven, Earth, Quarters and Subquarters.

65. Thus swelled the mountain peak with Devas, Yakṣas, Siddhas and others everywhere like the ocean in high tide.

66. Wafted by the wind, the trees showered flowers over the gods assembled in the peak.

67. The Gandharvas sang, Apsarases danced and the birds warbled in delight.

68. The wind was blowing gently and fragrant and pleasant.

69. When all the gods flocked there led by Viṣṇu, they saw the resplendent Nandī in front of them.

70. Seeing the Gandharvas, Apsarases and other celestials there with Indra, he prostrated before them.

71. After saluting all of them, he spoke to them words of welcome, offered *arghya* and *pādya* and requested them to be seated.

72. Watching all this carefully, the gods began to return him the honour.

73. The Ādityas, Vasus, Rudras, Maruts, Aśvins, Sādhyas, Viśvedevas, Gandharvas and Guhyakas honoured him.

74. All Gandharvas like Viśvāvasu, Hāhā, Hūhū, Citrasena and others and Nārada and Tumburu honoured him.

75. All the chiefs of serpents like Vāsuki honoured Nandī.

76. Siddhas, Cāraṇas, Vidyā(dharas) and Apsarases honoured him who was already honoured by the great lord.

77. The Siddhas, sages and rivers like Gaṅgā blessed him in great joy.

The gods said:

78. "O sage, let the great god Śiva be always pleased with you. Let there be unhindered supremacy for you.

79. You are now greater than gods.

80. You will be moving about in all the seven worlds together with Śiva without disease or death."

81. Thus said by the gods, Nandī spoke again.

Nandikeśvara said:

82. "Now that I am blessed by you all with your benedictions, I have become one worthy of commands from you. Please tell me what I may do for you.

83. O great gods, let me know your command". Hearing this, Indra said:

Indra said:

84. "Where is the great lord Śiva gone ? Where can we see him ?

85. If you know where he is, please tell us soon, O sage".

86. Hearing these words of Indra, Nandī replied contemplating on Śiva for a while.

Nandikeśvara said:

87. O lord of gods, you deserve to know this.

88. In this mountain Muñjavān, I worshipped lord Sthāṇu. He was pleased with me and gave me several boons.

89. Then he left this place and I am afraid to find out where he has gone.

90. But if you so desire, O Indra, we shall make a search for him."

CHAPTER TWO HUNDRED AND FIFTEEN

Greatness of Śaileśvara[1]

Brahmā said:

1. Then Indra and all other gods decided to start on a search of Śiva.

2. They all rose from the mountain and moved in the sky along with Nandī.

3. Wishing to find out Rudra, they moved about in heavens, in the world of Brahmā and in the world of serpents.

1. In the text this is given as Jaleśvara.

4. Searching him in all the seven islands of the earth with their mountains and forests, they became extremely tired, but could not trace him.

5-6. Not a blade of grass was left out in their intensive search in the caves of mountains and in their high peaks, in the bowers and woods.

7. But nowhere could they know anything about his whereabouts.

8. They searched again in spite of disappointment, but became afraid when they could not find him still.

9. Then they discussed among themselves about their predicament and decided again to seek my help.

10. I then entered into single-minded concentration on Śiva in order to get a means for finding out where he was.

11. Then I told them that a serious search has been made everywhere except the Śleṣmātaka forest and we may now go there.

12. When said thus, they all agreed and we proceeded to that place.

13. Soon we reached there in quickly moving aerial cars and saw the Śleṣmātaka forest resorted to by Siddhas and Cāraṇas.

14. There were in it many beautiful and pure places for meditation.

15. Near the penance groves and the caves there were beautiful streaks of forests and brooks with clear water.

16. The place was full of sounds of lions, tigers, bisons, bears, bulls, monkeys, elephants and deer.

17-18. Leaving the chariots and other vehicles, they all walked to the place led by Indra with a view to finding out Rudra anywhere in the caves, peaks or thickets.

19-21. As the gods entered one part of the forest full of plantain groves and flowering trees, they saw a stream and in its sands white like the swan, jasmine and moon, smelling sweet with the fragrance of flowers and honey, a beautiful damsel playing in the sand resembling powdered pearl.

22. Seeing this, they asked me, being the first among them, how this could be.

23. Meditating for a while, I could know that she was none other than Umā, the universal goddess, the daughter of Himavān.

24. Then they all climbed up the peak, and on looking down, saw the great lord (Śiva) there.

25. He was in the midst of a herd of deer as if their protector, having but one horn and one foot, lustrous like molten gold,

26. With beautiful face, eyes and teeth, having white dotes on the back, silverwhite on the belly,

27. With stout and raised up waist and neck and bent shoulders, rosy lips, brown tongue and slightly projecting canines.

28. Seeing that deer, all the gods quickly descended there to catch hold of it.

29. The tip of its horn was caught by Indra, the middle by me and the lower part by Viṣṇu.

30. Then the horn broke into three pieces.

31. The tip was in the hand of Indra, the middle in mine and lower part in Viṣṇu's hand.

32. When the horn was thus in our hands in three pieces, the lord naturally became hornless.

33. He instantly became invisible and spoke to us from the sky. "O gods, know that you are deceived by me.

34. I am here with my body. You got my horn alone. So I say you are deceived.

35. If you had caught hold of me with the entire body and placed me then the whole *dharma* with its four feet would have been established.

36. Now, O you gods, you may install the pieces of the horn here in this Śleṣmātaka forest for the sake of the world.

37. There will be great sanctity in this place because of my prowess.

38. For my sake the tīrthas in the world and rivers and the sea will make their presence here.

39. I will emerge by myself from earth in holy Nepal at the foot of the Himālaya,

40. With four faces and resplendent head and body, known as Śarīreśa in all the three worlds.

41. There I will remain within the water in the deep pond known as Nāgahrada for thirty thousand years.

42. When Kṛṣṇa who will be born in the clan of the Vṛṣṇis, smashes the mountain with his disc at the request of Indra, and kills demons, then that place will become peopled by the Mlecchas.

43. Then the Kṣatriyas born in the solar race will kill them and settle Brahmins there.

44. They will then establish in that country *dharma* permanently.

45. The Kṣatriya kings of the solar race will establish in the void the worship of liṅga.

46. The place will then become great with Brahmins and all other castes observing different āśramas in life.

47. The kings will do their duty well by *dharma*.

48. In that place thus well settled, every being will always worship me. Those who see me in that form or duly worship me there, will go to my abode and see me there, being freed from all sins.

49. Fourteen yojanas of land to the north of Gaṅgā and south of Aśvinīmukha is my region.

50. River Vāgmatī rising from the peaks of Himālaya is a hundred times more sacred than Gaṅgā.

51. Those who bathe there reach my world through the world of Viṣṇu after death.

52. Even sinners who live in this place, certainly go to the world of Indra.

53-54. The gods, demons, Gandharvas, Siddhas, Vidyādharas, Apsarases, sages, Yakṣas and others are deluded by my *māyā*, and so they are unable to know where I am.

55. This is known as Siddhakṣetra and is frequented by ascetics for penance. It is superior to Prabhāsa, Prayāga, Naimiṣa, Puṣkara and Kurukṣetra.

56. The great Himavān, my father-in-law is here.

57. From here arise great rivers like Gaṅgā. In this holy place all rivers are sacred, all springs are sacred, all rocks are sacred.

58. A hermitage resorted to by Siddhas and Cāraṇas will arise here and the spot where I remain will be known as Śaileśvara.

59. The river Vāgmatī flowing from here is very sacred, and (like) river Gaṅgā, cleanses one of all sins.

60. The utterance of its name brings about purification, its sight confers prosperity, and drinking its water and bathing in it liberates ten generations in the family.

61. Those who bathe in this famous tīrtha are never reborn after their death.

62. I raise from the ocean of worldly life those that bathe here every day and worship me.

63-64. He who takes from here at least one pot of water with devotion and purity of mind, gets the result of performing Agnihotra, particularly if he is learned in Veda and Vedāṅga.

65. A spring will arise there because of me. It will be known as Mṛgaśṛṅgodaka and it will be a favourite of ascetics.

66. Those who bathe there with concentration of mind will get free from all sins they commit.

67. Those who bathe in the tīrtha Pañcanada here gain the merit of performing Agniṣṭoma sacrifice.

68. Those who guard Vāgmatī (against defilment) get (the merit of gifting) six thousand cows.

69. The sinful or the ungrateful shall not go to Vāgmatī, but only the pure, the honest and the devoted.

70. The afflicted, the fear-stricken, the tormented and the diseased get beatitude by bathing in Vāgmatī.

71. Those who bathe in Vāgmatī and see me in devotion, get great peace of mind.

72. By my power the sins of those who bathe here disappear and natural calamities do not affect them.

73. Those who bathe in the Vāgmatī (in the particular tīrthas) get the result of Rājasūya and Aśvamedha sacrifices.

74. The place (actually occupied) by me (Rudra) should be taken as one yojana.

75. At the north-eastern side remains the great serpent Vāsuki surrounded by thousands of other serpents.

76. He will obstruct persons coming to this place.

77. He should be first saluted. Then there will be no difficulty for those coming here.

78. He who worships me here in full devotion, becomes a king in this world honoured by all.

79. He who worships my idol here with sandal and garlands, becomes a god.

80. He who offers me a lamp in this mountain with due devotion, will be born as a solar deity.

81. He who renders me service with vocal or instrumental music or dance, uttering praise and keeping awake at night, becomes my own.

82. He who bathes me with milk, curd, ghee, honey or water, overcomes old age and death.

83. He who feeds Brahmins in Śrāddha with due attention (here) becomes a god honoured by Indra.

84-85. Those who propitiate me through vows, pilgrimages, offerings of food and offerings in fire with attention, remain in heaven for sixty thousand years and are then born in this world in all prosperity.

86. Brāhmaṇas, Kṣatriyas, Vaiśyas, Śūdras, and women who resort with devotion to Śaileśvara here, get the position of my attendants.

87. Śaileśvara is the supreme secret, Śaileśvara is the supreme resort. There is no place superior to Śaileśvara on earth.

88. Even the man who has incurred the sins of killing a Brahmin, killing a teacher or killing a cow, gets purified by coming to this place.

89. There are various tīrthas here with various deities, and the touch of water in them removes all sins.

90. There is the tīrtha called Krośodaka built by the gods by condensing the form extending over a krośa.

91. By bathing there with purity, self-control and truthfulness, all sins disappear and abundant merit is achieved.

92. There is Anāśaka to the south of Śaileśvara and the person who goes there gets beatitude.

93. He who throws himself down from there without desire or anger, goes in an aerial car to heaven surrounded by Apsarases.

94. At the bottom of the precipice there is a tīrtha known as Brahmodbheda built by Brahmā. Know what merit it gives.

95. He who bathes there for one year with control of senses, doubtless goes to the world of Brahmā.

96. There is the Gorakṣaka dug by the feet of cows and bulls. Seeing it procures the benefit of a thousand cows.

97-98. By going to the peak there called Gaurīśikhara resorted to by Siddhas and seeing, touching or bowing to the universal mother Pārvatī who remains there for protecting the world, one attains her own world.

99. He who throws himself down from there to the bank of Vāgmatī, quickly goes to her world in an aerial car.

100. He who bathes in the pond called Umāstanakuṇḍa becomes lustrous like fire and goes to the world of Skanda.

101. By bathing in Pañcanada resorted to by great sages, the merit of Agnihotra is obtained.

102. He who makes others bathe there, will be reborn with memory of his previous lives.

103. To the north of this is another tīrtha resorted to by the pious called Prāntakapāniya guarded by Guhyakas.

104. He who bathes there for one year, becomes a Guhyaka and an attendant of Rudra.

105. To the north-east of this temple of Pārvatī and to the south of Vāgmatī, there is a holy tīrtha called Brahmodaya into which water flows from a cave.

106. By touching its water, sprinkling it over the body or bathing in it, one avoids seeing the world of death and is never put to any misery.

107. By bathing with due rites in the Sundarikātīrtha, one attains beauty and brilliance.

108. By worshipping Sandhyā there during the three times of the day, a Brahmin gets free from all sins.

109-110. The pure Brahmin who remains for a whole day and reciting Rudrādhyāya at the confluence of Vāgmatī and Maṇivatī, becomes a learned man well-versed in Vedas and liberates his entire family.

111. Even if a person belonging to an inferior caste bathes there and offers water with sesamum, no doubt, propitiates his manes.

112. By bathing anywhere in the Vāgmatī, one avoids taking birth as an animal, and becomes born in an affluent family.

113. The wise man may go to this confluence of Vāgmatī and Maṇivatī with his mind free from desire and anger.

114. And bathing there, he will acquire ten times the merit of bathing in the place of the emergence of Gaṅgā.

115. This is frequented by Vidyādharas, Siddhas, Gandharvas, sages, gods, Yakṣas and serpents for bath.

116. Even a little money given to Brahmins here, produces eternal merit.

117. The deities should be worshipped here with all effort, because there is no holy place superior to this.

118-119. In this holy Śleṣmātaka forest resorted to by the gods, wherever I have, in my form as deer, moved about, stood, slept or played, all that has become particularly sacred.

120. This horn broken into three will become famous in the world as Gokarṇeśvara.

121-122. Thus telling gods, the great Lord, still remaining invisible to them, bounded to the north.

CHAPTER TWO HUNDRED AND SIXTEEN

Greatness of Śṛṅgeśvara

Brahmā said:

1-2. When the great lord Tryambaka in the form of deer left, the gods were consulting one another and me as to where the three parts of the horn could be duly consecrated.

3. Indra installed the tip in one place. I installed the middle part also in the same place.

4. Devas, Devarṣis, Brahmarṣis and Siddhas proclaimed it as Gokarṇa.

5. Then Viṣṇu installed the base of the horn in Devatīrtha. It then came to be known as Śṛṅgeśvara.

6. When the three parts were thus installed in two places, the Lord bestowed two (of his hundred parts), one on each.

7. In the deer he had divided his energy into hundred parts. Two of these were bestowed on the three parts of the horn.

8. With the rest of the deer form, the Lord went to the foot of the Himālaya.

9. To worship the Lord in these three pieces of the horn is to get hundred times the benefit of worshipping him elsewhere.

10. Devas and Asuras worshipped him with severe penance and got many boons.

11. Devas, Asuras, Gandharvas, Siddhas, Yakṣas and Uragas went round the whole Śleṣmātaka region in pilgrimage.

12. Proclaiming the benefits of that region and of the tīrthas therein, they returned from there to their own places.

13-14. When the gods had left, Rāvaṇa with his brothers and other Rākṣasas came there and began to worship the great Lord Gokarṇeśvara with severe penance.

15. Śiva became pleased with him and offered him boons.

16. He sought the boon of victory for him in the three worlds.

17. Getting it from the great Lord, he immediately set out for the conquest of the three worlds.

18. He conquered the three worlds and defeating Indra, pulled out the tip of the horn installed by him and carried it away along with his son Indrajit.

19. On the way, Rāvaṇa placed it on the shore of the ocean for a while and went for performing Sandhyopāsanā.

20. When he returned he found that it had fixed itself on the ground.

21. His attempt to pull it out with all his might simply failed because it had so strongly cemented itself, and so leaving it there, he returned to Laṅkā.

22. That place came to be known as Dakṣiṇagokarṇa (Southern Gokarṇa) where Śiva, the lord of all beings, consecrated himself.

23-24. Thus have I told you in detail about Uttaragokarṇa, Dakṣiṇagokarṇa, Śṛṅgeśvara and Śaileśvara and how the Lord came to be in each of these places.

25. I have told you, O son, about the greatness of these places and tīrthas there. What else do you wish to know?

CHAPTER TWO HUNDRED AND SEVENTEEN

Benefits of Recitation

Sanatkumāra said:

1-2. You have cleared all my doubts after well thinking about them a lot and told me about Lord Śiva of universal form and unmatched glory who took the form of the deer and also about the installation of its horn and the body in holy places for the good of the world.

3. Now you may be pleased to tell me about the significance of this.

Brahmā said:

4. Whatever there is still to be told, will be narrated by Pulastya.

5. He will say that before the sages in the Kuru country. He will say about the importance of all tīrthas.

6. O my son, you are equal to me and have known the true essence of Vedas and Vedāṅgas. (By listening to what I have said) one gets cleansed of all sins, attains fame and becomes honoured in this world as well as in the world beyond.

7. This should always be listened to by people of all castes.

8. It is sacred and auspicious and brings about Dharma, Karma and Artha and all prosperity, long life and success everywhere.

9. It removes all sins and bestows wealth, fame, happiness and peace. So by listening to it one gets free from all that is bad and evil.

10. By getting it recited, one gets over the effects of Kali age and goes to heaven.

Sūta said:

11. Having thus told Sanatkumāra, the great lord Brahmā retired.

12. O virtuous ones, I have thus told you in essence the conversation between Varāha and Bhūmi.

13. He who recites this or listens to it with devotion, becomes free from all sins and gets beatitude.

14. This confers a crore times the merit acquired in Prabhāsa, Naimiṣāraṇya, Gaṅgādvāra, Puṣkara, Prayāga, Brahmatīrtha and Amarakaṇṭaka.

15. The merit of gifting a cow is acquired by listening even to one chapter of it.

16. Listening to ten chapters with attention confers the merit of Agniṣṭoma and Atirātra sacrifices.

17-18. He who listens always to the narration of utterances of Varāha acquires the merit of all sacrifices, all gifts and all tīrthas.

19. Varāha himself has declared: "He who listens with devotion to the narration of this greatness of mine gets sons if he has none, and also good grandsons".

20. He who keeps in his house a written copy of this, always gets the favour of Lord Nārāyaṇa.

21. He who always listens to it with deep devotion,

22. And performs pūjā to the work as for the great Viṣṇu with sandal, flowers and clothes and feeds Brahmins,

23. And the king who does so with gifts of villages according to his capacity, and honours well the discourser of the Purāṇa,

24. Become free from all sins and attain merger in Lord Viṣṇu.

CHAPTER TWO HUNDRED AND EIGHTEEN

Contents of the Purāṇa

1. This Purāṇa spoken by Varāha was written at Kāśī by Mādhavabhaṭṭa with the assistance of Vīreśvara in the Vikrama year one thousand six hundred and seventythree.

2. The contents of the Varāhapurāṇa are now given. First the occasion is mentioned and then the primordial origin.

3. Primary creation is then detailed followed by the story of Durjaya and place of narration and rules of Śrāddha.

4. In the narration of old legends we get the story of Saramā and the story of Mahātapas.

5. Then the origin of Agni, Aśvins, Gaurī, Vināyaka and Nāgas,

6. The origin of Skanda and Sūrya are given, followed by the origin of Devī.

7. Then we get the origin of Kubera, the determination of relative priority, and the origin of Dharma and Rudra,

8. Then the secret of the origin of Soma and briefly the origin of earth, then the ancient legend and the story of the hunter.

9. Then is the story of Satyatapas and later the rules for observance of Matsyadvādaśī, Kūrmadvādaśī, Varāhadvādaśī,

10. Nṛsiṁhadvādaśī, Vāmanadvādaśī, Bhārgavadvādaśī, Śrīrāmadvādaśī,

11. Kṛṣṇadvādaśī, Buddhadvādaśī, Kalkidvādaśī and Padmanābhadvādaśī.

12. Dharaṇīvrata, Agastyagītā, the story of Paśupāla and the Vrata for obtaining a good husband follow.

13. Then are given Śubhavrata, Dhanyavrata, Kāntivrata, Saubhāgyavrata, Avighnavrata,

14. Śāntivrata, Kāmavrata, Ārogyavrata, Putraprāptivrata, Śauryavrata and Sārvabhaumavrata,

15. The glorification of Purāṇa, the praise of Lord Nārāyaṇa by Lord Śiva, Rudragītā, and the determination of Prakṛti and Puruṣa.

16. Then follow the descriptions of the universe, the limits of Jambūdvīpa.

17. The extent of Bhārata and the various things there. Then we get the conversation between Nārada and Mahiṣa,

18. The account of the greatness of Śakti and the killing of Mahiṣāsura, followed by the description of Rudra's glory and the Parvādhyāya.

19. Then occurs Śvetopākhyāna. This is followed by the rites of Tiladhenu, Jaladhenu, Rasadhenu, Guḍadhenu,

20. Śarkarādhenu, Madhudhenu, Dadhidhenu, Lavaṇadhenu, Kārpāsadhenu and Dhānyadhenu.

21. Then we get the nature of devotion to the Lord, the praise of Lord Viṣṇu and the numerous questions put to him.

22. The nature of the devotees is then described, as also the nature of joy and sorrow and the thirtytwo offences in worship.

23. The rules and the mantras for worship are then given and also for permitted and prohibited food and the rules for Sandhyopāsana.

24. Observances for freedom from rebirth, the greatness of Kokāmukha, the importance of sandal and flower in worshipping the lord,

25. Māyācakra, the greatness of Kubjāmraka, the rules relating to different castes,

26. And the mantras for offering collyrium and mirror follow.

27. The expiations for eating the king's food, for not cleaning teeth, for touching dead body, for non-utterance of mantras,

28. For wearing blue cloth, worshipping with anger, for wearing red cloth, for worshipping in darkness,

29. For wearing black cloth or unclean cloth, for eating meat like pork,

30. For worshipping with the stain of the burnt oil in the lamp in hand, for going to the cremation ground,

31. For eating oil cake, for worshipping with foot-wear on, for not observing what is laid down by Śāstra are then stated.

32. Then follow the account of the greatness of Sūkarakṣetra, the story of jackal and the eagle, and that of Khañjarīṭa,

33. The greatness of Kokāmukha again and of Badarī, the importance of secret worship, the greatness of Mandāra and Guhya tīrthas and of Śālagrāma,

34. Of Someśvara, Muktikṣetra, Triveṇī and Gaṇḍakī,

35. Of Cakratīrtha, Harikṣetra, Devahrada and Rurukṣetra,

36. The importance of Goniṣkramaṇa, Dvārakā and its tīrthas, Lohārgala,

37. Mathurātīrtha and its origin, Yamunātīrtha, Akrūratīrtha are given.

38. Then occur the accounts of Devāraṇya, Cakratīrtha, Kapila, Govardhana,

39. Viśrāntitīrtha, the story of Gokarṇa,

40. The greatness of Sarasvatī, Yamunodbheda, Gaṅgodbheda and the curse of Sāmba.

41. This is followed by rules for installation of idols for worship made of wood, stone or clay,

42. And the same made of copper, bronze, silver or gold,

43. The origin of Śrāddha, piṇḍa and saṅkalpa and details of Pitṛyajña are then given.

44. Then we get the importance of Madhuparka, the description of Saṁsāracakra, the miseries of evil and pleasures of good,

45. The torments inflicted by Yama's men, the various hells,

46. The transformations consequent on the nature of actions, and sinful deeds.

47. The account of good and bad, the allurements in life and the wonderful story of Nimi are then given.

48. The sacred story of Gokarṇeśvara, the boons to Nandī, the greatness of Jaleśvara, Śaileśvara and Śṛṅgeśvara are then narrated.

49. By listening to this Anukramaṇikā, one attains the merit of listening to the Varāhapurāṇa.

GLOSSARY

The figure in black refers to a Chapter
The figure in white refers to a Verse

Abhāva, non-being **6**.15, **9**.3;—son of Unnetā **74**.9.

Acchodaka, a mountain in Krauñcadvīpa (same as Andhakāra) **88.1**.

Acyuta, a name of Viṣṇu **6**.16, **174**.74, **211**.84.

Adharā, deity representing downward direction **29**.4.

Āditya, Sun-god **80**.7, **113**.41; origin of the name **26**.7;—a law-giver 121.18; —a sage **170**.62.

Ādityas, a group of gods **17**.24-25, 41, **18**.1-3, **21**.10, 18, 19-20, 49, **73**.33, 48, **93**.27-28, **94**.6-9, 15, **124**.13, 24, **141**.24, 26, 27, **151**.12, **157**.10, **187**.21-22, 25, **214**.73.

Ādityatīrtha, a tīrtha in the Gaṅgā at Saukara, **138**.16.

Agastya, a sage **49**.7, 10-11, 13, 16-18, 41, **50**.1, **70**.12, 28, **72**.1.

Āgnāyī, another name for Kapilā cow **112**.15.

Agnī, god of fire **28**.14-15, 16, **87**.1, **110**.13-15, **113**.41, **124**.15, **128**.90, **174**. 71;—fire in the body **17**.24-25, 28-29, **18**.1-3;—guardian deity of south-east **29**.12-13, **99**.26, 36, 43;—a law-giver **121**.17.

Agnibāhu, son of Priyavrata **74**.7.

Agnidatta, a warrior in the army of Hetṛ-Prahetṛ (also Agnidaṁṣṭra) **11**.93-95, 100;—a Brahmin turned Brahmarākṣasa **155**.62.

Āgnīdhra, a special priest **21**.15-17;—son of Priyavrata and lord of Jambūdvīpa **74**.7.

Agnihotra, a sacrifice, **112**.6, **215**.63-64, 101.

Agnimān, a mountain in Kuśadvīpa **87**.1.

Agnimedha, a sacrifice **126**.73.

Agniprabha, a tīrtha in Śālagrāma **145**.56-59.

Agnisaras, a holy lake in Kokāmuhka **140**.34;—a tīrtha in Lohārgala **151**.54-56.

Agnisatyapada, a tīrtha in Badarī **141**.7-9.

Agniṣṭoma, a sacrifice **140**.18, **141**.5, **145**.58, **152**.40, **156**.13, **217**.16.

Agnitejas, a warrior in the army of Hetṛ-Prahetṛ **11**.93-95, 100.

Agnitīrtha, a tīrtha in Kubjāmraka **126**.66, 72.

Agniveśya, a sage **214**.43-45.

Āgrahāyaṇī, a month **178**.5-6.

Āhavanīyāgni, one of the three sacrificial fires **190**.15.

Ahaṅkāra, ego **17**.59, **25**.1, 5, 35.

Aindrī māyā, a form of Māyā **125**.37.

Airāvata, a minor mountain in Bhārata **85**.3.

Ajayā, a carrier goddess of libation **190**.29-30.

Ākāśa **17**.59.

Ākhyāvatī, a river **82**.4.

Akrūratīrtha, a tīrtha in Mathurā **155**.4-5, 13, 71, **168**.14.

Akṣayā, a carrier-goddess of libation **190**. 130.

Alakanandā, a stream in Meru **82**.1.

Alaṁśarmā, chief minister of Mahiṣāsura **93**.2.

Āmalaka, a holy tree in Bhūtagiri **148**.67-71.
Amaragaṇḍikā, a river on the side of Gandhamādana **82**.2.
Amarāvatī, city of Indra **75**.78-80, **76**.3-5, 6, **168**.9, **205**.5.
Amāvāsī, tithi **34**.7.
Āmbikeya, a mountain in Śākadvīpa **86**.2.
Ambhodhara, a serpent-chief **214**.57-63.
Amitākṣarā, a name of Brāhmī **91**.3.
Amṛtā, a goddess created by Vaiṣṇavī **92**.9-12.
Aṁśumayī, a form of Māyā **125**.44.
Āmuṣyāyaṇa, disciple of Sālaṅkāyana **144**.88, 90, 91, **145**.28.
Ananta, a name of Viṣṇu **174**.74, **186**.11, **211**.84;—a serpent-chief **24**.6-7, **214**. 57-63;—son of Pṛthu **74**.9.
Anantamāyā, a form of Māyā **125**.46.
Anantatīrtha, a tīrtha in Mathurā **155**.1-3.
Anaraṇya, king **62**.5-6.
Ānarta, a region in Krauñcadvīpa (same as Dundubhi) **88**.3.
Anāśaka, a vrata **141**.13;—a tīrtha near Śaileśvara **215**.92-93.
Andhaka, a demon **27**.1, 2, 5, 11, 19, 25, 26, 27, 39, **33**.19, **90**.15, **144**.23.
Andhakāra, a mountain in Krauñcadvīpa **88**.3;—a region of Krauñcadvīpa **88**.3;—one of the eight main hells **200**.1-2.
Andhakāraka, son of Dyutīmān **74**.7.
Andhakas, a class of people **149**.11, 19.
Andhatāmisra, utter darkness **2**.28.
Anekaparvatas, a group of Gandharvas **81**.5.
Aṅga, Maṇija king Sundara reborn **36**.5.
Aṅgāraja, a settlement in Naiṣadha **83**.2.
Aṅgāravāhinī, a river **82**.4.
Aṅgiras, a law-giver **197**.82;—a sage **2**.44, **21**.15-17, 18, **124**.16-17, **170**.62, **214**.43-45.
Āṅgirasa, a law-giver **121**.14;—a sage, husband of Tārā **32**.10;—preceptor of gods **16**.10-11.
Āṅgīrasī, a form of Māyā **125**.34.
Aniruddha **99**.30;—one of the four Vyūhas **148**.14.
Anityāśrama, a holy place in Kokāmukha **140**.31.
Añjana, a Rākṣasa **94**.5.
Annakūṭa, a holy spot in Govardhana, **164**.10, 11, 16, 23, 26, 45.
Antyā, a river arising from Vindhya **85**.5.
Apāna **17**.58, **20**.1, 18.
Aparājitā, a goddess created by Vaiṣṇavī **92**.9-12;—a goddess installed in Mathurā **160**.15.
Apsarases **54**.4, **75**.59, **76**.3-5, **77**.10, **79**.18-19, **100**.18, **105**.18, **110**.19, **124**.11, **125**.69, **126**.32, **145**.69, 84, **148**.47, 51, **149**.25, 77, **158**.11, **206**.5, **213**.20, **214**.28, 67, 70, **215**.53-54.
Apsarastīrtha, a tīrtha near Govardhana **164**.21.
Āpastamba, a law-giver **162**.34, **197**.17.
Arbuda, a serpent-chief **214**.57-63.
Ardhacandra, a tīrtha in Mathurā **169**.6, 16, 17, 18, **175**.15.

Atri, a sage 2.44, **21**.15-17, **35**.1, **214**.43-45;—a law-giver **197**.17.
Aṭṭahāsa, a holy place **122**.12.
Auddālaki, a law-giver **197**.17.
Audhra, son of Dyutimān **74**.7.
Augrasenā, a goddess installed in Mathurā **160**.16.
Aurva Prajāpati **147**.5, 10, 15, 20, 28.
Avanti, a country **3**.3-4.
Avasara, a mountain in Gomedadvīpa **89**.4.
Avatāras of Viṣṇu, list **48**.17-19, results of worshipping each **48**.20-22.
Avīci, a hell **7**.20.
Avidyā, ignorance **6**.11.
Avighnavrata, rituals **59**.1-4, results **59**.5.
Avimukta, a tīrtha in Mathurā **152**.33, **168**.16.
Avyakta, **25**.2, **99**.1.
Ayodhyā **97**.32, **163**.46, 49, 51, **178**.4.

Bābhravya, saṁhitā relating to Pāśupata, **71**.54;—a vrata relating to Rudra **97**.39, 43, origin of the name **97**.39.
Babhru, a name of Rudra **97**.5.
Badarī, a holy place in the Himālayas **48**.6-7, 23, **140**.4, **141**.1, 52, 55, 57 **175**.9.
Baḍavā, submarine fire **125**.39-40.
Bāhu, a warrior in the army of Hetṛ-Prahetṛ **11**.93-95.
Bāhudā, a river rising from Himālaya **85**.4, **214**.46-49.
Bahulā, a river in Krauñcadvīpa (same as Puṇḍarīka) **88**.5;—a river in Naiṣadha, **83**.3;—a tīrtha in Bṛndāvana in Mathurā **157**.8-9.
Bāhuvāhinī, a river rising from Ṛkṣa **85**.5.
Bāhuvana, a garden in Mathurā **161**.7.
Bāhyakāverī, a river rising from Sahya **85**.5.
Bakulavana, a garden in Mathurā **153**.39.
Balabhadra **99**.30, **160**.45, **164**.22.
Balādhana, a division of Kuśadvīpa **87**.2.
Bali, son of Virocana **152**.51-52, **159**.9, **193**.45.
Balihrada, a tīrtha in Mathurā **160**.34.
Bāṇagaṅgā, a holy waterfall near Someśvara **144**.70-74.
Bhadra, a banyan tree on the bank of Puṣyabhadrā **98**.6, 10;—a mount near Asitoda **78**.18-19.
Bhadrā, a stream in Meru **82**.1.
Bhadrakarṇa, a holy place **122**.12.
Bhadrākara, a region on the western side of Kuru **84**.12.
Bhadranadī, a river in Naiṣadha **83**.3.
Bhādrapada, the month Kanyā **48**.1, **150**.40, **153**.34, 36, **157**.45, **164**.17, **174**. 53-54.
Bhadrāśva, a country **10**.39;—the kingdom of Bhadrāśva **49**.6;—name of a king **49**.6, **50**.1, **51**.5;—the region on the eastern side of Mālyavān **82**.**2**, **83**.1;—a region on the east of Meru **74**.8, **75**.61.
Bhadravana, a garden in Mathurā **153**.40, **161**.7.

Bilvaprabha, a tīrtha in Śālagrāma **145**.38-40.

Bilvasthalī, a place in the valley between Sumūla and Vasudhāra **80**.5.

Bilvavana, a garden in Mathurā **153**.45, **161**.9.

Brahmā **1**.8, 19, 22, **2**.13, 16, 42, 46, 48-49, 51, 77, **3**.26-27, **4**.24-25, 27, **5**.6, **7**.36, **8**.30, 48, **13**.9, 12, **15**.4, 5, **17**.23, **18**.1-3, **19**.2, 9, **20**.1, 2, 35, **21**.4-9, 12, 13, 14, 18, 21, 28, 38, 51, 60, 73, **22**.31, 47, **23**.11-15, 17, 23, 27, **24**.4, 22, 30, **25**.6, 13, 14, 15, **26**.12, **27**.2, 3, 8, 31-32, 43, **28**.6-7, 19, 36-37, **29**.1, 2, 10, 14, 16, **31**.12, **32**.2, 14, 16, 19, 28, 31, **33**.5, 28, 31, 33, **34**.2, 5, 6, 7, **35**.1, 14, **37**.7, **39**.66, **44**.20, **55**.22, **70**.15-16, 17, 20, 26, 40, 47, **71**.12, 66, **72**.2, 9, 11, 13, 16, **73**.2, 10, 15, 23, 28, 29, 30, **74**.6, **75**.15, 69, 71, **77**.30, **81**.4, 6, 7, **82**.2, **90**.1, 13, 14, 17, 18, 22, 29, 37, 38, 39, 43, 45, **91**.8, **92**.15, **93**.57, 61, **96**.3-4, 63, **97**.2, 3-4, 8, 11, 37, 45, 46, **99**.1, 2, 44, **104**.19, **105**.16, **110**.13-15, **111**.3, 10, **112**.3, 6, 13, 68, 69, **113**.1, 9, 20, 30, 37, **124**.15, 24, **125**.9, 51, **126**.57, **128**.61, **129**.8, 58, **134**.55, **140**.36, **141**.20, 39, 41, 54, 59, 60, **144**.112, 114, 116, **147**.41, **148**.76, **150**.22, 23, **151**.12, 26, 77, 78, **152**.67, **153**.45, **154**.18, 19, **157**.17, 20, **159**.8, 17, 21, **160**.21, **163**.21, **174**.81, **177**.36, **182**.26, **186**.26, **187**.13, 14, 19, 20, 21-22, 24, 27, 82, 83, **188**.10, **190**.58, 59, 68, 73, 75, 80-81, 85, 86, **191**.7, 9, 10, 13, 15, **193**.42, **204**.26, **206**.26, **213**.4, 11, 53, 55-56, **214**.17, **215**.3, 94, 95, **217**.11;—identity with Viṣṇu and Śiva **70**.26-27, 39-40, **71**.6-7, **72**.14, 16, 41.

Brāhma, a sacrifice **8**.31.

Brahman, the supreme being **2**.24, **9**.4, **13**.13, **20**.28, **36**.10, **50**.24, **62**.24, 30, **72**.12, **98**.35, **139**.50, 100, **144**.46, **177**.51, **187**.41, 45;—a special priest **21**.15-17.

Brāhmaṇas, see Brahmins;—rules of worship for **115**.23-26.

Brāhmaṇī, a mother goddess representing pride **27**.35-36.

Brahmins **3**.19, **9**.15, **37**.15, 17, 25, 26, 28, 32, 33, 34, **39**.10, 50-53, 57,59, 68, **40**.8, **68**.5-6, 8, 9, 44, **71**.43, **75**.16, 82, **84**.2, **98**.29, 44, **99**.59, 66, 82, **112**.81, **116**.22, **121**.6, **122**.101, 102, **123**.23, **125**.173, 174, 176, **137**.98, 193, 196, 266, **138**.30, 102, **139**.51, **141**, 45, **145**.54, 118, **152**.47, **153**.22-23, **163**.2, **165**.39, **169**.13, **174**.40, 46, **176**.30, 34, **178**.1-2, 5-6, **180**.31, 74, 130, **182**.33, 35-36, **184**.17, 18, **185**.26, 28, 31, **186**.28, 29, **187**.21-22, 27, 37, 73, **188**.7, 11, 35, 75, 81, 103, 107, **189**.2, 48, 56, **190**.23-24, 43-44, **192**.10, 12, **194**.13, **195**.3, 5, 6, **200**.65, **205**.23, **206**.18, **207**.10, **208**.8, 18, 19, **211**.4, 22, 35, **215**.43, 46, 83, 86, 116, **217**.22;—initiation into Bhāgavatadharma **127**.9-24, 36, **128**.38, **114**.29-30.

Brahmadatta, king of Kāmpilya, **137**.67, **152**.44;—the chief judge in Yama's hall of justice **197**.20.

Brahmahā, a Rākṣasa **94**.10-12.

Brahmakuṇḍa, a tīrtha in Badarī **141**.4-6;—a tīrtha in Lohārgala **151**.73-78.

Brahmāṇḍa, the universe **9**.8, **18**.13.

Brahmapāra, a hymn in praise of Brahmā by Aśvins **20**.27-30;—a hymn in praise of Viṣṇu by Nārada **3**.9-20.

Brahmapada, a tirtha in Goniṣkramaṇa, **147**.40-43.

Brahmarākṣasa **139**.35, 37, 40, 57, 58, 63, 65, 73, 77, 80, 82, 84, 88, **155**.14, 44, 45, 47, 51, 54, 59;—liberation by an outcaste **139**.32-100.

Candrasena, a king of Mathurā **180**.2, 37.
Candrāvartā, a river in Candradvīpa **84**.10.
Candravatī, a river in Naiṣadha **82**.4, **81**.3.
Cāndrāyaṇa, a purificatory rite **130**.23, **134**.6, **137**.251, **151**.65, **174**.34, **179**.13, 14, 17, **187**.30.
Candrodaya, a mountain **81**.2.
Cāṇūra **15**.17.
Cāraṇas, a group of celestials **25**.15, **75**.8, 26, **79**.14-15, **92**.34, **158**.12, **215**.13, 58.
Carcikā, a goddess installed in Mathurā, **160**.16, 28.
Carmaṇvatī, a river rising from Pāriyātra **85**.4, **214**.46-49.
Cārubhāgā, a river **214**.46-49.
Cārukanyā, a goddess created by Vaiṣṇavī **92**.9-12.
Cārukeśī, a goddess created by Vaiṣṇavī **92**.9-12.
Cārumukhī, a goddess created by Vaiṣṇavī **92**.9-12.
Catuḥsāmudrika, a tīrtha in Mathurā, **158**.42-43.
Catuḥsāmudrikā, a holy well in Mathurā **165**.29, 55.
Catuḥsrotas, a tīrtha in Badarī **141**.17-19.
Caturdaśī, tīthi **33**.29-30, **166**.22, **174**.39.
Caturyuga **39**.62-63.
Chāyā, shadow of Saṁjñā, wife of Mārtaṇḍa **20**.7, 8, 12, 14.
Citrā, a river in Kuśadvīpa **87**.3.
Citravatī, a river **214**.46-49.
Citragupta, minister of Yama **194**.30, **198**.26-27, 28, 30, **200**.76, **201**.1, 4, 6, 12, 40, 55, 56, **202**.1, **203**.1, **204**.1, 25, **205**.1, **206**.1, 23-24.
Citrakūṭa, a minor mountain in Bhārata, **10**.20, 34, **12**.2, 3-4, **85**.3, **214**.53-55.
Citrakūṭā, a river rising from Ṛkṣa **85**.5.
Citrasena, a Gandharva **214**.74.
Citraśilā, a slab on the bank of Puṣyabhadrā, **98**.6.
Citrotpalā, a river rising from Ṛkṣa **85**.5.
Cittayoga **142**.42.
Cohabitation, rules relating to **142**.31-41.
Collyrium, offering of **128**.73.
Comb, offering of **128**.70-72.
Copper, origin of **129**.26-49.
Copper vessels, importance in rituals **129**.21, 41, 42.
Consecration of images **181**.9—**186**.36.
Coraka, a settlement in Naiṣadha **83**.2.
Cosmology **74**.1—**89**.7.
Creation, of gods **187**.7-27, primary **2**.4-53.
Cūḍamala, a settlement in Naiṣadha **83**.2.
Cyavana, a sage **214**.43-45.

Dadhidhenu **106**.1, 7, 8.
Daivikā, a river **214**.46-49.
Dakṣa **21**.12, 18, 26, 39, 63, 84, 87, **22**.3, **24**.5, **33**.5, **35**.1, 4, 8, **57**.2;—son of Brahmā **74**.6.

Dhanyā, a goddess created by Vaiṣṇavī **92**.9-12.

Dhānyadhenu **110**.1, 3, 17, 18.

Dhanyavrata, rituals **56**.1-2, results **56**.13-16.

Dharaṇīvrata, another name for Matsyadvādaśīvrata **39**.60;—origin of the name of **50**.27; ritūals **50**.4-22; results **50**.23-28.

Dhārāpatanaka, a tīrtha in Mathurā **154**.8-14.

Dharma, division among the four castes **32**.6; origin **32**.3; feet of **32**.7; three horns of **32**.8;—a law-giver **121**.16;—name of Yama **17**.71.

Dharmāraṇya, a forest on the bank of Gaṅgā **5**.18-19.

Dharmodbhava, a holy place in Kokāmukha **140**.44.

Dharmavyādha 6.39.

Dhātaka, son of Savana, **74**.7.

Dhātakīkhaṇḍa, the region of Dhātaka **74**.7.

Dhātus, vital elements in the body **17**.37, 59.

Dhenu, a river in Śākadvīpa **86**.3.

Dhenuka, a demon **157**.39.

Dhenuvaṭa, a holy place in Kokāmukha **140**.40.

Dhṛtarāṣṭra, a serpent-chief **214**.57-63.

Dhṛti, a river in Kuśadvīpa (same as Mahatī) **87**.3;—son of Jyotiṣmān **74**.8.

Dhruva **11**.61, **49**.16-18, 39-40, **159**.8, 22, **160**.6, **186**.11, **214**.40;—a region at the northern end of earth **171**.20;—son of Priyavrata **74**.7;—son of Medhātithi **74**.8.

Dhruvatīrtha, a tīrtha in Mathurā **152**.59-61, **180**.1, 7, 19, 25, 93, 106-107, 110, 123, 124.

Dhūmajanma, a settlement in Naiṣadha **83**.2.

Dhūtapāpā, a river rising from Himālaya **85**.4;—a tīrtha in Bhūtagiri **148**.58-62.

Dhvāṅkṣa, a Rākṣasa **94**.6-9.

Dhvastakarṇa, a Rākṣasa **94**.6-9.

Dhyānayoga **129**.8, 58.

Diks, the quarters **17**.24-25, **18**.1-3, **29**.16.

Dīptatejas, a warrior who came out of Gauramukha's gem **11**.83-84, 97; Maṇija king reborn as Śānta **36**.3.

Dīrghabāhu, a king **37**.25;—a Rākṣasa **94**.6-9.

Dīrghaviṣṇu, a deity installed in Mathurā **169**.41.

Diti, mother of Asuras **187**.26.

Divākara, a name of Sun; origin of the name **26**.7.

Divya, a sacrifice **8**.31.

Draviṇoda, a name of fire **18**.22.

Dṛḍhavrata, a king **55**.22;—a vow, requisites of **117**.37-42.

Droṇa, a division of Kuśadvīpa **87**.2;—a mountain (same as Hemaparvata) **87**.1, **214**.53-55.

Dṛṣadvatī, a river rising from Himālaya **85**.4.

Dundubhi, a region in Krauñcadvīpa **88**.3;—son of Dyutimān **74**.7.

Durga, a holy place **122**.14.

Durgā, opulence in the body **17**.24-25, 44, **18**.1-3;—a river rising from Vindhya **85**.5.

intercourse **132**.8-11; for touching a woman during her monthly course **132**.24-26; for touching idol after adultery **134**.29-30; for using saffower in food **136**.81; for waking up the deity without beating the drum **136**. 110; for wearing black garment **135**.20-21; for wearing cloth of another **136**.86-90; for wearing red garment **135**.5-6; for wearing unwashed cloth **135**.31-33; for worship after eating oil-cake **136**.58; for worship after eating pork **135**.48-52; for worship after going to cremation ground **136**.53; for worship in darkness **135**.12-14; for worship with forbidden flowers **134**.69-71; for worship with undigested food in stomach **136**. 116-119.

Five propagators of Bhāgavatadharma **148**.12.
Five sacrifices 8.31.
Four castes, origin from Lord's form **9**.15-16.
Four vyūhas **148**.14, **152**.25.

Gabhastī, a division of Bhāratavarṣa **85**.1;—a river in Śākadvīpa.
Gabhīraka, a tīrtha in Mandāra **143**.42-44.
Gadādhara, a form of Viṣṇu 7.29-40,47.
Gadākuṇḍa, a tīrtha in Sālagrāma **145**.53-55.
Gaja, a mountain **81**.4.
Gajamūla, a mount near lake Mānasa **78**.14-16.
Gambhīrā, a goddess created by Vaiṣṇavī **92**.9-12.
Gaṇāntika, rosary **128**.42, 69, 77; eligibility for **128**.79; materials of **128**.81; number of beads in **128**.80; place in worship **128**.50-63.
Gaṇapati, ākāśa **17**.24-25, 35-36, **18**.1-3;—a name of Vināyaka **23**.1, 25, **24**.2.
Gaṇas **213**.47, 53, 69, 76, 77.
Gaṇḍakī, a river rising from Himālaya **97**.17, **85**.4, **144**.39, 41, 58, 61, 95, 96, 122, 124, 131, 142, **145**.89, 112, 114, 115, **146**.50, 51, 59, **214**.46-49, story of its origin **144**.107-128.
Gandhakālī, a celestial damsel **214**.41-42.
Gandhamādana, a mountain on the southren part of Meru **10**.45, **48**.6-7, **74**.8, **77**.9, **214**.50-52.
Gandharvas **2**.47, **10**.41, **13**.30, **21**.19-20, **25**.7,15, **75**.59, **77**.21-22, 25, **79**.18-19, **80**.3, 4, **81**.5, **91**.12, **92**.25, **34**, 36, **93**.27-28, 29, 30-31, **95**.45, **98**. 11, **124**.11, **141**.60, **145**.69, 84, **146**.24, **151**.37, 38, **158**.12, **163**.14, **187**.50, **188**.25-26, 38, 42, **190**.33, **196**.17, **206**.5, 29, **207**.7, **213**.23, **79**, 85-86, **214**.67, 70, **215**.53-54, 115, **216**.11;—a division of Bhāratavarṣa **85**.1;—a tīrtha in Śālagrāma **145**.72-74.
Gandharvakuṇḍa, a holy spot in Asikuṇḍa in Mathurā **163**.13-14.
Gandhavatī, city of Vāyu **76**.12.
Gaṇeśa, a name of Vināyaka **23**.28-29, 37, **25**.20, **59**.4, **144**.36, **160**.13, 49, 52, **186**.41.
Gaṅgā, a river rising from Himālaya **13**.46, **22**.11, 30, **71**.30, 38, **82**.1, **85**.4, **97**.16, 29, 35, **99**.83, 84, 86, **125**.24, 75, 125, **137**.7, **118**.15, 88, **144**.25, 101, 127, 128, 169, **145**.103, **147**.10, 65, **152**.30, **154**.5, **160**.50, **162**.14-15, **164**.46, **187**.115, **193**.1-5, **206**.31, **215**.49, 50, 57, 59;—a tīrtha **214**.50-52.

Gomatī, a river rising from Himālaya **13**.46, **85**.4, **97**.17.
Gomeda, one of the seven islands of the world **74**.7, **89**.4, **140**.27.
Gomedha, a sacrifice **16**.10-11, 38, **111**.13.
Goniṣkramaṇa, a place at the top of Himālaya, **147**.4, **148**.1;—a tīrtha in Goniṣkramaṇa, **147**.9, 31-33, 54.
Gopa, a tīrtha, in Mathurā **160**.61.
Gopis **157**.21, 23, 25, 26, **160**.52.
Gopīśvara, a holy spot near Saptasāmudrika in Mathurā **157**.21.
Gorakṣaka, a tīrtha near Śaileśvara **215**.96.
Gori, a celestial damsel **214**.41-42.
Govardhana, a holy hill near Mathurā **164**.1, 11, 14-15, 17, 42, 46, **165**.23, **168**.14.
Govinda, name of Viṣṇu **36**.11, 22, 23, **153**.49, **174**.74;—a mountain in Krauñcadvīpa **88**.2.
Gṛdhravaṭa, a tīrtha in Saukara **137**.59, 74, 237.
Guḍadhenu **102**.1, 7, 13, 22.
Guḍākeśa, an Asura devotee transformed into copper and other materials **129**.26, 31, 33, 40, 44.
Guha, a name of Skanda, **25**.5.
Guhyakas, a group of celestials **10**.41, **80**.5, **213**.25, **214**.40, **215**.103.

Hāhā, a Gandharva, **22**.41, **214**.38-39, 74.
Hairaṇvatī, a river in Hiraṇmaya **84**.5.
Haṁsā, a river **82**.4.
Haṁsakuṇḍa, a tīrtha in Maṇipūra hill in Dvārakā **149**.47-52.
Haṁsakūṭa, a mount near lake Mahābhadra **78**.21-23.
Haṁsatīrtha, a tīrtha near Kāmika **144**.173-178.
Haṁsavatī, a river **82**.4.
Hanumān **159**.8, **160**.10, 13.
Happiness, actions leading to **116**. 26-44.
Haraṇa, a Rākṣasa **94**.10-12.
Hari, a name of Viṣṇu **15**.9, **58**.3, 7, **68**.19, **70**.17, **73**.51;—a division of Kuśadvīpa (same as Droṇa) **87**.2.
Haridatta, a Vaiśya **49**.22.
Harihara, a holy place **97**.31.
Hariharaprabha, a holy spot on the bank of Gaṇḍakī **144**.164.
Harikṣetra, the place where Gaṅgā meets Bhāgīrathī, **145**.113.
Harita, a mount in Naiṣadha **83**.1.
Haritoyā, a river **82**.4.
Harivarṣa, a region in Niṣadha **10**.37-38, 74.8, 75.32.
Haryaśva, a king **43**.9.
Hastināpura **157**.50.
Havya, son of Priyavrata and lord of Gomeda **74**.7.
Havyavāhana, a name of fire **18**.17, 19.
Hayamukti, a holy place in Mathurā **160**.23-25.
Hell, actions to avoid going to **207**.19-31.
Hemakūṭa, a mountain in Jambūdvīpa **74**.8, **75**.12, **27**, 32, **214**.53-55.

Initiation, of the Brahmins **127**.9-74; of the Kṣatriyas **128**.1-13; of the Śūdras **128**.25-36; of the Vaiśyas **128**.14-24.
Intellect **2**.7, 36.
Irāvatī, a river rising from Himālaya **85**.4.
Īśāna, guardian deity of north-east **29**.12-13, **99**.28, 39.
Itihāsa **170**.60, **180**.77, **193**.10-11.

Jaigīṣavya, a sage **4**.13-14, 22, 27, 32-33.
Jājali, a sage propagator of Bhāgavatadharma **148**.12.
Jalabindu, a holy waterfall in Kokāmukha **140**.16.
Jaladhāra, a mountain in Śākadvīpa **86**.2;—a region in Śākadvīpa **86**.3.
Jaladhenu **100**.1, 17, 18, 19, 20.
Jaleśvara, a holy place **122**.14;—a king **144**.150.
Jālmeśvara, a holy place **122**.15.
Jamadagni, a sage **15**.15, **214**.43-45.)
Jāmadagnya, an incarnation of Viṣṇu **44**.2-3.
Jāmadagnyadvādaśī, rituals **44**.1-7, results **44**.9-21.
Jāmbavatī, wife of Kṛṣṇa **149**.15.
Jambū, the principal tree at the peak of Gandhamādana **77**.17.
Jambūdvīpa, one of the seven islands of the world, **2**.57, **10**.40, **74**.7, **75**.1, 6, 11, 24, **76**.21-22, **85**.6, **86**.1, **139**.112, **140**.67, 68.
Jāmbūnada, a mountain and region in Śālmalidvīpa **89**.3.
Jana, a loka **7**.10, **9**.6, 19, **11**.15, **32**.22.
Janaka, king of Mithilā **163**.2, **207**.3;—Maṇija Soma reborn **36**.7.
Janamejaya, last king of the Kuru line **193**.1-5, **194**.36.
Janārdana, a name of Viṣṇu **4**.20, **5**.51, **7**.44, **10**.67, **11**.17, **12**.11, **36**.14, **39**.29-31, 50.19-20, **55**.33, 42, **70**.29-30, 34, **99**.34, **125**.135, **126**.19, 223-224, **127**.1, **128**.66, **130**.21, **132**.35, **134**.53, **137**.62, **155**.68, **157**.7, **158**.32, **159**.1, **167**.28, **174**.74, **179**.20, **181**.7, **211**.56, **74**, 92.
Jāruji, a mount near lake Mahābhadra **78**.21-23.
Jaṭākuṇḍa, a holy lake in Sānandūra **150**.48-54.
Jaṭāyu, a bird in the northern Dhruva **171**.28.
Jaṭhara, a mountain at the eastern extremity of Meru **77**.**4**.
Jātuccha, a mountain **81**.7.
Jaya, doorkeeper of Viṣṇu **113**.62;—son of Tṛṇabindu **144**.133, 139, 140.
Jayā, doorkeeper of Vaiṣṇavī **95**.27;—a goddess created by Vaiṣṇavī **92**.**9**-**12**.
Jayadā, a goddess installed in Mathurā **160**.17.
Jayanta, a minor mountain in Bhārata **85**.3;—a mount in Naiṣadha **83**.**1**.
Jayantī, a goddess created by Vaiṣṇavī **92**.**9**-**12**.
Jīmūta, a division of Kuśadvīpa (same as Valāhaka) **87**.2.
Jīmūtavāhana, son of Jyotiṣmān **74**.7.
Jñāna **142**.29, 44.
Jñānanidhi, a name of Brāhmī **91**.4.
Jvara, a manifestation of Rudra **201**.38, 41, 44, 48.
Jyeṣṭha, the month of Mithuna **45**.1, **141**.30, **147**.53, **152**.69, **157**.3,7, **163**.66, **176**.81-82.
Jyotirathā, a river rising from Ṛkṣa **85**.5.

Kānyakubja, a city **162**.5.
Kapāla **97**.38.
Kapālamocana, a tīrtha in Gaṅgā in Vārāṇasi **97**.30, 34, 36.
Kāpālīka, the naked form of Rudra **97**.21-22.
Kāpālikavrata **97**.10.
Kapālin, a name of Rudra **97**.5.
Kapardin, a name of Rudra **33**.24.
Kapi, a mount near lake Mānasa **78**.14-16.
Kapila, a sage **4**.13-14, 22, 27, 32-33, **112**.72, **163**.25, 27, **214**.56;—propagator of Bhāgavatadharma **148**.12;—a mount near lake Asitoda **78**.18-19;—a settlement in Naiṣadha **83**.2;—son of Jyotiṣmān **74**.8.
Kapilādhenu, tawny cow **111**.1, **112**.2, 7, 13, 14, 16, 19, 20, 33, **121**.25, 27.
Kapilavarāha, an idol installed in Mathurā **163**.32
Kapiñjala, a mount near lake Mahābhadra **78**.21-23;—a mount in Meru **80**.10.
Karālī, a name of Raudrī **96**.54.
Karambhavālukā, a furious river in Yamaloka **200**.27.
Karaṇṭakā, a river in Naiṣadha **83**.3.
Karatoyā, a river rising from Ṛkṣa **85**.5, **214**.46-49.
Karavīra, a tīrtha in Kubjāmraka **126**.53.
Kardama Prajāpati **80**.3, **114**.11.
Kārkoṭaka, a serpent-chief **24**.6-7, **214**.57-63, installed in Mathurā **160**.69.
Karmakāṇḍa, scripture of ritualistic action **52**.9, 11.
Karmayoga **142**.42.
Karṇāṭa, a settlement in Naiṣadha **83**.2.
Karṇikā, a settlement in Naiṣadha **83**.2.
Kārpāsadhenu **109**.1.
Kārtavīrya, king son of Kṛtavīrya **50**.24.
Kārttīka, month **123**.36-37, **138**.79, **139**.34, 102, **145**.99, **155**.74, **160**.1, **176**.67-68, **211**.29.
Kārttikeya, a name of Skanda **17**.24-25, **27**.31-32.
Kārttikeyakuṇḍa, a tīrtha, in Lohārgala **151**.63-65.
Kāsā, a river **82**.4.
Kāsavatī, a river in Naiṣadha, **83**.3.
Kaseru, a division of Bhāratavarṣa **85**.1.
Kāśmīra, kingdom of Vasu **6**.7;—of Sumanas **6**.33-34.
Kāśyapa, sage, son of Marīci **13**.30, **20**.3, **24**.4, **79**.20, **214**.43-45;—a law-giver **121**.16.
Kāśyapī, a carrier goddess of liberation **190**.29-30, 130.
Kātyāyanī, a name of Durgā **28**.1.
Kaumāra, a vrata performed by Vaiṣṇavī **92**.14;—a mother goddess representing stupefaction **27**.35-36.
Kaumuda, a month **123**.34, 35, **126**.29, 34, 67-68, **128**.57, **147**.42;—the region of Kumuda **74**.7.
Kauśikī, a river rising from Himālaya **85**.4;—a river in Kokāmukha **140**.53, 62, **187**.115, **214**.46-49.
Kāverī, a river **82**.4.

Kṛṣṇāṅga, a settlement in Naiṣadha **83**.2.
Kṛṣṇapāda, a settlement in Naiṣadha **83**.3.
Kṛṣṇatoyā, a river **82**.4.
Kṛṣṇavatī, City of Nirṛti **76**.11.
Kṛta, a sage **170**.62.
Kṛtānta, a Rākṣasa **94**.10-12.
Kṛtasthalā, a minor mountain in Bhārata **85**.3.
Kṛtasurā, a settlement in Naiṣadha **83**.2.
Kṛtavīrya, a king of Haihaya **50**.24.
Kṛtayuga **2**.53, 62, **3**.3-4, 18, **7**.35, **9**.1, **10**.15, **12**.21, **17**.4, **32**.5, 30, **36**.2, **47**.8, **49**.6, 30-31, **66**.16, **68**.3, **70**.24, **72**.9, **137**.66, **163**.22, **208**.28.
Krūra, a minister of Mahiṣāsura **93**.3-4.
Kṣatriyas **3**.19, **9**.16, **49**.16-18, 34, **66**.12, **68**.5-6, 7, 8, 9, **75**.18, 24, **116**.22, **128**.6-7, 13, 38, **134**.29-30, **152**.24, **163**.2, **165**.39, **180**.31, **183**.26, **187**.23, **193**.29, **200**.65, **206**.30, **215**.43, 45, 86; initiation into Bhāgavata dharma **128**.1-13; rules of worship for **115**.27-30.
Kṣemaka, a region in Śākadvīpa **86**.3.
Kṣetrapāla, the guardian god of Mathurā **168**.6.
Kṣiprodā, a river in Krauñcadvīpa (same as Khyāti) **88**.5.
Kṣīradhenu, **105**.1, **9**, 12.
Kṣīrodā, a river **82**.4.
Kubera, lord of wealth **10**.50-52, **28**.17, **113**.41, **125**.36, **139**.106-107, **108**, **174**.80, **185**.14, **213**.19, **214**.32; guardian deity of north **29**.12-13, **99**.28, 38, **158**.18;—a law-giver **121**.18;—the vital air in the body **17**.24-25 46, 59, 70, **18**.1-3.
Kuberamāyā, a form of Māyā **125**.36.
Kubja, a settlement in Naiṣadha **83**.3.
Kubjāmraka, a holy place on the bank of Gaṅgā **125**.75, 76, 139, **124**.3, **28**, 59, 66, 72, 89, 102, 108, 183, 187, 197, 199, 288, 234, **137**.4, 6, **152**.22, **179**.28, 32, 35; origin of the name **126**.6-14; dying creatures becoming human beings in **126**.109-227.
Kubjikā, a goddess installed in Mathurā **160**.40.
Kuha, a settlement in Naiṣadha **83**.2.
Kuhū, a river rising from Himālaya **85**.4.
Kuja **185**.14.
Kulapañjāka, a settlement in Naiṣadha **83**.2.
Kulika, a serpent-chief **24**.6-7.
Kumāra, a name of Skanda **25**.41, **151**.64.
Kumārā, a river in Śākadvīpa **86**.3.
Kumbha, a mount near lake Aruṇoda **78**.11-12.
Kumbhīpāka, a hell **200**.17, **202**.46.
Kumuda, a month **154**.5, **155**.73, **159**.22, **160**.80;—a division of Kuśadvīpa **87**.2;—a mount near lake Asitoda **78**.18-19, **79**.1, **80**.9;—a mountain in Gomedadvīpa **89**.4;—a mountain in Kuśadvīpa **87**.1.
Kumudvatī, a river in Krauñcadvīpa **88**.4;—a river rising from Vindhya **85**.5.
Kumudavana, a garden in Mathurā **153**.35-36.
Kundavana, a garden in Mathurā **161**.6.

Madhumān, mount near lake Asitoda **78**.18-19.

Madhuparka **114**.25, 26, 27, 61, **127**.71, **187**.108, 110, **189**.10,**191**.3, 6, 11, 15, **192**.3, 18, 30, 32, 35, 36; ingredients in **191**.21,**192**.19-21; offering of **192**.22-34; origin of the Devatā **191**.7-12.

Madhureya, a settlement in Naiṣadha **83**.2.

Madhuvana, a garden in Mathurā, **153**.33-34, **161**.6.

Mādhyandinīyaka, a sacrifice for Sūrya **177**.48; —a tīrtha in Mathurā **177**. 49.

Māgha, the month Kumbha **41**.4, **126**.57, 112, **214**, **145**.98, **149**.57, **177**.60, **187**.34.

Mahābhadra, a lake in the mountain Supārśva **78**.9.

Mahābhāgā, a name of Durgā **64**.3.

Mahābhūta, great cosmos **18**.6.

Mahādeva, a name of Rudra **17**.51, **213**.38, **44**;—mahattattva **17**.72.

Mahādruma, a region in Śākadvīpa **86**.3.

Mahāgṛhodaya, a city **162**.2.

Mahākadambā, a river in Naiṣadha **83**.3.

Mahākāla, a name of Śiva **144**.23;—a doorkeeper of Śiva **213**.77.

Mahākāya, a Rākṣasa **94**.6-9.

Mahāmāyā, a name of Durgā **28**.29, 32, **64**.3;—a river in Naiṣadha **83**.3.

Mahāmegha, a mount in Meru **80**.10.

Mahāmoha, extreme illusion **2**.28.

Mahānāha, a settlement in Naiṣadha **83**.2.

Mahānāma, a Brahmin living near Saṅgama in Mathurā **174**.2.

Mahānīla, a mount near lake Aruṇoda **78**.11-12, **79**.21, **81**.2.

Mahāpadma, a serpent-chief **24**.6-7.

Mahāprabhā, a name of Durgā **64**.3.

Mahāraurava, one of the eight main hells **200**.1-2.

Mahas, a loka **9**.5, 17-18, **11**.15.

Mahāśṛṅga, a mount near lake Mānasa **78**.14-16.

Mahāsthala, a holy spot in Vasatputra in Mathurā **160**.20.

Mahat, intellect **2**. 36;—ahaṅkāra, **25**.3.

Mahātapas, a sage **17**.7, **22**.49, **33**.1,

Mahātapta, one of the eight main hells **200**.1-2.

Mahatī, a river in Kuśadvīpa **87**.3.

Mahāvaktrā, a river **82**.4.

Mahāvana, a garden in Mathurā **153**.43, **161**.8.

Mahāvetra, a Vidyādhara-king **81**.1.

Mahāvidyeśvarī, a goddess installed in Mathurā **160**.42.

Mahāvīṭi, son of Savana **74**.7.

Mahāvrata, **113**.52.

Mahendra, a major mountain in Bhārata **15**.9, **85**.2, 6, **214**.53-55.

Maheśvara, a name of Śiva **90**.11, 18, 22, **213**.27, 60, **214**.7, 22.

Maheśvarakuṇḍa, a tīrtha in Lohārgala **151**.69-72.

Maheśvarī, a mother goddess representing anger **27**.35-36;—a name of Durgā **28**.29.

Māheyācala, a settlement in Naiṣadha **83**.2.

Naiṣadha, a mountain (same as Niṣadha) **74**.8, **83**.1.
Naiṣṭhuraka, a hunter **5**.20, 25.
Nāka, a settlement in Naiṣadha **83**.2.
Nala, a king, son of Vīrasena **44**.17, **61**.11;—a Rākṣasa **94**.10-12.
Namuci, a demon killed by Indra **96**.5.
Nanda, a serpent-king **81**.7;—son of Medhātithi **74**.8.
Nandā, a name of Durgā **28**.44, **99**.1, 4;—a river in Śākadvīpa **86**.3, **214**.46-49.
Nandana, garden of Indra **10**.50-52, **126**.32, 120, **137**.235, **139**.27, **148**.47, 48, **149**.77, **213**.13.
Nandikeśvara, same as Nandin, **145**.25, **27**.
Nāndīmukhas, Pitṛs with faces upwards **34**.6.
Nandin, Śiva born as son to Śālaṅkāyana **144**.77, 80, 84, 89, 164, **213**.30, **214**.1, 12, 21, 22, 81, **215**.2.
Nara **48**.8.
Nāra, water, **3**.23.
Naraka, a demon **113**.2.
Nārada, a sage **2**.44, 58, 81, **3**.23, **4**.9, **10**.41, **22**.41, 46, **27**.22, **32**.13, **54**.4, 19, **66**.3, 17-18, 20, **70**.10-11, **92**.15, 18, 19, 23, 29, 36, **93**.1, 4, 6, 10, **95**.30, 35, **124**.16-17, **151**.40, 41, **159**.8, **166**.4, 5, 6, 7, **177**.2, 4, 17, 23, 29, 32, 44, 46, **187**.58-59, 61, 69-70, 79, **188**.106, **207**.1, 4, **208**.4, 22-23, **209**.2, **211**.1, **212**.5, **214**.38-39, 74.
Nāradakuṇḍa, a tīrtha in Lohārgala **151**.39-41.
Naramedha, a sacrifice **145**.49.
Nārāyaṇa **1**.25, **2**.12, 21, 22, 24, 25, **3**.8, 11, 14, 16, **4**.1, 8, 17, 18, 19, 35, **5**.17, 45, **6**.26, 27, **7**.36, **9**.1, 2, 28, **10**.15, **12**.21, **13**.5, 6, 9, **17**.73, **18**.5, 14, **20**.4, 22, **21**.54, **25**.6, 27, **30**.2, **38**.12, 21, 31, **39**.15, 17, 19, **40**.4-5, 8, 11, **41**.44, **48**.8, 16, **50**.6-9, **55**.38, **66**.6, **70**.13-14, 19, 23, 39, 47, **72**.10, **73**.12-13, 21-22, 50, **74**.6, **81**.7, **89**.5, **90**.1, 17, 18, **98**.37, **99**.10, **112**.79, **113**.50, **114**.1, 48, 63, **115**.1, **118**.11, **123**.36-37, **124**.5,18, 22, **125**.1, **128**.43, 44-45, 61, 63, **129**.16, 22, **130**.1, 13, **132**.2, **134**.9, 24, 47, **136**.29, **137**.60, 228-229, **138**.34, 36, 57, 59, 60, **139**.59, **143**.4, **147**.25, 26, **148**.3, 4, 72, **149**.13, **158**.33, **160**.39, **163**.35, **174**.73, **182**.6, **187**.1, 109, **190**.5, **192**.29, **211**.31, 84, **217**.20; image of **166**.25.
Nārāyaṇamantra **4**.11.
Nārāyaṇasthāna, a sacred spot in Mathurā **160**.39.
Nārāyaṇī **6**.28-29.
Narmadā, a river **85**.5, **95**.17, **214**.46-49.
Nartanācala, a holy spot near Someśvara **144**.73.
Nāśadācārā, a river rising from Pāriyātra **85**.4.
Navamī, tithi **28**.40, 41, **159**.22, **160**.8, 80, **176**.81-82.
Navanābhā, a maṇḍala for pūjā **99**.23.
Navanītadhenu **107**.1.
Naya, son of Gaya **74**.9.
Nepāla, a country **97**.18, **145**.86-87.
Nikhāta, son of Pratihartā **74**.9.
Nīla, the chief of Durjaya's army **11**.76, 78, 80-81;—a demon **27**.14;—a moun-

Paṅkinī, a river rising from Ṛkṣa **85**.5.

Pāpapramocana, a holy spot in Kokāmukha **140**.51.

Parāka, an expiatory rite **179**.13, 14.

Parama, a tīrtha in Mandāra **143**.45-47.

Parameṣṭhī, son of Indradyumna **74**.9.

Paranandā, a river **214**.46-49.

Parāparā, a name of Sañjñā 8.20.

Parāśara, a sage **214**.43-45.

Paraśurāma, an incarnation of Viṣṇu (same as Jāmadagnya) **48**.20-22, **55**.37, **112**.69, **113**.24, **150**.41.

Parāvasu, a Gandharva **214**.38-39;—a sage **124**.16-17.

Pāriyātra, a major mountain in Bhārata near lake Asitoda **78**.18-19, **85**.2, 3, **214**.53-55.

Parjanya, a minister of Mahiṣāsura **93**.3-4,

Parṇāśā, a river **214**.46-49.

Parvata, a sage **22**.46, **124**.16-17.

Pārvatī **22**.15, 19, **25**.20, **27**.12, **71**.50, **90**.6, **147**.19, 25, **213**.28.

Paryuṣita, a ghost **174**.16, 24, origin of the name **174**.18.

Pāśā, a river rising from Vindhya **85**.5.

Paśupāla, a king **51**.9, 23, **52**.6, **53**.3-4,

Pāśupatas **122**.18.

Pāśupataśāstra **70**.42, **71**.56, **97**.44.

Paśupati, a name of Rudra **21**.82, **33**.28, origin of the name **21**.82.

Pataṅga, a mount in Meru **80**.1-3.

Pātāla, a netherworld **24**.24, 31, **36**.13.

Paurṇamāsī, tithi **35**.14.

Pauṣa, the month Makara **40**.1.

Pāvaka, a mountain in Krauñcadvīpa (same as Mānasa) **88**.1; a region in Krauñcadvīpa **88**.3.

Payoṣṇī, a river rising from Vindhya **85**.5, 5, **187**.115.

Penance, benefits of **207**.37-39.

Phālguna, the month Mīna **42**.1, **124**.1, 7.

Phālgunaka, a holy place in Mathurā **157**.35-36

Pinākin, a name of Rudra **71**.1.

Piṇḍāraka, a holy place **144**.10.

Piṅgala, a mount near lake Asitoda **78**.18-19.

Piñjara, a mount in Meru **80**.8.

Pippalā, a river rising from Ṛkṣa **85**.5.

Pippalāda, a sage **160**.67.

Pippalādeśvara, Śiva installed in Mathurā **160**.67.

Piśācas **124**.12, **187**.50, **188**.25-26.

Piśāca, a tīrtha in Yamunā in Mathurā **174**.98.

Pitṛ-devas, manes—gods **190**.31-32, **65**.

Pitṛ, a law-giver **121**.19.

Pitṛs **17**.24-25, **18**.1-3.

Pitṛmāyā, a form of Māyā **125**.52.

Pratiṣṭhāna, a city in Dekkan **41**.17, **165**.1, 8, 38.
Pratoyā, a river in Kuśadvīpa **87**.3.
Prayāga, a tīrtha **99**.51-52, **144**.100, **145**.98, **152**.13;—a tīrtha in Mathurā, **152**.38-41, **176**.67-68, **215**.55, **217**.14;—the confluence of Gaṅgā and Yamunā **152**.30, **155**.5.
Priyavrata, son of Svāyambhuvamanu **2**.56, 62, **4**.9, **74**.6, 7.
Pṛthu, son of Vibhu **74**.9.
Pulaha, a sage **2**.44, **21**.15-17, **124**.16-17, **144**.97, 130, **214**.43-45;—a law-giver **197**.18.
Pulastya, a sage **2**.44, **21**.15-17, **124**.16-17, **144**.97, 130, 155, **214**.43-45, **217**.4;—a law-giver **197**.18;—son of Brahmā **112**.69.
Puloma, a king of Vidyādharas **80**.4.
Puṇḍarīka, a mountain in Krauñcadvīpa, **88**.2;—a river in Krauñcadvīpa **88**.4;—a tīrtha near Govaradhana **164**.19;—a tīrtha in Kubjāmraka **126**.59, 223-224;—a sacrifice **126**.62, 64.
Puṇḍarīkākṣa **6**.10, 11.
Puṇḍarīkākṣapāra, hymn in praise of Viṣṇu uttered by Vasu **6**.10-16, 35-36, 40.
Puṅkhā, a river in Naiṣadha **83**.3.
Puṇyanadī, a tīrtha in Śālagrāma **145**.69-71.
Puṇyasthala, a holy spot at Vasatputra in Mathurā **160**.20.
Puṇyodā, a river in Naiṣadha **82**.4, **83**.3.
Pura, body **3**.14.
Purāṇas **36**.19, **38**.28, **58**.3, **73**.29, **74**.4-5, **81**.8, **95**.63, **159**.18, **170**.60, 73, **175**.15, **176**.79, **179**.30, **180**.77, **193**.10-11, **217**.22; contents of **2**.4; list of **112**.74-77.
Pūrṇasukha, a tīrtha in Kabjāmraka **126**.42, 43.
Puruṣa **144**.45, 48, **210**.30; the highest Tattva **25**.2, 4;—the supreme soul **17**.39, 53-55, 57;—a river **214**.46-49;—the spirit **3**.14;—a tīrtha **214**.53-55.
Puruṣasūkta **66**.10.
Puruṣottama, a name of Viṣṇu **8**.45, 72.12. **184**.13, **185**.10, 15, 19, **186**.23;—a tīrtha **8**.41-42.
Pūrvā, deity representing East **29**.4.
Pūrvagaṇḍikā, a river on the eastern side of Mālyavān **82**.2.
Pūṣā, a deva **21**.45, 46, 71, 77, **33**.10, 31.
Puṣkara, a lake **6**.6, 40;—a tīrtha in Mathurā **49**.41, **99**.51-52, **152**.10, 15, **174**.6-7, **176**.67-68, **215**.55, **217**.14;—one of the seven islands of the world **2**.57, **74**.7;—a mount in Meru **80**.10;—a mount near lake Mahābhadra **78**.21-23.
Puṣkaradvīpa **89**.4, **139**.10, **140**.32.
Puṣpasthala, a holy spot near Saptasāmudrika in Mathurā **157**.19.
Puṣpavahā, a river in Krauñcadvīpa (same as Gaurī) **88**.5.
Puṣpavān, a mountain in Kuśadvīpa **87**.1.
Puṣpāvatī, a river rising from Malaya **85**.6.
Puṣpodaka, a river in the city of Yama **196**.13.
Puṣyabhadrā, a river on the northern side of Himālaya **98**.6, 12-15.
Put, hell **193**.27.

Rebirth, conduet for avoidance of **121**.4-29.
Revā, river Narmadā, **144**.33, 34. 38.
Revākhaṇḍa, a tīrtha **144**.38.
Ṛgveda **2**.76, **3**.17, **11**.16, **39**.50-53, **71**.4, **72**.16, **145**.8, 11, **151**.75, **184**.6, **185**.23.
Ṛkṣa, a major mountain in Bhārata **85**.2, 5.
Rodhaka, a ghost **174**.16, 23, origin of the name **174**.21.
Rohiṇī, a form of Māyā **125**.58.
Rohīpāra, a river rising from Pāriyātra **85**.4.
Rohita, a mountain and region in Śālmalidvīpa **89**.3.
Romaharṣaṇi, disciple of Vyāsa **112**.73.
Romaśa, a Vidyādhara king **81**.2.
Romāvata, a country **10**.39.
Rosary, see Gaṇāntika.
Ṛṣabha, a mount in Meru **80**.9;—son of Nābhi **74**.9.
Ṛṣikulyā, a river rising from Mahendra **85**.6.
Ṛṣis **187**.27.
Ṛṣikā, a river rising from Śuktimān **85**.6.
Ṛṣitīrtha, a tīrtha in Mathurā **152**.62-63.
Ṛṣyamūka, a minor mountain in Bhārata **85**.3.
Rudra **1**.16, 2.16, 43, 48-49, 51, 79, **4**.24-25, 27, **7**.36, **8**.48, **10**.12, 16, **20**.30, **21**.3, 12, 21, 24, 25, 36, 41, 44. 45, 47, 48, 53, 54, 61, 64, 70, 85, **22**.1, 4, 6, 22, 28, 36, 44, 47, **23**.5, 8, 11-15, 31, 32, **25**.14, 27, **27**.7, 25, 27, 29, **28**.36-37, **33**.1, 4, 5, 13, 15, 25, 34, **35**.9, **58**.3, 5-6, 13-14, **59**.7, **70**.5-6, 7-9, 10-11, 36, **71**.58, **73**.12-13, 39, 43-44, 47, **74**.1, **82**.4, **89**.7, **90**.1, 4, 13, **91**.6, **93**.27-28, **94**.10-12, 15, **95**.48, **96**.37, 71, 72, **97**.2, 3-4, 5, 8, 10, 11, 27, 38, 45, 47, **99**.44, **108**.13-14, 17, **110**.21, **122**.18, **123**.12, **125**.9, 51, **126**.103, **127**.49, **129**.8, 58, **136**.13, 15, 24, 28, 39, 49, **151**.71, 72, **153**.36, **190**.59, 92, **191**.7, 11, **193**.42, **201**.57, **204**.26, **205**.22, 26, **211**.89, **213**.48, **215**.3, 17-18, **74**, 104; origin of the name **83**.4; identity with Vedas **72**.16;—the subtle cause of beings **17**.24-25;—a law-giver **121**.15.
Rudras, a class of gods **21**.10, 18, **124**.13, 24, **151**.12, **187**.21-22, 25, **214**.73.
Rudramahālaya, a holy place in Mathurā **160**.51, 56.
Rudrasaras, a tīrtha in Puṣyabhadrā **98**.12-15.
Rudravrata **97**.1.
Rūpavatī, wife of Mithi **208**.28.
Rūpī, a serpent-chief **214**.57-63.
Ruru, an Asura king **96**.3-4, 14, 21, 30, 32;—daughter of Devadatta **146**.3, 62, origin of the name **146**.62.
Rurukhaṇḍa, same as Rurukṣetra **145**.111.
Rurukṣetra, a holy spot on the bank of Gaṇḍakī **146**.87, **147**.1.

Sabhaṅga, a holy spot on the bank of Gaṇḍakī **11**.6, 58.
Śacī, wife of Indra **76**.7, **110**.13-15, **137**.93.
Sādhyas **10**.6-7, **214**.36.
Sagaja, a settlement in Naiṣadha **83**.2.
Sagara, a king **59**.6.

Sanātana, son of Brahmā **74**.6.
Sanatkumāra, son of Brahmā **7**.10, **70**.7-9, **74**.6, **77**.30, **113**.1, 5, 13, **134**.45, **151**.32, **213**.5, **217**.11.
Sandhyā **14**.2-3, **21**.32-33, **120**.23, **137**.263; worship of **5**.18-19, **120**.4-23, **129**.6-15, 54-60;—a river in Krauñcadvīpa **88**.4.
Śāṇḍilya, a sage **71**.20; propagator of Bhāgavata dharma **148**.12;—a law-giver **121**.18;—a Saṁhitā relating to Pāśupata **71**.54.
Saṅgamana, a holy spot in the Maṇipūra hill in Dvārakā **149**.43-46;—a tīrtha in Sānandūra **150**.27-33.
Saṅghasa, a warrior in the army of Hetṛ-Prahetṛ **11**.93-95.
Śani, son of Mārtaṇḍa and Chāyā **20**.8, 14, **185**.14.
Śaṅkara, a name of Śiva **9**.7, **81**.3.
Saṅkarṣaṇa, a name of Viṣṇu **40**.4-5;—one of the four Vyūhas **148**.14;—a tīrtha near Govardhana **164**.22.
Saṅketeśvarī, another name for Siddheśvarī **160**.46.
Śaṅkha, a law-giver **121**.16, **197**.18;—a serpent-chief **24**.6-7.
Śaṅkhakūṭa, a mount in Meru **80**.9.
Śaṅkhaprabha, a holy spot in Sālagrāma **145**.51-52.
Śaṅkhavarcas, a serpent-chief **214**.57-63.
Śaṅkukarṇa, a minister of Mahiṣāsura **93**.3-4;—a Rākṣasa **94**.6-9.
Sāṅkhya **113**.50, **140**.93, **142**.44, **152**.22, **179**.35.
Sannyāsayoga **142**.14-30, 42-44, 54-62.
Śānta, Maṇija Dīptatejas reborn **36**.3.
Śāntabhaya, son of Medhātithi **74**.8.
Santānaka, loka of manes—gods **13**.18.
Śantanu, a king **157**.49, 50.
Sāntapana, a purificatory rite **114**.33, **130**.23, **134**.29,30.
Śānti, a ritual **192**.5-61.
Saparṇa, a settlement in Naiṣadha **83**.2.
Saprakāśa, a region of Krauñcadvīpa (same as Uṣṇavān) **88**.3.
Saptamī tithi **26**.17, **174**.39, **177**.60.
Saptarṣikuṇḍa, a tīrtha in Lohārgala **151**.48-50.
Saptasāmudraka, a tīrtha in Kubjāmraka **126**.95.
Saptasāmudrika, a tīrtha in Mathurā **157**.13-14;—origin of **157**.24-30.
Saptatāla, one of the eight main hells **200**.1-2.
Śāra, a minor mountain in Bhārata **85**.3.
Śarabhaṅgā, a river in Lohārgala **151**.51.
Śarabhaṅgakuṇḍa, a tīrtha in Lohārgala **151**.51-53.
Sarala, a mount near lake Mānasa **78**.14-16.
Saramā, the dog of Devas **14**.11-39.
Sarasa, a mount near lake Asitoda **78**.18-19.
Sārasvata, a tīrtha in Yamunā in Mathurā 3.5, 7, **174**.87;—name of Nārada in his former life 3.3-4.
Sarasvatī, a goddess **17**.58, **206**.29;—a name of Brāhmī;—a river rising from Himālaya **85**.4, **97**.16, **144**.101, 169, **160**.48, 59, **170**.4, 16, 92, **173**.13, **214**.46-49.
Sarasvatītīrtha, a tīrtha in Mathurā **154**.23.

188.42, **213**.25, 85-86, **214**.40, 65, **215**.13, 53-54, 58, 97-98, 115, **216**.4, 11.

Siddhā, a name of Brāhmī **91**.13.

Siddhakṣetra, a holy place to the north of Gaṅgā and south of Aśvinīmukha **215**.55.

Siddhamukha, name of Śiva installed in Mathurā **160**.22.

Siddhāśrama, a holy spot in Śālagrāma **145**.91-100.

Siddhavaṭa **151**.7.

Siddheśvarī, a goddess installed in Mathurā **160**.44-46.

Śīghraga, a ghost **174**.16, 24, origin of the name **174**.20.

Śīghrodā, a river rising from Vindhya **85**.5.

Siddhiśaila, a mount in Meru, **80**.8.

Śīlamaṇḍitā, a goddess created by Vaiṣṇavī **92**.9-12.

Śilpas **95**.63.

Sindhu, a river rising from Himālaya **85**.4, **97**.17, **214**.46-49.

Sindhudvīpa, a king manifestation of Varuṇa **28**.2, 5;—son of Supārśva and father of Mahiṣāsura **95**.3, 7.

Sindhuparṇā, a river rising from Pāriyātra **85**.4.

Singing in praise of the Lord, release of a Brahma-rākṣasa by its power **139**. 32-100.

Śiśira, a mount near lake Mānasa **78**.14-16, **80**.1.

Śiśiramukha, son of Medhātithi **74**.8.

Śiśumāra, a constellation **210**.52.

Śita, a mountain **81**.1.

Sītā, a stream in Meru **82**.1, 4, **214**.46-49.

Sītātīrtha, a tīrtha **179**.30.

Śiva **5**.49, 55, **15**.9, **18**.1-3, **25**.2, **16**, **27**.5, 8, 11, 12, 15, 18, **28**.17, **33**.24, **36**. 20, **81**.7, **90**.1, 5, 16, 17, **91**.1, **94**.14, **95**.61, **99**.3, **107**.13, **108**.16, **110**. 13-15, **113**.30, **126**.57, **136**.13, 21, 28, **137**.119, **141**.54, **144**.11, 12, 13, 15, 18, 20, 26, 32, 33, 37, 69, 73, 77, 79, 82, 116, 167, 180, 181. **145**.20, 25, 86-87, 88, 106. 107, 108, 109, 110, **146**.53, 54, 55, 59, 60, **147**.9, 11, 13, 14, 19, 24, 27, 28, **154**.34, **157**.19, **158**.19, **160**.41, 47, 51, 64, **163**.40, **168**. 3, **169**.35-36, **174**.80, **175**.7. **206**.26, **213**.30, **33**, 35, 36-37, 51, 81, **214**.9, 18, 19, 21, 78, 84, **215**.1, 10, **216**.11, 22; association with cremation-ground, reason for **136**.16-50; identity with Viṣṇu and Brahmā **70**.26-27, 39-40, **71**.6-7, **72**.14, 16.

Śivā, a river in Kuśadvīpa **82**.4, **87**.3.

Śivadūtī, a goddess created by Vaiṣṇavī **92**.9-12.

Śivakṣemaka, son of Mahātithi **74**.8.

Śivakuṇḍa, a tīrtha in Mathurā **153**.1, **160**.26.

Śivanadī, a river in Dekkan **175**.11-12.

Skanda, son of Śiva and Pārvatī **25**.39, 46, 49, **27**.21, **114**.24, **141**.48, **151**.12, **214**.37, **215**.100;—ego **17**.39, **18**.1-3.

Śleṣmātaka, a serpent **214**.23;—the forest of its penance **214**.26, **215**.11, 13, 36, 118-119, **216**.11.

Smṛtis, codes of conduct **2**.67-68.

Snānakuṇḍa, a tīrtha in Mandāra **143**.17-20.

Raibhya **7**.31-40, by Rudra **73**.18-38, by Supratīka **12**.5-13; of Yama, by Naciketas **198**.9-20.
Sthāṇu, a name of Rudra **33**.17.
Sthūlaśiras, son of Aśvaśiras **5**.46-47.
Strīghna, a Rākṣasa **94**.10-12.
Stutasvāmī, a holy place **148**.9, 73-74, 77-78, 82, **149**.1, 4,;—origin of the name **148**.75-78.
Śubha, a warrior who came out of Gauramukha's gem **11**.83-84, 100;—Maṇija king born as Saṁvaraṇa **36**.6.
Śubhā, a river rising from Vindhya **85**.5.
Śubhadarśana, a warrior who came out of Gauramukha's gem **11**.83-84, **97**;—Maṇija king born as Pāñcāla **14**.4.
Śubhavrata, rules **55**.2-7, rituals **55**.8-9, results **55**.20-21.
Subrahmabhāgā, a river **82**.4.
Subrahmaṇya, a special priest **21**.15-17.
Subtle elements **2**.36-37.
Sūcīmukha, a ghost **174**.16, origin of the name **174**.19.
Sudānta, a warrior who came out of Gauramukha's gem **11**.83-84, 100;—Maṇija king born as Daśaratha **36**.7.
Sudarśana, a region of Krauñcadvīpa (same as Pāvaka) **88**.3;—Viṣṇus disc **11**.107-108, **12**.1;—son of Durjaya and Miśrakeśī **10**.77.
Sudhana, a pious merchant, his liberation of a Brahmarakṣas **155**.7-70.
Sudharmā, the assembly hall in Amarāvatī **76**.6.
Sudhīmān, son of Virāṭa **74**.9.
Sudyumna, Maṇija king born as Turu **36**.5;—son of Supratīka **10**.31;—a warrior who came out of Gauramukha's gem **11**.83-84.
Śuddhaśaiva, a vrata relating to Rudra **97**.40, 43, origin of the name **97**.40.
Śuddhavatī, city of Varuṇa **76**.12.
Śūdras **3**.19, 9.**16**, 13, 26, 27, **49**.16-18, 37, **66**.12, **68**.5-6, 7, 8, 9, **75**.17, **112**.16, 17, 20, 24, **128**.25, 29, 30, 38, **137**.265, **140**.45, **163**.2, **165**.39, **180**.31, **186**.49, 50, 51, **187**.23, **188**.57, 92, 103, **193**.29, **200**.65, **211**.4, 5, **215**.86; initiation into Bhāgavatadharma **128**.25-36; rules of worship for **115**.36-40.
Sughoṣa, a warrior in the army of Hetṛ-Prahetṛ **11**.93-95, 98.
Sugrīva **159**.10.
Suguhya, a tīrtha in Bhūtagiri **148**.57.
Sujātā, a goddess created by Vaiṣṇavī **92**.9-12.
Śuka, a settlement in Naiṣadha **83**.2;—son of Vyāsa **170**.60, 69;—Śukodara turned into a parrot **171**.16, 20, 29, 30, 39, 51, 53-54, **173**.1, 6-7, 10;—a temple of Śiva in Mathurā **173**.8.
Śukanadī, a river in Naiṣadha **83**.3.
Sukānti, warrior who came out of Gauramukha's gem **11**.83-84, 98.
Sukeśī, daughter of Hetṛ married by Durjaya **10**.74.
Śukeśvara, name of Śiva in the temple of Śuka in Mathurā **173**.9.
Śukeya, a settlement in Naiṣadha **83**.2.
Sukhā, a river in the valley between Mahānīla and Kakubha **79**.21.
Sukhada, a warrior who came out of Gauramukha's gem **11**.83-84, 100.

Suśīla, a warrior who came out of Gauramukha's gem **11**.83-84;—Maṇija king born as Vasudāna **36**.6;—a wealthy Vaiśya in Pratiṣṭhāna turned into a ghost **165**.2-54.
Sutala, a nether-world **24**.24.
Sutantu, a sage **170**.62.
Sutejas, another name for Dīptatejas **11**.97.
Suvāhinī, a river **82**.4.
Suvarṇataṭa, a settlement in Naiṣadha **83**.2.
Suvidyut, an Asura **10**.47-48, **16**.1-4, 6.
Suvindu, a mount near lake Aruṇoda **78**.11-12.
Suvrata, a name of Rudra **97**.5.
Subhīma, a Rākṣasa **94**.5.
Svadhā, **28**.31, **91**.11.
Svāhā **28**.31, **91**.11.
Svara, son of Paśupāla **51**.5.
Svarbhānu, a Rākṣasa **94**.5.
Svayambhū, a law-giver **121**.19.
Svāyambhuvamanu **2**.56, **12**.17, **25**.6, **74**.6, **187**.100, **188**.85, 98.
Svāyambhuva manvantara **74**.12, **99**.4.
Svayamprabhā, a goddess created by Vaiṣṇavī, **92**.9-12.
Śveta, a division in Kuśadvīpa (same as Kumuda) **87**.2;—a mountain in Meru **74**.8, 5, **80**.4;—a king in Ilāvṛta **99**.56, 57, 69-70, 73.
Śvetadvīpa **72**.8, **122**.103, 104, 110-111, **125**.179, **124**.225-226, 227, **137**.17, **137**.231, 233, **138**.95, 99, **139**.17, 21.
Śvetagaṅga, a settlement in Naiṣadha **83**.2.
Śvetagaṅgā, a river **145**.88.
Śvetaka, a mountain in Śākadvīpa **86**.2.
Śvetodana, a mount near lake Mānasa **78**.14-16.
Śyāmā, a river in Naiṣadha **83**.3.
Syamantapañcaka, a tīrtha in Mandāra **143**.48.
Svarloka, a world **9**.17-18, 20.

Taittirīya, a sage **170**.62.
Takṣaka, a serpent **27**.14.
Talātala, a neṭherworld **15**.12.
Tālavana, a garden in Mathurā **161**.6;—a palmyra grove on the bank of river Sukhā **79**.22.
Tamas, one of the three guṇas **2**.7, **3**.17, **7**.37, **32**.23, **66**.15, **68**.4, **70**.15-16, 18, 19, 22, **187**.88, 89;—darkness **2**.28, 35, 38-39.
Tāmasa **4**.5, **10**.10, 13, **130**.15.
Tamasā, a river rising from Ṛkṣa **85**.5.
Tāmrā, a river **214**.46-49.
Tāmrābha, a mount near lake Mānasa **78**.14-16, **80**.3.
Tāmraparṇī, a river rising from Malaya **85**.6.
Tāmravarṇa, a division of Bhārata **85**.1.
Tanmātras, subtle elements **2**.37.
Tantu, a sage **170**.62.

Triyāmā, a river rising from Mahendra **85**.6.
Tṛṇabindu, a sage **144**.133.
Tṛtīyā, tithi **22**.51.
Truth, praise of **193**.36-49.
Tryambaka, a name of Śiva **216**.1-2.
Tumburu, a sage **22**.41, **214**.38-39, 74.
Tuṅgā, a river in Naiṣadha **83**.3.
Tuṅgabhadrā, a river rising from Sahya **85**.5, **97**.17.
Tuṅgakūṭa, a holy waterfall in Kokāmukha **140**.29.
Tuṅgaprastha, a minor mountain in Bhārata **85**.3.
Turaga, a mount near lake Mānasa **78**.14-16.
Turu, Maṇija Sudyumna reborn **16**.5.
Tvaṣṭā **20**.5, **28**.5.
Twelve Ādityas **214**.35.

Udama, son of Medhātithi **74**.8.
Udarākṣa, a Rākṣasa **94**.5.
Udaya, a mountain in Śākadvīpa **86**.2; a region in Śākadvīpa **86**.3.
Udbhida, son of Jyotiṣmān **74**.8.
Uddālaka, a sage **191**.12, **198**.21.
Udgātā, a special priest **21**.15-17;—son of Abhāva **74**.9.
Ugra, a disciple of Paraśurāma **112**.70.
Ugrāśva, a king son of Haryaśva **43**.15.
Ujjayinī, a city **167**.3, 25, 26.
Ulūka, a Vidyādhara king **81**.2.
Umā, daughter of Himavān **9**.4, **21**.73, **22**.5, 10, 13, 45, 47, 48, **23**.8, **25**.4, 17, **58**.3, **73**.40, 46, **82**.4, **144**.20, 117, **151**.68, 69, **158**.22.
Umākuṇḍa, a tīrtha in Lohārgala **151**.66-68.
Umāstanakuṇḍa, a pond near Śaileśvara **215**.100.
Unhappiness, actions leading to **116**.9-24.
Unmattākṣa, a warrior in the army of Hetṛ-Prahetṛ **11**, 93-95, 99.
Unnetā, son of Nikhāta **74**.9.
Upala, a mount near lake Aruṇoda **78**.11-12.
Upaniṣads **9**.34, **38**.29, **177**.33-34.
Upasāyaka, a sage, propagator of Bhāgavata dharma **148**.12.
Upasparśana, ritualistic washing with water **134**.10-23.
Uragas **145**.84, **187**.50, **188**.25-26, **216**.11.
Ūrdhvā, deity representing upward direction **29**.4.
Ūrdhvasrotas, beings with upward growth **2**.32, 38-39.
Urvaśī, a celestial damsel **214**.41-42;—a goddess created by Vaiṣṇavī **92**.9-12.
Urvaśīkuṇḍa, a tīrtha in Badarī **141**.51-66.
Uṣṇavān, a region in Krauñcadvīpa **88**.3.
Utpalāvatī, a river rising from Malaya **85**.6.
Uttānapāda, son of Svāyambhuvamanu **74**.6.
Uttarā, deity representing north **29**.4.
Uttarāgni, one of the sacrificial fires, **190**.15.
Uttaragokarṇa, same as Gokarṇa **216**.23-24.

Vañjukā, a river rising from Ṛkṣā 85.5.
Vañjulā, a river rising from Sahya **85**.5.
Vapantī, a river rising from Pāriyātra **85**.4.
Vapuṣmān, son of Priyavrata and lord of Plakṣa **74**.7.
Varāha, the boar-incarnation of Viṣṇu **24**.1, **41**.1, 4-5, 11, **112**.52, **113**.1, 2, **119**.3, **123**.2, **126**.1, **128**.1, 88, **130**.20, **140**.21, **152**.9, **163**.26, 59, **166**.12, 16-17, **176**.72, 73, **182**.5, **210**.64, **211**.32, **217**.12, 17-18, 19; image of **166**.25.
Varāhadvādaśī, rituals **41**.2-13, results **41**.14-16.
Varāhakalpa **114**.12.
Varāhamāyā, a form of Māyā **125**.47.
Varāhapurāṇa **112**.67, 80, **141**.52; as the cream of all śāstras **148**.21; merits of listening to **99**.50-55; transmission of **112**.67-73.
Varāhatīrtha (a tīrtha in Mathurā **166**.24; four images in **166**.25;—a tīrtha in Piṇḍāraka **187**.115.
Vārāhī, a mother goddess representing tolerance **27**.35-36.
Vārāṇasī **16**.5, **97**.28, 32, **99**.51-52, **122**.12, **152**.10, 14, **162**.67.
Vārandhama, a minor mountain in Bhārata **85**.3.
Vardhamānā, a mount in Naiṣadha **83**.1.
Varṇā, a river in Kuśadvīpa **87**.3.
Varṣyaghāta, a tīrtha in Mathurā **160**.30.
Varuṇa **28**.2, 16, **39**.34-37, **113**.41, 57, **126**.89, **127**.51, **149**.48, 49, **174**.80, **183**. 19, **185**.14, **214**.31;—guardian deity of west **29**.12-13, **99**.27, 38, 43, **158**.18;—a law-giver **121**.17;—lord of the sea **125**.35;—a division of Bhāratavarṣa **85**.1.
Varuṇamantra **39**.38.
Varuṇatālī, a river **82**.4.
Varuṇatīrtha, a tīrtha to the west of Govardhana **164**.3, 7-8.
Vāruṇīmāyā, a form of Māyā **125**.35.
Vasatputra, a holy spot in Mathurā **160**.20.
Vasiṣṭha, a sage **21**.15-17, **42**.10, 13, **44**.6, **62**.16-17, 29, **99**.56, 58, 59, 62, 64, 72, 75, **112**.66, **151**.43, 44, **174**.60, **214**.43-45.
Vasiṣṭhakuṇḍa, a tīrtha in Lohārgala **151**.42-44.
Vasu, a Brahmin of the Pāñcāla country **175**.10;—a king of Kashmir, son of Sumanas **5**.5, 12, 14, 15, **6**.1, **8**.1.
Vasus **1**.16, **18**.6-7, **21**.10, 10-20, **73**.33, **81**.3-4, **93**.27-28, **94**.5, 15, **124**.13, 24, **151**.12, **187**.21-22, 25, **214**.73;—manes—gods **11**.30.
Vasudāna, Maṇija Suśīla reborn **36**.6.
Vasudeva, father of Kṛṣṇa **46**.6, 8, 14, **144**.5, 6, **148**.10.
Vāsudeva, a name of Viṣṇu **15**.17, **55**.37, **99**.30, **123**.38, **127**.45, **129**.8, 58, 59, **144**.7, **153**.47, **157**.43, **160**.38, **163**.35, **174**.74, **186**.26, **192**.14, **211**.84;—one of the four Vyūhas **148**.14.
Vasudhāra, a mountain in Meru **80**.5, 6, **81**.3, 5.
Vasukarṇa, father of Gokarṇa, **170**.1, 59.
Vāsuki, a serpent-chief **24**.6-7, 16, **27**.14, **35**.9, **180**.72, **214**.57-63, 75, **215**.75.
Vasumān, a sage **170**.62.
Vasumatī, a goddess installed in Mathurā **160**.15;—a river **82**.4.

Vidyādharas **80**.3, **81**.2, 5, 8, **93**.27-28, **124**.12, **145**.67, 68, **206**.16, **213**.23, **214**. 40, **215**.53-54, 115.

Vidyeśvarī, a goddess **169**.38-39;—a name of Brāhmī **91**.3, 13.

Vidyujjihva, a Rākṣasa **94**.6 9;—a serpent-chief **214**.57-63.

Vidyullā, a river in Kuśadvīpa **87**.3.

Vidyullatā, a mountain in Krauñcadvīpa **88**.1.

Vidyunmāli, a minister of Mahiṣāsura **93**.3-4;—a Rākṣasa **94**.6-9.

Vidyut, an Asura **10**.47-48, **16**.1-4, 6.

Vidyut-prabha, an emissary of Mahiṣāsura **93**.24, **95**.1;—a warrior in the army of Hetṛ-Prahetṛ **11**.93-95, 98.

Vidyutprabhā, a goddess created by Vaiṣṇavī **92**.9-12, 16-17, 18;—queen of Supratīka **10**.19.

Vighasa, a minister of Mahiṣāsura **93**.3-4, 12, 18, 25;—a warrior in the army of Hetṛ-Prahetṛ **11**.93-95, 97.

Vighnakara, a name of Vināyaka **23**.28-29.

Vighnarāja, a name of Vināyaka **154**.29, 30;—a tīrtha in Mathurā **154**.29-31.

Vijaya, door-keeper of Viṣṇu **113**.62;—son of Tṛṇabindu **144**.133, 139, 140, 141, 142.

Vījayā, a goddess created by Vaiṣṇavī **92**.9-12.

Vikaṅka, a mount near lake Aruṇoda **78**.11-12.

Vilāsinī, a river **82**.4.

Vimalavana, a garden in Mathurā **153**.38.

Vimati, a king, son of Sumati **166**.3, 12.

Vinata, a serpent-chief **214**.57-63.

Vināyaka **23**.20, 23, 25, 31, 33, **160**.40, **214**.37.

Vindhya, a major mountain in Bhārata **85**.2, 5, **113**.49, **143**.2, 24,39,49, **214**. 53-55.

Vindhyavinissṛta, a tīrtha in Mandāra **143**.30-32.

Vipāśā, a river rising from Himālaya **13**.46, **85**.4, **214**.46-49.

Vipracitti, an Asura **25**.7.

Vipula, a mountain on the western part of Meru **77**.9.

Vīrabhadra, chief of Śiva's army **27**.16.

Virādha, a warrior in the army of Hetṛ-Prahetṛ **11**.93-95.

Vīradhanvā, a king **41**.17, 28.

Virāja, a celestial region **65**.14-15;—a mount near lake Mahābhadra **78**.21-23.

Virajā, a river rising from Ṛkṣa **85**.5.

Vīrasena, a king **44**.9.

Vīrasthala, a holy spot near Saptasāmudrika in Mathurā **157**.16, **160**.20.

Virāṭ **13**.25.

Virāṭa, son of Naya **74**.9.

Virocana, minister of Durjaya **11**.70-71.

Virūpākṣa, commander-in-chief of Mahiṣāsura **93**.27-28, 32.

Virūpanidhi, servant of Prabhāvatī **180**.38, 98.

Viṣa, a mount near lake Mānasa **78**.14-16.

Viśākha, a mountain in Meru **80**.4;—a mount in Naiṣadha **83**.1.

Viśāla, a city **7**.13-14;—a country **7**.13-14, 16-17, 31;—a king **7**.13-14;—a king of Kāśī **48**.6-7;—a name of Badarī **48**.23.

Vitala, a netherworld **24**.24.
Vitastā, a river rising from Himālaya **85**.4, **97**.17, **214**.46-49.
Vivarṇā, a river in Naiṣadha **83**.3.
Vivasvān, son of king Vasu **6**.5.
Vṛndakāvana, a garden in Mathurā **36**.11, **161**.10.
Vṛṣabhāñjanaka, a temple in Phālgunaka in Mathurā **157**.37-38.
Vṛṣahaṁsa, a mount near lake Mahābhadra **78**.21-23.
Vṛṣṇis, a class of people **149**.11, 19, 23, 53.
Vṛṣotsarga, ceremony of letting loose a bull **155**.74.
Vṛtra, a demon killed by Indra **125**.37.
Vyāsa, a sage **112**.72, **175**.3, 8;—a lawgiver **197**.17.
Vyoma **2**.7.

Women in monthly period, rules relating to **142**.6-10, 45-51.
Worship, in autumn season **123**.7-14, in rainy season **124**.45-59, in spring season **124**.1-40, in summer season **124**.41-44, in winter season **123**.15-20; expiations for offences in **179**.11-19; food permitted in **119**.4-18, grains and vegetables **119**.8-11, flesh of animals **119**.12, flesh of birds **119**.17, fruits **119**.5; offences in **117**.5-36, **179**.3-10; rituals in **118**.1-58;—of Sandhyā **120**.4-23, **129**.6-15, 54-60.

Yādavas, a clan **144**.8, **149**.6.
Yadus, a clan **144**.4.
Yajña **66**.19.
Yajñahā, a Rākṣasa **94**.10-12.
Yajñahanus,a Rākṣasa **95**.43.
Yajñamūrti, a form of Viṣṇu **10**.16.
Yajñapuruṣa, name of Viṣṇu in Naimiṣāraṇya **11**.111, **41**.41-42.
Yajurveda **2**.77, **3**.17, **39**.50-53, **71**.4, **72**.16, **145**.12, **151**.76. **185**.23.
Yakṣas, a group of celestials **9**.17-18, **16**.5, **20**.29, **33**.7, **76**.3-5, **77**.21-22, **79**.18-19, **80**.9, **81**.5, 7, **91**.12, **92**.25, 32 **98**.11, **112**.59, **124**.12, **190**.33, **213**.**79**, 85-86, **214**.33, 40, 65, **215**.53-54, 115, **216**.11.
Yakṣadhanus, a king of Saurāṣṭra **153**.9-10.
Yakṣatīrtha, another name for Haṁsatīrtha **144**.180.
Yayāti, a king son of Nahuṣa **43**.16-17;—a king of Mathurā **152**.24.
Yama, god of death **21**.43, **26**.12, **27**.31-32, **28**.14-15, 16, **113**.41, **137**.258, 261, **153**.26, **155**.31, **174**.71, **185**.14, **188**.47, **193**.7, 14, 25, 50-51, **194**.7, **13**, **195**.19, **197**.10-11, 29, **198**.1, 21, **199**.7, 20, **201**.47, 50, 55, **202**.1, **206**.6, **207**.1, **208**.22-23, **211**.96, **212**.8, **214**.34;—guardian deity of the south **29**.12-13, **99**.27, 37, **158**.18;—a law-giver **121**.17, **137**.121;—principle of dharma **17**.24-25, 48, 49, **18**.1-3;—son of Mārtaṇḍa and Saṁjñā **8**. 6, 10, 12.
Yamacullī, a fire-place in Yamaloka **200**.36.
Yamadaṇḍadharā, a mother goddess representing malignity **27**.35-36.
Yamaloka, city in **196**.2-35; sinners in **195**.3-18.
Yamana, a tīrtha in Mathurā **168**.16.
Yamanadī, a river in Yamaloka **200**.46.

INDEX

(Figures refer to the number of page)

—o o o—